UNIFYING GERMANY

1989-1990

UNIFYING GERMANY 1989-1990

MANFRED GÖRTEMAKER

First published 1994 by
THE MACMILLAN PRESS LTD
Houndmills, Basingstoke, Hampshire RG21 2XS
and London
Companies and representatives
throughout the world

ISBN 0-333-61969-2

A catalogue record for this book is available
from the British Library.

Printed in the United States of America by
Haddon Craftsmen
Scranton, PA

■ TABLE OF CONTENTS ■

■ FOREWORD ■

JOHN EDWIN MROZ

The experts had it wrong. Only months prior to the collapse of the German Democratic Republic (GDR), the leading experts on Germany were writing that the question of Germany could no longer be one of reunification, but rather was one of the nature of the relationship between the two German states and the impact of that relationship on East-West stability and European security. In the spring of 1989, the Institute for EastWest Studies published with St. Martin's Press what turned out to be a surprisingly controversial volume, edited by F. Stephen Larrabee and entitled *The Two German States and European Security*. Leading German scholars and some officials in both German states criticized the Institute's decision to publish the book due to the "subtle challenges" that its authors were making about the long-term viability of the GDR. Most of all, they were unhappy with the editor's call for a reassociation between the two German states in the context of new European security requirements. One German member of the Institute's board, a distinguished scholar and government advisor to Bonn, said that such a volume "could only cause bad feelings and arouse new tensions between the two Germanys."

The experts have been wrong about many other things as well. Those experts who spent time in the GDR during the 1980s needed to venture outside Berlin. In the mid-80s, Leipzig residents would sarcastically tell me to come back later in the year, when the Politburo "prepared" for the Leipzig Trade Fair. Then stores and restaurants would be stocked to impress the visitors and the dreariness of daily life would appear less so for some weeks—until the Trade Fair guests had departed and all would return to normal. Graduate students in prominent universities would explain how they were trying to go to Moscow to study as the Gorbachev era brought "fresh air" to the social sciences in the USSR, but not in Berlin. A manager of a small factory quietly explained that his production figures always "grew substantially" when Berlin bureaucrats got their hands on them. From Dresden to Wiemar, one could feel the seething discontent. Yet most visitors traveled only to the capital. They returned to the West having concluded that things were not that bad. Even Western officials seemed to buy the propaganda that the economy was the world's tenth strongest.

In this volume, *Unifying Germany*, Manfred Görtemaker addresses such misconceptions in a straightforward and hard-hitting manner that is both refreshing and educational. His book is not so much a history of the reunification process as it is a roadmap to better understanding the nature of the German character and what Europe can expect from the new Germany. As such, it is an important tool for Americans and others to use in coming to grips with the new Germany. While remembering the atrocities of the past century, most Germans today are focused on building a new European civil society. To understand Germany and the new Europe, it is imperative to understand how Germany was reunited and what this new Germany sees as its role for the future.

As Krupp Foundation senior associate at the Institute in New York, Professor Görtemaker undertook an exhaustive research program to determine the causes of the reunification. He convincingly demonstrates that the sudden reunification was not the result of carefully crafted policies in Bonn but rather a genuine uprising of the 16 million people of the German Democratic Republic. The revolution was made possible by the restrained policies of Mikhail Gorbachev and the surprising actions of neighboring Warsaw Pact states, particularly Hungary. The author's argument is convincing and carefully documented.

Görtemaker explains the fast-breaking events on the ground and why the phenomena were not "Germanic" but rather similar to those being expressed in the other East European countries under Soviet domination. Indeed, this time German reunification was caused by a revolution from within. No one was prepared for it, and many in the West as well as in the East were unhappy to see it come. Professor Görtemaker clearly demonstrates that Western fears about a reunified Germany further muddied the confusing waters of late 1989. He is generous in describing the French paranoia about a reunified Germany and how the French, British, and others wanted to bring the German reunification process under some form of international control. It seems that only the Americans had genuinely come to accept the Federal Republic of Germany unreservedly as a responsible pillar of the democratic West. One senior French official told me in March 1990 that this was because "you Americans are so bad at history and are so naive to believe a people like the Germans can change."

The French view was certainly shared in the United States following World War II. Görtemaker brings to light a fascinating private memorandum written by John Foster Dulles in November 1944 arguing that the only way to ensure that Germans behave would be to "assimilate them into other societies." Dulles proposed a European Federation of States as the vehicle to do that. This view is not much different from that held by many Frenchmen, Poles, and other Europeans even today. Professor Görtemaker deals with this line of argument directly and presents a solid case for understanding that the new Germany sees its future in a unified Europe where it seeks not to be dominant but to play a role compatible with its size and level of economic development. The reader can determine for himself whether the arguments are convincing. Based upon my experience with policymakers in this region since the 1970s, the arguments ring true. Throughout the 1980s, the Institute for East-West Security Studies played a quiet background role in negotiations between the two Germanys. German experts from the two states worked together each year in New York on specific issues that would help develop a closer working relationship. We worked carefully with Foreign Minister Genscher and other politicians. This book's author notes the historic excitement when party leader Erich Honecker visited his birthplace in West Germany. The IEWS was able to arrange the first official visit of a West German leader to the GDR—in this case the much publicized visit to Potsdam in 1988 of Deputy Chancellor Hans-Dietrich Genscher. Having worked closely with many of the Hungarian, Polish, and other leaders described in this volume, my colleagues and I are able to vouchsafe for the accuracy of insights provided by Professor Görtemaker in this study. The Institute is proud to sponsor this volume as an important bridge between the revolutionary period of 1989-90 and the future of Europe.

■ ACKNOWLEDGMENTS ■

The Institute is deeply grateful to the Alfried Krupp von Bohlen und Halbach Stiftung for its generous support of Manfred Görtemaker's research as a Krupp senior associate in New York. The $1.2 million provided during the 1980s by the Krupp program enabled the Institute to bring scores of leading experts from East European and Western countries to work together and to convene meetings and dialogue when this was neither easy to do nor common. The Institute and the author also wish to thank the Carnegie Corporation of New York for supporting the publication of this volume as part of its long-term core support for the Institute's Security Program. Carnegie continues to be a leading force both in the public policy study of the changing security needs in Europe and in the practical strategic dialogue among parties in Europe about their future. The impact of this book in contributing to this should not be underestimated: Three Russian members of Parliament have requested a synopsis of the Görtemaker volume. One member justified his request as stemming from the need "to fill in our ability to respond to ultra-nationalists about the new Germany and its possible threat."

Finally, the IEWS is grateful to the core funders of our public policy work during the past decade. The Görtemaker study drew upon a wide variety of sources provided by the IEWS over the past four years. Among those core funders are the Ford Foundation, the John D. and Catherine T. MacArthur Foundation, the Rockefeller Brothers Fund, the William and Flora Hewlett Foundation, the Arcana Foundation, and the Scherman Foundation.

JOHN EDWIN MROZ
Founding President
Institute for EastWest Studies
New York

■ INTRODUCTION ■

This book tells the story of German unification in 1989 and 1990, analyzes its historical dimensions, and outlines future prospects. My work on this project began in the early afternoon of November 9, 1989, when I was sitting quietly in my office at the Institute for East-West Security Studies in New York, now the Institute for EastWest Studies, where I spent an academic year as a Krupp Foundation Senior Associate. Suddenly the phone rang. On the line from Washington was the Institute's president, John Edwin Mroz. He had just been informed that a few minutes earlier in East Berlin, Günter Schabowski, a member of the East German Politburo, had announced the opening of the border between East and West Germany. Now CNN wanted John to comment on what was likely to become a revolutionary event, and he asked me—a German scholar-in-residence—for advice.

None of us was instantly ready, of course, for a balanced ad hoc assessment of the move. We had followed the developments in Eastern Europe and the German Democratic Republic (GDR) closely throughout the summer and autumn of 1989, but there were still many surprises every day. Poland, Hungary, the Soviet Union—reforms, even radical transformations—were imminent everywhere. And the refugee movement from the GDR via Hungary and various Western embassies in East European capitals indicated a growing desire for change in East Germany as well. The possible consequences of the opening of "the Wall," however, went beyond anyone's imagination: How could the economically deadbeat GDR survive with an uncovered, unguarded flank vis-à-vis booming West Germany? Was a confederation of the two German states even possible? And how could the Soviet predominance in Eastern Europe be sustained if the East German pillar of its empire collapsed?

I agreed with John that the information he had just received from East Berlin was truly a surprise that could change the world, and I decided immediately—encouraged also by Peter Volten, the Institute's research director—to start collecting material on the events that would evolve in my country in the days, weeks, and months ahead. Later, as the chimera of a unified Germany gradually became a reality, I made up my mind not only to describe the process of German unification but to look at its implications in the context of Germany's past behavior as a unified state as well. Naturally, the storytelling aspect of the book, including a rather detailed description of specific episodes, was going to prevail, as it was much too early—historically speaking—to provide an in-depth structural analysis of the complex developments that were still unfolding.

One analytical topic nevertheless emerged from the narrative account rather quickly and was soon to form the real thread of the story: the contrast between the past experience of the former German Reich striving for European hegemony and the current trend to embed the newly united Federal Republic of Germany in the process of European integration. The simple but important question was: Would Germany become an assertive colossus in the middle of Europe again, with a position and policy similar to the tradition of the German Reich between 1871 and 1945, or was the background of the unification process in 1989-90 so different from the history of the Reich in the nineteenth and early twentieth century that any direct comparison would only be misleading?

For nearly half a century after the fall of Hitler and Nazism, it had hardly been necessary to raise this question. Germany had been divided between East and West, and although both Germanys—the Federal Republic even more so than the GDR—had been able to exercise considerable influence, particularly in multilateral fora where they could universalize or regionalize their national interests to make them less obtrusive, they had been only "semisovereign" and had not possessed all of the postwar trappings of power. Now, with unification, Germany was returning to a position of greater responsibility. Its new weight as a unified power in the center of Europe could even exceed the influence it had exerted in the past and determine the fate of the continent in the decades to come.

The opening of the border between East and West, the collapse of the Soviet empire in Eastern Europe, and the liberation of Germany from the constraints of the "German question" actually brought the Federal Republic to the core of the search for a new European architecture, transcending former blocs, alliances, and ideologies. The new phase in European history will therefore be marked by the contrast, rather than the similarities, with the familiar patterns of post–World War II politics, dooming the structure of a predominantly bipolar international system that was based on American power, Soviet force, and the division of Germany to a relic of the past.

Yet, within the new Europe, the unification of Germany is as much a matter of anxiety as it is an expression of hope. German unification could bring new attention to the idea of "Mitteleuropa" as a bridge between East and West, thus promoting an all-European understanding and identity apart from traditional structures of East-West partition and bipolarity. Given the disorientation of Eastern Europe and its need for economic assistance and cooperation, the unified Germany could establish a link between the capitalist democracies of the West and the transforming societies in the East, providing economic strength and political weight alike. On the other hand, the notion of putting Germany in the driver's seat of Europe again could provoke feelings of uneasiness, if not outright rejection. History remains a burden, even if European cooperation takes precedence over memories of the past and gradually revises the German image.

In any case, the question of a new European architecture is an issue of imperative importance. What kind of order can we expect? What role is Germany going to play? Will it become a subject, rather than an object, of international relations again? And what are the implications for Eastern Europe and Russia, for the Atlantic Alliance and the United States, and for the process of European integration and the European Community? Will there be a return to a balance-of-power system among the nations of Europe, resembling the order that was established at the Congress of Vienna in 1815? Or can a new structure be implemented, stretching from Vancouver to Vladivostok, in which Europeans, Americans, and Russians alike would be united by their determination to preserve stability and peace via new mechanisms of security and cooperation?

Within the framework of revising the *ancien régime* of European politics, the unification of Germany marks the beginning of a new formative period in European history. On the threshold of the 21st century, we are witnessing an evolution in state, society, and economy that is about to revolutionize the face of the European continent, if not the world. The following study, though focusing primarily on the German aspects of change, also explains this development of a new international order.

The book begins with an analysis of the historical dimensions of the German question to gain a better perspective for assessing current events. The introductory section argues that Germany's striving for hegemony in the nineteenth and early twentieth centuries was more a matter of time and circumstances than the result of a specific German nature and mentality. I also suggest that Germany's position in the international arena has changed dramatically after World War II and that the unification process of 1990 was caused not by a new German nationalism but by the collapse of communist power in Eastern Europe. In fact, the unification of Germany was more a side effect of the gradual decline of Soviet influence after the beginning of comprehensive reform processes in Poland and Hungary earlier in the 1980s and Mikhail Gorbachev's policy of glasnost and perestroika than the product of German policies.

The events leading from the resignation of Erich Honecker and the opening of the border to the downfall of the Socialist Unity Party (SED) regime and the unification of the two German states form the heart of the book. The account shows that any theory linking Chancellor Kohl and his government to the beginning of the unification process is false. Germany's unification actually did not emerge from *outside* the GDR, but from the Monday demonstrations in Leipzig and other East German cities—that is, from a growing unification movement *within* the GDR and from the rapidly increasing flow of refugees who left East Germany for the Federal Republic and soon began to create economic problems in both East and West. The West German government in Bonn, on the other hand, was anything but prepared for a quick unification. Kohl's ten-point confederation proposal of November 28, 1989, was more an improvisation than a master plan. And not until his visit to Dresden on December 19-20 did the chancellor become convinced that unification would occur in a matter of months rather than years.

The negotiations for the establishment of the German Economic and Monetary Union on July 1, 1990, and the talks between the two German states and the four victorious powers of World War II—"two-plus-four"—resulting in the unification and full sovereignty of Germany on October, 1990, eventually concluded the revolution of the political, economic, and social order in the center of Europe. Again, the details reveal the differences between the former German Reich and the new Federal Republic. The central thesis of the book therefore remains that the new Germany has little, if anything, in common with the former Germany of Bismarck or Wilhelm II—not to mention Hitler.

The thesis is also supported by the concluding "implications" part of the book, which broadens the perspective and resumes the historical argumentation of the introductory chapter. Its economy strained by the tremendous dual task of financing German unification and helping to rebuild the countries of Eastern Europe, Germany is not likely to attempt establishing a "Fourth Reich." Rather it should continue the Federal Republic's policy of European integration and transatlantic cooperation. Accordingly, the new European architecture should not be dominated by a restored system of nation-states with Germany at its center, but should be based on the interlocking institutions of the European Community, North Atlantic Treaty Organization, Western European Union, and the Conference on Security and Cooperation in Europe.

In other words, the Germany of 1990 is not the Germany of 1871, 1918, or 1933. The new Germany is not only more democratic; it is also more stable and more accepted. And while the collapse of Soviet communism and the end of the Soviet empire in Eastern Europe have led to crises and conflict in the ensuing process of transformation, resembling in many ways the problems of former times, in Germany the past will eventually give way to a better future.

MANFRED GÖRTEMAKER
Berlin-Potsdam
October 1993

The German Question
in Historical Perspective

reed for power and struggle for hegemony are neither peculiar German phenomena nor have they ever been confined to the horizons of Europe. The history of mankind is filled with examples demonstrating the rise and fall of empires and the constant fight to balance the interests and ambitions of competing forces.[1] Ancient China, medieval Mongolia, the Ottoman Empire, and the great wars of early modern history associated with the names of Charles V, Philip II, Louis XIV, and Napoleon I all indicate that the execution of power is anything but a German privilege.

Yet from the 1870s until after World War II, it was Germany that was perceived as the main threat to European and world peace. During this period, even apart from the Nazi crimes, the prevailing German image was characterized by militaristic aggressiveness, political boundlessness, and an overall lack of sensitivity for the concerns and interests of others.

This view was largely shaped by the course of history between 1871, when Germany became a unified Reich under the leadership of the Prussian squire Otto von Bismarck, and 1945, when German ambitions were finally curbed with the defeat of Nazism, partition, and the integration of the divided country into the emerging power blocs led by the Soviet Union and the United States.

The history of the Reich since 1871 seemed to prove that a united Germany was simply too big and dynamic for any stable European state system and that the German tendency toward political aggressiveness was not simply an expression of legitimate pursuit of German national interests, but also a reprehensible sign of the internal character of the German nation.[2] Reminiscent of 74 years of German unity, two world wars, Nazism, and nearly 65 million people killed either by warfare or in concentration camps, it was now said that Germany's political, economic, and military power inevitably threatened the independence and well-being of its neighbors and that the German nature had not only made Germany aggressive abroad but also susceptible to totalitarianism at home.[3]

After World War II, the partition of Germany and the Soviet-American duopoly over Europe seemed to have resolved the "German Problem." By dividing and containing German power and ambition, thus keeping the German menace at bay and the German people safe from themselves, Europe and the world were thought to be safe from the Germans once and forever.[4]

Now Germany is united again. Even if history does not tend to repeat itself, fundamental questions therefore arise: Is there any proof that the Germans possess a distinct personality that makes them essentially different from other nations? Does the fact that the unified Reich of 1871 exercised supreme power, challenging the European equilibrium of 1815 until it was destroyed, indicate that the unified Germany of the 1990s could once again become a destructive force in Europe? And will the geopolitical position of Germany in the center of Europe, an issue of such eminent magnitude in the past, be a destabilizing factor again, or could the geographic location of Germany also be turned into an advantage for both the Europeans and the Germans themselves?

MODERN GERMANY AND THE EUROPEAN BALANCE OF POWER

Until the late nineteenth century, Prussia and Germany did not constitute a threat to European security, nor did they provide a model for any specific form of Germanic aggressiveness.[5] Despite the notion of Prussian militarism, which was the result of the country's rise into the ranks of the great European powers through the use of military force in the eighteenth century and the internal organization of Prussia along the lines of military discipline, Germany remained an essentially fragmented and powerless group of relatively sovereign states until 1871.[6]

Dreams of a united Germany that had emerged in the late eighteenth and early nineteenth centuries, and particularly during the struggle against Napoleon and French occupation between 1806 and 1813, did not even materialize at the Congress of Vienna in 1815. There the Austrian and British foreign ministers, Graf Metternich and Viscount Castlereagh, put forward their concept of "restoration" that was designed to overcome the ideas of the French Revolution by reinstating absolutism and re-creating the European pentarchy of powers, consisting of Britain, France, Prussia, Austria, and Russia.[7]

Metternich and Castlereagh believed that restoration would be more effective than any new system in bringing about lasting peace in Europe.[8] Their so-called European concert was designed to maintain a balance of power—in other words, a system to defend the status quo.[9] While France, after a struggle of 150 years for European hegemony, was assured of an honored place in the restored order (for it represented an essential factor in the general balance of power), Germany remained divided into four free cities and 35 sovereign states, among them two European great powers—Prussia and Austria. The creation of a "German Federation" turned out to be essentially meaningless, since this was an organization with few competencies, little power, and almost no central authority.[10] It became clear during the revolution of 1848-49, if not earlier, that the federation was designed to prevent, rather than to promote, the foundation of a German nation-state.[11]

As a result, Germany was unable to participate in Europe's evolution into national states, which increasingly seemed the only effective political formula for organizing stable government over modern societies. Indeed, Germany was the last of the great European national states to be formed. In retrospect, the successful attempts of classical European diplomacy, beginning with Metternich and Castlereagh and continuing with French policy until 1870, to undermine the German unification movement were in the long run counterproductive—to say the least.[12] Also, the failure of German liberals to satisfy the aspirations of German nationalists in the revolution of 1848-49 is probably one of the major tragedies of German and European history. For the failure of liberalism in 1849 soon caused a growing number of Germans to turn their hopes to Prussian conservatism and its determined leader, Otto von Bismarck.

Bismarck, who was nominated prime minister of Prussia by King Wilhelm I in 1862, was well aware of the dilemma facing Prussian and German policy: While Germany was impatiently awaiting unification, which also seemed necessary for economic reasons, unification under Prussian dominance would be possible only if Austria's influence in German affairs was eliminated and French resistance was crushed—even if this meant war.[13] Moreover, it had been argued since 1815 that the continued partition of Germany was a prerequisite of a stable European balance of power, because a unified Germany would be too strong and powerful not to pose a threat to the stability and peace in Europe.

Therefore, Bismarck pursued a dual strategy designed to address the national goal of unification as well as the European concerns about the impact of a united Germany. In other words, he did not hesitate to use force against Denmark in 1864, Austria in 1866, and France in 1870 to establish the Reich, but after 1871 he was strictly opposed to expanding influence beyond the limits of traditional German boundaries or to assume a global, rather than European, role for the new German empire. As a result, Bismarck's policy was characterized by controlled aggressiveness until 1871 and by a remarkable degree of moderation and self-restraint thereafter.[14]

Bismarck's experience as a Prussian delegate at the Bundestag in Frankfurt (the parliament of the German Federation) from 1851 until 1859 and as an envoy at the Prussian legations at St. Petersburg and Paris from 1859 until 1862 had made him familiar with the rules of internal German affairs and the principles of European balance-of-power politics. Thus he reached the conclusion that it was necessary, first, to establish the German Reich without the participation of Austria (kleindeutsche Lösung, or small-German solution) and, second, to integrate the united Germany firmly into the existing European system. Germany, Bismarck argued, was supposed to work for, not against, the status quo. Indeed, Germany was supposed to assume the function of a stabilizing center in the middle of the European continent.

The performance of the German Reich in foreign affairs during the Bismarck era furnished evidence that a united Germany was not per se predetermined to undermine the balance of power in Europe. On the contrary, Germany even became a major defender of the existing order—with Bismarck playing the role of an "honest broker," acting as a mediator between the competing powers of the European order, as he did with much-admired success at the Congress of Berlin in June-July 1878.[15]

After Bismarck's dismissal in 1890, however, a new generation, of which young Kaiser Wilhelm II was the most typical and representative symbol, assumed responsibility. Clumsy, bigmouthed, and arrogant, he immediately turned his attention outward to pursue noisy German Weltpolitik.[16] The Kaiser, like many of his associates, felt that Germany had a natural right to expand; Britain, France, and the other colonial powers had already presided over vast empires, yet they expected Germany—the national latecomer—to remain locked within the tight frame of Europe's traditional balance of power. The perception of unjustified restrictions on Germany was magnified by the prospect of the emerging American and Russian empires, as David Calleo has stated rightly: "From a German view, preserving the European balance, while extra-European giants formed all around, meant condemning Germany to mediocrity and, ultimately, all of Europe to external domination. That was the 'German Problem' as the Germans saw it."[17]

In any event, Bismarck's diplomatic mastery did not suffice to shape a foreign policy of reconciliation that would outlast its creator. In domestic affairs, too, the "Iron Chancellor" was unable to control factors that led to future aggression and expansion: the dynamic forces of nationalism that Bismarck himself had summoned to consolidate his Reich; the evils of

Prussian militarism that had been aggravated by the triumphs of 1864, 1866, and 1871; and the rapid economic growth that would soon overshadow France and challenge Britain.

While German imperialism in the late nineteenth century was more a matter of time and circumstances—and not the product of an abnormal political culture essentially different from that of any other nation in Europe—and while Germany's "aggressiveness" against the international order was more the result of geography and history than the consequence of a demonic state of the German mind, this does not imply that Germany lacked any specific elements that could link historical roots to the events in the first half of the twentieth century. The opposite is true: First, the unification process from 1864 to 1871 led to a previously unknown emphasis on military power, which was soon perceived as a major threat to the European order. Second, the lack of political influence of the middle class hindered the development of democratic institutions and enabled the aristocracy to secure their rule and maintain the Prussian tradition. Third, the rapid industrialization of the authoritarian Reich created a dangerous mix of economic strength and military might in a political environment that combined the absence of effective parliamentary control with a conservative public opinion of nationalist pride and an expansionist mood, paving the way for German Weltpolitik under Wilhelm II. And finally, the presence of anti-Semitic parties and a certain brand of racially and nationally based anti-Semitism—though not unusual in Europe in the nineteenth century—indicated that the Germans too were susceptible to slogans and demands for the persecution of minorities in general and Jews in particular.[18]

The Weltpolitik aspirations of a "world mission" were cultivated by, among others, the powerful Navy League, founded in April 1898, and by Admiral Alfred von Tirpitz, who was confident that a well-armed Germany at sea would be able to exploit the opportunities in world politics promised by the expected waning of English influence.[19] Tirpitz's appointment as state secretary in the Navy Ministry in March 1897 coincided by chance with Bernhard von Bülow's assumption of the Foreign Ministry; together, the two men changed the course of history.[20] Bülow, member of an old and famous German aristocratic family, son of a diplomat, and a career diplomat himself, ordered the acquisition of Kiautschou, the Caroline Islands, and Samoa and promoted building the Baghdad railway line, thereby furthering German expansion in Southeast Asia, the Pacific, and the Middle East. Tirpitz, a senior naval officer with a brilliant career in command posts as well as staff positions, designed and implemented a fleet program to make Germany a leading naval power in the world.

Bülow's and Tirpitz's policy was emphatically supported by Kaiser Wilhelm II and a great majority of the German public, as imperialism proved to be a powerful force for the political integration and mobilization of the middle and lower-middle class. Calleo even argues that "imperialism grew with the democratization of politics," as the "stunning rise of the Social Democrats, with their organized mass base, pushed the other parties to find a popular base of their own." Thus, Calleo says, "as the conservative parties used the agrarians and anti-Semites for support, and the center relied on the various Catholic associations, the National Liberals turned to imperialism."[21] The long-term effect of these developments on public opinion, however, was alarming: "By the second decade of the twentieth century, bourgeois opinion was thoroughly impregnated with the notion that for future growth Germany required a major territorial sphere of its own in the world, a sphere comparable to those of Britain, Russia, and the United States."

The extent to which imperial Germany was attempting to achieve world hegemony has been a matter of considerable dispute among scholars studying the pre-World War I period.[23] The discussion was greatly influenced by a comparison of Luigi Albertini's *The Origins of the War of 1914* with Fritz Fischer's *Germany's Aims in the First World War.* As a result, it seems to be clear that Germany was trying to ensure a preeminent position for itself in the future world system of states—a position for which it claimed to have legitimacy, indeed the natural right as one of the leading powers of Europe.[24]

Even earlier, by the turn of the century, the dichotomy of perception and reality had already led to a German image that was characterized by what was thought to be standardized Prussianism: a high work ethic and an inclination to efficiency and performance, combined with formal stiffness, total lack of humor, and a militaristic mentality that provided the basis for uncommon aggressiveness and a constant readiness to use force in the pursuit of political and economic goals. When World War I began in 1914, all the negative assumptions about the German character seemed to be amply demonstrated.

In Germany—as elsewhere—power and military ambition had their way, losing all restraint. Fantasies of a new German Reich stretching from the Rhine through Central and Eastern Europe to the Ukraine and the Caucasus were dreamed as late as August 1918, by which time American entry into the war—and, more important, into combat—showed the ultimate futility of continued fighting. And when the war ended, the generals did not admit their own responsibility and guilt, but rather felt deserted by the politicians on the home front; the Kaiser went into exile in the Netherlands, while many senior military figures went into unrepentant internal or external exile.

The revolution of November 1918 and the establishment of the Weimar Republic marked the beginning of a new era. The question was: Would the collapse of the imperial regime have a sedative effect on Germany's policy? Or would the dynamism of change only lead to new aspirations and demands? There is probably no more concise characterization of the fate of the Weimar Republic than Peter Gay's remark that it "was born in defeat, lived in turmoil, and died in disaster."[25] However, defeat also meant a fresh start, the turmoil provided for opportunities, and the end was by no means predetermined. The choice of the Weimar Republic, therefore, was "neither quixotic nor arbitrary; for a time the Republic had a real chance."[26]

The defeat of Germany in World War I implied military surrender as well as a political revolution. When Germany first asked for an armistice in October 1918, it did so on the basis of a declaration by US president Woodrow Wilson of January 8, 1918, which came to be known as the "Fourteen Points."

Wilson's general concept of peace did not incorporate a renewal of the European system—with its wars for hegemony—nor the establishment of a world system with its corresponding dangers, but the far-reaching abolition of foreign policy in the old sense of the term—the abolition of a multitude of sovereign states, each ready to wage war, and their replacement by a peaceful grouping of nations within the organizational framework of a League of Nations. Specifically, Wilson called for the end of secret diplomacy, freedom of navigation on the seas in peace and war, removal of barriers to international free trade, reduction of armaments, and the right of national self-determination.[27]

If Wilson's program had been implemented, Germany's defeat on the battlefield might have turned into a European victory on the political stage. Unfortunately, however, the conditions for a new international order were much less favorable than desired: At the Versailles peace conference in 1919, Wilson's idealism collided with the bitter realism of French premier Georges Clemenceau, British prime minister David Lloyd George, and Italian prime minister Vittorio Orlando.

From a German viewpoint, the Fourteen Points were nothing less than a face-saving device to get out of the war with honor. To the British and Italians, however, and even more to the French, who demanded revenge and suppression rather than reconciliation and equality, Wilson's ideas seemed almost absurdly inadequate to serve the Allied war aims.[28] As a result, a war-guilt clause, ascribing sole German responsibility for the outbreak of the war, and extensive reparation agreements constituted the core of the peace treaty with Germany that was signed at Versailles on June 28, 1919.[29]

This treaty almost immediately became a major obstacle to the stabilization of the new democracy in Germany. The reasons were both economic and psychological: The reparation payments helped prevent the quick economic recovery that could have broadened public acceptance of the Weimar system; the war-guilt clause led a majority of the Germans to regard the treaty as the exact opposite of the just and fair peace promised by President Wilson in January 1918; both made it an easy task for extremists from left and right to demand significant revisions. Many Germans felt particularly cheated by the eventual withdrawal of America. And since the treaty was neither signed nor supported by the militarists who had really been responsible for the catastrophe of 1914 to 1918, but by the only recently appointed and innocent foreign minister Hermann Müller and transportation secretary Johannes Bell—the former a Social Democrat, the latter a member of the Catholic Zentrum party—the critique was soon also extended to the representatives of the new republic.

Thus the Versailles treaty provided for a bad start even if it was not the only reason for the failure of the Weimar regime. Germany's acceptance of the terms of the treaty depended on domestic political and economic factors as well as on the interplay of external influences upon the life of the German nation. On both levels, conditions were rather unfavorable between 1919 and 1924. At that time internal and external circumstances improved to the extent that pacification of the country became more likely. However, after 1929, the republic experienced rapid decomposition, ending with the collapse of the regime and the establishment of the Third Reich in January 1933.[30]

Economic distress, the increase in the number of déclassés, and even the abolition of the monarchy resulted in a loss of focus. While the Weimar Republic had been able to preserve a united German national state, its ability to promote national interests had been limited by restrictions from the Versailles treaty, an economy in shambles, social disintegration, and a weak international position. So, in the absence of a democratic tradition, millions of Germans voted for a strong national leader—Adolf Hitler.

When general elections for the Reichstag were held in September 1930, the Nazis achieved their political breakthrough. In their competition with communism, the nationalists gambled on the collapse of the entire Western order established in 1919. Their concept was based on radical hostility to Versailles and uncompromising hatred of "Jewishness." They felt that they had a unique historical opportunity to gain bourgeois and European support for wiping out the Bolshevik revolution and in so doing create completely new conditions for the expansion of German power and territory.[31]

A further factor, reinforcing the dynamism of Hitler's so-called National Socialism, was the racial irredentism that originated in the nineteenth-century writings of Joseph Arthur Count de Gobineau, Georges Vacher de Lapouge, and, above all, Houston Stewart Chamberlain.[32] The race theories of the Nazis were a blend of the ideas expressed in the works of these authors as well as of common Darwinism and dark emotions from the southeast of Europe.[33] Nazism transformed the idea of racial superiority into a most powerful weapon for leadership and political pretensions.

Between September 1930 and the summer of 1932, the Nazis became the largest political party in Germany and Hitler emerged as a charismatic enemy of German democracy. After July 1932, an absolute antirepublican majority paralyzed the legislature of the republic, whose government now tended even more than before to rule through abuse of Article 48 of the Weimar Constitution, which gave presidential decrees the force of law. The president from 1925 on was former field marshal Paul von Hindenburg, anything but a determined defender of the republic. Acting on the advice of antirepublican intriguers, Hindenburg appointed Hitler head of the government on January 30, 1933.[34]

Meanwhile, outside Germany—above all in Benito Mussolini's Italy—caesarism had already proven its capacity to rally national feelings and provide a third form of government between predatory communism and confused bourgeois democracy. Inside Germany, however, the new Führer grew into an infinitely larger figure than his peers in other European countries, except in Joseph Stalin's Russia. His methods of terror and propaganda, though possibly modeled on methods practiced elsewhere, reached unprecedented heights of horror. The "movement" of Nazism won every position of power and authority; the seizure of power did not sober it, however, as had been expected by so many of those who cheered it on. On the contrary, success raised the demonic nature of the regime to a still higher pitch and injected it violently into the emotions of the masses.[35]

Carried along by the dark wave of the economic crisis and continually spurred on by the worldwide aspirations of the Bolsheviks (or the perception thereof), Hitler quickly expanded the power he just had been granted and promised to seek a proper place for the German Reich by destroying the "unjust system of Versailles." As with his totalitarianism at home, there eventually seemed to be nothing he could not achieve through aggression abroad in pursuit of his historic mission, which he saw as resolving the German geopolitical problem of being entangled in middle-European narrowness.[36]

Thus Hitler set out for boundless territorial expansion to create a Grossdeutsches Reich, as opposed to Bismarck's kleindeutsche Lösung (small-German solution) of 1871. And he left little doubt what he was up to. As early as the mid-1920s, he had outlined the main goals of the foreign policy that he was going to pursue "by the force of a victorious sword" in his book *Mein Kampf*: reclamation of the territories that Germany had lost after World War I; annexation of all areas outside the Reich where Germans lived;

conquest of new space in the East (Lebensraum im Osten); and German world supremacy.[37]

While the immediate goals of Hitler's foreign policy—Germany's emancipation from the restrictions of the Versailles treaty, the restoration of the eastern frontiers, and the annexation of Austria—were supported by a vast majority of the German people and more or less accepted by foreign governments, the long-term claims of Nazism—conquest of space in the East and German world domination—were not taken very seriously by the Germans themselves and by the world abroad. At the very least, the Western appeasement policy vis-à-vis the Nazis until 1939 demonstrated a basic readiness to allow the Germans to "correct" the mistakes of Versailles.

But Hitler was dead serious about his long-term goals. He believed that his predecessors had been far too weak in making use of Bismarck's foundation of a united Reich. The necessity, as he saw it, to provide adequate space in lands contiguous to Germany for the German people to grow had been fatally neglected. Therefore, the mere restoration of old borders would be dangerously inadequate and strategically irrelevant. The eventual aim of the new foreign policy of his strong government, Hitler stated again and again, was to solve the old German problem of living space by seizing new lands—even if this meant war.[38]

Such a war, he believed, would have to be fought mainly against France and the Soviet Union, whereas Italy and Britain might be won over as allies.[39] Britain was particularly critical, as World War I had shown, but if Britain joined Germany or could be kept out of the struggle, there was no reason to assume that the war could not be decided in favor of Germany. Therefore, when British prime minister Neville Chamberlain, after talks with Hitler in Berchtesgaden and Godesberg, accepted the Munich agreement of September 29, 1938, and one day later even signed an Anglo-German declaration to settle all future problems "consultatively," the Führer could be confident that his strategy would succeed.

If it had, Germany would have gained hegemony over the European continent and Britain would have been confirmed in its empire. Thus, Hitler can hardly be regarded as entirely irrational. His goals as well as his strategy were clearly defined and, from a geopolitical point of view, rationally conceived. To be sure, until Britain's sudden firmness over Poland, which came as a genuine surprise to the German leader, Hitler's foreign policy must be described as successful beyond the fondest dreams of the German people.[40]

With the beginning of World War II, however, Hitler's megalomania and obstinacy began seriously to interfere with the rationality—within a strictly German context—of his foreign policy. In domestic affairs this had always been the case: Ever since his coming to power (the so-called Machtergreifung), Hitler had acted brutally to eliminate political opposition, persecute Jews and other minorities, and apply totalitarian force as an instrument of terror, thus making any resistance to his regime suicidal. Now the criminal internal methods of Nazism were extended to foreign affairs as well. The system that did not recognize the legal constraints of a constitution at home could hardly be expected to respect international law abroad. Thus the European war that began in 1939 was destined to be fought until total victory or total defeat.[41]

PARTITION AS A SOLUTION

As early as 1941, the countries at war with Germany, notably the United States, Britain, and the Soviet Union, began discussing the future of Germany once defeated. German militaristic aggressiveness, political unscrupulousness, and moral abjectness had reached such unprecedented heights under Nazism that sober reflections about leading Germany back into the community of nations was anything but easy. Not surprisingly, considerations long fluctuated between reeducation and rehabilitation on the one hand and a punitive settlement on the other.

Between the beginning of World War II in September 1939 and the German attack on the Soviet Union in June 1941, there was hardly any postwar planning at all. Even after the launching of "Unternehmen Barbarossa" —which was the code name for the German invasion of the Soviet Union— Stalin, in a telegram to Winston Churchill, stated on November 8, 1941, that there existed "no definite understanding between our two countries on war aims and on plans for the post-war organization of peace."[42] Subsequently, the British prime minister proposed to send Foreign Secretary Anthony Eden to Moscow to discuss with Stalin the whole range of war and postwar issues.

In his meeting in December 1941 with Eden and at the Teheran Conference two years later, Stalin toyed with the idea of German dismemberment. Churchill also long favored Germany's partition, proposing above all a decisive weakening of historic Prussia, a division of Germany along the Main River, and the creation of a Danuvian Confederation in the south. Yet the experts at the Treasury and the Foreign Office kept insisting that such a solution would be, from a British budgetary standpoint, economically unsound and, in view of the Soviet advance to East-Central Europe in the course of the war, politically dangerous.[43]

The US "Advisory Committee on Post-War Foreign Policy" that was established in February 1942 under the chairmanship of Secretary of State

Cordell Hull also focused mainly on the dismemberment of Germany. However, no partition plan ever received the support of a majority of the committee. On the contrary, the final recommendation—entitled "The Political Reorganization of Germany" and submitted to President Franklin D. Roosevelt in September 1943—argued strongly in favor of maintaining German unity.[44]

But Roosevelt, pursuing a policy concept of global dimensions, felt it necessary to accept Soviet domination in large parts of Eastern and Central Europe as a price for Moscow's cooperation. In a conversation with Francis Cardinal Spellman in September 1943, the president admitted that communism was likely to expand and that the nations of Europe would have to adapt to Soviet leadership.[45] Subsequently, at the heads-of-government meetings at Teheran in November-December 1943, Roosevelt proposed a partition of Germany into five separate states and two regions under international control—a proposal close to the ideas Stalin had put forward in his December 1941 talks with Eden.[46]

At Teheran, Roosevelt, Churchill, and Stalin were still operating under the assumption that the restoration of a united Germany would constitute a threat to world peace and that only a divided Germany could eventually become an acceptable partner on the international scene again. In the United States, this conviction was shared particularly by the secretary of the treasury, Henry Morgenthau, who in September 1944 put forward his own plan for German partition and deindustrialization.[47] Since Morgenthau had already earned a reputation of being rigidly anti-German, his views came as no surprise to anybody. The fact, however, that John Foster Dulles, who had worked closely with the German banking and business community as a corporate lawyer during the 1920s and 1930s (and later, as secretary of state, was to become a cordial friend of Chancellor Konrad Adenauer), expressed similar ideas in a private memorandum in November 1944 would have been a great surprise—had it been known to the public. Dulles, who at the time was not just a private citizen but an associate of Republican presidential candidate Thomas E. Dewey in the election campaign against Roosevelt, noted:

> It has been found that when the German is assimilated into other societies he makes a good citizen. It is only when he is *en masse* that he rises to white heat over the idea of racial superiority and all that heinous philosophy means. Let us, then, draw the life of the Germans into surrounding countries, leaving only a nucleus of Prussia. Let the Rhineland be drawn into France, South Germany into Austria, Eastern Germany into Poland. Then let us encourage a European Federation of States that will ally itself against the rise of the war spirit in the Prussians to police them.

All this time let us endeavor to educate the young and the old. Let us re-write their history books, giving them the truth. Let us recognize that they have to be ruled with a heavy hand or they will have nothing but scorn for their rulers. Let us give them a religious training. Let us train them as we would have them trained and not leave them to their own methods, which have brought about destruction such as we never thought possible and which could bring about a more horrible war than we have yet experienced. Let us make it impossible for them to murder the world. Let us make sure that civilization conquers and is not conquered.[48]

Apparently, the German struggle for hegemony had developed both the material and the spiritual forces of destruction to such a degree that even friends of Germany found it difficult to make a distinction between Nazism and long-term aspects of German politics.

By the time of the Big Three meeting at Yalta in February 1945, however, it had already become obvious that the nearing surrender of the German Wehrmacht and the subsequent collapse of the Nazi Reich would not put an end to the play of power politics. The fall of Germany liberated the peoples of Western Europe from the danger of totalitarianism; on the other hand, the peoples of Eastern Europe, including East Germany, were now exposed to it with a vengeance. This, too, was ultimately a result of the German urge to achieve hegemony, whatever the more specific reasons may have been. Therefore at Yalta, Churchill, who had grown up in the tradition of classical British and European balance-of-power diplomacy, warned against an approach, including the partition of Germany, that opened the floodgates to Soviet hegemony in all of continental Europe.[49]

Stalin quickly bent to Churchill's new attitude when he realized that President Roosevelt, already visibly ill and under strong pressure from the experts in his own administration who agreed in large part with the British assumptions and conclusions regarding Germany's dismemberment, did little to thwart the arguments of the prime minister. At the victory parade in Moscow on May 9, 1945, the Soviet leader publicly declared that "the Soviet Union is celebrating the victory but is not going to dismember or destroy Germany."[50] The instrument of joint occupation, Stalin now seemed to believe, would enable the Soviets to influence events in the Western zones to achieve security against a future German threat, and the option of an all-German framework would provide the basis to exact reparations from their own zone as well as from the Western industrial areas, particularly from the Ruhr, for the recovery of the Soviet economy.

From July 17 through August 2, 1945, new US president Harry S. Truman, Stalin, and Churchill (who was replaced very early on by Clement Attlee when the British elected a Labour government) met again at Potsdam to confirm earlier decisions reached by the European Advisory Commission (EAC). The Allied leaders addressed the German occupation statute and the division of Germany into American, British, Soviet, and French zones as well as respective sectors of occupation for the area of Greater Berlin. Agreement was also reached on the dissolution of the Nazi Party and the demilitarization of Germany. A Council of Foreign Ministers (CFM), including representatives of the Soviet Union, the United States, Great Britain, France, and China, was entrusted with preparing a peace settlement for Germany "to be accepted by the Government of Germany when a government adequate for the purpose is established."[51]

In the meantime, the four military governors were to form an Allied Control Council to deal with questions relating to Germany as a whole. Furthermore, the Potsdam agreements stipulated that "so far as practicable" the population was to be dealt with uniformly throughout the country and Germany treated as a single economic unit—a principle that clashed with the supremacy of each zone commander within his own domain and would soon lead to conflict, emerging most sharply over the issue of reparations.[52]

Other matters discussed at Potsdam concerned the revival of political life, Germany's new borders, and access to Berlin. Denazification and democratization were accepted as desirable principles, but the conference failed to provide specific definitions or guidelines for implementation, thus leaving it to the respective occupation regimes to apply their different ideas on what they felt constituted reeducation and democracy.[53]

Regarding the question of borders, the eastern boundary of the Soviet zone was fixed along the Oder and Görlitzer-Neisse rivers. Former German territories east of this line were placed under Polish administration. Poland was thereby compensated for land lost on its own eastern border to the Soviet Union. The settlement was formally provisional, as the final peace settlement was to be concluded with a future German government. However, none of the powers present in Potsdam expected a revision of the agreement reached there.[54]

Arrangements for Berlin also were preliminary, as the conference failed to devise a satisfactory formula for access and joint Allied occupation. An extensive study prepared by the planning staff of the Supreme Headquarters Allied Expeditionary Force (SHAEF) entitled "Command, Organization and Administration of the International Zone, Berlin," forwarded to the State Department by the US Embassy in London on June 28, 1944, had already foreseen the problems of access. Under the heading "Access into the Zone," the paper stated:

It must be recalled that Berlin lies some 100 miles from the North-West zone and 150 miles from the South-West zone. Movement into the Berlin zone by road, rail and air of all personnel and supplies must therefore necessarily be through the RUSSIAN zone. Agreement with the RUSSIANS as to how this is to be effected is consequently a first essential.[55]

Yet Washington never sent any instructions to its representative in the EAC, Ambassador John E. Winant, who discussed the matter with his counterparts from the Soviet Union and Britain in the autumn of 1944. Winant was confident anyway that concrete provisions could be negotiated in the EAC without great difficulty; the Soviet representative had repeatedly stated that arranging for transit through the Soviet zone to Berlin was no problem and that the presence of US and British forces in Berlin "of course" carried with it all necessary facilities of access.[56] But no written agreement was signed, and in Potsdam the issue still remained without binding Soviet guarantees of access by land and water across their zone to Berlin; only three air corridors were formally approved, and those not until November 1945.

In view of these hardly satisfactory settlements, George F. Kennan, then US ambassador W. Averell Harriman's deputy in Moscow, reflected about the future of the defeated Germany and wrote in the summer of 1945:

> The idea of a Germany run jointly with the Russians is a chimera. The idea of both the Russians and ourselves withdrawing politely at a given date and a healthy, peaceful, stable, and friendly Germany arising out of the resulting vacuum is also a chimera. We have no choice but to lead our section of Germany—the section of which we and the British have accepted responsibility—to a form of independence so prosperous, so secure, so superior, that the East cannot threaten it.[57]

Kennan's analysis—indeed prophecy—could not have been better defined. Although Stalin had told the leader of the London-based Polish exile government, Stanislav Mikolajzik, in 1944 that "communism fitted Germany as a saddle fitted a cow," the Soviets were determined to consolidate their own power and that of their German communist assistants in their own zone from the very first days of occupation.[58] And since the Western powers also wasted no time in restructuring their own spheres of influence in Germany according to their political views, ideological convictions, and economic necessities, partition was imminent, if not already an established fact, in late 1945.

A major quarrel occurred over reparations. Indignant at the Soviets' refusal to supply food and other commodities to the Western zones in exchange for reparations deliveries from the West as agreed upon at Potsdam, the US

military governor, General Lucius D. Clay, unilaterally suspended dismantling operations and deliveries to the Soviets from the American zone in May
1946. Both sides began seeking to take advantage of the opportunities and
ambiguities of the wartime agreements to readjust their policies to contain
each other's power rather than continue approaching postwar reconstruction
cooperatively.[59]

The shift in American policy toward Germany was signaled by the July
1946 proposal of Secretary of State James F. Byrnes to unify the economy of
the American zone with that of any of the other zones and by his reconcilia-
tory speech in Stuttgart of September 6, 1946.[60] In effect, Byrnes's initiative
was an expression of his government's commitment to the economic recovery of Germany, a policy that conflicted with Soviet insistence on the priority
of reparations from current production over the German standard of living.
On January 1, 1947, the British and American zones were formally merged
into "Bizonia."

The crumbling of Allied unity in Germany also doomed to failure the deliberations on a peace treaty for Germany at the four-power conference of foreign
ministers in Moscow in March 1947. Soon after the commencement of the conference, President Truman enunciated his doctrine in which he promised US
support to the "free peoples" of the world and vilified the communist way of
life as one "based upon the will of a minority forcibly imposed upon the majority."[61] Subsequently, the European Recovery Program (ERP)—commonly
known as the Marshall Plan—was announced in June 1947, formally offering
aid to both Eastern and Western Europe, although the United States probably
never seriously intended to include in the program the Soviet zone in Germany
or the newly established "people's democracies" in Eastern Europe.[62]

Regarding Germany, the application of the Marshall Plan implied an economic and political restructuring of the Western zones, including the introduction of a separate West German currency and the creation of a separate
West German state, regardless of the consequences for German unity. As
could be foreseen, the Soviet Union, afraid of losing reparations from the
industrial heart of Germany at the Ruhr, protested against this development.
In March 1948, the Soviet representative withdrew from the Allied Control
Council, forcing the four-power control over Germany to collapse. Six
Western nations agreed at a conference in London on June 7 that the West
Germans could draft a constitution for a separate state. Finally, on June 18,
the worthless reichsmark was replaced by the new deutsche mark in order to
spur economic recovery and political stability.

The Soviet reaction to the London conference and the Western currency
reform was to sever all road, rail, and canal links to the Western sectors of

Berlin on June 24, 1948. The Western powers responded by deciding to provide supplies for West Berlin's population of over 2 million by means of an airlift.[63] The operation was so successful that the Soviets eventually called off their blockade in May 1949.[64] But the Western perceptions of the aggressive Soviet behavior in the Berlin crisis still hastened the final establishment of a West German state. A constitution (the Basic Law) came into force on May 23, 1949, the first elections for the Federal Parliament (the Bundestag) took place on August 14, and a government was constituted under Konrad Adenauer in the following month.

In the Soviet occupation zone, decisive steps toward the creation of an East German state were taken at the sessions of the German People's Congress (Deutscher Volkskongress) in May 1949. The Congress elected a 330-member People's Council (Volksrat), in which the Socialist Unity Party (SED) and mass organizations subservient to it held 210 seats. The council then prepared a constitutional draft and constituted itself as a provisional People's Chamber (Volkskammer) on October 7, 1949, in response to the emergence of the West German Federal Republic, while on October 10 the legislatures of the five East German Länder elected delegates to a provisional upper house. The two chambers, meeting jointly, proclaimed the German Democratic Republic (GDR) and approved the constitution. Otto Grotewohl, who had been the leader of the Social Democratic Party in the Soviet zone until its merger with the Communist Party, was entrusted with the formation of a government, and the veteran communist Wilhelm Pieck was elected provisional president of the new republic. General elections, which were put off until 1950, were then held for a single list of candidates, with seats distributed in advance among the parties and mass organizations.[65]

Within three years of the war's end, Germany's division had become a fact of European and world politics. Surprisingly, however, the partition had not been decided on by the great powers uniformly as an act to once and for all destroy the basis of German might. On the contrary, for reasons of power politics—Britain and the United States needing a united Germany as a bulwark against further Soviet expansion in Europe; the Soviet Union preferring a united Germany as the only chance of getting reparations from the Ruhr—the preservation of German unity had been declared a common goal of Allied postwar policy at Yalta and Potsdam. Thus the division of Germany after 1945 was more a result of disunity among the Allies over occupation policies and growing conflict in the emerging Cold War than the logical conclusion of lessons taught by the German history of the nineteenth and early twentieth centuries.

ADENAUER'S POLICY OF WESTINTEGRATION

In 1949, as the Federal Republic of Germany was established and Konrad Adenauer was elected chancellor, the country still found itself under Allied occupation, without sovereignty, mistrusted by nations worldwide, and only beginning to realize the extent of the Nazi regime's atrocities. The defeat in World War II had destroyed the prerequisites for a significant German role in world politics; Hitler's expansionism and crimes against humanity had demolished the moral basis of Germany's position in the community of nations; Germany was divided, part cause, part symptom of the East-West confrontation; indeed, it was a country in ruins in almost every respect.

Adenauer had no reason for optimism, as very little, if anything, remained of Germany's political, economic, and military institutions, and the development of the Cold War between East and West had led to a difficult climate for negotiations. Yet the division of Germany, the 1948 communist coup in Czechoslovakia, the Berlin blockade, and the outbreak of the Korean War in June 1950 were all conducive to anticommunist policies, which at the same time brought West Germany closer to a political understanding with the West European nations as well as with the United States.

Adenauer realized that the Federal Republic had something of vital importance to offer the West during this period of apparent communist aggressiveness: repulsion of communist expansion into Western Europe through making West Germany a bulwark against the East by means of political and economic stabilization, rearmament, and a firm alignment with the West.[66] Coming from the Rhineland, Adenauer had always held the Western nations of Europe in higher esteem than the East. After World War I, in 1918-19, he had even supported the idea of a "Rhenish Republic" and its separation from Prussia, but not from the German Reich.[67] Now, after World War II, Adenauer concluded that Germany, at the crossroads of Eastern and Western Europe, had to end its tendency to seesaw back and forth between the two. For the chancellor, history clearly dictated which side to align with; in his opinion, the only way to prevent all Germany from falling under Soviet dominance was to root the free part of the country firmly in the Western community. There it might stand some chance of eventually regaining its sovereignty and respect.[68]

Adenauer, therefore, pursued a policy of Westintegration. Between World War I and II, Germany had not been able to establish balanced relations with its former enemies. After World War II, the extent of destruction caused by the war and the shocking annihilation of millions of people for political, religious, or racial reasons could have prevented integration again. In contrast to developments after World War I, however, it was widely recognized that

Germany had to be included when "Europeanists" were marching for the unification of Europe; Germans, like other Europeans, were eager to avoid the consequences of the isolation—self-imposed and forced upon them by others—that had characterized their situation before the war. An early example of the Europeanist approach toward the "German Question" was taken by Winston Churchill, who in a speech in Zurich on September 19, 1946, pleaded for reconciliation between Germany and France as a first step to create, on the basis of the ideas of the League of Nations, "something like the United States of Europe."[69]

The Cold War finally put pressure on governments and people in both East and West to accept the integration of the two parts of Germany into the new spheres of influence. History remained a burden, but the strength of West Germany and the necessity for West European collaboration took precedence over fears and memories and gradually revised the German image.

Within this framework of West European integration, Adenauer sought to win back German sovereignty piecemeal through a policy of rearmament while concurrently making progress toward a European supranational political union. Rearmament of Germany would require respect and consideration of German wishes and might be used to expedite an end to the existing occupation statute. By rearming Germany, Adenauer could strengthen Western defense and, simultaneously, achieve his goals of national sovereignty, external security, and internal stability.[70] The price, however, was giving up the idea of reunification, now out of reach, at least for the foreseeable time.

Whether reunification would have been possible under the circumstances of East-West confrontation and Soviet presence in Central Europe remains an open question.[71] Adenauer, to be sure, sought to develop West Germany as a "magnet" for East German citizens. Economic success and political freedom in the West, Adenauer hoped, would inspire East Germans to undermine their system, or to escape, thereby weakening the East German regime. In the end, reunification would be the fruit of a policy of strength, not a result of weakness.[72] In other words, reunification would certainly not be bought for the price of Soviet domination. Instead, Western integration was to provide the basis of Western strength that finally would lead to the restoration of unity as was stated in the Basic Law: "The entire German people is called on to achieve by free self-determination the unity and freedom of Germany."[73]

Thus the chancellor's priorities were "Freedom-Peace-Unity"— in that order. German influence on Western policy was largely a function of its intimate relationship with the United States, aided by the considerable trust between Adenauer and US secretary of state John Foster Dulles.[74] It was mainly based on their parallel thinking, shared conceptions of internal democratic order, and resistance to Soviet expansionism. At that time, the United States was the major Western power, essential to military security and economic stability. US institutions were deemed ideal. The "American way of life" was widely imitated. The identification was domestic as well as international—the United States became an ersatz nation, that is, an alternative role model, for the deflected national feelings of West Germans—so did the idea of "Europe."

To the Soviet Union, such close German identification with the West was unacceptable. Moscow therefore offered reunification under some form of neutrality, apparently hoping that this might be a sufficient temptation for the West Germans to vote against permanent integration into the Western alliance.

In a note of March 10, 1952, to the three Western powers, Stalin proposed negotiations on German reunification and the signing of a peace treaty with an all-German government. Free elections would be permitted and a neutral Germany would be allowed armed forces in relation to its defense requirements.[75] Stalin's initiative, which amounted to nothing less than the possibility of dismantling the GDR, was obviously designed to forestall the entry of the Federal Republic into the European Defense Community (EDC)—that is, the attempt to build an integrated West European defense force, following a December 1950 proposal by French prime minister Rene Pleven—then under discussion. But the sincerity of the offer to negotiate was not put to the test since neither Adenauer nor the Western powers were prepared to sacrifice German Western integration at the price of an insecure state of neutrality.[76] Eventually, after the June 1953 revolt in East Germany, Moscow seems to have abandoned any hope of securing dominant influence in a unitary German state.[77]

West Germany's subsequent entry into the North Atlantic Treaty Organization (NATO) and the 1956 upheavals in Eastern Europe then forced the Kremlin to entrench along the entire length of the Iron Curtain. At the same time the Federal Republic gained sovereignty and self-respect (with the Paris Treaties of October 1954), began a program of compensation (more than DM90 billion between 1952 and 1993 in the form of direct financial compensation, restitution, and reparations) for victims of Nazism, and enjoyed the benefits of an economic miracle, which finally led to a propitious position in world politics that bore little resemblance to the situation shortly after World War II. It was a rather astonishing rise from the ruins of defeat to political stability and economic prosperity, with growing leeway in foreign affairs and the development from a nonmilitary status in the late 1940s and early 1950s to a medium-size power of considerable strength that made an important contribution to Western defense.

The Federal Republic's initial stance vis-à-vis the East reflected a strong sense of diplomatic grievance: With regard to Eastern Europe, however, Adenauer adopted a policy of political, territorial, and economic claims that made cooperation and reconciliation almost impossible with Poland, because it had been awarded one-quarter, or 40,000 square miles, of the former Reich by the Potsdam agreement (pending final settlement in a peace treaty); with the Soviet Union, because it had received sections of East Prussia and the Baltic port of Königsberg; with Czechoslovakia, because it had expelled 3.25 million Sudeten Germans from their homeland; and, last but not least, with the GDR, because the legality of the communist rule in East Germany was not recognized by the Federal Republic. The FRG claimed to be the only legitimate successor of the former Reich and insisted on representing all Germans within the country's 1937 boundaries.[78]

Although Adenauer did establish diplomatic ties with Moscow in September 1955, his policy toward the East remained fragmentary and insignificant—even if this meant continuation and deepening of German division.[79] When, at the Geneva foreign ministers conference of the Four Powers in December 1955, British diplomacy moved toward a position that the Western powers should sign any reasonable security treaty with the Soviets, provided Germany was unified by means of free elections and provided the unified German government had freedom in domestic and foreign affairs, Adenauer let the British know that he would oppose such a position. In a "Top Secret" memorandum dated December 16, 1955, the British permanent under secretary of state for foreign affairs, Sir Ivone A. Kirkpatrick, explained Adenauer's motives for rejecting any deal with the Soviets. Kirkpatrick, the former British high commissioner for Germany, who had been informed about the chancellor's attitude by the German ambassador in London, noted that:

> The bald reason was that Dr. Adenauer had no confidence in the German people. He was terrified that when he disappeared from the scene a future German Government might do a deal with Russia at the German expense. Consequently he felt that the integration of Western Germany with the West was more important than the unification of Germany.[80]

And Kirkpatrick concluded by adding: "In making this communication to me the Ambassador naturally emphasized that the Chancellor wished me to know his mind, but that it would of course be quite disastrous to his political position if the views which he had expressed to me with such frankness ever became known in Germany."[81]

The British naturally kept the secret, and Adenauer could be at ease, as he did not have to shift the focus of his policy from Westpolitik to Ostpolitik until his resignation in the autumn of 1963. On the contrary, his policy was fully endorsed by Bonn's allies, who argued in accordance with the chancellor's own convictions that only a firmly held position of superiority could induce the Soviet Union to relax its stand regarding Eastern Europe in general and German unification in particular. Accordingly, the policy of Westintegration was viewed as an instrument for strengthening Bonn's leverage against Moscow and East Berlin.[82]

Yet unification never became the guiding principle of Adenauer's policy—despite the public notion that he was more conservative, that is, more nationalistic, than his SPD counterparts Kurt Schumacher and Erich Ollenhauer. The chancellor never dreamed of re-creating the Reich. He thought little of Bismarck's Great Prussia and Stresemann's revisionist attempts to overcome the Versailles order. If history had taught Germany a lesson, Adenauer believed, it was that a nation like Germany, located in the center of a politically fragmented continent, simply could not afford to be surrounded by hostile powers but instead had to win the trust and friendship of neighboring countries. Freedom and democracy, it followed, were the best guarantees against renewed militarism and national delusions.

Adenauer's policy always reflected these basic convictions. He was a determined European and, to a certain extent, Atlanticist; he was not a nationalist. And his commitment to individual rights of freedom and political pluralism was real, not expeditious. Therefore, the integration of Germany with the West and Adenauer's rigidity and limited flexibility toward the East must be understood as a logical result of ideological convictions and the historical circumstances of the Cold War and East-West confrontation. The chancellor's reliance upon the United States and his personal alliance with John Foster Dulles were particular examples of this basic orientation: a democratic order at home and formerly unknown cooperation and harmony abroad—including the change of the spiked-helmet image to the notion of moderation and sobriety.

The West German identification with the United States was gradually modified, however, after the inauguration of President John F. Kennedy in January 1961, when US foreign policy visibly began moving toward rapprochement with the Soviet Union. The Federal Republic, restricted in its maneuverability in foreign affairs by the German question, could not follow in that direction so swiftly. Until this time, West Germany had been the main support and even the spearhead of US policy in Central Europe against the Soviet Union. But with the emerging US-Soviet détente, Bonn had either to look for other partners to fill the vacuum or to adjust to the new strategy of détente in order to avoid the danger of East-West negotiations over German heads (Adenauer's "Potsdam trauma") and international isolation.[83]

The construction of the Berlin Wall in August 1961 can be seen as an example of the change. On the one hand, it demonstrated the determination of the Soviet Union and the GDR to preserve the status quo and contain Western influence; on the other, the reluctance of the US response also was an indication of the limited value the new administration in Washington attached to German reunification.[84] Thus the construction of the Wall was a crucial step in consolidating the superpowers' spheres of influence. It physically divided Germany and confirmed that both the United States and the Soviet Union had a vital interest in preserving the viability of their respective spheres. Neither side, however, appeared any longer interested in the liberation of the other sphere, as had been proclaimed throughout the 1950s by John Foster Dulles in his rhetoric about liberating the "captive peoples" of Eastern Europe and by Stalin and Khrushchev in their rhetoric about communist world revolution.[85]

In Germany, when the Treaty on German-French Cooperation was signed in January 1963, the "Gaullist" option was debated. Would it not be possible to reduce political, economic, and military dependence on the United States by concentrating on the strength of Western Europe or even by returning to the old "Europe of Fatherlands"—across the Iron Curtain to the Urals? But the dream of a rejuvenated Old Europe vanished quickly, as the indispensability of the United States was underlined by the security dilemma of Western Europe after the French withdrew from the NATO integrated military structure in July 1966.[86] Subsequently, the question of how German foreign policy should respond to the new direction in US-Soviet relations became even more urgent, indeed imperative.

WILLY BRANDT'S NEW OSTPOLITIK

Among the first who perceived that the Berlin Wall would eventually force Bonn to alter the priorities of its German policy was the philosopher Karl Jaspers. In a book published in 1963, he criticized Adenauer's policy toward the East, calling for the entire abandonment of the program for reunification through the establishment of common institutions and proposing instead that greater stress should be placed on the welfare of the German people in the GDR.[87]

In fact, several developments were already pointing in that direction: the failure of Konrad Adenauer's attempt to reunify Germany through a policy of strength—a failure that had become visible only with the building of the Berlin Wall in 1961; President Kennedy's "strategy of peace" aimed at reducing the risk of nuclear war through a policy of arms control and negotiations with the Soviet Union; and a growing desire of many West Germans—including politicians of all major parties, intellectuals, and church members—to improve relations with the neighbors in the East. When Adenauer resigned as chancellor on October 15, 1963, vague ideas were converted into concrete measures. The new chancellor, Ludwig Erhard, and Foreign Minister Gerhard Schröder immediately began to introduce a "policy of movement" with regard to Eastern bloc countries—focusing mainly on cultural and economic aspects. Simultaneously Willy Brandt, then governing mayor of West Berlin, began a "policy of small steps." Brandt, whose people were particularly hard hit by the East's policy of sealing itself off from the West, felt that an improvement in human contacts between the two Germanys could make division of the country easier to bear and would also help to preserve the cohesiveness of the German nation.[88]

Brandt's thinking had been shaped largely by the construction of the Berlin Wall. But as early as February 1959, in a speech commemorating Abraham Lincoln's 150th birthday, the mayor had stated that "there is neither an isolated nor a sudden solution and we must hope for gradual changes."[89] Now, as visits between the western and eastern parts of the divided city were no longer possible, Brandt launched talks between representatives of the Berlin Senate and the government of the GDR aimed at allowing West Berliners to visit the eastern sector again. Very much to the dislike of the federal government in Bonn, a temporary agreement was worked out at the end of 1963.

According to the first protocol on visitors' passes, "despite differing political and legal standpoints, both sides were guided by the principle that it should be possible to realize this humanitarian aim," although both sides, in a so-called saving clause, also determined that "an agreement on designations for places, authorities and offices could not be reached." Thus it was possible to avoid what might otherwise have seemed like a recognition of the GDR and a violation of Bonn's official "policy of non-recognition."[90] By 1966, three further visitors' pass agreements were concluded for limited periods of time. Then the GDR government refused to continue to accept the saving clause, while the Senate had to insist on keeping it for political more than legal reasons. As a result, no further agreement was reached, and the inner city border remained closed for Berliners until 1971.

Whereas Brandt's "policy of small steps" was focusing on humanitarian issues, Schröder's "policy of movement" gave cultural exchanges a new impetus and helped to establish permanent West German trade delegations in all East European capitals except Prague, making the Federal Republic the leading Western trading partner for East European countries.[91] Additionally, the contacts were broadened by exchanges at semiofficial levels. On October 14, 1965, the Evangelical Church of Germany published a memorandum criticizing the Federal Republic's position on the Oder-Neisse line and encouraging a formal renunciation of territorial claims against Poland.[92] In the spring and summer of 1966, the West German social democrats and the East German communists prepared for an exchange of speakers of the SPD and SED, which had been proposed by the SED newspaper *Neues Deutschland* on March 26, to give both sides an opportunity to publicly unfold their views about the German question at respective political rallies. The SED eventually withdrew from its offer, but the project as such was once again evidence of the new flexibility in East-West relations.[93]

In fact, the changing atmosphere could be felt on many occasions. Even Konrad Adenauer offered an example in his farewell speech before the Christian Democratic Union party congress on March 21, 1966, when he stated that the Soviet Union had now "entered the ranks of those countries that want peace in the world."[94] Only four days later, his successor as chancellor, Ludwig Erhard, delivered a diplomatic note to 115 states, including those of Eastern Europe, proposing a reduction of nuclear weapons in Europe, an agreement prohibiting the transfer of nuclear weapons to nonnuclear powers, and finally, that agreement should be reached with the East European governments prohibiting the use of force in international disputes.[95]

Yet this so-called peace note did not alter the legal position of the Erhard government regarding the German question, which had been expressed by Foreign Minister Schröder in October 1965:

> No German government, constitutionally sworn as it is to act on behalf of all Germans and to restore German unity, could abandon the policy of reunification. . . . If there is to be a real relaxation of tension, Germans throughout the whole of Germany must be able, as again stated in the joint declaration of the three Western Powers, June 26, 1964, to exercise the right of self-determination. To achieve this elementary human right, our policy must be, not to arouse false hopes, but to establish relations between East and West based on mutual trust and thus enable us to remove, first of all, the minor sources of tension, [and] subsequently the major ones as well.[96]

In other words, Erhard and Schröder insisted that Germany continue to exist in international law within the boundaries of December 31, 1937, so long as a freely elected all-German government did not recognize other frontiers.

Such a position was incompatible with the view of most East European governments that all existing boundaries in Europe, including the border between the Federal Republic and the GDR, had to be acknowledged by Bonn before a policy of cooperation could be introduced. Several East European countries—for example, Hungary and Romania—however, seemed tempted for economic reasons to accept Erhard's and Schröder's offer for improving relations with the Federal Republic even without Bonn's formal recognition of the GDR. And since the Erhard government appeared to be determined to secure concessions "collectively if possible, individually if necessary," without making the slightest move toward accommodating the strategic interests of the Warsaw Pact, the German peace offensive actually heightened what was still regarded to be the "German danger."[97]

The Soviet Union reacted by promoting the idea of an all-European security scheme in order once again to internationalize the issue of the German question. At a meeting of the Political Consultative Committee of the Warsaw Pact in Bucharest in July 1966, Moscow proposed a European Security Conference aimed at reaching an all-European solution to the questions of borders, security, and cooperation in Europe. In the ensuing discussion it soon became clear that, despite differences of opinion in many respects (for instance, regarding the participation of the United States and Canada), the development of East-West détente had gained new momentum and the Eastern policy (Ostpolitik) of the Federal Republic was at the very heart of it.

Then came the fall of Erhard's government and the formation in December 1966 of the Christian Democratic (CDU)/Christian Socialist (CSU) Grand Coalition with the Social Democratic Party (SPD). Kurt Georg Kiesinger as chancellor and Willy Brandt as foreign minister accelerated Bonn's efforts to improve relations with the East. In his initial policy statement before the Bundestag—his government declaration of December 13—Kiesinger promised to promote détente as the foundation of his own Ostpolitik and emphasized the Federal Republic's desire to establish diplomatic ties with Germany's eastern neighbors. He acknowledged that Germany could not exclude itself from the trend toward détente: "If we stay on the defensive . . . we will find ourselves hopelessly isolated. For this reason we must act. We must get things moving."[98]

Subsequently, diplomatic relations were established with Romania in January 1967 and with Yugoslavia in January 1968, although these countries did not break off their ties with the GDR. This marked the end of the "Hallstein Doctrine," which stated that with the exception of the Soviet Union, no nation officially recognizing the GDR would enjoy diplomatic relations with the Federal Republic. Regarding Poland, however, Kiesinger said already in his initial government declaration that Poland's "claim to live finally in a state with assured boundaries" had to be fulfilled within the context of German reunification.[99]

As far as the GDR was concerned, Kiesinger continued to claim the right to speak for the entire German people on the basis that the Federal government was the only freely elected government in Germany. Yet Kiesinger was also the first West German chancellor to take official note of the GDR. He not only suggested extended contacts in the economic, cultural, and technical fields but, in May 1967, reached a cabinet decision to accept letters sent by the GDR and to answer them. Up to that point, letters from the GDR government had always been sent back unopened and, of course, unanswered.

Kiesinger's motive to increase contacts with East Germany, including greater freedom of travel, broader trade and credit facilities, joint economic projects, and cultural and educational exchanges, was "to prevent the two parts of our people from drifting away from each other during the period of separation," as he himself said, and to ease the life of all Germans.[100] Thus he repeatedly outlined specific proposals for expanding inter-German relations and, during the spring and summer of 1967, exchanged a series of notes with GDR prime minister Willi Stoph to continue to establish Bonn's de facto acceptance of the GDR. Indeed, Kiesinger offered, in his State of the Nation speech in March 1968, to negotiate on German problems directly with Stoph if sufficient progress could be made in preliminary discussions to assure success.[101]

Yet the Federal Republic's "new opening to the East," which was largely determined by the ideas of Foreign Minister Willy Brandt, was anything but undisputed. As a matter of fact, there was considerable bureaucratic infighting within the Bonn government, notably between Brandt and Kiesinger's state secretaries, Karl Carstens (CDU) and Karl Theodor Freiherr von und zu Guttenberg (CSU), about basic principles of the new Ostpolitik.[102]

At the core of the dispute was the formal recognition of the GDR as a second German state. Brandt was convinced that the new Ostpolitik was doomed to failure without such recognition. Carstens and Guttenberg, representing the nationalist wing of the CDU and CSU, insisted on maintaining the legal position the Federal Republic had taken ever since the formulation of the Basic Law. To them, "Germany as a whole" still existed and the responsibility of the Four Powers to look after the rights and interests of Germany was an expression of a still existing executive power for all of Germany that could not be exercised by either of the German states at the time.[103]

It turned out, however, that Brandt's concern was justified, since most East European governments criticized the Ostpolitik of the Grand Coalition for not making real significant concessions, especially regarding the GDR. As Brandt predicted, Bonn's policy toward Eastern Europe and the GDR was stalemated. As a result, the terms and general direction of Ostpolitik became a major issue in the campaign for the Bundestag elections that were scheduled for September 28, 1969.

Brandt himself had long paved the way for a general reform of West Germany's policy toward the East. Ever since the Berlin Wall crisis, he had continuously met with friends and advisors, among them Egon Bahr, Klaus Schütz, and Dietrich Spangenberg, to design a new policy that would recognize the European status quo without jeopardizing the Federal Republic's own security, improve relations with the GDR, acquire security guarantees and a more defined status for West Berlin, and provide—in context with international efforts toward détente—an atmosphere of greater mutual trust in Central Europe as a precondition for an envisaged European peace order.[104]

In abandoning the "reunification first, then détente" policy, Brandt opted for a Friedenspolitik to create, as he himself stated, "a climate in which the status quo could be changed—in another word, improved—by peaceful means."[105] Like Adenauer, Brandt did not accept that German division was to last for ever. Yet he was prepared to acknowledge "the facts of today" as a basis for an active, dynamic strategy of cooperation and long-term Wandel durch Annäherung ("change through rapprochement"), a phrase Egon Bahr had coined in a speech at the Evangelic Academy in Tutzing in July 1963.[106]

Though Brandt recognized that fluctuations in world politics could endanger the spirit of negotiations, the desire to preserve German national unity by way of peace in Europe remained a primary goal of his new policy. By fostering cooperation and agreement with the West as well as an understanding with the East, the Federal Republic could remain a reliable member of the Western alliance and seek to ease tensions with the Soviet Union and Eastern Europe. Brandt's overtures to the East were therefore carefully worked into the complex scheme of Western détente with the Soviet bloc.[107]

In March 1969, the Political Consultative Committee of the Warsaw Pact signaled unconditional readiness for détente.[108] Simultaneously, at an international communist gathering in Budapest commemorating the 50th anniversary of the Comintern, Moscow called for cooperation with the West German SPD as the most plausible means of curbing German rightist tendencies.[109] Among the first who followed the Soviet proposal for exploring ways to support the SPD without damaging its election prospects was Poland's communist party chief, Wladyslaw Gomulka. In a major speech on May 17, 1969, dealing with the declining German threat and the need to reexamine Polish interests in an accommodation with Bonn, Gomulka acknowledged recent indications that West Germany was moving in a new direction. He referred specifically to a demand by the SPD to formally recognize the Oder-Neisse line as the Western border of Poland:

I have in mind here, first of all, certain statements made by the leaders of the West German Social Democrats . . . particularly those made by the chairman of the party, Vice Chancellor of the Federal Republic, Willy Brandt. . . . One cannot fail to appreciate the fact that, from the political point of view, the SPD formula on the recognition by the Federal Republic of the frontier on the Oder and Neisse constitutes a step forward in comparison to the stand taken on this issue by all the previous Federal Republic governments.[110]

Gomulka added that it was now appropriate to explore ways to establish diplomatic relations with Bonn on the condition that the Federal Republic formally recognized the Oder-Neisse line as the Western boundary of Poland.[111] The Polish party chief would not have delivered his declaration without prior consultation with Moscow. Yet the necessity to normalize relations with West Germany for economic reasons had already been stressed at a plenary session of the Central Committee of the Polish United Workers Party as early in April that year. By April 11, a Polish government delegation headed by Prime Minister Józef Cyrankiewicz and Gomulka himself had informed a dismayed East German government under Walter Ulbricht that the establishment of diplomatic ties between Warsaw and Bonn was inevitable.[112] Brandt responded to Gomulka's offer of May 17 for talks, two days later calling the Polish leader's suggestion "remarkable" and stating that "we regard the reconciliation with Poland as being just as important historically as the similar reconciliation with France."[113] Brandt knew, however, that little would be achieved if there was no basic understanding with the Soviet Union. Therefore he was eager to renew the dialogue with Moscow. On July 3, Brandt's state secretary for foreign affairs, Ferdinand Duckwitz, handed over a formal diplomatic note to Soviet ambassador Semion Zarapkin in Bonn to continue the discussion on a renunciation-of-force treaty that had begun with Ludwig Erhard's peace note of March 1966.

In Moscow, Foreign Minister Andrei Gromyko responded to Brandt's new proposal in a policy declaration before the Supreme Soviet on July 10, 1969. He said that a turning point in relations between the Soviet Union and the Federal Republic could occur if the Federal Republic followed "the path of peace."[114] Brandt noted on the same day that relations with the Soviet Union were approaching normality for the first time since 1955.[115]

On September 12, still more than two weeks before the Bundestag elections, Moscow formally replied to Bonn's note of July 3, indicating its interest in continued negotiations with Bonn regardless of the election outcome. It was quite apparent, however, which outcome the Soviets preferred. Therefore the fact that a new coalition was formed after September 28, consisting of the

SPD and the Free Democratic Party (FDP) rather than CDU and CSU, and with Brandt as the new chancellor, made the new German Ostpolitik even more promising.[116]

When, subsequently, the West German Ostverträge (Eastern treaties) with Moscow, Warsaw, East Berlin, and Prague and the Quadripartite Agreement on Berlin were signed between August 1970 and December 1973, the ground for progress in a relaxation of tension in Europe was laid. This also allowed the Conference on Security and Cooperation in Europe (CSCE) to conclude the Helsinki accord of August 1, 1975. In the treaties with the Soviet Union, Poland, the GDR, and Czechoslovakia, the Federal Republic supported the renunciation-of-force principle; acknowledged the existing border in Europe, especially the Oder-Neisse line as the Western boundary of Poland; established semidiplomatic relations with the GDR; and accepted a Four-Power solution for Berlin.[117]

All these regulations could be reversed, if mutual agreement on a peaceful settlement was reached; peaceful change, therefore, remained possible. In other words, the Ostverträge were not a substitute for a German peace treaty and, as a result, could not be regarded as a final settlement of the German question. But they provided a modus vivendi and allowed a search for practical solutions with respect to humanitarian issues, economic cooperation, and East-West cultural exchange.[118]

However, the new Ostpolitik led to an immediate increase of options with regard to the foreign policy of the Federal Republic. Until 1969, the unresolved German question had resulted in a great many restraints on West German foreign policy; above all, the Hallstein Doctrine had posed serious problems. Designed to isolate the GDR, this doctrine actually had promoted GDR reliance on, and solidarity within, the Warsaw Pact. It even had restrained West Germany's relations with Third World countries, as those countries seeking more development aid had effectively blackmailed the Federal Republic with the threat of recognizing the GDR.[119] Abandoning the Hallstein Doctrine meant diplomatic relief. West Germany's foreign policy was no longer focused on the issue of nonrecognition of the GDR, but became one in which leeway and maneuverability were introduced all the way around—toward the West, the East, and the Third World.

Within this new maneuverability, Germany also gradually rediscovered its traditional place in the center of Europe. Based on a firm commitment to the West, the Federal Republic was able to negotiate and collaborate with the East. Common interests—the imperative to maintain peace and military stability, the need for economic cooperation, and the desire to develop existing ties among families and friends—indicated that the East was not merely a hostile communist neighborhood. After all, there were Germans living on both sides of the Iron Curtain. And the Poles, Czechs, Slovaks, and Hungarians, as well as the other East European nations, were as European as the people in the western part of the continent. Europe, to be sure, did not end at the Elbe River. In this respect, the new German Ostpolitik, with its middle-European perspective and its all-European approach, contributed to promote a new vision of Europe across existing lines of tension and separation.

It was also clear, however, that lessons of Germany's past had to be drawn regarding the new options and constraints in the 1970s and thereafter. Germany's geopolitical "in-between" position between East and West, its volatile relationship with the Soviets, its being too strong to fit into the European state system and too weak to play a real hegemonical role, the complexity of its domestic issues and its inconsistency in confronting the past at home after 1945, particularly in dealing with the enormity of the Third Reich's crimes—including, above all, the "Final Solution"—and promoting the value of ethnic diversity, all made a new approach necessary, indeed imperative.

Chancellor Willy Brandt, a former political refugee himself (he had been expelled from Nazi Germany as early as 1933 and subsequently even lost his German citizenship), now seemed to be poised to open a new chapter in German history. Brandt's all-European, antinationalist approach, building on Adenauer's policy of Western integration, was one important lesson that was drawn from Germany's past. But after the improvement of Franco-German relations and the inclusion of West Germany in a variety of Atlantic and Western European institutions under Adenauer, reconciliation with the East came next. The extent to which Germany would be able to catalyze all-European integration while the East-West conflict was still in progress, however, remained as much an open question as the depth and direction of the long-overdue transformation and democratization of the German society. There was hope, at least, that after the physical reconstruction of West Germany had been completed, a renewal of ideas and values would follow to support democratic stability that had been so lacking in the history of Germany in the nineteenth and early twentieth centuries.

Preparing for a
Democratic Revolution

By the 1970s, the German question reached a new dimension. Memories of the historical Reich had gradually faded, and the idea of German reunification was overshadowed by the continued integration of the two Germanys in their respective alliances and by the developing relations between the two states. As a result, the German image changed: Germany and the Germans no longer seemed to pose a threat to the international order, the world got accustomed to the reality of German partition, and the "normal, good-neighborly relations" spoken of in the 1972 Basic Treaty between the FRG and GDR were almost taken for granted.[1]

Reunification, however, remained on the agenda. For the government of the Federal Republic it was a constitutional mandate, irrespective of the apparent distance between the reality of the division and the dream of this goal. For its part, the GDR leadership argued that reunification would be possible only if and when socialism emerged victorious in the Federal Republic. Even the pragmatic SED secretary general Erich Honecker, who himself originated from the West German town Wiebelskirchen in the Saarland, voiced a belief that the renewed unification of Germany would be certain: "And when the day comes when the working class begins a socialist restructuring of the Federal Republic, then the question of uniting the two German states will be seen in a completely different light. There should be no doubt in your minds, dear comrades, as to what our decision would be like then."[2]

In his case, as in many others, common history, language, and culture, as well as the continuing bonds among families and friends across the Wall, provided a strong impetus "to work for a state of peace in Europe in which the German nation will recover its unity in free self-determination." A free vote on the matter might have furnished evidence that a large majority of

Germans in both East and West was still in favor of reunification 35 years after World War II.[3]

Yet for the political leaders of the GDR, the development of inner-German relations always remained part of the global class struggle between socialism and capitalism. "Peaceful co-existence"—that is, détente—was only a form of class warfare. The West German adversaries continued to be "class enemies" rather than relatives of a common German nation. Moreover, the new Ostpolitik of the Federal Republic threatened to endanger the internal stability of the GDR, as the series of agreements concluded between 1971 and 1973 radically changed the GDR's political environment and inner-German relations.

True, the GDR could derive much satisfaction from the fact that in the year following the signing of the Basic Treaty on December 21, 1972, 68 states established diplomatic relations with the GDR, whereas only 19 countries had done so between 1949 and 1972. In September 1973 both German states also became members of the United Nations. In April 1974 even the Nixon administration in Washington formally recognized the GDR. At the signing of the Final Act of the Helsinki Conference on Security and Cooperation in Europe (CSCE) in August 1975, SED general secretary Erich Honecker sat proudly between West German chancellor Helmut Schmidt and US president Gerald Ford. The GDR had finally breached the political and diplomatic "wall" that Bonn had thrown up around it.[4]

The new policy also had its flaws, at least in view of the GDR leadership, for the treaties eased contacts between East and West Germans. Whereas 2 million people from the Federal Republic and West Berlin had visited the GDR and East Berlin in 1970, the figure soared to about 8 million in 1973. Telephone calls from West to East rose from a mere 700,000 in 1970 to 23 million in 1980. Bearing in mind that the GDR was already heavily penetrated by the Western media (most GDR citizens outside the Dresden region and parts of northeastern Mecklenburg were able to watch West German television), the leadership in East Berlin was seriously worried about the potentially destabilizing effect of the dramatic increase in personal contacts, which were regarded as more influential, and therefore more dangerous, than the effects of simply watching television.[5]

"Demarcation" (Abgrenzung) between the two German states was invoked as the formula for addressing the new challenge. SED Politburo member Hermann Axen proclaimed on September 13, 1970, shortly after the first two meetings between Chancellor Willy Brandt and GDR prime minister Willi Stoph in Kassel and Erfurt, that the GDR had "a duty to continue to demarcate herself from the imperialist Federal Republic in all areas."[6] On October 6, 1970, Stoph himself rejected the "fiction of the so-called unity of the nation."

He maintained that "in view of the antagonism of the systems of state and society an objective process of demarcation, rather then rapprochement, is taking place inevitably."[7]

Subsequently, key groups of people, including party and state functionaries and conscripts, were forbidden contact with foreign visitors. A "visitors' book" was introduced in which the names of foreign visitors had to be registered. In addition, Honecker also announced at the 1971 SED Party Congress that two separate nations were developing in Germany: the socialist nation in the GDR and the capitalist nation in the FRG. Historians and party ideologues were mobilized to refute Bonn's thesis of the continuity of the German nation based on a common history and a feeling of still belonging together even in separate political entities.

Thus it was anything but a coincidence that on the day before the state secretaries Egon Bahr of the West German Chancellery and Michael Kohl of the GDR Council of Ministers initialed the Basic Treaty, on November 8, 1972, the SED Politburo passed a resolution on new principles for agitation and propaganda. Ten days later, on November 16-17, a major "agitation conference" was held, with Politburo member Werner Lambertz declaring there was "no truce at the ideological front but intensified fighting" and that "peaceful co-existence is not ideological co-existence."[8]

Finally, steps were taken to remove references to the apparently offensive term "German." In the new East German constitution of 1974, the GDR was defined as a "socialist state of workers and peasants," not, as in the constitution of 1968, a "socialist state of the German nation." The national anthem, penned by Johannes Becher while in Soviet exile in 1943, could no longer be sung in its original form, as it contained the words: "Arisen out of the ruins and headed for the future, let us serve Germany, our united fatherland." Since the abrupt change of course regarding the nationality question encountered widespread opposition, even among SED officials, however, Honecker was forced to "clarify" his position at a meeting of the Central Committee of the SED on December 12, 1974. Now he proclaimed: "The name of our socialist state is German Democratic Republic, because the majority of its citizens are, according to their nationality, Germans. . . . Citizenship—GDR, nationality—German. These are the facts."[9]

From a Western point of view, the East German attempts to contain the unwanted side effects of détente through a policy of demarcation constituted a violation of the spirit of cooperation. For the West, the increase of personal contacts and the "special nature" of inner-German relations were major assets, not flaws, of the détente process. Willy Brandt in particular had undertaken great efforts to defend his policy as a means of bridging, rather than widening or deepening, the gap between East and West. Although this was not understood correctly, or was intentionally misinterpreted, by many opponents of the new Ostpolitik during the ratification debate in the spring of 1972, the establishment of semidiplomatic relations and the intensification of political, economic, and human contacts with the GDR did not imply a farewell to the idea of German unity and eventual unification. Instead, it reopened new possibilities for "change through rapprochement," the slogan Egon Bahr had coined in July 1963, underlining the policy's dynamic rather than static aspects.[10] The same view had been expressed by another architect of the new Ostpolitik, Peter Bender, who called for "offensive détente" in the title of a book published in 1964.[11]

The question now was whether the dynamic forces of the policy would prevail, as was hoped for in the West (and possibly by many in the East as well), leading even to a democratic revolution in the GDR and some form of reunification. Or would the East German leadership be able to contain the destabilizing effects of the policy and transform it into a vehicle for international recognition and domestic stability? The development of Ostpolitik and inner-German relations during the 1970s and into the 1980s would provide an answer to these questions.

OSTPOLITIK AND INNER-GERMAN RELATIONS

In the early 1970s, the GDR leadership seemed confident that the potentially dangerous implications of accepting the terms of West German Ostpolitik could be kept under control. Moreover, the benefits of international recognition and economic cooperation with the West were too important to be missed.

Such an "opening" to the West had to be analyzed in the context of recent history. More than 400,000 residents of the Soviet Occupation Zone had fled to the West before the GDR was established in 1949; moreover, between 130,000 and 330,000 East German citizens every year thereafter had left their state, fleeing to the Federal Republic, until Erich Honecker supervised the building of the Berlin Wall on August 13, 1961. The Wall, as well as the security stripes, fences, barricades, and antipersonnel devices along the 1,377 kilometers of border between the two German states and the 160-kilometer border around West Berlin, reduced the number of refugees to less than 5,000 per year.[12]

This hemorrhage had truly been a traumatic experience for the East German communists: Until 1961, a total of 2,689,942 of their citizens had left the country and were registered in West German refugee camps—about 14 percent of the GDR's 1949 population.

But the 1970s were thought to be different from the 1950s. The Cold War between East and West had been replaced by a policy of détente; the SED had assigned the improvement of East German material and cultural living standards to a central place in party policy; and Honecker himself had retreated from Ulbricht's orthodox style of leadership and cultivated an image of flexibility and pragmatism, apparently concerned more about the well-being of the people than about the purity of Marxist-Leninist ideas.[13] Moreover, the available data indicated considerable improvement in the GDR's economic situation as well.[14]

Additionally, many aspects of détente seemed to be controllable, since Honecker had carefully consolidated his own authority within the SED by the time of Walter Ulbricht's death on August 1, 1973. He had promoted into the Politburo several of his former associates in the Free German Youth Movement (the Freie Deutsche Jugend), of which he had been chairman between 1946 and 1955. Among them were Erich Mielke, the minister of state security since 1957, and Heinz Hoffmann, the minister of national defense since 1960, who had both known Honecker for many years. On the other hand, Willi Stoph, a potential rival, was demoted from chairman of the council of ministers (prime minister) to chairman of the council of state (head of state).[15]

After consolidating his internal position, Honecker felt he could implement measures aimed at reducing the undesired human implications of détente. In particular, contacts between East and West Germans were made more difficult—that is, more expensive. On November 5, 1973, the GDR finance minister issued a decree raising the so-called minimum daily exchange requirement per person and day for visits to the GDR from DM10 to DM20, and for visits to East Berlin from DM5 to DM10. The exchange requirement exemption for pensioners and young people was dropped; children and retired citizens now too were obliged to exchange currency before entering the GDR or East Berlin.[16]

This meant that trips to the East became so expensive that many FRG citizens, particularly those with families, often could no longer afford them. Consequently, the number of visits to the GDR and East Berlin decreased from 6.1 million in 1973 to 4.5 million in 1974. The correlation between mandatory exchange and visits was quite apparent.[17]

However, the GDR did not impair telephone communication between the two German states; nor did it hinder the development of trade and economic cooperation or the contractual settlement of bilateral issues according to Article 7 of the Basic Treaty. More than 70 agreements were concluded in compliance with Article 7 between 1973 and 1986, the last one being the

Cultural Agreement signed on May 6, 1986. The trade volume of the two German states more than doubled between 1970 and 1980, from DM4.5 billion to DM11.7 billion.[18]

Yet the explosion in the price of oil and other raw materials in the 1970s caused a dramatic deterioration in the terms of trade of the GDR, a country heavily dependent on imports of raw materials. First, the oil crisis following the Yom Kippur War between Israel and its Arab neighbors in October 1973 and the subsequent confusion in the international business world shadowed the economic prospects of the GDR. Second, the higher prices for oil and natural gas charged by the Soviet Union put even more serious strains on the GDR economy. Finally, recession in the West compounded the GDR's trade problems; net indebtedness to the West grew at a rate of more than 20 percent per annum, reaching a staggering $11.66 billion in 1981. From 1975 onward, a trade deficit was even recorded with the Soviet Union, the GDR's main supplier of raw materials.[19]

Both the mandatory exchange policy of the GDR and the economic crisis after 1973 eventually contributed to a certain degree of stagnation in inner-German relations, especially since Helmut Schmidt, who succeeded Willy Brandt as West German chancellor in May 1974, seemed to be more concerned with managing the implications of the oil price explosion than with providing new incentives for improving ties with the GDR. On December 12, 1979, in accordance with a plan advocated and strongly supported, if not invented, by Schmidt, NATO agreed to deploy Pershing II and cruise missiles in Western Europe in response to the Soviet Union's installation of new mobile medium-range nuclear missiles (SS-20) in the western part of the Soviet Union. Further damage to East-West relations was done by the Soviet invasion of Afghanistan two weeks later. Superpower tensions thus imposed yet more strain on the delicate fabric of inner-German détente.[20]

Despite combined efforts by Chancellor Schmidt and French president Valéry Giscard d'Estaing to limit the negative effects of these events, a general decline of the détente process could not be averted. Specific ramifications in Germany included a raising, on October 13, 1980, of the mandatory amount that West Germans were obliged to change into GDR-marks when visiting East Berlin or the GDR again—to a uniform level of 25 marks per day for extended stays in East Germany as well as for daylong visits to East Berlin. On the very same day, Honecker in a speech at Gera demanded West German recognition of a separate GDR citizenship and the upgrading of the permanent representatives to the status of ambassadors.[21]

Linking increasing East-West tensions and deteriorating inner-German relations, Honecker proclaimed that one could hardly participate in NATO's missile decision and then expect ties between the two Germanys to be un-affected. He stated:

> We too, share the view that progress in economic relations is good and right. But with all clarity, one is forced to add that the securing of the peace is above all a political question. It is oriented to those steps that directly lead to the solution of the most important task of our time, to the halting of the arms race and to disarmament.[22]

It soon became clear, however, that the decision of the East German gov-ernment to once again raise the mandatory exchange amount, making the cost of entry almost prohibitively high for West Germans and West Berliners, was not just another expression of bloc tensions. The GDR's mea-sure against the West was followed by a similar decision vis-à-vis the East: On October 30, 1980, the SED regime decided to end nine years of visa-free traffic between the GDR and Poland and to impose strict conditions on those citizens still wishing to travel between the two states in order to limit possi-ble effects of the Polish democratization movement in the GDR.[23]

Yet both German states had too many vested interests in their détente not to attempt a salvage operation. The West German government could not afford to sacrifice the human achievements of détente, which were so sub-stantial for millions of Germans in both parts of the country, at a time when the policy of the US administration under President Ronald Reagan was widely regarded as irresponsible. Moreover, 1981-82 was a period of deep-ening economic crisis for the GDR. Its debts to the West of about $12 billion and inability to rely on acquiring new credits from Western banks in the wake of the failure of Poland and Romania to honor their obligations were also affected by a cutback of Soviet oil supplies from 19 million tons in 1981 to 17.7 million tons in 1982.[24]

In the early 1980s, therefore, the Federal Republic and the GDR entered a new phase of trying to improve mutual relations—not the least because of an all-German grassroots peace movement in both protesting the danger of a nuclear holocaust.[25] The visit of Chancellor Schmidt to the GDR and his meeting with Honecker at Lake Werbellin on December 11-13, 1981, despite the imposition of martial law in Poland at the time of Schmidt's stay in East Germany, was a first step in this reorientation process, which continued even after Helmut Kohl replaced Schmidt as chancellor on October 1, 1982.[26] An invitation to Honecker, issued by Schmidt at Lake Werbellin, to visit the Federal Republic and especially his hometown of Wiebelskirchen in the Saarland was renewed by Kohl immediately after taking over as chancellor in a personal telephone conversation with the East German leader.

Yet this visit, scheduled for September 1984 but eventually postponed due to prevailing East-West tension and Soviet pressure, was of lesser importance than the vital economic assistance the Federal Republic provided for the GDR in 1983 and 1984 in the form of two large government-backed credits of DM1 billion and DM950 million. The GDR honored the assistance by easing the procedures at the border checkpoints for West German citizens and by reducing the mandatory daily exchange rate for GDR and East Berlin visits from DM25 to DM15. More significantly, the East Germans also dismantled 54,000 automatically triggered shooting installations (SM-70) and landmines along the inner-German border.[27]

When Honecker finally visited Bonn, Munich, and Wiebelskirchen in September 1987, he was formally received by Chancellor Kohl and President Richard von Weizsäcker. A band played the GDR national anthem upon his arrival. It was the first visit by a leader of the SED to the "other" German state and a significant personal triumph for Honecker. Yet it was already known at this time that the internal situation in the GDR was seriously deteriorating and that the economic assistance provided by the Federal Republic could fill gaps but would not be able to improve the structural deficiencies of the GDR system.[28]

The increasing social instability of East Germany found expression in many forms: the expulsion of GDR citizens, notably intellectuals and artists; the formation of grassroots opposition, beginning with the peace movement and environmental groups, later focusing around the East German Protestant Church; and the growing number of people asking for exit visas, soon amounting to hundreds of thousands. The SED's enforced expatriation of the satirical balladeer Wolf Biermann in November 1976 set a dangerous precedent: It ended the cultural Tauwetter (thaw) of the first half of the decade, during which many intellectuals had hoped for détente in both the external relations of the GDR as well as within East Germany itself. With Biermann's expatriation, the disappointed members of the GDR's cultural elite became more critical of the SED regime. Subsequently, many were themselves expelled and forced to follow Biermann on his voyage to the West.[29]

Others set a precedent of a different kind: On January 20, 1984, six GDR citizens entered the US Embassy in East Berlin, refused to leave, and, in a letter to President Reagan, asked for political asylum and protection against GDR security organs. After two days of intense negotiations between East German lawyer and Honecker confidant Wolfgang Vogel and representatives of the embassy and the Bonn government, the refugees were allowed to resettle in the Federal Republic.[30] It was only the beginning of a series of attempts by East German citizens to force their way out of the GDR via diplomatic missions. The most prominent example was Ingrid Berg, a niece of Willi Stoph, who, on February 24, 1984, fled to the West German Embassy in Prague, where 14 other East Germans had already asked for asylum. In October of the same year the embassy even had to be temporarily closed when more than 100 GDR citizens sought refuge there. Similar incidents were reported from Bucharest, Budapest, and Warsaw.

One of the reasons why so many East Germans were desperately trying to leave the GDR was the fact that they had lost all hope for reform in the foreseeable future. According to a survey by the Munich-based communications research institute Infratest and the University of Wuppertal among 2,000 emigrants (Aussiedler) from the GDR, the motives why they had decided to leave East Germany were "a lack of freedom of opinion," "political repression," or "limited possibilities for traveling." Economic motives apparently had played only a minor role in their decision to emigrate, although the motivation was generally a mix of several factors.[31]

REFORMS IN POLAND AND HUNGARY

The frustration of the East German population about the absence of reform in the GDR was multiplied by examples of change in Poland, Hungary, and the Soviet Union. Even if most GDR citizens initially preferred their relative economic security over Polish chaos, Hungarian confusion, and Soviet sloppiness, it would be wrong to assume that the reform policies in these countries had only marginal impact on developments in the GDR. To the contrary, the failure of the SED leadership to implement similar reforms contributed significantly to the loss of hope among GDR citizens that finally provided the basis for the East German revolution of 1989.

Developments in Poland, in particular, had an effect on the GDR as early as the summer of 1980, when worker unrest escalated in the shipyards of Gdansk and Gdynia and the "Solidarity" movement presented a dangerous challenge to the established communist party rule.[32] As James McAdams has pointed out, Poland's problems threatened East German domestic stability, which was a fundamental precondition on which the traditional form of the détente policy of the 1970s had rested. The disturbances in neighboring Poland shattered the confidence of the GDR leadership and caused many SED functionaries to wonder whether the sense of internal calm that had been imposed on the country during the 1970s could be maintained.[33] Nationwide protest strikes and the organization of independent labor unions by East German workers seemed unlikely but not impossible. And the timing of the events—just as the GDR was opening to Western ideas and influences —added to the uneasiness of the SED political establishment.

True, the July strikes and the downfall of Edward Gierek's leadership were not the first serious political crisis in postwar Poland. In fact, crises seemed to have become a "political ritual" in a country that was continuously plagued by economic decline and mismanagement.[34] But in August 1980, the communist Polish United Workers' Party (PZPR) was, for the first time, forced to meet with representatives of the Solidarity movement, an organization independent of the government and representing 10 million people demanding fundamental political changes. It was a nightmare not only for the PZPR but for the watching SED as well.

Therefore it could only be interpreted as a sign of insecurity when the official SED organ *Neues Deutschland,* in its first editorial assessment of the Polish developments, accused the Federal Republic of "now relying upon American missiles in order to realize its revanchist goals against the GDR as well as against Poland."[35] Privately, most experts in East Berlin at the time stated that they were convinced that the relatively high living standards in the GDR, compared with Poland, and traditional East German-Polish animosities and prejudices would prevent GDR citizens from following the Polish example immediately. In the longer run, however, it was quite uncertain if the SED regime could continue its "delicate balancing act" of exposing its population to regular contacts with the outside world "when at the same time the Poles next door were questioning the fundamental principles of socialist order."[36]

Thus, as has already been mentioned, the SED leadership decided on October 30, 1980, to end visa-free traffic between the GDR and Poland and to impose strict conditions on travel between the two states. *Demarcation* to the West was now complemented by *delimitation* to the East. The process of the GDR's external self-isolation began. Simultaneously, internal security was stepped up. Minister of State Security Erich Mielke publicly vowed to increase the activity of security agencies throughout the country. This was necessary, he argued, to combat the "inhuman and anti-socialist plans and machinations" of the forces of counterrevolution, the chief representatives of which appeared to be "imperialist forces in the West." Mielke added that "we must heighten mass vigilance, enforce socialist legality, guarantee state secrecy, and make sure that order, security, and discipline prevail in all branches of our economy."[37]

Mielke's reference to "economic security" indicated that there was concern among SED leaders about the possibility of worker unrest similar to that in Poland. But new security measures were also imposed on other potential opposition groups in the GDR, particularly those connected with churches.

In November 1980, for the first time in years, East German Lutherans were not allowed to send representatives to their church's annual meeting in West Germany. Additionally, church publications came under heavier government censorship, and Western reporters found themselves suddenly denied entry to the GDR to cover church proceedings.[38]

There were also indications in late 1980 that the regime was ready to apply additional pressure on the country's artistic community. In a key speech, SED Politburo member Kurt Hager explicitly attacked the Federal Republic for allegedly trying to undermine East German artistic standards and for abusing existing cultural exchange programs. "It would be unrealistic," Hager said, "if cultural relations with the FRG were in any sense construed to be separable from the larger political picture."[39] In other words, if there was going to be a dampening of the general political climate—for instance, in the wake of NATO's decision on medium-range missiles in Europe—Hager threatened that inner-German cultural relations also would suffer. Actually, however, Hager's attack was more likely directed against internal opponents in the GDR than against outside intervention from the Federal Republic.

Yet by the summer of 1981, East Germans had shown themselves to be relatively docile in the face of the Polish disturbances. There were even signs of resentment among the population that the GDR should have to make sacrifices to support the Poles. On both sides of the border traditional prejudices between the two nations rose to the surface again—the officially proclaimed socialist solidarity proved to be absent in the face of political turmoil and economic crisis. For the leadership in East Berlin this meant relief. The SED regime's level of anxiety was now lower than it had been a year earlier.

But the possibility of unrest remained, as demonstrated by the emergence of an all-German peace movement that was backed especially by young people and church representatives in East Germany. They regarded it as both a legitimate expression in favor of peace and a form of opposition against the SED regime. The East German government, however, found it difficult to crack down on the protests, since the GDR state was, in an official phrase, the "embodiment of the peace movement."[40] The government had in fact endorsed the movement by allowing a conference of international writers and scientists "for the promotion of peace" to convene in East Berlin in December. The conference had been organized by the chairman of the East German writers' association, Stephan Hermlin, upon Honecker's personal initiative. Among the participants were Bernt Engelmann, Günter Grass, and Luise Rinser from the Federal Republic, and Hermann Kant, Christa Wolf, Stefan Heym, and Thomas Brasch from the GDR. For the first time in years, GDR writers were allowed to criticize their government in public.[41]

A few weeks later, in January 1982, an East Berlin minister, Rainer Eppelmann, drafted a widely circulated petition calling for the removal of "occupation troops" from both parts of Germany. And on February 13, 1982, more than 5,000 young people gathered for a "Forum Frieden" (peace forum) in the Kreuzkirche in Dresden, commemorating the bombardment of the city in 1945.[42] They used an emblem that carried the "swords to ploughshares" summons of Old Testament prophet Micah and a diagram of the corresponding monument that the Soviet Union had donated to the United Nations and that had been set up in front of the UN building in New York. The situation was not without irony. With the Berlin conference for the promotion of peace in December 1981, Honecker personally had opened the floodgates for the emergence of a GDR peace movement. Now, only a short time later, the leadership in East Berlin was watching the new movement with displeasure and suspicion. The combination of biblical rhetoric and Soviet peace propaganda seemed to make the bearers of the "Swords to Ploughshares" stickers unassailable. Yet the East German officials looked upon them as provocative and reacted with reprisals. The conflict between a growing mass movement of dissidents and the SED regime had begun.[43]

The complexity of the situation could not have been better characterized than by the fact that on the very same day on which the conference for the promotion of peace convened in East Berlin, December 13, 1981, Honecker met with Chancellor Schmidt at Lake Werbellin and martial law was imposed in Poland. For the East German communists, the concurrence of these events caused optimism: The meeting with Schmidt promised progress in inner-German détente and economic cooperation; the conference in East Berlin was useful propaganda to demonstrate the GDR's peace-loving intentions; and the suppression of the Solidarity movement in Poland, including the detention of thousands of opponents of the Polish communist regime, assured the SED of calm and stability at the Eastern border.

Yet General Wojciech Jaruzelski, who had imposed martial law in Poland, turned out to be less orthodox than the GDR leadership had hoped for. In a 1982 conversation with American journalist Tad Szulc, he admitted that the only alternative to the suspension of Solidarity had been Soviet intervention, and he also acknowledged that the clock could not be turned back.[44] After martial law was lifted in July 1983, Jaruzelski quietly gave the Poles a degree of freedom and political pluralism unknown in other communist countries, and he personally became engaged in a dialogue with the Catholic Church.[45] The democratic opposition, though not allowed to organize formally, had little difficulty making its views known through clandestine publications, official newspapers and magazines under ever less censorship, and contacts with the foreign press. Soon even the Solidarity movement, still illegal but very much alive, again vividly pressed for reforms, giving new momentum to the democratization process and seriously threatening the PZPR's monopoly on power.[46]

By 1984, the spillover of reforms in Poland into the international arena was evident and slowly began to create new uneasiness among East Germany's leaders. In Hungary, meanwhile, where the "New Economic Mechanism" (NEM) had been introduced in 1968 as a means of improving economic efficiency without liberalizing the political regime, heated debate began about fundamental goals of Hungary's economic and political future. This debate was not the result of strikes or social upheaval, but was instead the consequence of widespread dissatisfaction with the existing structure of the society, economic system, and political regime—in other words, a situation similar to that in the GDR. Yet in contrast to East Germany, where the government seemed to be able to keep the opposition at bay, in Hungary the "Kádár compromise" of "Goulash communism"—that is, the strategy of decoupling economic reforms from political liberalization—showed the regime had already lost control.

Several factors brought about this development. These included growing assertiveness by some elite groups (economists, financial experts, and the farm and export lobby, among others) who had lost patience with the government's inept fumbling with economic policies; deteriorating living standards prompted by shrinking purchasing power; the rise of organized dissent, indeed a "para-opposition" (to use George Schöpflin's term); and, finally, the declaration of martial law in Poland, which had put an end to magic illusions held by many Hungarians since 1956 that "the reforms" would make progress under socialism still possible at least in one country in Eastern Europe "without the state resorting to force having its way."[47]

Moreover, by 1980-81, Hungary's "economic miracle" was running out of steam, as growth faltered and foreign debt grew to the largest per capita burden in Europe.[48] Eventually, between 65-70 percent of convertible export earnings had to be spent on debt service alone. Because of the debt burden and the failure to invest in productive sectors, Hungary's growth dropped to 1 percent in 1985. And with inflation running at anywhere from the officially admitted 17 percent to a more likely 25 to 30 percent, the real purchasing power of the people drastically declined.[49] The ill-advised central planning took its toll, and Hungary's relationship with the Council for Mutual Economic Assistance (CMEA) proved to be damaging to the economy.

Yet, the 1982 to 1984 debate about "reforming the reforms" did not lead immediately to spectacular results. János Kádár remained in power, if not in control, and was even able to issue a warning to those who tried to take advantage of the reform debate to position themselves around putative contenders for party leadership after his demise. But he had to agree to electoral reforms encouraging political participation, new economic measures promoting enterprise management, the further dismantlement of "industrial dinosaurs" (the ineffective industrial trusts and conglomerates created by the planning bureaucracy), and the principle of personal accountability for economic performance.

Strangely enough, however, these rather quiet reforms, which also required the "externalization" of the domestic economy by way of building up Hungary's commercial links with Western and Third World trading partners, had an immediate effect on the GDR—though in an unexpected manner. Mátyás Szürös, a secretary in the Central Committee of the Hungarian Socialist Workers Party (MSzMP) and former ambassador to the Soviet Union, advocated greater flexibility for Hungary in the conduct of its foreign affairs in the January 1984 issue of *Társadalmi Szemle,* the party's theoretical monthly. His article was met with great sympathy in the GDR, where Honecker's policy of—in his own words—"damage limitation" in view of the growing superpower hostility had led to considerable differences with the Soviet Union. Szürös's article was even reprinted in full in *Neues Deutschland.*[50]

The East German reaction to Szürös was all the more remarkable, as the official newspaper of the Communist Party of Czechoslovakia, *Rude Pravo,* stated in a lecturing response: "All elements of particularism in our community, any and all weakening of the socialist countries' uniform foreign policy strategy . . . merely harm the prestige of socialism in the eyes of the world, to say nothing of the fact that [these factions] actually harm the long-term interests of those who act in this way."[51] Moreover, this critique provoked a reply by Szürös that was again reprinted by the East German press, which incidentally ignored the Czechoslovak item.[52]

Ironically in this case, however, Honecker found himself aligned with Hungary against the Soviet Union (and Czechoslovakia, for that matter) at a time when Hungary was about to pursue a course of domestic reforms and external opening that eventually would contribute to the overthrow of the SED regime. This seemingly absurd constellation can be explained by the incongruence of the GDR's domestic and foreign policies in the early 1980s, when the containment of democratic movements at home coincided with a search for a renewed framework for détente abroad. Although two different models of reform had emerged, with a vengeance in Poland and more modestly in Hungary, Honecker's political formula of the 1970s—his balancing act of seeking contacts with the West while trying to prevent the intrusion of democratic ideas into East Germany that could undermine internal order—had not lost its validity yet. The situation would change, however, when Mikhail Gorbachev became the new general secretary of the Communist Party of the Soviet Union.[53]

THE GORBACHEV FACTOR

Despite various changes in tactics and political emphasis under Stalin, Khrushchev, Brezhnev, Andropov, and Chernenko, the USSR had been a bastion of Leninist orthodoxy. For the communist leadership of the GDR, the continuity in the nature of Soviet government had meant above all stability. The conservative Kremlin, afraid of revolutionary change and democratic upheaval, had insured, through the sheer presence of Soviet troops as well as through the application of psychological pressure and physical force, the power of the SED as the ruling force in East Germany. In fact, it seems almost certain that without Soviet backing the SED would never have been founded and the GDR would never have been established. At the very least, neither would have survived very long.[54]

Moreover, there had been a silent understanding between Moscow and East Berlin for 40 years that Soviet assistance was an essential element of maintaining the internal stability of the GDR. The role of the 380,000 Soviet troops stationed in East Germany had been as much directed at keeping the SED in power as it had been at providing external security for the GDR. As long as Soviet behavior did not put in doubt the disciplinary function of the Red Army presence—which constantly implied the readiness to use force to crack down on opposition—neither the stability of the GDR nor the existence of the Soviet empire in Eastern Europe were seriously at stake.

All of this changed when Gorbachev assumed power on March 10, 1985 —though not overnight. The new general secretary of the Communist Party of the Soviet Union (CPSU) did not possess a master plan for reform beyond the catchwords of glasnost and perestroika. Rather, his approach was to develop gradually, as an ongoing process dependent on challenges that called for improvised action, a concept for the transformation of Soviet policy, economy, and society.[55]

This was particularly true with regard to Soviet-East European relations. Whereas Gorbachev seemed to have general ideas—that is, a vision—about economic modernization and political reform in the Soviet Union as well as a general readiness for a return to détente and arms control with the West, his early policies toward the countries of Eastern Europe remained contradictory.

Professions of diversity alternated with demands for unity. Emphasis, however, was put on increasing political, economic, and military integration as a means of strengthening, rather than weakening, socialist internationalism—albeit on a more consultative basis.[56]

In other words, between 1985 and 1987, although Gorbachev called for the improvement of economic efficiency and changes for the CMEA in order to accelerate economic cooperation with foreign enterprises, he did not try to impose his "new thinking" on Eastern Europe. Most members of the Warsaw Pact, with the exception of Romania, therefore felt comfortable enough to ritually endorse the new party line emanating from Moscow. Yet the risk of instability associated with Gorbachev's policies prevented any of the East European countries from adopting the Soviet model. Here, due to history and tradition, even a policy of perestroika without the implications of glasnost—if such a separation was possible at all—could lead to demands for political pluralism, democracy, and greater independence. The risk was too great for the East European leaders, whose power depended on a firm hand in domestic affairs as well as reliable mutual links with the Kremlin.

Age, and a certain degree of the inflexibility that it implies, may have played a role as well. In 1987, Bulgaria's Zhivkov was 76, Hungary's Kádár 75, East Germany's Honecker 75, Czechoslovakia's Husák 74, and Romania's Ceausescu 69. Only Poland's Jaruzelski, 64, sincerely supported Gorbachev's reforms as a policy that coincided with his own. Jaruzelski did not want to adopt the Soviet model either, but he did welcome the same "historic current of change" in the two countries. "Poland," he declared in early 1987, "has not experienced such a happy convergence for the whole of the past millennium."[57]

In the GDR, Honecker made a distinction between the external and internal aspects of Gorbachev's policy; he embraced the efforts for a renewal of East-West détente but said there was no need for greater openness or economic reform in the GDR.[58] Time and again, Honecker and the SED leadership reaffirmed their own "correct course" past and present. They claimed that since their "streamlined" economy was performing well and since conditions in the GDR and the Soviet Union differed, further changes were both untimely and unnecessary. As to glasnost, there were no plans to link gradual economic improvements to political change. Officials privately rejected the Soviet argument for an inherent link between economic reform and political liberalization.[59]

The East German leaders apparently felt that Gorbachev's strategy was doomed to fail—and with it Gorbachev himself. The attempts at restructuring the Soviet economy were leading nowhere, and the situation had only gone from bad to worse. In other East European countries where reform policies had been implemented, the communist parties were about to lose their leading role. The GDR, however, could not afford an experiment that "looked like a prescription for disaster rather than a solution to the GDR's problems."[60] If the experiment failed, East Germany could not, like Poland and Hungary, fall back on nationalism. The GDR lacked a strong sense of identity and was exposed to the "magnet effect" of the Federal Republic's political attractiveness and economic abundance. Thus it had considerably less room to maneuver than any other East European nation, including the Soviet Union.[61]

Honecker, therefore, insisted that the GDR should not be forced to adopt the Soviet model, but should be allowed to develop socialism "in the colors of the GDR." SED Politburo member Hager, the party's chief ideologist, even stated in an interview with the West German magazine *Der Stern* on April 9, 1987, that "a policy of imposing the Soviet system on Germany would be false, such a policy does not correspond to the current conditions in Germany." He was quoting from Anton Ackermann's "Appeal of the German Communist Party" of June 1945, which had advocated a "special German road to socialism."[62] And by referring to Gorbachev's vision of a "Common European Home," Hager added, somewhat sarcastically: "If your neighbor chooses to rewallpaper the walls of his house, would you feel obliged to do the same?"[63]

One day later, when Hager's statements were reprinted in *Neues Deutschland*, on April 10, Gorbachev stressed in an address in Prague that he was ready to accept the idea of diversity among communist countries:

> We are far from calling on anyone to copy us. Every socialist country has its specific features, and the fraternal parties determine their political line with a view to the national conditions. . . . No one has the right to claim a special status in the socialist world. The independence of every party, its responsibility to its people, and its right to resolve problems of the country's development in a sovereign way—these are indisputable principles for us.[64]

The fact that Gorbachev made this statement in Prague was hardly accidental. The location was well chosen: Here, in 1968, Czechoslovakian communists under the leadership of Alexander Dubcek had tried to establish a system of democratic socialism until tanks of five Warsaw Pact nations had ended the experiment of the so-called Prague spring by force—and with it the hope of many idealists in both East and West that socialism and democracy might be compatible.[65]

Gorbachev reiterated the point in his speech commemorating the 70th anniversary of the Bolshevik Revolution on November 2, 1987, when he declared that "unity does not mean identity or uniformity."[66] Gorbachev was prepared to go even a step further and to do what seemed only consistent within the framework of his previous approach, but was likely to imply even more radical consequences: repudiate the "Brezhnev Doctrine" regarding the "limited sovereignty of socialist states" that had been used to justify the invasion of Czechoslovakia in August 1968; it had remained valid as a threat of intervention in the case of deviating behavior ever since.[67]

The communiqué issued at the end of Gorbachev's trip to Yugoslavia in March 1988, which expressed "respect for different paths to socialism" and stressed "the right of all countries to unimpeded independence and equal rights," was a first indication of Gorbachev's readiness to accept the repudiation of the Brezhnev Doctrine.[68] In a speech to the Council of Europe in Strasbourg in July 1989, he then stated explicitly "that any interference in internal affairs, any attempts to limit the sovereignty of states—both friends and allies or anyone else—is inadmissable."[69]

Without mentioning the Brezhnev Doctrine as such, he finally reinforced this point by referring to his idea of a "Common European Home"—a Europe of peace and cooperation, without the potential for war. He affirmed that "the philosophy of the Common European Home rules out the probability of an armed clash and the very possibility of the use of threat of force, above all military force, by an alliance against an alliance, inside alliances, or wherever it may be."[70]

The only thing still missing was an explicit repudiation of the doctrine. It finally came from Soviet Foreign Ministry spokesman Gennadi Gerasimov during Gorbachev's visit to Finland in October 1989. Here a humorous Gerasimov frankly declared that the Brezhnev Doctrine was "dead" and that it had been replaced by the "Sinatra Doctrine"—referring to a popular song by singer Frank Sinatra, "My Way."[71] Thereafter, each socialist country was free to decide on political, economic, and social reforms without the threat of Soviet interference—in other words: to do it "their way."

Apparently, the Soviet leadership did not realize immediately what eschewing the threat of intervention would do to their domination of Eastern Europe. The Soviet withdrawal from Afghanistan—beginning on May 15, 1988, and ending on February 15, 1989—was already perceived as a signal of reduced commitment to the "empire." It encouraged the reformist governments in Poland and Hungary as much as it put the more orthodox regimes in Czechoslovakia, Bulgaria, and especially the GDR in an awkward and embarrassing position. (Romania and Albania had already widely been written off as nations whose policies and political institutions could not be reformed at all).

In the GDR, the threat was increasingly felt by 1988. In November the Soviet journal *Sputnik,* which was available in GDR bookstores and was read by many reform-minded East Germans as an expression of Soviet openness, carried an article critical of the former Communist Party of Germany (KPD) in the 1920s and 1930s and put Stalin on a par with Hitler. The journal was banned from distribution in the GDR; in addition, five Soviet films were withdrawn from East German cinemas.[72]

Thus the GDR's self-isolation progressed. After the demarcation against the West in the 1970s and the delimitation against Poland in 1980, the SED now even isolated itself from the Soviet Union. At the same time, however, it did seek closer ties to orthodox members of the East bloc, such as Czechoslovakia and Romania, and even to communist heretics, such as Albania and China.

The antireformist course of the Honecker regime was not unanimously accepted among SED party officials. Alfred Kosing from the Academy of Social Sciences of the SED Central Committee, for instance, argued in July 1988 that "it would be a disastrous mistake to assume that the GDR had already carried out all necessary changes and that only the other socialist countries had to deal with these."[73] But the debate remained limited. Most functionaries kept their mouth shut, even if they quietly disagreed. The "cement-heads" at the top of the SED were thus able to carry through their course of resisting any initiative that could have led the GDR to join the East European reform movement.

The growing autism of the top leadership, however, contrasted sharply with the political development among the GDR population, especially the young people who had gathered under the protective roof of the evangelical churches, for whom Gorbachev was not a threat but a symbol of hope. Similarly for many who had lost their confidence in their own government a long time before, the policy of perestroika was the only hope that remained. Thus the SED's loss of contact with its own domestic sphere as well as with the surrounding world—including the Soviet Union and Gorbachev—was soon to become a major factor in its demise, because an increasing number of East Germans began to ask what was left to hope for.[74]

A second, even more significant factor in the downfall of the SED was the "reformist encirclement" of the GDR by the moves toward greater democracy and pluralism in Poland and Hungary. Encouraged by Gorbachev's own attempts at internal reform, they were free to move in an entirely new direction when Gorbachev's repudiation of the Brezhnev Doctrine liberated them from the fear of Soviet intervention.[75] And it did not take long before the speed and the range of the changes escalated. Renewed confrontation in April-May 1988 between striking steel mill and shipyard workers and the regime of General Jaruzelski in Poland, as well as Károly Grosz's ousting of János Kádár in Hungary on May 19, 1988, already indicated a "radicalization" of the reform process.[76] By the end of 1988, it remained to be seen just how long the GDR would be able to remain an island of orthodoxy in a sea of shifting political, economic, and ideological structures.

GROWING UNREST IN THE GDR

The nervousness of the GDR leadership about Gorbachev's reforms and his glasnost campaign was compounded by the problem of growing unrest in East Germany itself. There had been the potential for unrest ever since the beginning of the new Ostpolitik, which had opened the floodgates for Western ideas and ideals, although for more than a decade the SED regime had proven to be capable, through its policy of demarcation, of limiting the number of contacts with the West, or, through its policy of social pacification and social control, of diluting their impact on the GDR society. Western observers, therefore, had been lured into the false perception of stability and relative success.[77]

When the situation exploded in 1989, however, the sudden outburst of dissatisfaction demonstrated with a vengeance that the stability had been no more than superficial; the substance of the society had long undergone dramatic changes that had been overlooked by Western experts and Eastern politicians alike. To understand what happened, when and why the first changes did occur, and how they developed into open clashes between dissidents and the SED regime, requires a return, for a moment, to earlier periods of GDR history.

During the first two decades of the GDR, between 1949 and the early 1970s, East German society was kept under tight control, with little leeway for writers, artists, and opposition groups to express themselves freely. Prominent intellectuals such as philosopher Wolfgang Harich in the 1950s and writers Stefan Heym, Stephan Hermlin, and Christa Wolf in the early 1960s might occasionally protest against the provincialism of GDR culture, but the party's outlook was clearly stated by Honecker at the 11th Plenum of the SED Central Committee in December 1965.[78] Honecker, Walter Ulbricht's deputy for party affairs and at the time charged with supervision of the military and security forces, presented the report of the Politburo to the members of the Central Committee. He criticized "harmful tendencies" in film, television, theater, and literature, leading to "skepticism and immorality."[79] Lyricist Wolf Biermann, novelist Stefan Heym, and Professor Robert Havemann were particularly branded and denounced.[80]

After Honecker had replaced Ulbricht as first secretary of the SED, on May 3, 1971, he initiated a brief liberalization in cultural policy. In December 1971 he declared that "if one proceeds from the social premises of socialism, there can be no taboos in the realm of art and literature. This applies both to content and style—in short, to the concept of artistic mastery." Hager, Central Committee secretary for science and culture, provided further encouragement in July 1972 when he broadened socialist realism to encompass "scope for a wealth of forms, variations of presentation of style, and individual refinements."[81] And Honecker finally added, in May 1973, that the social development of the GDR allowed "a wide field for creative artistry." The spectrum of literature, art, and music as well as the work in theater, film, and television should be "broader and more colorful."[82]

The limits on the autonomy of intellectuals, writers, and artists were soon reached. Wolf Biermann was expelled in 1976 and, subsequently, so were friends and critics who opposed his expatriation, among them Robert Havemann and Rudolf Bahro.[83] As early as 1977, numerous prominent writers such as Bernd Jentzsch, Sarah Kirsch, Jurek Becker, and Hans-Joachim Schädlich, as well as the popular actor Manfred Krug and composer Thilo Medek, were either expatriated or were granted long-term exit permits. Others, like the expelled novelist Jürgen Fuchs and songwriters Christian Kunert and Gerulf Panach, declared publicly that they had not left the GDR voluntarily. Yet they were not the last to leave. Many more were to follow: Karl-Heinz Jakobs, Günter Kunert, Erich Loest, Klaus Poche, Klaus Schlesinger, Rolf Schneider, and Joachim Seyppel—just to mention a few. The exodus of prominent GDR writers in the late 1970s led to an intellectual drain, a disastrous manifestation of the SED's suppressive cultural policy as well as an unbearable loss for the quality of GDR literature.[84]

Uneasiness within the religious community also dated back to the early 1970s. Pastors who were distressed about the discrimination against their church under the communist regime, alarmed by the absence of dialogue among the various segments of the East German society, and encouraged by the normalization of relations with the Federal Republic began to address the concerns of young people. Church-sponsored discussions of sexuality, alcoholism, rock music, life in the GDR, and even the militarization of society became more common and often led to jammed church services, even in rural areas, as nonbelievers joined believers to hear popular preachers.[85]

The self-immolation of Pastor Oskar Brüsewitz in front of his church in Zeitz in August 1976 triggered off a major crisis. Before setting himself on fire, Pastor Brüsewitz explained that he was taking his life to protest the timidity of the church leadership under Bishop Albrecht Schönherr. Pastors

Rolf Günther of Falkenstein and Gerhard Fischer of Schwanewitz followed suit in September 1978.

Even before these self-immolations, the leadership of both the Evangelical Church and the SED had been willing to conclude, at a high-level meeting between Honecker and the church's trustee board headed by Bishop Schönherr, on March 6, 1978, an informal pact that designated the church as "an autonomous organization of social relevance."[86] But the accord merely established a working relationship. Its limits were clearly drawn by the secretary of state for church affairs, Klaus Gysi, who said in 1981 that cooperation was desirable where state and church agreed but that the church should respect the state's decisions in the event of disagreement.[87]

Yet the relationship deteriorated, despite "warm thanks" expressed by Honecker to the church for its past work at a second high-level meeting in February 1985. The new chairman of the League of Evangelical Churches, Bishop Johannes Hempel, also acknowledged at this meeting that relations had developed constructively since 1978, but he added the rider that "trust between us [church and state] will grow only to the extent that such trust is felt by ordinary believers."[88] It was precisely trust, however, that was lacking—on both sides.

Meanwhile, the church had become more outspoken on a variety of political topics mainly concerned with peace. It had openly criticized the Soviet invasion of Afghanistan and protested against "overly long belligerent reports" by East German media about Warsaw Pact maneuvers in the GDR —an act that had resulted in the confiscation by the authorities of an edition of the Evangelical News Service in September 1980.

In January 1982, East Berlin Pastor Rainer Eppelmann sent the so-called Berlin appeal, signed by several hundred East Germans, to Honecker, reproaching him for the programmatic distribution of war toys in the GDR, the glorification of army life in the schools, the regular visits of kindergarten groups and school classes to barracks, the incorporation of military spectacles into all national holidays, and the continued discrimination against those professing pacifist actions. In his appeal, Eppelmann said, "The weapons accumulated in both East and West will not protect us, but they will destroy us. . . . The balance of terror has prevented nuclear war only by postponing the war until tomorrow time and again."[89]

The church hierarchy felt constrained to distance itself from Eppelmann's unilateral action, which angered many dissidents who accused the church of needlessly compromising with the state. But in general, the church became increasingly active in expressing its position in favor of improving justice and freedom in East German society.

This was particularly true with respect to human rights. As early as October 1977, Bishop Hempel told a district synod in Saxony that the church would retain a "critical distance" from the SED on the subject of human rights and that the church considered respect for human rights a criterion for assessing the legitimacy of the state and the social order it represented.[90] Subsequently, the Evangelical Church became a major defender of human rights in the GDR and a watchdog against violations, which led to clashes with the authorities almost on a regular basis.[91]

In the autumn of 1980, when the GDR government embarked upon a delimitation course against the infiltration of Polish ideas about free trade unions and democratization, the East German churches also became a target of intensified state control. Press coverage of church synods at which political issues were discussed was banned; church papers that printed political statements were pulped and reprinted with sanitized texts; contacts between the Evangelical Church in the GDR and outside churches were curtailed; and, in mid-November 1980, the church was threatened with "administrative measures" unless it desisted from further political criticism.[92]

In response, Protestant parishes throughout the GDR held what proved to be the first of a serious of regular peace forums, during which thousands of youths gathered to hear the clergy speak out on peace and to participate in wide-ranging discussions. It was, as has already been mentioned earlier, the beginning of a massive protest movement in the GDR—within the walls of the church where political, philosophical, and ethical ideas could be expressed freely in an environment protected by the prestige and power of an institution that the state could no longer afford to challenge as it had done for so long.[93]

By 1982, the peace movement had gained momentum—with tens of thousands of mostly young East Germans participating in a series of events. Now almost every town and village had local clergy and peace groups involved in organizing discussions, meetings, and church services. From the vantage point of the SED, the movement had grown to dangerous proportions. In early 1983, about 20 East German pacifists were expelled from the country; in September of the same year, several demonstrators were arrested; one month later, Pastor Lothar Rochau of Halle was sentenced to three years in prison without probation for the "establishment of illegal groupings."[94] Eight more pacifists, all from Weimar, were behind bars by the end of January 1984. Shortly thereafter, 30-year-old theologian Wolf Quasdorf, another active pacifist, was imprisoned, ostensibly for "illegal contacts" in pursuit of emigration. Meanwhile, East German authorities continued their surveillance of unofficial peace rallies, obstructed access to them, and photographed those attending.[95]

In early 1984, the GDR government changed its tactics, pressuring pacifists and other dissidents to leave the country rather jailing them. In the first six months of 1984, some 31,000 citizens were allowed to leave for the West (compared with 7,729 in all of 1983). In July of that year, for the first time, 50 East Germans sought refuge in the Permanent Representation of the Federal Republic in East Berlin in order to get permission to leave the GDR.[96]

The protest movement continued, with the peace motive soon accompanied by environmental considerations, which were also expressed under the cover of the church walls. The three most prominent ecological centers in the GDR were all affiliated with the church: the Church Research Center run by Peter Gensichen in Wittenberg, the Theological Study Department of the League of Evangelical Churches in East Berlin, and the Church and Society Committee under the chairmanship of Dr. Heino Falcke. Criticism was directed at the SED leadership's pursuit of economic growth without due care for environmental protection, its emphasis on the performance principle and production volume, its misplaced faith in the benefits of science and technology, and the lack of popular participation in decision-making processes of the East German political regime, including the falsification of election results.[97]

Throughout the 1980s, the GDR government was unable to contain the protest movement, although the authorities consistently stiffened their approach toward the dissidents. Censorship of church journals and newspapers was stepped up, and the pattern of police crackdowns continued. In November 1987, state security forces raided the basement of the Church of Zion in East Berlin, where an environmental group had installed its library, suspected by the police as a center of protest; some of the group's members were arrested and a number of documents were confiscated. In January 1988, again more than 50 dissidents were arrested, some of whom were forced to emigrate to West Germany. The pattern repeated itself time and again.[98]

Writers and artists also continued to play their role in the protest movement. For them, controls had been tightened up in 1979 when reform of the penal law made it more difficult for authors to publish in the West. At the 11th Party Congress in April 1986, Honecker reaffirmed the hard line when he called for a clear stance by the cultural intelligentsia, which was expected to support communism: "Given the responsibilities of the arts community in a socialist society, the only valid position is that of a fellow-fighter, or a fervent protagonist who, with her/his own particular tools, spreads the ideas of peace and socialism among the masses."[99]

However, not many writers or artists bought these arguments. Those who had not been expelled after protesting against the expatriation of Biermann in 1976 or subsequently demonstrating against the lack of intellectual freedom in the GDR began quietly to organize meetings and discussion groups that eventually evolved into dissident organizations, such as Neues Forum, founded by Bärbel Bohley, a well-known painter and sculptor, in 1989.[100]

Apart from the rather spectacular and highly visible protests and demonstrations of the peace movement, the environmental groups, and the articulate intellectuals, however, there was yet another manifestation of dissent within the GDR society: the Übersiedler (resettlers). On October 15, 1983, a new emigration decree had become effective in the GDR that, in accordance with the Final Protocol of the Madrid follow-up meeting of the Conference on Security and Cooperation in Europe of September 6, 1983, permitted East Germans to file applications for a resettlement outside the GDR. In 1984, as has been pointed out before, more than 30,000 East Germans had been allowed to leave their country, though mainly for political reasons, as the government wanted to expel troublesome dissidents. In 1985, about 18,000 citizens received permission to leave—more than twice as many as in 1982 and 1983. And yet, even these relatively larger numbers after 1984 accounted for only a small portion of several hundred thousand East Germans who had already filed applications for resettlement. Many of them had been waiting for approval for up to five years.[101]

Although the resettlers protested rather quietly by "voting with their feet," they nevertheless gave a powerful indication of the amount of frustration and the lack of hope that existed in the GDR at the time. The sheer number of applications for resettlements made clear that in 1989, hundreds of thousands, and possibly millions, of East Germans were held back from emigration only by one factor: the insurmountable Wall that had been erected for precisely that purpose. Without the Wall, the SED regime was doomed to failure. In this respect, 1989 was no different from 1961.

MASS EXODUS, PROTESTS, AND DEMONSTRATIONS

In the spring of 1989, ethnic Germans from all over Eastern Europe were arriving in the Federal Republic. A majority of them were young and were therefore sociopolitically still regarded a plus for the FRG. On April 3, 1989, Horst Waffenschmidt, the parliamentary state secretary in the Interior Ministry and the federal government's commissioner for the Resettlement of Ethnic Germans, stated that the favorable age structure of the new arrivals would help improve the country's population structure. Only 4 percent of ethnic Germans who had arrived in 1988 were older than 65, while 43 percent were 25 years of age or younger. The young people would earn their own pensions during the course of their working lives in the Federal Republic and accordingly would not be a permanent burden but rather a benefit to the community.[102] Thus the mood of the federal government was generally optimistic. The German immigrants were welcome, and Bonn intended to play a constructive role in Eastern Europe as the reforms there progressed. Accordingly, on April 17, 1989, when the Polish free trade union movement Solidarity was legalized by a Warsaw court, Foreign Minister Hans-Dietrich Genscher immediately called for economic support for Poland and advocated granting the country "a breather" in repaying its debts.[103] The state minister in the Foreign Office, Helmut Schäfer, proposed a summit meeting of all heads of governments and finance ministers in the European Community to better coordinate economic and financial aid. Bonn should lead the aid efforts, he said. The efforts would concentrate primarily on easing the rescheduling of Polish debt, finding private lenders, and accelerating consultations between the World Bank and the International Monetary Fund.[104]

In East Germany, the new developments in Poland were viewed with suspicion and concern again—behind closed doors. In public, on May 1, powerful organized Labor Day demonstrations celebrated the victory of socialism—with some 700,000 claques in East Berlin, 270,000 in Dresden, and 300,000 in Leipzig. The next day, however, news agencies reported from Budapest that Hungarian forces had begun to dismantle electronic security devices and barbed wire at the Hungarian-Austrian border (the "Iron Curtain") near the town of Köszeg.

When the SED Politburo gathered on May 4 to evaluate the success of the Labor Day festivities, Defense Minister Heinz Kessler passed on "solid information" he had received from his military attaché in Budapest that the Hungarian government was reducing installations but that border checks would continue. The Politburo members felt relieved. They continued their session with a discussion about the outlook for the potash industry in the GDR and some speculation about possible adverse votes at the upcoming local elections scheduled for May 7.[105]

Günter Schabowski, a member of both the SED Central Committee and the Politburo, was present at the meeting on May 4. He later recalled that he had immediately had a hunch what "explosive force" the Hungarian dismantling of the Iron Curtain might have for the GDR, but that he, like the other members of the Politburo, had preferred to ignore his foreboding. General Kessler's spirited explanation had provided a comfortable "alibi."[106]

Yet questions remained. The Hungarians had not consulted the GDR government. Would they be prepared to go a step further and let East German citizens pass over the border into Austria? Was the Hungarian initiative only the beginning of general unpredictability in the Eastern bloc? Would it be necessary to prevent East German tourists from visiting their traditional vacation areas in Hungary, Romania, and Bulgaria? And what would be the effect of such a measure with regard to the internal stability of the GDR? For some time, the uneasiness deriving from these open questions was overshadowed by short-term political problems, Schabowski said. But in the long run the anxiety could no less be shooed away than "wasps from a plum tart."[107]

Among the short-term concerns were the upcoming local elections. All members of the Politburo agreed during their session on May 4 that the former "super percentages"—the 99 percent results—could no longer be expected, as the spillover effect of the democratization process in Eastern Europe and the growth of opposition in the GDR would take their toll. Even an unusual 5 percent of adverse votes against the candidates of the National Front seemed possible, especially since members of several opposition groups intended to monitor the elections to ensure the correctness of the electoral process.

But on May 7, when the results of the elections became known, the SED leadership reveled in euphoria. Egon Krenz, chairman of the electoral commission and also a member of the SED's Central Committee and Politburo, declared that again 95.98 percent of the votes had been cast in favor of the candidates of the National Front. Only 142,301 adverse votes, according to Krenz, had been counted in the whole country. Two days later, in the next session of the Politburo, Krenz praised the results as an expression of "the willingness of the electorate to continue to participate actively in the formation of the developed socialist society." Erich Honecker called the outcome "an impressive confession toward the policy of the SED aimed at peace and socialism."[108]

Few of the leaders doubted that the elections had been fixed. Kurt Hager even knew about the true outcome, at least about the counts at selected polling stations at the universities: with adverse votes of up to 51 percent, for instance, at the Kunsthochschule Berlin-Weissensee. Schabowski later stated that this election had been no different from previous elections by any means, that every election in the past had been manipulated. They had "just been organized this way, without special orders, automatically, like the big demonstrations."[109]

This time, however, something *was* different. Rumors spread quickly that the government had falsified electoral documents in order to get the desired results, and opposition groups set out to prove the forgeries. During the following weeks, Minister of State Security Erich Mielke was bombarded with reports about "domestic enemies" who intended "to seek 'proof' of an alleged forgery of electoral results." Mielke responded by decree No. 0008-38/89, ordering his security organs to inform any citizen complaining about the correctness of the electoral process that there were "no clues arousing suspicion of a criminal offence."[110]

How the election results had been fabricated, contrary to Mielke's brazen decree, was later exemplified by police testimony of Harry Klapproth, a member of the SED district leadership of Potsdam. In April 1989, at a meeting with the second secretaries of the 15 SED districts, Horst Dohlus, himself a member of the SED Politburo, had orally requested results that would be equal to, or "in points better," than the results achieved during previous elections in 1984 and 1986. In the district of Potsdam, the second secretary of the SED, Ulrich Schlaak, then conferred with election commissioners Harri Schindler and Klapproth about the results to be reached. After the meeting with Schlaak, Klapproth sat down with Schindler and, according to his own words, "on the basis of the results of the 1984 and 1986 elections we determined the percentages." "Let's see," he told Schindler, "where we want to arrive at." Valid and invalid votes and votes for opponents were laid down in exact numbers for the district, before counties, municipalities, and towns each received their fabricated results. Whatever happened in the polling stations was completely irrelevant. The results had already been determined by SED party officials well in advance.[111]

But the Politburo never bothered even to discuss the forgeries and did nothing to defuse the growing popular outrage about the blatant falsification. A recount of the votes was never seriously considered. Honecker later denied any responsibility of either the Politburo or the Central Committee for the manipulation. "For us," he maintained, "even a result of 65 percent would have been a great success. . . . I must say quite frankly that it is a complete mystery to me. . . . I regard election forgery as dreadful, since it is not only self-deceit but a deception of the people, for whose cooperation we are struggling."[112]

Amid the mounting criticism of vote fraud that was the starting point for protest demonstrations on the seventh day of every month, the East German government seized another opportunity to attract opposition. After troops of the Chinese People's Liberation Army had cracked down the student rebellion in Beijing on June 4 and had drawn protests from all over the world for the massacre at Tiananmen Square, the SED Politburo decided to come to the assistance of what was called "the hard-pressed Chinese people." First, the Volkskammer (the East German parliament) announced its support for the suppression of the "counterrevolutionary riots" in the Chinese capital. Then Foreign Minister Oskar Fischer emphasized the bonds between the GDR and China when his colleague from Beijing, Qian Qichen, visited East Berlin on June 12. Finally, a phalanx of prominent GDR politicians set out for solidarity missions to China during the following months: Hans Modrow in June, Günter Schabowski in July, and Egon Krenz in September.[113]

Mikhail Gorbachev's visit to the Federal Republic, on the other hand, from June 12 to 14, was regarded as yet another sign of decadence. His performance in Bonn was assessed by the SED Politburo as "hardly class warfare-like." Comrade Gorbachev, the East Germans stated, had failed to sufficiently oppose Chancellor Kohl's reunification talk and had only confirmed his already existing poor rating as a communist leader.[114]

Honecker himself contributed, unintentionally, to the political downfall of the GDR. On July 10, when he had to undergo a gallbladder operation that would keep him away from office for the rest of the summer while convalescing, he entrusted the responsibilities of his office to Egon Krenz. Like Honecker, Krenz had been chairman of the SED's youth organization for many years. He had been, as the party's secretary for security, youth, and sports, a member of the SED Central Committee since 1973, and had become a full member of the Politburo in 1983. Born in 1937, he was still relatively young, compared with his colleagues in the East German political elite, and had been treated as the logical successor of the aging Honecker for some time.

Yet now, in the summer of 1989, nearing the top of his career, Krenz quickly lost control. On August 1, he was confronted with a crisis not unlike the events in 1984 but different in size and proportion. Several hundred GDR citizens entered the West German embassies in Prague and Budapest and the FRG's representative office in East Berlin asking for permission to resettle in West Germany. About 170 East Germans sought refuge in the Federal Republic's embassy in Budapest alone. Within two weeks, Bonn's embassy in Prague had to be closed temporarily because of overcrowding. Krenz, as he had worked out with Honecker, took a tough stand and refused to grant exit permits. Instead, on August 12, *Neues Deutschland* published an article commemorating the building of the Wall on August 13, 1961, and printed a full page of pictures depicting "treacherously murdered" border guards.[115] But the situation continued to deteriorate.[116]

Meanwhile, on August 3, Krenz and Security Commissioner Wolfgang Herger had had a two-and-one-half-hour talk with Markus Wolf, the longtime head of the espionage department of the GDR Ministry of State Security. Wolf encouraged Krenz to renew the party and the state and provided a detailed list of proposals for political reform.[117] Krenz said he fully agreed with Wolf's arguments but, unfortunately, could not afford to utter such frank statements in his "party group" without being ousted immediately. Even Gorbachev, he noted, had become general secretary only because of the party discipline he had exercised under three of his predecessors.[118]

The conversation between Wolf and Krenz indicated, however, that Krenz knew how necessary reforms in the GDR were. In fact, the "crown prince" had warned Honecker several times about possible negative implications of the migration. But Honecker's response had always been brusque: "Why do you actually put these migration numbers together? What are you driving at, anyhow? Before the Wall was built, a lot more were leaving us."[119]

Now the necessity for change became even more evident. Herger gathered information about the reasons why, at this time, 120,000 East Germans had filed exit applications. The results, compiled in a classified paper for Krenz only, were devastating. The report stressed "the loss of perspective as mass protest." GDR socialism was "only smiled at," particularly among youths, including Free German Youth functionaries, while religiousness had risen 10 to 15 percent. Resignation had become a mass phenomena, and affection for the GDR was diminishing at an alarming rate. Honecker personally was blamed for the deplorable state of affairs.[120]

Krenz received the report just one day prior to his departure for summer vacation in Dierhagen at the Baltic Sea. He offered to postpone his holiday in view of the pending crisis. Honecker immediately rejected the suggestion, appointing his confidant and hunting partner, Günter Mittag, the Politburo economic expert, as acting general secretary. "Nobody is indispensable," Honecker coolly told Krenz. His decision in this critical situation to nominate Mittag as the acting head of the party was clearly a vote of no confidence for Krenz, who then disappeared from the scene for four weeks, enjoying his summer vacation at the Baltic Sea.[121]

Others went on vacation too. On August 19, some 660 GDR citizens used a "picnic" of the Pan-European Union near Sopron at the border between Hungary and Austria for their escape to the West. The Hungarian border guards watched carefully the other way and did not intervene.[122] Subsequently, between 100 and 200 East Germans arrived in West German reception camps daily. Among the GDR leadership, the grievance against Hungary increased. In the Politburo, Mittag accused the Hungarians of "treachery to socialism."[123] A GDR deputy foreign minister, sent to Budapest as an SED representative "to slow things down," returned empty-handed: The Hungarians were no longer in control and, moreover, apparently no longer had any intention of regaining control.[124]

The démarche in Budapest only confirmed the worst. The emissary reported that Hungarian foreign minister Gyüla Horn was the "driving force behind the development." The military continued to be "loyal to the expectations of the GDR," but was no longer united.[125]

Honecker ordered Foreign Minister Oskar Fischer to sound out Moscow if a Warsaw Pact meeting could be arranged to discipline the Hungarians. But Gorbachev declined: The time when a departure from the general line could be corrected by majority pressure was past. The GDR was alone.[126]

Finally, on September 5, the SED leadership was informed that six days later, GDR citizens would be permitted to cross over the Hungarian border into Austria legally. The news caused a heated debate in the Politburo. Mittag, the only member of the highest organ of the SED who had full knowledge of the seriousness of Honecker's illness (which included the secret implantation of a cardiac pacemaker), informed his colleagues that some 120,000 GDR residents were still vacationing in Hungary, all of them potential refugees. Erich Mielke, the head of state security, reacted as could be expected: He proposed ending the processing of travel applications.[127]

But then Werner Krolikowski, the Central Committee's secretary of agriculture, asked whether the Politburo should turn to the people with a proclamation. Krolikowski himself did not have the slightest new idea of what could be done. But his bewildering question provoked the first real discussion in the history of the Politburo, as Schabowski recalled, "during which faulty developments were not shuffled off to the incompetency of a combinat's director or the laziness of a minister, but where principles of the system were touched upon."[128] Unfortunately, the discussion led nowhere, since Kurt Hager asked for adjournment of the debate that, he said, had taken on "such a fundamental character" that it could not be continued without the general secretary being present.[129]

Thus the official response of the GDR government to the events in Hungary was predictable. The Federal Republic was accused of "organized slave trade," and Hungary was denounced for "breaching faith" in return for a DM500 million loan from Bonn promised by Chancellor Kohl.[130] Some of the more sensitive members of the Politburo, such as Schabowski, understood the deadly blow that Hungary's border opening toward Austria had dealt to the SED regime, but no conclusions were drawn.

Within a few days, as many as 12,000 East Germans escaped to the West, the single largest flow of refugees from the Eastern bloc since 1961, when the last mass exodus of East Germans had led to the decision to construct the Berlin Wall. Yet the SED leadership continued to view the exodus only as "illegal smuggling" and "an overt attempt" by West Germany to destabilize the GDR.

As John Edwin Mroz has noted, the unilateral suspension by Hungary of "certain paragraphs" of the 1969 Hungarian-East German treaty on tourism had more to do with the future evolution of Eastern Europe than the obligation to prevent citizens of an allied country from exiting to the West without the approval of their own government.[131] Hungary had acted not only to invoke its international obligations as a signatory of the Geneva Convention on the Status of Refugees, which bans the practice of forcibly sending refugees back to countries of origin if they are likely to face persecution, but, more important, it had responded to domestic pressures that could spell the fate of the leadership of the Hungarian Socialist Workers' Party (MSzMP) in the forthcoming parliamentary elections scheduled for the spring of 1990. Hungarian communist party officials estimated that at best they might capture 30 percent of the vote, with the remainder being divided among 10 opposition parties. However, if the government sent back the East German refugees against their will, one party official told a group of Western experts in September 1989, the MSzMP "would be lucky to get 5 percent of the vote."[132]

For the GDR, the Hungarian decision could not have come at a worse time. The question was not only whether the close links built with West Germany could be preserved while the most skilled young workers continued to leave the country via the Hungarian-Austrian back door to the Federal Republic, but also what would happen if East Germany became even further isolated among allies in the East than it had been in recent years.

As it was, within one month the number of East Germans who crossed from Hungary to Austria on their way to the Federal Republic climbed to 25,250. On October 10, the Ministry for Intra-German Relations in Bonn reported that a total of 110,000 East Germans had resettled in the Federal Republic with or without the consent of GDR authorities during the first nine months of the year. Some 32,500 GDR residents had registered in West German reception centers in September alone.[133]

The opening of the Hungarian-Austrian border contributed decisively to the swelling of the exodus. But the Hungary-to-Austria escape route was not the only one that existed. Thousands of GDR residents who had managed to get to Poland or Czechoslovakia sought refuge in the West German embassies in Prague and Warsaw, refusing to leave until the GDR granted them permission to resettle in the Federal Republic. On September 30, while the SED state put up decorations for its 40th anniversary celebrations, an agreement was reached among the West German, East German, Polish, and Czechoslovakian governments to allow some 5,500 East Germans in the Federal Republic's embassy in Prague and about 800 in Warsaw to resettle in the West.[134]

Formally negotiated in New York by Foreign Minister Genscher with his Soviet counterpart, Eduard Shevardnadze, the agreement was complemented by the efforts of other foreign ministers from both West and East, among them East Germany's Oskar Fischer and Czechoslovakia's Jaromir Johanes.[135] Actually, however, the breakthrough had been made possible by a personal decision of Honecker's.

The SED general secretary had returned to his office on September 25, after being absent for six weeks. Four days later, in view of the impressive but deplorable pictures showing people with suitcases and rucksacks jumping over the fence of the West German embassy in Prague and children in tents freezing in the rainy and cold autumn weather, he telephoned his Czechoslovakian colleague, Milos Jakes. Honecker proposed to transport the refugees under the cover of night from Prague via GDR territory to the Federal Republic. Jakes agreed that it would be the best solution if the GDR itself would settle the problem that had become such a great burden for both sides.[136]

During a "friendship meeting" between representatives of the GDR and the People's Republic of China at the opera that evening, Honecker informed the members of the Politburo who were present about his conversation with Jakes. He also indicated that he had made the decision to let the refugees go because of the forthcoming festivities in celebrating the GDR's anniversary on October 7. "We have no choice," he said, "if we want the thing to be disposed of by the 7th."[137]

Honecker was confident that the emptying of the FRG's Prague embassy would provide sufficient breathing space for a grandiose jubilee. But the polished logistics of the operation turned out to be not so flawless. The road just begun—a road that first led to the collapse of communist leadership in the GDR and eventually to German unification—soon became irreversible.

Even the prescient Genscher seemed unaware of the far-reaching implications of his policy at the time. In an interview published in *Der Spiegel* on September 25, he stated that the Federal Government did "not wish, now or in the future, to destabilize the GDR." Because it was "important to stay on course," he said Bonn would continue its policy "on the basis of the Basic Treaty concluded between the two states in 1972 and the Helsinki Final Act."[138]

To be sure, Genscher did not rule out unification in the long run. But his mention of this possibility made it appear to be a continuing tradition of West German foreign policy rather than a new option. He even avoided the terms "reunification" and "German unity":

> The fact that—as Willy Brandt puts it—what belongs together cannot be separated forever has determined the policy of all governments. Any policy which assumes the existence of two German nations is built on sand. There is neither a socialist German nation or a capitalist German nation. In keeping with the mandate of our Basic Law, the policy of the Federal Republic of Germany has always been directed toward striving, within the framework of a European peace policy, toward a rapprochement between the Germans in West and East.[139]

Two days later, in a speech at the United Nations, Genscher referred again to the relationship with the GDR—saying that "new and closer forms of cooperation" were needed "in many fields," while "national solo efforts" should be precluded in order "to work for a pan-European peaceful order from which no country may be excluded or exclude itself."[140] The West German foreign minister obviously felt that reforms in the GDR could not be avoided if the East German government was to give its citizens incentive to stay; the Federal Republic should continue to support the GDR in making the reforms possible, but a solution to the overall German question would come only in the form of a general transformation of the all-European system.

Genscher's approach, calling for reforms without radical shifts in the political structure of Europe, was best visible when he referred to the growing mass exodus from the GDR:

> The GDR can, under its own conditions, contribute through reforms toward greater openness in Europe, just as the Soviet Union, Poland and Hungary are already doing. Deeply moved, we witness the fate of young people who are sorrowfully leaving their homes and their familiar surroundings. Nobody can want that. A policy of reform would open up new prospects in the GDR as in other Central and Eastern European countries. This will encourage the people to stay.[141]

Quite similar to Genscher's belief that reforms could help to stabilize the GDR, Theo Sommer, one of West Germany's leading newspaper columnists, also asked for a sober analysis rather than emotional wishful thinking. Referring to a statement of Chancellor Kohl that the German question was "still on the agenda of world politics," Sommer wrote in an article published in *Die Zeit* on September 29: "We are not an inch closer to reunification than a year ago, or five or ten years ago. . . . The issue of German unity is not hotter than ever. On the contrary: It stays on one of the rear cooktops of world politics, and there is no fire under the pot."[142] Facts had not changed, Sommer argued, only the mood of the country. Therefore a new policy toward the GDR was not justified. Bonn should continue to pursue, with pragmatism and patience, its "critical dialogue."[143]

Yet when the agreement of September 30 permitted those 6,300 GDR citizens who had sought refuge in the FRG's embassies in Prague and Warsaw to resettle in the West, it became almost instantly clear that there was very little time left for reform. First of all, Erich Honecker and the leadership of the SED had yielded to the pressure of the embassy occupiers not for humanitarian reasons, but to save face: The whole world was watching Prague and Warsaw while East Berlin was preparing for its 40th anniversary celebrations. The decision to let the occupiers emigrate was widely understood not as a sign of greater flexibility and reform, but rather "a barely concealed capitulation."[144] Second, the calculation that by agreeing to the mass exodus the regime in East Berlin would gain not only peace on the anniversary front, but also maneuvering room and breathing space in domestic politics, quickly turned out to be wrong; the day after the 6,300 had left Czechoslovakia and Poland, another 1,200 GDR citizens entered the West German embassies in Warsaw and Prague.

These developments were particularly confusing to those East Germans who remained in the GDR and tried to improve the system from within. On the one hand, they realized that the regime's reaction was marked by confusion, contradictions, and helplessness, as the West German newspaper *Die Welt* noted: "Even the last semblance of a lawful government or at least of one that acts consistently is now gone. An edifice built on illusions and lies is now collapsing."[145] On the other hand, the unusually weak, erratic, and timid behavior of their government encouraged many people in the GDR to come forward with greater frankness than at any time since the uprising of June 17, 1953.

On October 2, 1989, more than 15,000 people demanding change by chanting "Gorby, Gorby" or "Gorby, help us"—referring to the Soviet general secretary—marched through Leipzig in the biggest of the "Monday evening demonstrations" in East Germany's second largest city. At the same time, the Federal Republic's embassy in Prague, which had been emptied of thousands of East German refugees only two days earlier, was overrun by almost 5,000 more and was forced to close its doors on Tuesday, October 3. Still, newcomers continued to arrive, gathering outside the embassy, even climbing onto roofs of adjacent buildings and dropping into the packed grounds. Others clashed with Czech police and broke through barriers to reach the fence.[146]

The SED leadership tried to contain the rapidly rising wave of mass exodus and protest by announcing on October 3 that visa-free travel to Czechoslovakia was being suspended because "certain circles in West Germany are preparing further provocations to mark the 40th anniversary of East Germany."[147] This measure was expected to be effective, since Czechoslovakia had been the only country to which GDR citizens could travel without restrictions. Yet closing the last major escape route for East Germans was not without risks either. Western diplomats in Bonn noted immediately that the decision to close the border to Czechoslovakia was certain to aggravate tensions. As one diplomat said, "It'll quickly turn East Germany into a pressure cooker, and it may explode."[148]

The Collapse of
Communist Power

On the evening of October 4, 1989, three sealed trains of the East German Reichsbahn pulled into the main railway station of Dresden. Their load was an open secret, as everybody in the GDR who could watch West German television or receive Western radio programs—that is, virtually everyone—knew what the trains were carrying. Nearly 7,600 GDR refugees from the Federal Republic's embassy in Prague had been allowed to emigrate to the West pursuant to the agreement reached by the foreign ministers of the two German states, the Soviet Union, and Czechoslovakia on September 30. The trains had been due to arrive in Dresden on October 3 but were delayed for 24 hours as tracks and stations along the route were cleared of people who tried to get a free ride to the West.

Hans Modrow, the local chief of the SED in Dresden, had repeatedly tried to convince the leadership in East Berlin that it was unwise to guide the trains through his city instead of sending them directly from Prague to Hof in West Germany. But the Politburo and the government insisted that the East German authorities had to provide correct exit papers for their citizens, because, they argued, "whoever leaves the GDR, regardless on what route, shall not do so as a citizen of the GDR."[1] Additionally, the minister of transportation, Otto Arndt, indicated that the crammed trains had already reached the border between Czechoslovakia and East Germany, and the occupants might become panicky if the trains were sent back to Prague.

Thus the local authorities in Dresden had no help in coping with an increasingly difficult situation, in which some 10,000 spectators and would-be emigrants from all over the GDR had attempted to stop the trains and join the refugees. As Modrow had anticipated, tumultuous scenes occurred when the transport appeared. The crowd clashed with the security forces, who had been ordered to protect the station and ensure the trains smooth passage.

Stones were thrown at the station building. Many people were injured, among them policemen from Dresden and the adjacent district of Halle, as well as soldiers of the National People's Army who had been sent by Defense Minister Heinz Kessler to support the police. The material damage was high. Fortunately, however, no shots were fired and no one was killed.[2]

After the transports had left the GDR, the official East German news agency ADN stated in a commentary that the refugees "have all trampled upon our moral values and have separated themselves from our society." When the chief editor of the SED organ *Neues Deutschland,* Joachim Herrmann, submitted the text to Honecker for approval, the general secretary paused for a second and then added by his own hand: "Therefore we should not drop a tear after them."[3]

The events in Dresden fit well into the general frame of an ever growing opposition to the SED regime. While the exodus of GDR citizens to the West was an important catalyst of change, it was hardly the cause of the protests. In fact, public demonstrations had already been held regularly on the seventh day of every month since June, drawing attention to the manipulation of the elections on May 7. In addition, weekly "Monday demonstrations" had begun in Leipzig on Monday, September 4, after some 1,200 people gathered for peace prayers in the Nikolai Church and attempted to march to Market Square in the downtown area, chanting demands for freedom of travel and the right of assembly. At the time of the events in Dresden, the Monday demonstrations had already become an established tradition and the focus of the opposition in the GDR. The number of participants had grown to about 5,000 on September 25 and as many as 20,000 on October 2.[4]

Encouraged by the success of the demonstrations, a number of political organizations had been formed. On August 26 in East Berlin, Ibrahim Böhme, Martin Gutzeit, Markus Meckel, and Arndt Noack had called for the foundation of a "social-democratic party in the GDR." On September 4, in Böhlen, near Leipzig, trade unionists, students, committed Christians, and members of the SED had passed a proclamation "For a United Left in the GDR." On September 9-10, Neues Forum (New Forum) had been established by some 30 dissidents in Berlin, among them Bärbel Bohley and Jens Reich. On September 12, another group in Berlin, with Wolfgang Ullmann, Konrad Weiss, Hans-Jürgen Fischbeck, and Ludwig Mehlhorn, had instituted Demokratie Jetzt (Democracy Now). And on September 14, a pastor from Erfurt, Edelbert Richter, had announced the formation of the group Demokratischer Aufbruch (Democratic Awakening).[5]

In other words, the SED leadership faced both a refugee problem and an increasingly powerful political opposition. This became all the more evident when, on October 4, at virtually the same time as the clashes at the railway station in Dresden, delegates of the various dissident movements met in Berlin. Their joint declaration spoke about "possibilities of common political action," with their primary goals free elections under control of the United Nations and, more generally, a "democratic renewal" of the GDR.[6]

As October 7, the day of the 40th anniversary of the GDR, drew nearer, public demonstrations and the combined activities of the opposition groups reached a new climax. On the eve of the festivities, Dresden was again the site of violent clashes between demonstrators and the police. Although no further refugee trains were led through the city after October 4, the demonstrations there continued for three consecutive nights, always countered by a massive police presence. But protest was now spreading from Berlin, Leipzig, and Dresden to other cities. A major demonstration with 800 participants was reported from Magdeburg, for instance, with 250 people arrested by the police and state security.[7]

For the SED, it was time to worry. Egon Krenz, who returned from China shortly before the anniversary, expressed concern about Honecker's exit policy and stated privately that "whatever may have happened at Tiananmen Square, nowhere should we move against demonstrators by military force. That would be our political and moral end."[8] On his way back from Beijing, he worked on a paper that he intended to submit to the regular Politburo session on October 10 for the opening of a general debate on future policies of the SED. In Berlin, he handed the text over to his confidant Wolfgang Herger, as well as to Siegfried Lorenz and Günter Schabowski for revision. Krenz said the Politburo should turn to the public with a declaration explaining the position of the leadership. In essence, his paper constituted such a declaration.[9]

For the time being, however, it was necessary above all to endure the anniversary weekend on October 6-7. Numerous actions by the opposition could be expected, including the regular monthly demonstration on the Alexanderplatz against the manipulation of the May elections. Honecker and Minister for State Security Mielke had already conferred about military measures to shield the festivities from disturbances. Schabowski therefore asked Krenz to use his influence to prevent "stupidities" by the security organs, and recommended that the SED district leadership of Berlin should send agitators to the demonstrations to diffuse the opposition politically.[10] It is clear that at this point neither Krenz nor the more farsighted Schabowski were aware how close the end of the Honecker era—and, for that matter, the communist regime—in the GDR was.[11]

THE RESIGNATION OF ERICH HONECKER

Meanwhile, Honecker continued to prepare for his ceremonial address, which would be delivered in the Palace of the Republic in East Berlin on Friday, October 6. More than 4,000 guests from the GDR and more than 70 foreign delegations, including a Soviet delegation headed by Mikhail Gorbachev, were scheduled to attend.

Gorbachev arrived on the morning of October 6 at Schönefeld airport, where he and his wife, Raissa, were welcomed by Erich and Margot Honecker as a sign of traditional Soviet-East German friendship. The SED leaders felt that the presence of the Soviet general secretary in the GDR at this time was a valuable asset, a respected celebrity casting the shining light of his international prestige on the anniversary celebrations. Yet Gorbachev was also a symbol of hope for the dissidents, who felt that he alone could help the reform process in East Germany succeed.

The official commemorative event in the afternoon passed without disruption—except for the fact that Gorbachev's congratulations resembled more an attempt at damage control than an homage to his hosts. While he bestowed compliments to the faithful comrades on their "historic road," he also referred to democratization and "the free development of all people"; moreover, he officially maintained his position of not departing from his principle of nonintervention.[12]

Honecker's speech, on the other hand, was characterized by smooth emptiness: no word about the refugees; no sentence about the internal problems of the GDR.[13] Schabowski's eleventh-hour advice to Honecker to respond to the feelings of insecurity and despair among the population and to offer a broad dialogue with the new political forces obviously had borne no fruit.[14] In the evening, however, spontaneous public ovations for "Gorby" during an Unter den Linden torchlight procession left no doubt to whom the sympathies of the people belonged.

The second day of the festivities, October 7, began with a military parade on Karl Marx Avenue. Subsequently, the members of the SED Politburo assembled at Niederschönhausen Castle for a meeting with Gorbachev. Prior to this gathering, the Soviet leader had a personal talk with Honecker. Günter Mittag, who had hoped to be included in the conversation but had been left unnoticed outside the conference room, noted Honecker's stern countenance when he returned from the tête-à-tête with the Soviet leader. Gorbachev had been very polite but quite frank in stating that "bold decisions" were necessary and that any delays would lead to defeat.[15]

A few minutes later, in his meeting with the SED Politburo, Gorbachev repeated his position regarding the necessity of reforms:

I think it to be very important not to miss the right time and not to waste an opportunity. . . . If we stay behind, life will punish us. . . . This is the stage of important decisions. They must be far-reaching decisions, they must be well thought through in order to bear rich fruit. Our experiences and the experiences of Poland and Hungary have convinced us: If the [communist] party does not respond to life, she will be condemned. We have only one choice: to go forward resolutely; otherwise we shall be beaten by life itself.[16]

After Gorbachev had concluded his insistent pleading for political and economic reforms, Honecker only praised the successes of socialism in the GDR again. Once more, no mention of the refugees, no sentence about the crisis in his country. Instead, the SED general secretary promised continuity: "Always forward, never backward." He then assured "the Soviet comrades" that he would "take notice of every hint which will help to develop socialism in the German Democratic Republic on an even stronger basis." Rhetorically, Honecker asked, "Do the comrades have any questions? I think we are united."[17]

Gorbachev gazed at the East German leader and smiled resignedly after Honecker had finished his statement. A click of the tongue was his only comment. Then Kurt Hager, Gerhard Schürer, Werner Krolikowski, and Werner Eberlein had their say. Everybody praised everybody. There were no critical, or self-critical, remarks from any of the East Germans, only socialist positives. Finally, Gorbachev took the floor again, talking at first about the difficult situation at the coal mines in the Donezk region and the failure of some of the party secretaries there, before generalizing that "you see, if somebody works badly, does not have the knack of the things, and we protect him, then such problems run wild. There are many signals for the party."[18] After that, the CPSU general secretary rose abruptly to indicate that the meeting should come to its close. Apparently there was nothing more to say.

The day ended with a reception at the Palace of the Republic, where Krenz and Schabowski expressed their opinion to Valentin Falin (Moscow's ambassador to Bonn from 1971 to 1978, now a CPSU Central Committee member) and Gennadi Gerasimov (the Soviet Foreign Ministry spokesman) that Honecker's utterances had been distressing and that the Soviet comrades could be sure that something would happen soon.[19] Gorbachev departed for Moscow directly after the reception, formally seen off at the airport by Mittag and Hermann Axen, the SED Central Committee's secretary for international relations. It is doubtful, however, as Krenz stated in his memoirs, that the Soviet leader encouraged ("Deistvuite!"—"Act!") the East Germans to overthrow Honecker.[20] First, no front against Honecker existed in the Politburo that could have been visible to Gorbachev at this time. Second, if he entertained any expectations in that direction, he presumably would not have shared them with Mittag and Axen.

Meanwhile, some 15,000 to 20,000 people had gathered at the Alexanderplatz, only a few blocks away from the Palace of the Republic. The strategy of the SED district leadership to reduce the tension by charging hundreds of "agitators" to discuss things with the demonstrators turned out to be effective. The talks were controversial, but nobody was arrested or beaten. Finally, the crowd began to disperse. While Honecker proposed his toast to the international notables and the domestic establishment in the large hall of the palace, demonstrators who returned from the Alexanderplatz on the opposite bank of the Spree River chanted "Gorby, Gorby" again, "Gorby, help us," and "We are the people."[21]

That the East German leadership had not only tolerated the demonstration in the center of the capital so close to the official anniversary festivities, but even had undertaken to debate with the demonstrators for several hours under the eyes of the international press, seemed to be a sign of hope that the government would talk eventually. Yet only a short time later the situation changed abruptly. Police and state security units, which had abstained from intervention at the Alexanderplatz, were awaiting the retreating demonstrators in the streets of the Prenzlauer Berg district. Violence, which had been avoided downtown, was now used without restraint. An investigation by the Office of the District Attorney later revealed that demonstrators and passersby alike were beaten, arrested, harassed, and psychologically maltreated. The minister for state security had personally shown up, inciting his forces to advance more brutally.[22]

West German chancellor Kohl quickly denounced the use of force as a sign of the "deep insecurity of those responsible in East Berlin," but he also called on the GDR leaders to institute reforms and to listen to the concerns and needs of the people. Kohl also repeated his offer to provide the GDR with "comprehensive and far-reaching" aid in all areas if fundamental political, social, and economic reforms were instituted there.[23] Foreign Minister Genscher said he could only hope that SED general secretary Honecker would use "the authority which he has in the GDR leadership to work for urgently needed reforms."[24]

Neither Kohl nor Genscher obviously felt at this time that a revolution in East Germany was imminent. Defense Minister Gerhard Stoltenberg and the chairman of the Free Democratic Party, Otto Lambsdorff, also stressed that the German question would not be "ripe for a decision" for many years. Anyone trying to give a different impression, Count Lambsdorff said in Tokyo, was laying the foundation for disappointment among Germans and irritation among Germany's neighbors. The FDP chairman declared that a reform policy by the leadership of the German Democratic Republic based on the Hungarian and Polish model would be the first step toward overcoming the division of Germany. If the GDR were oriented toward democracy, human rights, and individual freedoms, it could take part in the formation of a European peace order in a completely different way than it had in the past. Under these conditions, no one could deny Germans from East and West the right to decide on the question of German unity, Count Lambsdorff maintained, adding that this would be possible only with the agreement of Germany's neighbors in East and West and in accordance with the European policies of integration and peaceful coexistence.[25]

Stoltenberg also said in a speech in Washington on October 10 that Bonn could resolve the German question only "in the framework of positive developments in all of Europe." Only a free Europe without an Iron Curtain would make a reunified, free Germany possible over the long term. But, the minister declared, "it would be wrong and ill-conceived to give in to temptations to organize a common future only for us alone and the Germans in the GDR."[26]

Contrary to West German politicians who were reluctant to make bold statements about the possibility of new options in resolving the German question, journalists were less restrained in speculating about the future of the two Germanys. On the day of the anniversary of the GDR, the *Süddeutsche Zeitung* in Munich wrote:

> The state which celebrated this past weekend may still exist. But it has no future. For this reason, the question whether the GDR can exist on another level, in a different way, becomes much more important. . . . How great is the GDR's awareness of this possibility, given the fact that it little resembles what GDR leaders are trying to convey to their citizens? How heavily can this awareness be burdened? Of all the German questions, which are now becoming open questions again because of the force of developments, these are the ones which are most difficult to answer; at the same time, they are the most important questions.[27]

In fact, the position of the aging SED leadership was much gloomier than most observers in the West assumed at this time. In the morning after the anniversary celebrations, Mielke informed all district administrations of state security that on the previous day demonstrations had been held in various parts of the GDR, notably in Berlin, Leipzig, Dresden, Karl-Marx-Stadt, Halle, Erfurt, Plauen, and Potsdam.[28] Since further "riots" could be expected, Mielke ordered all units of his ministry to be "in full service until further notice." All members of state security who had permission to carry weapons were to have their weapons with them "permanently according to the given circumstances."[29]

At 10:00 Sunday morning, Mielke met with leading officials of his own ministry, the National People's Army, and the Ministry of the Interior. Krenz, Schabowski, and Wolfgang Herger, head of the security department of the Central Committee, were also present. Mielke explained how the security forces had managed to keep the anniversary largely free from disturbances. However, new provocations would follow as early as that day; therefore, the vigilance of the respective staffs and forces was not to wane.[30]

During the meeting Krenz pushed a paper down the table toward Schabowski. The five-page manuscript constituted the text Krenz intended to submit to the Politburo the following Tuesday as a proposal for a proclamation of the GDR leadership to the public. The paper contained no spectacular accusations or demands. At first sight, the text was hardly any different from usual party decrees. Only two sections expressed new ideas: the causes why so many people kept leaving the GDR were "manifold" and had to be looked for among the leadership, and that among the basic questions "to be solved today and tomorrow" were "a democratic togetherness and committed cooperation, a good supply with commodities and merit pay, life-oriented media, travel possibilities, and a healthy environment." Nobody could seriously object to such insights and imaginations, Schabowski thought. Only Honecker would be furious.[31]

An hour later, at his office on the floor of the Politburo, Krenz went through the text with Schabowski. The final draft, without major revisions, was delivered to Honecker in his Wandlitz home on early Sunday afternoon. This was necessary, as only the secretary general had the right to release submissions for discussion at the Politburo. At 3:00 P.M. Honecker telephoned Krenz, saying that he did not want the text to be debated. When Krenz insisted, however, that the leadership could no longer remain silent, he agreed to discuss the matter over again the next day.[32]

Only now, on late Sunday afternoon of October 8, did Krenz and Schabowski fully realize what they were up against and how dangerous their undertaking was. For the first time they began to weigh the risks and consider possible allies in the Politburo who might support them if Honecker refused to give in.

On Sunday evening further demonstrations were reported from Berlin and Dresden. The border between East and West Berlin, which had been closed on October 6 as a precaution against disturbances of the anniversary celebrations, was still shut. Thousands of tourists who applied for entry permits to visit East Berlin were rejected without being given any reasons.[33] In Dresden, where demonstrators had clashed with the police every night since the refugee trains had passed on October 4, representatives of the Evangelical Church and Superintendent Ziemer acted as mediators between the opposition and Mayor Wolfgang Berghofer, who turned to local SED chief Hans Modrow for advice and support. Modrow decided to support the talks in order to avoid an escalation of violence, and Berghofer opened his dialogue with a group of 20 Dresden citizens—the so-called Group of 20—whom the demonstrators had named as their negotiating delegation that evening.[34]

The following day Krenz not only conferred with Honecker about his submission to the Politburo, but was also confronted with a request of the SED district leadership in Leipzig to support an appeal for nonviolence initiated by the chief conductor of the Leipzig Gewandhaus orchestra, Kurt Masur, pastor Peter Zimmermann, cabaret artist Bernd-Lutz Lange, and the three local SED party secretaries, Kurt Meier, Roland Wötzel, and Jochen Pommert. The six were afraid that at the Monday demonstration a few hours later the state security organs might seek a "Chinese solution"—that is, a solution by use of force, as had happened at Beijing's Tiananmen Square in June—and hoped that an appeal for nonviolence might have a pacifying effect.[35]

As the Central Committee's secretary for security, Krenz was the appropriate authority for the request. Before he could discuss the issue with the ministers for state security, defense, and the interior, however, Honecker called him to talk about the declaration again. The talk was very contentious, but in the end Honecker realized that he could not prevent the debate Krenz was asking for. "Then just go ahead," he threatened, "but I can tell you right away that the Politburo will give you the proper answer."[36]

Despite his success, Krenz was upset by the dispute. The quarrel with his longtime chief had hit him hard, and he needed some time to compose himself before attempting to settle the Monday demonstration matter. It was already after 7:00 P.M. when he called Leipzig to inform the three secretaries of the SED district leadership that he agreed with the nonviolence appeal and that ministers Mielke, Kessler, and Dickel had instructed their forces accordingly.[37]

Yet even before Krenz called, it had become clear that the worst would not happen. Since the late afternoon, a crowd of more than 70,000 had marched through the streets of Leipzig, and the downtown area was filled with people; it was the largest spontaneous demonstration in the history of the GDR since June 17, 1953. The security forces seemed to have been put on a leash. The brutal use of police truncheons, which had ignited protests earlier, was not repeated. A cautious gaining of time seemed the new motto instead. Apparently the appeal had been successful.[38]

The Soviet 20th Motorized Guards Division, which was responsible for security in the Leipzig area, also kept its 13,300 men and 271 T-72 and T-80 tanks in the barracks. The troops complied with an order of the Soviet leadership, pushed through by Foreign Minister Eduard Shevardnadze in August 1989, not to interfere with mass demonstrations in the GDR and even to work upon the East German army to similarly refrain.

Shevardnadze had been convinced as early as 1986 that the German partition "by walls of ideology, arms and ferro-concrete" constituted a growing danger that ought to be defused politically. His position had been supported by scholars such as Vyacheslav Dashichev, who even had considered "the possibility of German unification" in a memorandum presented during an internal discussion among Soviet foreign policy experts on November 27, 1987.[39] Others, however, such as Falin and Alexander Bondarenko, head of the Central European department of the Foreign Ministry, had disagreed. East Germany, they felt, was too important as a cornerstone of the Soviet empire in Eastern Europe to be put at risk. But in August 1989, when the mass exodus of GDR citizens and the demonstrations began, Shevardnadze's proposal to instruct the 380,000 Soviet troops in the GDR not to intervene in the internal affairs of East Germany had been adopted by the Soviet political and military leadership upon Gorbachev's personal request.[40]

In the GDR itself the strategy to defuse the confrontation by political means also showed some effect. The use of party agents at the Alexanderplatz in East Berlin, Mayor Berghofer's talks with the Group of 20 in Dresden, and the nonviolence appeal in Leipzig actually provided the starting point for a dialogue between the GDR leadership and the opposition. An increasingly large number of mayors and lower SED functionaries went out to the streets and began to hear about the causes of the mass exodus and to listen to the wishes and demands of the people. Yet the sincerity with which the dialogue was sought was still doubted. For too long, the citizens of the GDR had been fooled by the leadership's unwillingness to reform. Now, as the party was vacillating and the pressures of the large numbers of emigrants and the protest meetings were beginning to have an impact, a semantic tactic was no longer suitable to mollify a population that was becoming more tenacious, demonstrating with a newly discovered courage and speaking with an audacity that had been inconceivable up until then.

The Politburo members, who gathered for their regular Tuesday morning meeting on October 10, seemed to be aware of the situation. Nearly everybody agreed with Krenz's draft public declaration that, in view of the recent events, a new role for the party and new ideas were necessary. When Honecker realized that Krenz's proposal was supported by a majority of the assembly, he stated—surprisingly—that there was "principal agreement on the text." He suggested that a commission of several Politburo members, including Mittag,

Krenz, Schabowski, and Joachim Herrmann (who, besides being the chief editor of *Neues Deutschland,* was the SED Central Committee's secretary for propaganda and agitation) should formulate the final version.[41]

Mittag also had prepared a paper. His text—ten pages with proposals for a social and economic reorientation—had been delivered to Honecker on October 9 and was now returned to Mittag for consideration by the editorial commission.[42] Schabowski, who did not have any knowledge of the Mittag paper at the time, probably catches the atmosphere of the moment best when he notes in his memoirs that after the decision to install the commission, an apparently angry Honecker "cast material to Mittag that was more voluminous than the draft of the declaration."[43] The "material" was in fact Mittag's own text. But the Krenz paper remained the basis for the declaration that was eventually published by the Politburo on October 11 and reprinted by *Neues Deutschland* the following day.[44]

Yet the declaration did nothing to restore the authority of Honecker or to save the communist regime. Despite its careful new tone, the declaration was disappointing: Too little substance was proclaimed too late. On the other hand, few people outside the inner circle of the SED leadership and even most Politburo members, who did not know the genesis of the text, realized that it represented a first step toward dismissing Honecker.

However, the downfall of the general secretary had become virtually unstoppable—with or without vague declarations of a new course. At a meeting with the district leaders of the SED on October 12, Honecker was sharply criticized by the local party chiefs. The secretaries from Neubrandenburg, Karl-Marx-Stadt, and Cottbus described the increasingly difficult situation in their regions. The secretary from Potsdam, Günter Jahn, tactfully reminded Honecker of Ulbricht's "honorable example" when he resigned in 1971. And Hans Modrow from Dresden launched a fierce attack for causing the trouble of the "refugee express Prague-Hof via Dresden" and then leaving the Dresden comrades in the lurch. Modrow claimed that the Politburo declaration contained "neither a realistic analysis of the situation nor a reform concept." He wondered if the Politburo actually still knew what was happening in the republic. "If so, then that would be proof of the failure of the leadership."[45]

Krenz, who was present at the meeting of the district party secretaries, later admitted that in the Politburo such harsh criticism of Honecker never had occurred. In a conversation with Modrow and Siegfried Lorenz, the party secretary of Karl-Marx-Stadt, he also stated that he now saw an opportunity to combine the factual evaluation of the events with changes of the personnel.[46] When Schabowski met by chance with Modrow at the rest room, he suggested that "we should talk together some time." Modrow agreed. But for the time being he had to return to Dresden, and Schabowski joined Krenz in preparing to jettison Honecker, an act that now seemed overdue.[47]

After the meeting with the district party chiefs, Krenz felt encouraged and decided to wage the final step at the next Politburo session on October 17. Meanwhile, he caused the secretary of the Defense Council, General Fritz Streletz, to sign an order that the state security organs would not use force at the forthcoming Monday demonstrations on October 16.[48] He also conferred with Schabowski and Herger, and spoke with Prime Minister Willi Stoph who, as everybody knew, hated Honecker and therefore could possibly be a useful ally. Finally, Krenz and Schabowski met with Harry Tisch, the chairman of the Free German Trade Union (FDGB), who wanted to get rid of Mittag—"the evil ghost of Honecker," as he liked to say.[49]

Krenz and Schabowski visited Tisch after dark on Sunday, October 15, at his home in Wandlitz. There Krenz reported about his talk with Stoph, who was prepared to come forward with a motion for dismissing Honecker at the next session of the Politburo. Stoph also had informed Krenz that he personally wanted, for reasons of age, to be released as prime minister—a post he had held from 1964 through 1973 and again, after a brief period as head of state, since 1976—and had proposed his deputy Werner Krolikowski as his successor. Schabowski and Tisch protested. Krolikowski, they said, was "not a capable economic expert" but a "phrase monger" who only tried to "fawn upon Mittag." Tisch suggested that he, as chairman of the trade unions, might be a better choice as the future head of government. That would be favorable internationally and, after all, Tisch praised himself, he was acquainted with the complexities of the economy as well as with the opinion of the workers. If the prime minister was a former trade unionist, the relationship between the state and the workers could only benefit.[50]

But Krenz avoided making any commitment. There was still some time left, he argued, before the parliament would have to vote on the issue. He was interested, however, in entrusting Tisch with an important mission during a routine trip to Moscow the following day. Tisch would not only visit his colleague Stepan Shalayev, but would ask for a brief meeting with Gorbachev as well. Krenz stressed that he did not expect a message, or even endorsement, from the Soviet leader, but he wanted Gorbachev to be informed about his plan.[51]

The next day, while driving through the Soviet capital, the members of the FDGB delegation were caught by surprise when Tisch's car suddenly left the convoy and headed for the Kremlin. Gorbachev took notice of the news without saying much himself. He asked Tisch to convey his best wishes to Krenz and the other comrades for the success of their undertaking.[52]

Meanwhile in Berlin, Stoph had indicated that he would be prepared to open the move against the general secretary in the Politburo only if Honecker could keep his representative position as chairman of the State Council. Krenz and Schabowski were upset. They knew that the credibility of the party's renewal depended on the complete removal of Honecker from the political scene. But how could Stoph be convinced? After a moment of perplexity, Schabowski called Soviet ambassador Vyacheslav Kochemasov in his Unter den Linden office on a special telephone line. Since Schabowski could not expect the diplomat to play a role in the coup and did not want to put the ambassador in an embarrassing position, he explained the situation and then closed his statement without waiting for a response: "You are a diplomat, Vyacheslav Ivanovich. And this is an unusual request. I am convinced that you will do whatever is possible for you to do." And Kochemasov merely replied: "I have understood you well." On this note, the "conversation" ended.[53]

The Monday demonstration in Leipzig on October 16, as large as usual, proceeded peacefully. The same was true for smaller demonstrations in Berlin, Dresden, and Magdeburg. The local security forces obviously complied with the instruction of General Streletz.[54]

Next morning, the Politburo gathered. Shortly before 10:00 A.M., Honecker received a phone call from Modrow, who tried to explain his behavior the previous Friday at the meeting of the district secretaries and asked for an appointment to look for a compromise.[55] After a minor delay, due to the talk with Modrow, Honecker entered the conference room of the Politburo and routinely shook hands with everybody present. As usual, the gathering opened with the reading of the protocol of the previous session. Then Honecker made a move to call up the first point of the agenda. Suddenly, Prime Minister Stoph raised his voice: "Erich, please . . . ."—"Yes," Honecker replied, apparently astonished. Stoph again: "I propose to release Comrade Honecker from his function as general secretary, and to remove Comrades Mittag and Herrmann from their positions as well."

At first, Honecker did not react at all. After a moment of silence, he tried to return to the agenda. Protests became audible. Eventually he gave in: "All right," he said, "let's discuss it!"[56] Everybody, including his hunting partner Mittag and state security chief Mielke, pleaded for his resignation. The final vote was unanimous. Twenty-five arms were raised in favor of the proposal. Honecker, Mittag, and Herrmann voted against themselves. The 26th member of the Politburo, Defense Minister Kessler, could not participate. He was on duty in Nicaragua.[57]

After the decision, Honecker went back to his office, where he informed his secretary and the other members of his personal staff. Then he called his wife and told her that "it" had happened. He was disappointed about the "breach of confidence" behind his back, but felt relieved as well.[58]

Thus, the Honecker era had come to an end. The Politburo advised the Central Committee to elect Egon Krenz as the new general secretary of the SED. The proposal was accepted on the following day, October 18, after only a brief, emotional, and unsystematic discussion.[59] Modrow, who had demanded a debate on the future course of the party, found himself in manifest opposition to the majority of the assembly, who wanted to return to the local organizations as quickly as possible to inform them about the changes that had occurred. Many delegates also felt that a public declaration by the new party leader was more urgent now than an endless and painful internal dispute. The cry "Egon must go on television" drowned any voices who asked for a rational consideration of the issues.[60]

In his televised address the same night, Krenz promised again to engage in dialogue with all groups in society and pledged open discussions between the public and top SED officials. However, the new general secretary merely repeated what he said to the delegates of the party a few hours earlier; he literally read his text again—as if he were speaking to a gigantically enlarged Central Committee.[61] He had already been criticized for his role in the vote manipulation in May and his support for the Chinese government's attempts to snuff out the democracy movement there. Now his appearance on television added to his image of a party functionary who had represented the old regime so well: a dark suit, clumsy moves, monotonous rhetoric. The speech turned out to be a flop, and the "reformers" missed their first, and maybe only, chance to give their attempt at renewing the party and its policies some credibility.[62]

Krenz and his comrades soon realized that the overthrow of Honecker had solved none of the problems. Only substantial reforms could help to improve the situation. Therefore, within a few days, the new leadership pledged to accept demonstrations as part of the political culture of the GDR. New travel laws were announced, changes in media coverage occurred, a debate on elections began, and formerly unknown critical and self-critical statements by SED-controlled organizations were heard.

Another important signal was a decision by the State Council on October 27 to issue an amnesty for emigrants and demonstrators.[63] The amnesty decision was most remarkable because it seemed "to represent an admission by GDR authorities that they had manipulated the law and applied its paragraphs according to opportunistic principles."[64] The amnesty did not change the basic problem, as there was still no legally guaranteed equal treatment of the population. Justice remained the province of the party, not of an independent branch of the constitutional system, with reforms being administered—if at all—through amnesties.[65]

Despite the announcement of reforms and signs of goodwill, the people in the GDR seemed to have little confidence in their new leadership. Egon Krenz, with the appearance and disposition of a functionary and a reputation as a narrow-minded, obedient henchman of Honecker, was unable to overcome his negative image and present himself as a reformer. And the SED proved equally or even more incapable of gaining credibility after more than four decades of monopoly power and authoritarian dictatorship.

As a result, demonstrations and protests continued. On the first Monday evening after Krenz's nomination as the new general secretary, more than 300,000 people marched through the city of Leipzig carrying anti-Krenz banners with such sayings as "Demokratie unbekrenzt" ("Democracy unlimited"—playing with the German word *unbekrenzt* instead of *unbegrenzt*) or "Sozialismus krenzenlos" ("Socialism without limitations"—playing with *krenzenlos* rather than the correct word *grenzenlos*). Another 40,000 demonstrators gathered in the industrial city of Plauen. Similarly large numbers showed up in Dresden, Halle, Zwickau, Neubrandenburg, and Jena. In East Berlin, 5,000 protesters in front of the Palace of the Republic demanded "Democracy—Now or Never."[66]

Regardless of such warning signs, however, Krenz still did not seem willing to share, let alone relinquish, power. At the end of October, he asked Hans Modrow only to pledge his cooperation with the party leadership. This was important primarily because Modrow had been portrayed by the Western media as a "champion of hope" for some time already. Additionally it was expected that Mikhail Gorbachev would raise the question of Modrow's future role in the process of reforming the GDR during Krenz's visit to Moscow on November 1.[67]

That meeting between Krenz and Gorbachev was ultimately devoid of substance. Krenz was still not capable of grasping the realities in his country, while the Soviets turned out to be astonishingly uninformed about the situation in Germany. With a naïveté that resurfaced concerning events in his own country over the next two years, Gorbachev seemed confident. Convinced that the government in East Berlin would be able to provide stability, he did not ask for new names, with the exception of Modrow, to replace the old guard. Nine days before the Wall was opened, there was not the slightest hint during the conversation that such a possibility even existed. In a diary entry of November 1, however, Krenz noted that he had talked with Gorbachev "about the existence of two German states as a stabilizing factor in Europe and about the perspectives of the German question. In connection with the construction of a common European home, the issue of a unification of the two German states was mentioned."[68]

In a statement following the meeting with Gorbachev, Krenz insisted on the SED's unique claim to power, giving the impression that the East Germans, unlike the Poles or the Hungarians, would continue to be deprived of the right to self-determination, political pluralism, and free elections. The fundamental shock to communism in the GDR, the first signs of democratization, and the need to develop a new relationship between the state, the churches, and the citizens' action movements all remained unnoticed.[69]

But while Krenz visited Moscow, the situation continued to deteriorate. When travel restrictions to Czechoslovakia, imposed by the GDR authorities at the beginning of October, were lifted at midnight on November 1, some 8,000 GDR citizens crossed the border within a few hours. Before the day had ended, an estimated 1,200 East Germans wishing to resettle in the West had entered the Federal Republic's embassy in Prague.[70]

On November 4, the demonstrations reached a new climax, when more than half a million people assembled at the Alexanderplatz in East Berlin, where Stefan Heym, one of the GDR's most prominent writers, proclaimed: "It seems as if a window has been thrown open after all the years of stagnation, of intellectual, economic, political stagnation, after all the years of gloominess and stuffiness, of twaddle and bureaucratic arbitrariness."[71]

Actors and artists had prepared for the demonstration for weeks. It was the first demonstration of its kind in the history of the GDR: officially approved, but planned and organized by independent cultural groups, with hundreds of thousands of participants who showed up voluntarily instead of being "detailed" by the regime. The atmosphere was characterized by a mix of nervousness and excitement: To go to "the demonstration" almost became a matter of honor. Yet because the reaction of police and state security was not predictable, the outcome was pretty much uncertain.

The list of the speakers was long: 27 names, among them dramatist Heiner Müller, actor Ekkehard Schall, writers Christoph Hein and Christa Wolf, Pastor Friedrich Schorlemmer and Professor Jens Reich of the New Forum, as well as the former espionage chief of the GDR, Markus Wolf. Gregor Gysi, a 41-year-old lawyer from Berlin who had defended several prominent dissidents in court but continued to support the cause of socialism, was also there.[72] Many of the speakers, however, demanded a truly democratic revolution and the resignation of the still largely unchanged state and party leadership. The yearning for a better, democratic GDR was expressed. Those who intended to emigrate were urged to stay and help with the reform. Nobody spoke of a unification of the two Germanys. But the regime of the "exalted ones" in the GDR, as Heym put it in his memorable speech, was asked to resign, and the *Frankfurter Allgemeine Zeitung* noted: "In this eleventh hour, Egon Krenz might get credit as the initiator of a change in course, and his intentions may not be all bad. Still, trust in the system he represents has been irrevocably destroyed."[73]

Günter Schabowski, who had been nominated by the Politburo to represent the SED as its official speaker at the event, experienced firsthand the extent to which trust had waned. Despite the microphone, he had difficulties making himself heard when he declared that the SED had begun the transformation "damned late" but now the party was ready for a change. He said, "We want to utilize the productivity of contradiction." In the end, however, when Schabowski pleaded "for a strengthened socialism which the people really want," his speech was drowned out by noisy boos.[74]

Now even the SED leadership realized that a more reform-minded approach was required. On November 6, 500,000 people gathered in Leipzig, 60,000 in Halle, 50,000 in Karl-Marx-Stadt, 10,000 in Cottbus, and 25,000 in Schwerin. The following day the entire government of the GDR (the Council of Ministers) stepped down, and on November 8 the Politburo also resigned as a group and was replaced by a new leadership that consisted basically of the anti-Honecker elements of the former regime, among them Krenz, Wolfgang Herger, Modrow, and Schabowski. Additionally, Modrow was eventually nominated as the GDR's new prime minister.[75]

Unlike Krenz, who did not possess a reputation as a reformer, Modrow seemed to represent a credible alternative to the old guard of the party, although it would have been greatly exaggerated to label him a dissident. The 61-year-old Modrow had been a member of the SED for four decades. Elected to the party's Central Committee in 1967, at the age of 39, he had even been appointed head of the committee's agitation-propaganda department in 1971. Honecker had sent him to Dresden in 1973, though, removing him from the more powerful position in the capital.

In Dresden, however, Modrow had gained considerable respect and popularity. Pursuing a policy of nonideological pragmatism that had earned him the reputation as a reformer, his superiors repeatedly but unsuccessfully tried to reduce his influence through personal criticism and examinations of his party organization in Dresden. Yet all such actions had only promoted his image as a credible alternative to the aging and encrusted leadership in East Berlin, making a growing number of people believe that he even might have the potential of becoming "the Gorbachev of the GDR."[76] Moreover, it was anything but a secret that the Soviets themselves had viewed Modrow as a promising figure in GDR politics for some time already. Thus his selection as the successor to Stoph was an almost logical step in the accelerating process of change.

THE OPENING OF THE WALL

Meanwhile, the GDR's room for maneuvering had become extremely limited. On the one hand, the leadership was faced with continuing demonstrations by a growing number of people who increasingly became more "radical" as they began to demand free elections and reject the SED's attempt at avoiding powersharing. On the other hand, large numbers of GDR citizens, most of them young and well educated, continued to emigrate to the West. Two days after the lifting of travel restrictions to Czechoslovakia on November 1, the GDR announced that its residents could travel directly from Czechoslovakia to the Federal Republic—a step that made the Wall practically irrelevant. Within one week, 48,177 East Germans entered the FRG.[77]

The indirect opening of the GDR border to the West began to create in the Federal Republic difficulties in accommodating the flow of newcomers. Already more than 225,000 East Germans and 300,000 ethnic Germans from Eastern Europe had resettled in the FRG in 1989—with many more still expected to come. West German interior minister Wolfgang Schäuble therefore urged East Germans to carefully consider the move to the West: While the Federal Republic would continue to accept every arriving German, the newcomers should understand that they might have to live for a relatively long period of time in inadequate housing.[78]

Chancellor Helmut Kohl, however, now characterized the promotion of fundamental political and economic change in the German Democratic Republic as a "national task." In his annual State of the Nation address on November 8, Kohl declared that the Federal Republic was prepared to support reforms implemented by the new GDR leadership. He called on the GDR's ruling Socialist Unity Party to abandon its monopoly on power, permit independent parties, and give binding assurances of free elections.[79] Bonn would be willing, Kohl said, to discuss "a new dimension of economic assistance" to the GDR, if there was a fundamental reform of the entire economic system, the removal of bureaucratic economic planning, and the development of a free market system. Yet in the absence of such reforms, Kohl maintained, any economic assistance would prove futile. Just as the current problems stemmed from causes existing exclusively in the GDR, so could their solutions only be created there: "In the final analysis it is up to the GDR leaders to offer the people there the prospect of a life worth living.

Only in this way can those who are still wrestling with the difficult step of leaving the GDR be induced to stay."[80]

Regarding the question of German reunification, the chancellor expressed the conviction that if given the opportunity, GDR residents would decide in favor of "freedom and unity." He stressed that it was Bonn's national duty to promote among its neighbors and partners in the world the right of self-determination for all Germans. "No one in East and West could ignore a vote of all Germans for the unity of their fatherland," Kohl asserted. He emphasized that Bonn continued to adhere to the preamble of the Basic Law, which called for the achievement of "the unity and freedom of Germany in free self-determination."[81]

The chancellor had been encouraged by French president François Mitterrand. The latter had supported the right to self-determination and the unification of Germany at a joint press conference with Kohl at the end of the 54th German-French consultations in Bonn on November 3. For his part, Kohl had assured the French president that the German place was "in the Western community of values and in European integration" and that the German question could only be resolved "under a European roof" and not in an anti-European spirit. For the West Germans, there was "no teetering or moving back and forth between different worlds."[82]

On the same day as his State of the Nation address, Kohl also gave assurances to Poland, where he was scheduled to arrive on November 9 for a six-day official visit. In a press interview, the chancellor reaffirmed the importance of the 1970 Warsaw treaty on relations between the Federal Republic and Poland. He stated that Bonn had declared in the treaty, which established the Oder-Neisse line as Poland's western border, that it had no border claims against Poland. At the same time Kohl stressed, however, that the Federal Republic could not make a binding declaration extending this treaty to Germany as a whole—although the Bundestag, almost simultaneously and with full knowledge of the chancellor, approved a resolution pledging that the right of the Polish people to live within secure borders "will not be called into question by Germans with territorial claims either now or in the future."[83]

During the debate that followed the address, all parties in the Bundestag expressed support for the calls from the people in the GDR for free elections, democratic reforms, and an end to the SED's monopoly on power. Members of both the governing coalition and the opposition parties made clear that they would accept the results of any decision by Germans in the GDR on German unification made freely. All parties also voiced a willingness to provide economic support for genuine reforms in the GDR.

The chairman of the opposition Social Democratic Party (SPD), Hans-Jochen Vogel, asserted that the reform processes in the East were interconnected. He appealed for support for all reform movements, maintaining that a setback for any single reform would have an effect on efforts in neighboring states. The SPD politician expressed "respect and sympathy" for the people in the GDR and cited Mikhail Gorbachev as having given an essential initiative for "revolutionary processes" in the GDR. Vogel also urged the West to continue to push the disarmament process forward, helping reduce the burden on the economies of the East bloc states and indirectly contributing to the success of reforms. With regard to the refugees, Vogel acknowledged that the Basic Law gave GDR residents the right to settle in the Federal Republic, but he appealed to the Germans in the GDR to consider whether there were not sufficient reasons to stay. It was important for both the GDR and the Federal Republic to end the flow of resettlers, he said, adding that a GDR "drained of its life blood" could not reform but would rather "sink into lethargy and chaos."[84]

But it was already too late. By the time Chancellor Kohl presented his State of the Nation address to the West German Bundestag, the number of refugees had increased to 500 every hour. Within one day, from Wednesday morning, November 8, until Thursday morning, November 9, more than 11,000 East Germans fled to the Federal Republic via Czechoslovakia.

Egon Krenz and the new SED leadership had been aware from the very beginning that a solution of the travel question would be of utmost importance, indeed imperative, if renewal of the regime were to have any chance of success. Therefore, Prime Minister Stoph had instructed the minister of the interior, Friedrich Dickel, to prepare a new travel law as early as October 19, only one day after Honecker's resignation. Another five days later, the Politburo had declared that "in the future all GDR citizens will be allowed to travel without hindrance."[85]

On October 31, a first draft of the new law was available for circulation among top officials of the party and government. The bill stipulated that all citizens of the GDR would be allowed to travel abroad for a maximum of one month per year without hard currency, provided they had a passport and visa (to be issued by the police within 30 days after application).[86] When Schabowski received the draft in his office at the SED district leadership, he was coincidentally with Gregor Gysi, whom he had asked to establish a line of communication with Bärbel Bohley of the New Forum. Schabowski used the opportunity to hear Gysi's comments on the draft. Gysi noted that the bureaucratic application procedure, the fixing of time limits, and the refusal to provide hard currency for tourists were problematic and that, strictly speaking, the law on the whole was more or less superfluous anyway. "If you give passports to the people, that would be sufficient as an exit permit," he said. "If the people have a passport, let them travel."[87] Schabowski agreed with Gysi's analysis and informed Krenz about his position. Yet on November 6 the draft was published despite its deficiencies because the Politburo felt it necessary to present the bill to the public as a quick gesture of goodwill. The government expected the draft to be discussed until the end of November, with the revised bill eventually becoming law after normal legislative procedures some time in December.

But the draft met with massive resistance. The same day it was published, several hundred thousand people demanded "a travel law without restrictions" at a mass demonstration in Leipzig. In addition, the mood was more aggressive than ever. "The Internationale," the communist anthem, was not sung. Representatives of the SED were no longer allowed to speak at the event. "Too late, too late," the crowd roared. And, for the first time: "We don't need laws—the Wall must go!"[88]

Protests in other GDR cities were also directed against the new travel bill. Even the censored official East German television broadcast critical statements by GDR citizens. And the Politburo was particularly worried about previously unheard strike warnings from workers in factories throughout the country, who felt discriminated against by the planned law because it did not provide them with the hard currency that would be necessary for trips abroad. Consequently, the draft was rejected the following day by the legal committee of the Volkskammer as "insufficient."[89]

Bad news also came from Czechoslovakia. Milos Jakes let Egon Krenz know that his government was no longer prepared to allow GDR citizens to enter the West German embassy in Prague or to travel without delay across the Bavarian border into the Federal Republic. The relief that the Czechoslovakian communists provided for their East German comrades, Jakes argued, was grist to the mill of Czechoslovakia's own dissidents. If the GDR did not close its border with Czechoslovakia, he stressed in the tone of an ultimatum, Czechoslovakia would close its border to the GDR.[90]

Thus, on November 7, the SED Politburo continued its discussion with even greater urgency. There was concern that if the government in Prague went ahead with its threat, thousands of East German families would soon camp out along the border with Czechoslovakia or even start mass attacks against it. It was clear to everybody that the new leadership in East Berlin would not have the stamina to hold out against such pressure. Therefore it seemed necessary to establish the desired freedom of travel at once, in a provisional step that later could be approved by a regular law of the parliament.[91]

Prime Minister Stoph, who resigned that day but remained in office until the new cabinet under Modrow was formed on November 17, was ordered to obtain a government decision that would include both the right to leave the GDR—the so-called permanent exit—and the normal practice of visits abroad with exit and reentry.

On the afternoon of November 9, Krenz informed the Central Committee —rather casually, as participants of the meeting later recalled, as he did not want to provoke the assembly majority, still regarded as orthodox—that the government had just reached a decision on the new travel regulation.[92]

At 6:00 P.M., Krenz handed two sheets of paper over to Schabowski, the Central Committee's new secretary of information. He was on his way to the International Press Center to inform journalists about the outcome of the meeting. "Make this known," Krenz said. "That will be a scoop for us." The text was a copy of the government submission on the advance travel regulation, not an approved decision, which was still pending. (Schabowski still claims today he did not know this at the time.[93])

At 7:07 P.M., shortly before the end of the press conference, which had been broadcast live on television and radio, Schabowski announced that the GDR had opened its borders. His tone of voice implied that this was a routine message or an inadvertent declaration. Yet the crowd in the International Press Center instantly burst into wild excitement. "Does that mean," a reporter inquired, "that every GDR citizen can now travel to the West freely?" Schabowski then cited from the text that "private trips to foreign countries can be applied for without meeting requirements." Everybody could get a visa after 8:00 the next morning. The authorities had been advised to issue passports and visa "fast and unbureaucratically." The regulation would become effective "at once."[94]

Schabowski hustled through the text. He did not want to accentuate more than necessary that the GDR was beginning to breathe its last gasps. But his message was unmistakable: The border was open. After 28 years, the Wall had come down for all GDR citizens.

In Bonn, where a plenary session of the Bundestag was still in progress after 7:00 P.M., the CSU deputy Karl-Heinz Spilker, instead of reading his prepared speech about the furtherance of club activities, informed his colleagues about the news that he had just received. Most of the deputies, except for members of the Green Party, rose from their seats to sing the national anthem: "Einigkeit und Recht und Freiheit" ("Unity, Justice, and Freedom").

Many East Germans and East Berliners, who had heard the news in the media, soon tried to find out personally what the announcement was worth. The magic "at once" at the end of Schabowski's declaration—and perhaps the mild November evening—inspired a particularly large number of East Berliners to turn off their televisions, put on a light jacket, and set out for the border. Small groups of people gathering at the checkpoint soon grew to massive crowds.

The guards were perplexed but circumspect. Thus far they had not received any instructions regarding the new settlement and depended more on rumors and instincts than on official guidance. The members of the Central Committee and the government had gone home after a long day of intense meetings. Most participants of the Central Committee plenum were not even aware that a major decision had been taken. The cabinet ministers believed that the matter was still pending. Yet even Krenz and Schabowski did not expect the announcement of the new regulations to have an immediate effect. Of course, people could apply for visas after 8:00 the next morning. But this would certainly happen in an orderly manner, as from now on there would always be the possibility to travel freely. Why, then, should there be any panic? While the crowds already began to move to the checkpoints, Schabowski drove home to Wandlitz.

The first information Krenz received about the events at the border came in at about 9:00 P.M. in the form of a phone call from Minister for State Security Mielke. Several hundred people, Mielke reported, were demanding exit, referring to Schabowski's press conference. Krenz responded, "Let them pass!"[95]

Yet at the borders, the situation slowly turned into chaos. At midnight the border guards lost control. Still without full directions, the officers on location spontaneously opened the gates. Suddenly the border was open. First hundreds, then thousands of people stormed across the long-impassable dividing lines between East and West. At Heinrich Heine Strasse, Bornholmer Strasse, Invaliden Strasse, people crossed the border unhindered, laughing, crying, singing, and dancing.

Outside Berlin the situation was even more confusing. In Oranienburg, north of Berlin, for instance, the Border Guards Training Regiment No. 40 was ordered to "heightened combat readiness" shortly after midnight. While the checkpoints in Berlin had already been opened on the personal initiative of the respective commanders on location, other units of the GDR Grenztruppen prepared for military action. Although no clear orders were being given by the Central Border Command in Rummelsburg or the chief of the border troops in Pätz near Königs Wusterhausen, the vehicles of the border regiments around Berlin were loaded with ammunition, and the companies received weapons for all-out engagement against the forces of "counter-revolution." At 2:00 A.M., however, when television reports had shown the extent of the border crossings and had made it clear that military action would lead to carnage, the "combat-ready" companies were sent back to their quarters.

The following morning, the mood among the Politburo members was gloomy when they gathered for a cup of coffee before the third day of the Central Committee meeting began. "Who on earth has got us into that mess?" Krenz asked rhetorically. Mielke shook his head. They either had not foreseen what might happen or now shrank back from their own courage.[96]

Krenz then phoned Soviet ambassador Kochemasov. The Soviets had also been taken by complete surprise and saw their immediate interests in Berlin violated. Earlier there had been discussion about the opening of several checkpoints to the Federal Republic in the south of the GDR, and the Soviet government had not objected to such plans as part of the travel law intended to be made public on November 10. But now it was too late for such considerations. Once again events had overtaken all plans.[97]

At the same time, in the Federal Republic, President Richard von Weizsäcker called the developments in the GDR "a significant turning point in postwar history," which showed that freedom could not be contained behind walls forever. He added, however, that it was now necessary "to go forward . . . with the task of reaching the point where Germans in the German Democratic Republic and Germans in the Federal Republic live together in freedom and dignity."[98]

Kohl interrupted his visit to Poland for one day because of the developments in the GDR and Berlin. At a November 10 rally in front of the Schöneberg City Hall, the seat of the West Berlin city government, he also stressed how important it was "to remain calm, act with prudence and ignore radical voices." But in a tone that differed markedly from Weizsäcker's cautious approach, Kohl concluded that Germans would now be put to a test, that this was a "great and historic hour," and that the people of the GDR should continue their fight for freedom, because, Kohl said, "You are not alone. We are at your side. We are a nation."[99]

Speaking at the same rally, Foreign Minister Hans-Dietrich Genscher, who had returned from Poland with the chancellor, expressed the hope that further steps forward would be taken in the GDR, because freedom of speech and free elections were now needed. Willy Brandt, who had been the governing mayor of Berlin when the Wall was first erected in August 1961, emphasized that much would now depend on whether the Germans were able to cope with the situation. German-German rapprochement was taking place in a manner different from what most people had expected. A new relationship had arisen, Brandt said—a relationship in freedom. "What belongs together, will grow together."[100]

While Brandt was still speaking, Horst Teltschik, Kohl's foreign policy advisor, was called to the telephone. On the line was Yuli Kvitsinsky, the Soviet ambassador in Bonn, with an urgent message from Gorbachev. The Soviet leader was concerned that the demonstrations in both parts of Berlin might create "chaos," and he asked Kohl to bring his reassuring influence to bear on the people.[101] Obviously Gorbachev was afraid that the politicians might completely lose control and would quickly be up against a fait accompli if the Berliners turned the demonstrations into a reunification event.

Yet the chaos did not occur and Kohl returned to Bonn, where he phoned British prime minister Margaret Thatcher and US president George Bush. At about 11:00 P.M., when Kohl was still conferring with his staff at the Chancellery, National Security Advisor Brent Scowcroft called Teltschik to inform the German government about a telephone conversation between Gorbachev and Bush earlier in the day. Gorbachev had classified the situation as "very sensitive" and had instructed Ambassador Kochemasov in East Berlin to get in touch with his three Western power colleagues instantly. On the other hand, Scowcroft said confidentially, Gorbachev also had called upon the SED leadership to ensure a "peaceful transition" in the GDR.[102] This hint, which was corroborated in another telephone conversation between Kohl and Gorbachev on November 11 at noon, confirmed the view that the chancellor had already held since the very beginning of the crisis: The Soviet leader was not thinking of a "Chinese solution" in East Germany.

However, only Gorbachev and his adherents were against military intervention. After the Wall had been breached, his opponents in the party, and especially in the military, wanted "to line up the strike forces and barrage divisions along the borders, and start the tank engines," Eduard Shevardnadze later revealed.[103] Among those proposing military intervention was Valentin Falin, who threatened privately in the Soviet Embassy in East Berlin that "we will send a million troops who will close the border again." Publicly, in a *Pravda* article, Falin called for an "emergency brake" against German unity. And in a subsequent interview with the German newsmagazine *Der Spiegel,* he stressed that "if Gorbachev intended to execute his will in an iron manner, it would take him, or his successor, only a few hours."[104]

Falin found much support among the generals, party bureaucrats, and the orthodox wing of the CPSU led by Yegor Ligachev, who rightly feared the loss of the western bastion of the socialist camp. But Foreign Minister Shevardnadze pointed to the possible consequences of military action in the center of Europe. "We were moving at the brink of war," he later told Fyodor Burlatsky. "Yes, yes. Don't be surprised—at the brink of a World War III." Fortunately, Gorbachev had backed him up in his confrontation with the proponents of a military solution, leaving no doubt that he was not ready to use force again. Military conflict, with incalculable risks, had been avoided.[105]

THE MODROW GOVERNMENT: STRUGGLE FOR "SOCIALISM WITH A NEW FACE"

In Germany, the battle in the Kremlin about military intervention went unnoticed. On November 13, the East German parliament elected Hans Modrow as the new prime minister. After a weekend of joyous and relaxed scenes, which seemed almost like a fairy tale in view of decades of lethal action along the intra-German dividing line, the new self-assurance with which GDR citizens were using the sudden opening of the border for exuberant excursions to Berlin and the Federal Republic could also be felt in the Volkskammer. Even though it still needed the legitimacy of free elections, the GDR parliament for the first time in its 40-year history behaved like a popular representative body. The controversial nomination of the new parliamentary president, Dr. Günther Maleuda of the Democratic Farmer's Party, fit into the changed picture; the fact that he won only after a run-off election was something unheard-of previously. Modrow's election proceeded as usual, with only one opposing vote; the parliament apparently wanted to provide demonstrative support for a politician who was open to reform.[106]

Since the beginning of the crisis, Modrow had stated that he hoped to become a stabilizing factor during the uncertain time of transition to a "socialist democracy." His eventual goal, however, remained a subject of speculation and suspicion. Privately, the new prime minister spoke of Krenz as a "Kania or Jakes solution"—that is, an interim settlement like the temporary replacement of Edward Gierek by Stanislav Kania in 1980 in Poland or Gustav Husak by Milos Jakes in 1987 in Czechoslovakia.[107]

It is also noteworthy that Modrow and Dresden's mayor, Wolfgang Berghofer, had maintained close relations with Markus Wolf, head of the espionage department of the GDR ministry for state security until 1987. Wolf proclaimed that he had left his post only to administer the artistic bequest of his brother, the movie director Konrad Wolf.[108] Wolf may have given up the secret service career for a different reason, however: namely, to "clear" his resumé—by writing a book on a nonpolitical subject—in preparation for a new role in the post-Honecker era.[109] And, coincidence or not, when Markus Wolf's colleague from Moscow, Vladimir Kryuchkov, then deputy head of the KGB, visited Dresden in 1987, he apparently met with Modrow.[110] At that time, the KGB and Wolf had already concluded that

Honecker was bound to fail and that the GDR needed an East German Gorbachev if the country was to remain a cornerstone of the Soviet security system in Europe.[111] But in 1987 the time to act had not come yet, Kryuchkov told Professor Manfred von Ardenne, with whom he discussed reform proposals the latter had submitted to Egon Krenz for implementation of a policy of perestroika in the GDR. Subsequently, however, Western media suddenly began to speak of Modrow favorably as a potential candidate for launching a reform policy in the GDR. It is not at all unlikely that at least some of these reports were "influenced" by KGB agents to build up Modrow as a credible alternative to Honecker: modest, reform-minded, and likable.[112]

The Kryuchkov-Wolf-Modrow connection, if correctly interpreted, implies that the foreign divisions of the Soviet and East German secret services may have pursued a long-term strategy of implementing some form of perestroika in the GDR to salvage stability, socialism, and Soviet influence in the eastern part of Germany, all of which seemed threatened by Honecker's stubbornness and lack of flexibility. In the framework of this strategy, Modrow would certainly play a key role as the future leader of the GDR; the functions of Berghofer and, above all, Markus Wolf himself would depend on the influence Modrow could gain over the SED apparatus and the government and his ability to assign people of his own choice to prominent positions.[113]

For his part, Wolf realized at the demonstration in East Berlin on November 4 that his past could not be overcome easily. During his speech, the crowd of 500,000 people yelled and whistled at the person who had been a leading member of the state security organ for 33 years; they understandably identified him with the hated service. "Stop it," they had cried, and "Hang him."[114] Modrow, on the other hand, had compromised himself less. For the time being, he even enjoyed some popularity and respect. But most GDR citizens saw the change of leadership as only a beginning. True reforms had not yet been made. And the East Germans, increasingly self-confident, seemed to be more determined than ever to accomplish them.

Officials in the Federal Republic also made their willingness to cooperate with the new leadership of the GDR dependent on the further development of the reform process. Only reforms leading to freedom in the political and economic arenas could lay the foundation for West German economic assistance, Economics Minister Helmut Haussmann wrote in a position paper issued by his ministry on November 14 in Bonn.[115] To facilitate talks on Western economic aid, he added, the GDR should remove several obstacles that stood in the way of intra-German economic relations. As examples, he called upon GDR authorities to permit direct contacts for business people in order to improve their work opportunities. He also suggested progressive legislation to make joint ventures possible. If the East German government specified the radical economic reforms announced as a general goal, Bonn would open special federal funds of the European Recovery Program—that is, the still-existing remnants of the 1947 Marshall Plan that provided loans by the German Kreditanstalt für Wiederaufbau—for investments in the GDR, Hausmann said, noting that in 1990 some DM4.8 billion in credits could thus be available to business.[116]

Others were even blunter. During a television interview on November 14, Finance Minister Theo Waigel said that the flow of West German capital into the East German economy was conditional on the establishment of a market economy there. A "wide array of aid possibilities" would then be available, the minister said, similar to those initiated in Poland. The chairman of the Free Democratic Party, former economics minister Otto Lambsdorff, noted that overall conditions had to change in the GDR as soon as possible for assistance to be effective. As two of these conditions, he named currency reform and the free convertibility of the GDR-mark. The opposition Social Democrats and the Greens, on the other hand, cautioned against "selling off the GDR" if the currency differences between the "hard" D-mark and the nonconvertible "soft" GDR-mark were not adjusted.[117]

In contrast to the West German government, the private sector very early displayed great willingness to cooperate with the GDR, as a news agency poll of major West German businesses conducted the day after the opening of the East-West borders showed. A spokesperson for Daimler-Benz said the enterprise was expecting business activities to take on a "qualitatively new dimension," adding that "in the face of the current developments, new horizons may open up which we did not consider possible up until a short time ago." According to the head of Thyssen, Dieter Spethmann, many German and other Western companies were "ready to act swiftly" by starting up plants in the GDR.[118]

Since the help, as outlined by the government in Bonn, was largely conditional on East Germany's adopting a market economy, opposition politicians in Bonn as well as a majority of the GDR leadership charged that this amounted to blackmailing East Berlin, requiring that it abandon its separate system and accept economic absorption by West Germany. The SED remained dead set against reunification. New Forum and other opposition movements in the GDR, composed largely of reformist socialists, also declared themselves opposed to union, insisting that their goal was to create a new form of democratic socialism in East Germany.[119]

For Hans Modrow, however, this was anything but easy to achieve. The same day Modrow was chosen prime minister by the East German parliament, departing finance minister Ernst Höfner disclosed that East Germany's budget deficit amounted to about US$70 billion, causing gasps of amazement in the hall. The efficiency of factories producing goods for export had sunk by almost 50 percent in the previous nine years, Höfner said, and he predicted further deficits of up to $35 billion in the 1990s. Höfner also told the deputies he could not confirm an estimate by a member of parliament that East Germany's inflation rate stood at 12 percent. But a party economics expert said the rate was much higher than that.[120]

Gerhard Schürer, the departing head of the State Planning Commission, claimed before the Volkskammer that East Germany's foreign debt was still a state secret. But on November 15 the *Berliner Zeitung,* the organ of the SED in East Berlin, cited the Swiss Central Bank as saying that East Germany's short-, middle-, and long-term obligations to Western creditors totaled $20 billion, putting East Germany's per capita foreign debt close to or ahead of Hungary's and Poland's. In other words, the GDR's economy, battered by the flight to the West of 200,000 people in 1989 alone (among them more than 100,000 highly skilled workers), was in much worse shape than almost anyone had known.[121]

The beginning of Modrow's term as prime minister was characterized by both alarming revelations about the economy and by practical difficulties as well. In the period between Modrow's election on November 13 and the confirmation of his cabinet on November 17, Stoph—a man of Prussian strictness and formality—insisted categorically that his successor not set foot in the prime minister's office or to interfere with any government affair, because the constitution of the GDR stated that the departing prime minister remained on duty until the new government was established. Modrow later complained, however, that during this critical period Stoph had been completely inactive and had not even shown up in his office, leaving the country to its fate.[122]

Thus the new prime minister took up temporary quarters at the Berlin hotel An der Spree, where he developed his political strategy and selected the members of his cabinet and personal staff. As an economist, he quickly realized that the financial and economic situation of the GDR was miserable and required first priority on the agenda of his administration. His advisors, among them Dieter Klein of Humboldt University and Christa Luft of the Institute of Economics in Karlshorst, told him that the results of an exact analysis were "critical."[123] Successful reforms would have to be part of a general strategy, including a qualitatively new relationship with capitalist countries. Gerhard Beil, an expert on East Germany's external economic position and minister for foreign trade, even stated that the GDR would survive only if it could quickly establish "confederative relations" with the Federal Republic.[124]

Therefore, Modrow proposed in his inaugural speech on November 17 a Vertragsgemeinschaft ("contractual community") between the Federal Republic and the GDR similar to the arrangements between West Germany and the European Community.[125] In an interview with *Der Spiegel* published on December 4, he also considered the idea of a "German confederation." The term had already been mentioned by Egon Krenz in the Volkskammer a few days earlier. But, Modrow said, "If we want to talk about the confederation, we have to be realistic. . . . At first, we need a basis we can build upon. We live in a Europe and in a world that are watching us. . . . We need trust for what is happening. . . . The word reunification will not be the word for characterizing the future."[126] Modrow admitted, however, that the GDR was reassessing its economic development "with a view of the European market." Because the Hungarians had already arrived at Strasbourg (the Council of Europe, although Budapest would not gain full membership until the following year) and were on their way to Brussels, and as the Poles and others were struggling to get there, the GDR would be no exception.[127]

Apparently Modrow hoped that East Germany would be able to attract economic assistance from the Federal Republic within the proposed contractual community and would even get access to the European Community (EC) without being politically absorbed by the Federal Republic into a unified Germany. In addition, the new GDR prime minister also believed that his country would be able to develop a market-oriented socialist economy that would dispose of "state property, mixed property, joint ventures, and everything else that we have to offer." Modrow even referred to a new "socialist entrepreneurship" that he felt was necessary.[128]

How all this was to be achieved remained unclear. Modrow had been in office for only two weeks at this time, and most of his work was a series of experiments and improvisations. Moreover, the political and economic situation continued to erode. The mass exodus of East Germans went on and new political forces, such as the New Forum and the emerging Social Democratic Party, gathered for "Round Table" talks—following the Polish example—on a variety of issues, in essence constituting a "side government" to Modrow's official administration.[129]

Coming to grips with the GDR past turned out to be at least as difficult as economic reforms. Erich Honecker, Günter Mittag, and Joachim Herrmann had been the first to lose their positions on October 18. Harry Tisch—who had participated in their overthrow and hoped to succeed Willi Stoph as prime minister—followed on November 2; the executive board of the FDGB, under pressure from the trade union's local organizations, agreed to his resignation.[130] Kurt Hager had already asked to be released from his positions in the party and the state at the end of October; on November 7, the Politburo complied with his request. Erich Mielke, Alfred Neumann, Hermann Axen, and Erich Mückenberger were also convinced by Krenz to resign "voluntarily." A few days later, Horst Sindermann and Werner Krolikowski threw in the towel.[131]

But the issue was not simply one of personalities. The Socialist Unity Party, identified with four decades of GDR history, lost all its support among the East German people and more than half of its 3 million members within two months after Honecker's resignation. Nearly 600,000 comrades returned their membership books within five days of a television broadcast on December 1 that dealt with party corruption being investigated by a special committee of the Volkskammer. Numerous former SED leaders now went to jail, among them Mittag and Tisch, accused of corruption, fraud, and other felonies or misdemeanors. On December 1, the East German parliament decided to change Article 1 of the GDR constitution, eliminating the formulation about the leading role of the "Marxist-Leninist party."[132]

It was noteworthy in this respect that Modrow, who had become a member of the Politburo on November 8, never really participated in the investigations on unwarranted privileges, abuse of authority, and criminal offenses of party leaders under Honecker. Whenever such issues were being discussed, the prime minister was intently leafing through his files.[133] This passivity may have been tactical: Each new scandal that was unveiled not by the official party committees but instead by the newly emancipated media strengthened his position against Krenz and the rest of the discredited old guard. In fact, if the Kryuchkov-Wolf-Modrow connection still existed, then Krenz's downfall had to be a primary goal in the process of stabilizing the GDR.

On December 3, the complete Politburo and Central Committee of the SED gave up and resigned as a group. A "working committee" was entrusted with the preparation of an extraordinary party convention. Herbert Kroker, SED party secretary from Erfurt, was elected chairman. Not surprisingly, several participants, and perhaps a majority of them, were allegedly close to the "connection"—among them Wolfgang Berghofer, Markus Wolf, Gregor Gysi, Dieter Klein, and Roland Wötzel. On the other hand, not Krenz, Schabowski, or any other former member of the Politburo was a member of the working committee. Consequently, and hardly unexpectedly, one of the committee's first moves was to pass a vote of confidence in Modrow and his government.[134]

Modrow stated before the committee that the problems of the country could "only be solved with the SED" and that he would fly to Moscow the following day to consult with Gorbachev and to participate in a Warsaw Pact conference that had been convoked for information about the Bush-Gorbachev summit at

Malta. Krenz joined Modrow on his trip to Moscow—but only as chairman of the State Council, not as party leader.[135] The working committee, on the other hand, had authorized Modrow to speak on behalf of the party. The prime minister had become the predominant figure in the GDR's transition toward a "socialism with a new face," whereas Krenz's brief era had virtually ended.[136]

On December 6, Krenz also resigned from his positions as chairman of the State Council and chairman of the National Defense Council of the GDR. Three days later, at the extraordinary party convention, Gregor Gysi was elected as the new leader of the SED.[137] In a resolution, the delegates apologized to the people of the GDR "that the former leadership of the SED has led our country into this existence-threatening crisis."[138] On the second day of the convention, after a one-week interruption, on December 16, the name of the party was changed into "Socialist Unity Party—Party of Democratic Socialism" (SED-PDS).

Gysi, however, turned out to be a loyal party functionary. At the rally in East Berlin on November 4, he had proclaimed "the best state security is legal security." But now he tried to use the still-existing party apparatus for gathering new support and even sought to maintain and restore some of the remnants of the Staatssicherheitsdienst ("Stasi"), the former Ministry for State Security, as a means of keeping developments under control.[139] When the opposition protested against such orthodox communist power ploys (carrying banners with slogans such as "Gysi-Stasi-Nazi"), the SED-PDS finally decided after an emergency session on January 21, 1990, to purge several more former leaders but rejected calls that it dissolve altogether. Those ousted included Krenz and 13 other former Politburo members.

In an interview with the West German tabloid *Bild,* Krenz complained that he had been given no credit for leading the change. "What I did for the change counted for nothing," he said. "We were all measured with the same yardstick as Honecker."[140] Günter Schabowski, the East Berlin party leader who had announced the opening of the border on November 9, and Heinz Kessler, the former defense minister, also were among those ousted.

The weekend emergency meeting had been called after dissident members from East Berlin's Humboldt University, the Academy of Sciences, and other institutions had requested the party's dissolution on the grounds that it had become a "security risk." In addition, wildcat strikes, increasingly angry demonstrations, and a continuing flight of almost 2,000 East Germans daily to West Germany had made the economic and political situation more and more difficult, bringing it close to the brink of chaos. After 15 hours of heated battle, Gysi acknowledged that the party had failed to rid itself of its Stalinist past in the five weeks since he had taken charge. But, he said, "after long, mature and sometimes controversial debate," the party's ruling council had decided "that disbanding would lead to greater social tension, not less."[141]

The tensions that existed within the party and had been expressed during the emergency meeting became even more visible to the public when a group of 40 party members from Dresden led by Wolfgang Berghofer, the vice chairman of the party since its regrouping in December, declared their departure. In a letter to Gysi published on the day of the emergency meeting, Berghofer stated that he had concluded that the party could not get rid of its past and so could not be a credible source of renewal. Any attempt to take a new path with the old party would only increase the popular suspicion that it was trying to get back to power, he said.[142]

Modrow and Gysi tried to recover from these setbacks by making public Modrow's offer to give the 15 seats the SED-PDS held on his 27-member cabinet to the opposition. Gysi also announced plans to move up a party congress, scheduled for mid-March, and at that time to change its name to simply the "Party of Democratic Socialism" (PDS). But the new PDS also suffered from its SED heritage, as the transition was burdened by memories of the past as well as current behavior, such as illegal attempts to transfer state-owned SED property to PDS accounts.

Another matter of concern for Modrow and the East German communists was the previously almighty and ubiquitous Ministry for State Security (MfS). The so-called Stasi had been particularly active in suppressing the opposition in the GDR and had become almost synonymous with the brutality of the SED dictatorship. Thus the MfS had become an object of public anger and exasperation as soon as the Honecker regime had crumbled. Under Modrow the MfS was now called Amt für Nationale Sicherheit (AfNS)—Office for National Security—but except for the new name, little had changed. Even officials of the AfNS complained about the lack of reforms in the service. Markus Wolf later also described the passivity of the AfNS leadership and its inability to comprehend the demands of the people of the GDR.[143]

More important, however, the agents of the MfS-AfNS, who were worried that the revolution would seize the security organ as well and hold its members personally responsible for their deeds, began first gradually, then systematically, to destroy the service's files as the party began its freefall. When the public realized what was happening, offices of the MfS-AfNS were raided by demonstrators who tried to protect the files and prevent their destruction or deportation. The first demonstrations of this kind were reported on November 29 from Frankfurt (Oder), Ilmenau, and Limbach-Oberfrohna. On December 5, several thousand people occupied the AfNS district office in Dresden. On the same day, citizens in Suhl, Erfurt, and Gera, in cooperation with the respective offices of the district attorney, attempted to stop the persistent disappearance of files in their cities.[144]

On December 6, New Forum asked the government to "completely dissolve the structures of state security that are directed inwards."[145] The Round Table, which began its talks on the following day, agreed with the request and demanded also "the subordination of the Office of National Security to civilian control.[146] Modrow, who still proceeded on the assumption that the GDR would continue to exist as a sovereign state, responded by proposing two different organs instead, an Office for the Protection of the Constitution and a "news service" for espionage. But the Round Table insisted that a scaled-down internal security agency—if necessary at all—should be reestablished only after national elections and that the AfNS had to be dissolved at once.[147]

On the same day, however, as the Round Table asked for the elimination of the security organs, Modrow secretly sanctioned, indeed ordered, the destruction of files. A telegram to the district councils from the Council of Ministers stated that "the Government entrusts the Head of the Office for National Security to destroy immediately all documents that have been set up without authority."[148] The head of the AfNS, Lieutenant General Wolfgang Schwanitz, instantly sent instructions to all his services defining the categories of files that were to be erased. In another telegram the same evening at 8:15 P.M., the AfNS leadership once more referred to the government decision, urging its officials to "promptly destroy unauthorized documents."[149]

Modrow also proceeded with the establishment of the AfNS "news service" he had proposed—which was nearly identical with the former espionage division of the Ministry for State Security that had been headed by Markus Wolf—and the creation of the Office for the Protection of the Constitution. Both organizations were specifically referred to in an internal resolution that was passed by the Council of Ministers on December 14.[150] In this respect it could only be regarded as cynical that on the same day Modrow and his government decided to take charge of the dissolution of the AfNS themselves. Essentially, Modrow's double-track strategy seems to have been designed to provide sufficient delay for the destruction of compromising files and to help members of the discredited regime cover their tracks.

Finally, however, after further initiatives of the Round Table and massive protests and demonstrations, including the threat of a general strike, Modrow agreed to abandon the state security services—at least for the time being. "Let me specify here once again," he said during a debate in the Volkskammer on January 12, "that until May 6 no Office for the Protection of the Constitution will be established."[151] Subsequently, the AfNS was actually dissolved as well.[152] But valuable time for taking evidence and the prosecution of criminal offenses had been lost.[153]

INCREASING PRESSURE FOR UNIFICATION

As Germans from both parts of their divided country stood laughing and dancing atop of the Berlin Wall in front of the Brandenburg Gate, the world realized that a revolution had occurred. The Iron Curtain had been lifted, a new national awareness of the German people had come into being.

A united Germany remained a distant prospect, though. Unification had not been a principal demand of the millions whose demonstrations had forced the SED to its knees; moreover, the process of disentangling the two Germanys from a web of separate alliances and economic systems was staggering.[154] But although the Wall was down, the writing on it was still clear to some. Henry Kissinger, for one, pointed to an already visible future. In a *Newsweek* article on December 4, he cited the 19th-century Austrian foreign minister Count Metternich, who once had written: "Policy is like a play in many acts which unfolds inexorably once the curtain is raised. To declare then that the performance will not go on is an absurdity. The play will be completed either by the actors or by the spectators who mount the stage."[155]

Where would the historical revolution in the GDR lead? Would the East Germans now launch into a headlong rush toward reunification, or were they only seeking a kinder, gentler socialism, as the opposition groups maintained? Would West Germany fulfill its promises to Poland and Hungary, or rather focus all its wealth and might on reviving its Eastern kinfolk? And would a united Germany maintain its allegiance to the North Atlantic Treaty Organization (NATO) and West European integration, or would it seek its future in a renewed version of its old Schaukelpolitik, not necessarily neutral, but shifting between East and West, maintaining the illusion of being the center of gravity in the middle of Europe?

There was anxiety, as the West Berlin daily *Der Tagesspiegel* noted on November 15, "about the future path of the Federal Republic—the fear that the Federal Republic might concentrate too much on aid and support for the reform process in Eastern Europe, that it will neglect its engagement to Europe and European union."[156] There was anxiety, too, that the momentum could push the two Germanys inexorably together, as the direct contacts now possible made East Germans increasingly frustrated with their lesser lot. And there were fears that in the absence of a broader arrangement worked out with their allies, the Germans could be tempted to go it alone, shaping a German solution that might alienate allies and conceivably even destabilize the European continent.[157]

West German foreign minister Genscher addressed these concerns as early as November 13, at a one-day meeting in Brussels of the Council of Foreign Ministers of the Western European Union (WEU), where he underscored the fact that the Federal Republic would undertake no efforts in the future at a "national solo in foreign policy." The Bonn government was committed to a policy of integration within the European Community and NATO and would pursue this consistently, Genscher said, emphasizing that the West did not intend to patronize Germans in the GDR or give them unnecessary advice. "They alone set the standards for reforms," the foreign minister added, "and we intend to respect that."[158]

Chancellor Kohl, who had returned to Poland to continue his state visit after one day of celebrating the breach of the Berlin Wall and dealing with its immediate implications, was still in Warsaw when he began to tackle the anxieties about the future course of Germany. On November 14 he signed a joint declaration with Polish prime minister Tadeusz Mazowiecki that renewed Bonn's guarantee of Poland's western border and outlined a number of West German economic aid measures. The two sides pledged to fulfill in "letter and spirit" the 1970 Warsaw Treaty, in which the two countries had declared "the inviolability of their existing borders now and in the future" and had promised to harbor no territorial claims against each other. In the section of the joint declaration dealing with economic matters, Bonn pledged to support Polish efforts for credits from the International Monetary Fund and the World Bank.[159]

After the declaration, the Poles could be confident that the developments in Germany would neither threaten the security of their western boundary nor impair their economic relations with the Federal Republic. But the new Polish government, under internal pressure, had wanted even more, namely a final German commitment to the Oder-Neisse border. By the end of the visit, however, Mazowiecki had realized that, in view of the immense economic problems and the significant progress that had been made in German-Polish relations during Kohl's trip, it would not be prudent to insist on a more precise formulation of the German position. Kohl at that point could not or did not want to provide one because of opposition to his policy in his own country. And so the border issue remained a topic for debate and even for mistrust—as absolute clarity had not been reached.[160]

The domestic pressure on Kohl was twofold. On the one hand, the Social Democrats were accusing him of being too passive in view of the dramatic changes in Eastern Europe and East Germany; on the other, the right-wing Republican party had been remarkably successful in recent local elections, and it was threatening to absorb conservative support for Kohl's government in the upcoming 1990 Länder and Bundestag elections. Together, this opposition from both left and right dangerously reduced the CDU/CSU-FDP coalition's chances of maintaining the necessary majority in the Bonn parliament for Kohl to prevail as chancellor beyond 1990.

Apart from such considerations about the play of domestic forces in the Federal Republic, Kohl also had to take into account "German question" developments in the GDR. The first faint choirs calling for "Deutschland, einig Vaterland" ("Germany, united fatherland") had been heard at the Monday demonstration in Leipzig on November 6. By the following Monday, the slogan had already become the motto of placards, albeit accompanied by whistling and voices of protest and dissent.[161]

Yet when the chancellor stepped before the Bundestag on November 16 to present a government declaration on his state visit to Poland and comment on the new developments in the GDR, he remained as reluctant as he had been in his State of the Nation address on November 8. Instead of indulging in euphoria about the possibilities of German reunification, Kohl only stated the facts in a sober and concise analysis. Even the Greens applauded when he confirmed that the Federal Republic would "of course respect any decision that the people in the GDR come to in free self-determination."[162]

A few hours later, Teltschik informed the US ambassador in Bonn, Vernon A. Walters, about the results of the chancellor's trip to Poland and his views regarding the situation in the GDR. Walters, a patriarchal-looking friend of the Germans whose steadfastness had made him a reliable factor in the shaping of recent US-German relations, told Teltschik that he had visited the Glienicke Bridge between Berlin and Potsdam a few nights earlier. As a soldier he had experienced four wars, Walters said, but never had he seen so many men crying than on that evening. He had realized that this was more than a reunion or the meeting of friends, a family had come together again. "Therefore," the ambassador emphatically stressed, "I believe in reunification. Whoever speaks out against it will be swept away politically." This assessment he had transmitted to the president, too.[163]

On the following day, the government in Bonn received the text of a speech Gorbachev had made before students in Moscow on November 15. In his address, the Soviet leader had used the term "reunification" as well, which was all the more remarkable as he had not referred to it as a matter to be settled in 50 or 100 years from then; he had only excluded it for "today." In principle, Gorbachev said, the question of reunification was an "internal affair" of the FRG and GDR, adding that "how history will continue—comes time, comes advice." He welcomed what was happening in East Germany, and supported it.[164]

Four days later, on November 21, when Nikolai Portugalov showed up in Bonn, it turned out that Gorbachev's reference to German unification had been no accident. Portugalov was an outstanding Soviet expert on German politics, with excellent contacts to the SPD as well as the CDU. He was a counselor in the Central Committee of the CPSU and a member of Falin's staff. Despite Falin's well-known skepticism about German unity, however, Portugalov had been a frequent visitor to Bonn who always stressed before leaving that he would return soon, because, as he used to say, "everything between the Soviet Union and the FRG is so important."

Now he was back once again, on a mission. With a solemn face, Portugalov presented a handwritten note, hastily translated into German, consisting of two parts: The "official" section, compiled in a joint effort by Falin, Portugalov, and Anatoli Chernayev, foreign policy advisor to Gorbachev, had been initiated by the Soviet leader himself; only Falin and Portugalov, the latter claimed, had coordinated the more far-reaching second part.[165]

The note opened with a brief assessment of the situation in the GDR, stating that Moscow had foreseen the developments in East Germany "since the dawn of perestroika"; further, Gorbachev assumed Bonn understood that recent events would not have happened against the will of the Soviet Union. The memorandum then noted concern that the inner-German relations might take an undesired and even dangerous course. In this respect, the chancellor was asked several general questions: what he personally thought of the changes in the GDR; what his priorities were; whether the construction of an all-European peace order continued to be more important than the resolution of the German question; if the Ostverträge of the early 1970s, including the Basic Treaty between the FRG and GDR, were still valid; and if Modrow's proposal of a "contractual community" could be a modus vivendi.

The second part of the paper then raised specific questions regarding the cooperation between the two German states, particularly about reunification, the GDR's accession to the EC, membership in alliances, and the possibility of a peace treaty. "As you can see, we are pondering over everything in the German question alternately," Portugalov added, "even . . . the unthinkable." And he could imagine, he told Teltschik, that under certain conditions the Soviet Union "in the medium term" could give a German confederation the green light.[166]

Teltschik was electrified. Apparently, the considerations within the Soviet leadership on German unification had proceeded much further than had hitherto been assumed in Bonn. Since the West Germans themselves so far actually had no plans in this respect that could be referred to, Teltschik's responses to the Soviet questions had to be kept evasive and circumspect. Thus he diverted the conversation to gain time and suggested a meeting between Gorbachev and Kohl, probably in an "unofficial setting," such as Gorbachev's vacation spot in the Caucasus Mountains, to talk quietly about the implications of the dramatic changes in Europe.

Immediately after his meeting with Portugalov, Teltschik informed the chancellor that Gorbachev and his advisors were discussing the possibility of reunification already and that it was high time for the Germans to follow suit. The chancellor, hurrying on his way to another appointment, agreed that it was necessary to deal with the issue soon.

In a nightly round at the Chancellery on November 23, Kohl and his advisors decided to develop a concept for the unification process. At 10:00 A.M. next day, Chancellery Minister Rudolf Seiters, Claus-Jürgen Duisberg, and Teltschik joined for a brainstorming session to discuss possible answers to the questions Portugalov had presented. At the end, they had put together exactly ten points, much to their own delight. During the following weekend the ten points were incorporated in a speech that Kohl would deliver to the Bundestag on Tuesday, November 28, during the debate on the budget.

When Kohl eventually stepped before the Bundestag, only the US administration had been notified in advance. In an 11-page letter transmitted to the White House earlier in the morning, the chancellor had explained in detail his plan for a German confederation and had asked President Bush for support. The Soviet ambassador in Bonn, Yuli Kvitsinsky, only received the text at 11:00 A.M., while Kohl was still speaking at the parliament. The ambassadors of the three Western powers were informed soon thereafter.

Kohl's "ten-point program" called for the removal of "unnatural barriers between Eastern and Western Europe," which he said were manifested "in the clearest and ugliest fashion in the division of Germany." The Federal government was prepared, Kohl assured, to provide "immediate concrete aid" to the GDR and to continue its cooperation in all areas if "fundamental change of the political and economic system of the GDR is firmly agreed upon and put irrevocably into effect." The Federal government also accepted Prime Minister Modrow's thoughts of a contractual community, Kohl declared, but wished "to take a further decisive step, namely, to develop confederative structures between the two states in Germany with the goal of creating a federation, a federal state order in Germany."[167]

Nobody knew, the chancellor said, how a reunified Germany would look. He was, however, sure that unity would come if the German nation wanted

it. First, a legitimate democratic government within the GDR was "an unre-
linquishable prerequisite." After free elections, several institutions could be
formed, including a common governmental committee for permanent consultation and political harmonization, common technical committees, and a
common parliamentary body. Finally, with this sweeping policy and the
attainment of freedom within Europe, the German people could, via self-
determination, restore their unity. "Reunification, the reattainment of German
state unity," remained "the political goal of the Federal government."[168]

With respect to the external aspects of his proposal, Kohl stated:

> The future of Germany must fit into the future architecture of Europe as a
> whole. The West has to provide peace-making aid here with its concept for
> a permanent and just European order of peace. . . . The European
> Community is now required to approach the reform-oriented states in
> Central, Eastern and Southern Europe with openness and flexibility. . . .
> This of course includes the GDR. The Federal government therefore
> approves the quick conclusion of a trade and cooperation agreement with
> the GDR. This would expand and secure the GDR's entry within the com-
> mon market, including the perspectives of 1992.[169]

In addition, the chancellor said, the CSCE process was and remained "a
crucial part of the total European architecture" and must be further advanced.
Moreover, surmounting the separation of Europe and the division of Germany
demanded "far-reaching and speedy steps pertaining to disarmament and
arms control."[170]

During the debate following Kohl's address, all parties in the Bundestag
with the exception of the Greens expressed support for the proposition for a
confederation of the two German states. Speaking for the Free Democrats,
Foreign Minister Genscher voiced the FDP's approval and said ties between
the two German states must be supplemented through the relationship between
the GDR and the European Community. The GDR recently had obligated
itself in a memorandum to the EC to free elections; this opened the way for
negotiations on a trade agreement and an accord on cooperation between the
GDR and the EC.[171] The chairman of the FDP, Otto Lambsdorff, however, criticized the chancellor for failing to consult with the Allies, the Soviet Union,
and the GDR before releasing the ten-point proposal. He also said that the proposal lacked a clear statement of West German recognition of the Polish western border. The chancellor's concept was "sound," Lambsdorff said, but the
manner in which it was presented required "further discussion."[172]

The next day, the executive committee of the SPD faction in the Bundestag
announced that it would draft its own resolution in which, contrary to the

chancellor's proposal, the recognition of the Oder-Neisse line as Poland's western border would be an "indispensable prerequisite" for closer cooperation with the GDR. Green Bundestag deputy Jutta Österle-Schwerin said her party saw "not a single sensible reason which speaks for reunification." She described the Federal government as "ignorant and arrogant" in its dealings with the GDR. Green executive committee member Jürgen Maier rejected the chancellor's plan on the grounds that "the people of the GDR did not take to the streets to be reunited in a pan-German confederation in NATO."[173]

Despite the criticism, the Federal government wasted no time in following up Kohl's proposal. On November 29, Economics Minister Haussmann outlined a three-step plan to improve intra-German economic relations. For the first, short-term step, he proposed that the GDR create the legal framework allowing joint ventures and reducing trade barriers. The minister maintained that there were signs that the GDR would be willing to come to a joint venture agreement quickly. He added that West German trade organizations offered to bring East German vocational training up to the latest standards. The second step, continuing up to the planned elections in the GDR on May 6, would involve improving contacts between West and East German firms, particularly small- to medium-size ones. Haussmann said he intended to discuss this with his East German colleague before the end of the year. In the third step, basic economic reforms in the GDR should be tackled. This, however, he stated, was up to the East Germans alone. So far the SED and all of the other official parties and the East German opposition groups had only "very vague" ideas about their country's future economic order. Nevertheless, Haussmann concluded, it already seemed to be clear that "the broken fragments of 40 years of centrally planned economy cannot be glued together by generous amounts of financial aid; it must instead be cleared up and disposed of thoroughly."[174]

While the Germans were still arguing whether the two Germanys should continue to exist either in the form of a "contractual community" or by way of a confederation, former US secretary of state Henry Kissinger allowed himself to think ahead, as has been said already. "German unification in some form has become inevitable," he stated on December 4, "whatever the misgivings of Germany's neighbors and World War II victims."[175] In fact, Kissinger had expressed this conviction as early as November 15, when he had addressed the World Affairs Council in Philadelphia.[176]

Other former top US officials took a more cautious view. George F. Kennan, the former US ambassador to the Soviet Union and professor emeritus at the Institute for Advanced Study in Princeton, New Jersey, wrote in an article in *The Washington Post* on November 12 that there was "no reason for an immediate German unification" and that this was "not the time to raise the subject."[177] Similarly, Paul H. Nitze, a top national security figure in Republican and Democratic administrations since World War II, stressed that the reunification of Germany would "scare a lot of people" and added that US policy should be to encourage an alternative arrangement of close cooperation between the two German states.[178]

Zbigniew Brzezinski, on the other hand, President Jimmy Carter's national security advisor, found himself agreeing with Kissinger when he recommended that the Bush administration ought to strive to develop a new security arrangement in Europe in which there would be a confederation of the two Germanys. "You cannot end the division of Europe without ending the division of Germany," Brzezinski said. "If you want to end the division of Germany, you need to end the fears that it generates."[179]

In principle the administration agreed. However, neither the White House nor the State Department were conceptually prepared for the change. US officials, like everyone else, had been caught by surprise when the pillars of the postwar order in Europe began to crumble, but they also had failed to develop new ideas after the collapse had become self-evident. Now they were literally steamrollered by Kohl's ten-point plan. President Bush and White House chief of staff John Sununu showed themselves particularly annoyed about Kohl's lack of advance consultation with the Allies. At a NATO meeting in Brussels on December 4, President Bush spelled out his differences with the chancellor quite explicitly by outlining four conditions for German reunification: that it must be accomplished on the basis of free elections in both East and West Germany; that it be in accordance with the 1975 Helsinki Final Act; that a unified Germany remain in the Western alliance as a member of NATO and the EC; and that unification must come about gradually and peacefully.[180]

In other words, Bush tried to tie developments in Germany to negotiations between East and West, and made it plain to the chancellor that he would not support the idea of an early confederation of the two Germanys before the Europeans, Soviets, and Americans had been consulted.

However, as events in Eastern Europe and Germany were moving so quickly that the administration felt it could no longer speak in generalities about the future of the continent, Secretary of State James Baker was dispatched to Berlin on December 11 to receive firsthand information about the situation and to meet with Kohl and Genscher and with GDR prime minister Modrow. En route to Berlin, at a hastily arranged stopover in London, Baker met with British prime minister Margaret Thatcher, who had indicated publicly that she was even more worried than the United States about the prospect of a unified Germany not bound to the Western alliance, and tried to help patch up intra-EC differences over how the community might be better integrated so as to anchor a unified Germany firmly to the West.[181]

In a speech at the Berlin Press Club on December 12, Baker repeated the four conditions for German unification that President Bush had outlined previously.[182] But more significantly, Baker also conferred with Ambassador Walters, after Walters himself had met with his colleagues from Britain, France, and the Soviet Union. This was anything but accidental, of course, as Baker made clear in an impromptu statement at a press conference in London: "Our policy position is that there are certain responsibilities reserved under the Allied powers that have to be considered when you deal with the question of German reunification. These things have to be considered and dealt with."[183] Privately one of the ambassadors explicitly stated that the purpose of the meeting had been "to put an anchor on Bonn." And in Paris, a French official was even more blunt when he declared that "the purpose was to remind the Germans who's in charge of Berlin."[184]

In Moscow, Mikhail Gorbachev also expressed his displeasure at Kohl's proposal. In a December 10 telephone conversation with the new chairman of the SED-PDS, Gregor Gysi, Gorbachev stated that the Soviet Union would reject any attempt by the West to infringe on East German sovereignty. "The stability of the German Democratic Republic depends, in no small degree, on the stability of the European continent," he told Gysi, according to an account by ADN, the official East German press agency.[185]

The chancellor responded quickly to the criticism. In a speech to the national leadership of his party on December 11, Kohl claimed that he had not laid down a rigid schedule of steps toward unification and that many had misunderstood his plan or taken the elements out of context.[186] The chancellor particularly attacked the Social Democrats who—according to Kohl—were willing to consign the more than 16 million people of East Germany to communism permanently. Therefore, the chancellor said, the voting at the national elections for the Bundestag in December 1990 would be "crucial, even fateful" with regard to the German question.[187]

The SPD had in fact put itself in an awkward position by pursuing a dialogue with the SED for several years, going so far as to produce a statement on areas of agreement in 1987. With the East German communists discredited or revealed as corrupt, the West German Social Democrats now had to move away from them as quickly as possible. Yet in December 1989 the SPD was still undecided about what to do. On the one hand, the party claimed that many elements of the outline Kohl advanced in his proposal of November 28 actually came from them. On the other, some of the SPD leaders, most notably party chairman Hans-Jochen Vogel, hesitated to impose any Western concepts, even ideas, upon the East German people, as they felt the GDR citizens eventually should have not only the right but also the leeway to decide about their destiny. Furthermore, most of the SPD superiors also misread the mood of the East Germans in concluding that reunification was not an issue. A statement of December 11 carefully avoided the term "reunification," using "unity" or "unification" instead, and also blamed Kohl for having raised German unity in a national rather than an international context.[188]

Former chancellor Willy Brandt, who had attracted tens of thousands of East Germans to attend his rallies in the GDR in early December, was one of very few SPD leaders who quickly comprehended the emotional value and political significance of the subject. Brandt saw that at the traditional Monday evening demonstrations, which had helped to bring down two East German communist leaders since October 18, the number of people who carried banners demanding reunification was increasing steadily. As a matter of fact, on December 11, as many as 300,000 people took to the streets of Leipzig and Dresden in huge demonstrations, more than in previous weeks, calling for unification and waving black-red-and-gold German flags, some with the West German eagle emblazoned in the center, chanting "Deutschland! Deutschland!" A survey published by the local *Leipziger Volkszeitung* that day showed that three-quarters of the city's 547,000 people were in favor of unity.[189]

This increasing pressure for unification was a movement too powerful for anyone, including the Social Democrats, to ignore. During a three-day SPD convention in West Berlin in mid-December, a declaration on Deutschlandpolitik, passed by a large majority of the approximately 440 delegates, not only supported many elements of Kohl's ten-point program but urged the "speedy" establishment of a confederation, stating that such a move would be possible even if the two German states at first remained members of their respective alliances. The December 18 declaration also called for the recognition of Poland's western border "without any ifs, ands, or buts," for an emergency aid program for the GDR, and a "contractual community," as proposed by Modrow, as a preliminary step to a confederation. Hans-Jochen Vogel stressed that a confederation of the two German states was the most reasonable solution, but added that a step-by-step demilitarization of both NATO and the Warsaw Pact and drastic conventional and nuclear disarmament measures would be necessary before German unity could be achieved.[190]

Weeks before the Social Democrats finally agreed to the idea of a German confederation, Kohl and Genscher personally undertook the difficult task of trying to convince the Allies and the Soviet Union of the necessity to finally solve the German question. Genscher explained Kohl's ten-point proposal during talks with Gorbachev and Shevardnadze on December 5 in Moscow, shortly after Gorbachev and President Bush had discussed the issue at their Malta summit. Kohl stressed in his meeting with Secretary of State Baker in Berlin on December 12 that a solution to the German question would have to be integrated "in the architecture of Europe." And both Kohl and Genscher brought the European Community to recognize explicitly the right of Germans to unity through free self-determination during a meeting of the leaders of the EC countries on December 8-9 in Strasbourg, where a declaration was issued stating that the German people must reattain unity "in a democratic and peaceful way while preserving the agreements and treaties on the basis of all principles established in the Helsinki Final Act and in connection with dialogue and East-West cooperation."[191]

In addition, Kohl wrote a detailed letter to Gorbachev, dated December 14, informing the Soviet leader about the Federal Republic's policies with regard to Germany and Europe. Once again the chancellor explained the intentions of his ten-point proposal. When Kohl returned to Bonn after a three-day visit to Hungary on December 18, however, he found on his desk a brusque letter from Moscow in which Gorbachev reminded him that the Soviet Union would do everything necessary to "neutralize" any interference in the internal affairs of the German Democratic Republic. The GDR, Gorbachev stated, was a "strategic ally" and member of the Warsaw Pact. Therefore the future peaceful cooperation between the GDR and the Federal Republic had to be based on "the grown realities and the existence of two German states."[192] Gorbachev was apparently concerned about the tempo and the finality of the German unification process, and he worried about its implications with respect to the strategic situation of the Soviet Union.

Minister President Lothar Späth of Baden-Württemberg experienced how far the mood in the GDR had in fact shifted toward unification during a brief visit to Dresden on December 10. Späth had initially been invited by Hans Modrow in late September. At that time Modrow, then SED district secretary of Dresden, had spent several days in Stuttgart exploring new possibilities for closer cooperation with Baden-Württemberg, a state known for its economic success.

When Späth arrived at Dresden Klotsche airport, his 30-member delegation was welcomed by some hundred citizens and a placard displaying the slightly modified phrase of Field Marshal Illo from Friedrich Schiller's *Wallenstein*: "Spät(h) kommt ihr—Doch ihr kommt! Allein der weite Weg entschuldigt euer Säumen."[193] ("You're late—But you came! Only the long way excuses your delay.") While touring the Striezel-Markt, a traditional Christmas bazaar, Späth was continuously approached by people with tears in their eyes who merely wanted to touch him and make sure that he was real—as if he might be a mirage. When his delegation later left the Cross Church, a large crowd had gathered, waving black-red-and-gold flags and chanting "Deutschland, Deutschland" time and again. Späth and everyone in his party understood that the wishes of these men and women, young and old, who were expressing their emotions with such a vengeance, were irresistible and that anything short of German unification would not live up to their demands.[194]

Upon his return to the Federal Republic, Späth immediately informed the chancellor about his trip and let Kohl know what he could expect when he himself traveled to Dresden to meet with Modrow and representatives of the churches and the opposition groups on December 19. In Bonn, Späth's report caused some anxiety. Dresden had been chosen as meeting place because it had seemed to lack the historical associations of other available sites. Chancellery Minister Seiters, who had prepared Kohl's trip to the GDR on behalf of the Federal government, had insisted that Kohl not visit East Berlin, the capital of the SED regime; the "heroic city" of Leipzig had not been acceptable to the East German government; and both sides had thought Wartburg Castle to be overly symbolic, as it was identified not only with Martin Luther but with the prelude to the unification of the German Reich in the 19th century, as well. Dresden had been assumed to be relatively free of such historical recollections. Now the situation looked different, as the chancellor's trip to East Germany was likely to stir emotions of unwelcome proportions. When Soviet ambassador Kvitsinsky called Teltschik on the eve of Kohl's departure to ask what the Federal government intended to do to prevent uproar and turmoil, Teltschik could merely respond with a mix of hope and trust in God, saying that there was "no cause for such fear."[195]

The talks between Modrow and Kohl began at 10:00 A.M. on December 19 at the Hotel Bellevue. The West German chancellor had been greeted by many thousands of people along the ten-kilometer route from the airport to the hotel, forcing the convoy to drive at a walking speed. The East German prime minister, with the SED party badge in the lapel of his suit, opened the meeting by reading a lengthy typewritten manuscript—an obligatory act that reminded the members of the West German delegation of similar compulsory exercises during the old days of Brezhnev, Andropov, and Chernenko, who always had begun their talks with dull and dreary statements. Although Modrow's voice was hectic, his face pale and pinched, and his sparse hair was churned up, he showed almost no emotion and no smile appeared on his face during the conversation. With a considerable degree of success, he tried to avoid eye contact with the other persons in the room. It was quite apparent he was very worried that the situation in his country was desperate.[196]

During the talks, agreement was reached about a joint declaration on the shaping of a contractual community and also about visa-free travel between the two Germanys after December 24 and the opening of the Brandenburg Gate in Berlin on December 22 for pedestrians. Negotiations at the ministerial level on the contractual community would begin after January 1. Also, the GDR would receive compensation for financial losses in connection with the new travel regulations.[197]

But at the Bellevue, Kohl was also confronted for the first time with Modrow's demand that the FRG should support the GDR economy with an "equalization of burdens" of DM15 billion. Modrow argued that with the opening of the borders, the GDR had come under strong pressure from West Germans who profited by a favorable exchange rate and high state subsidies for East German goods. Additionally, Modrow said, the GDR needed the money to modernize its industry and agriculture and reconstruct its infrastructure.[198]

Kohl expressed "understanding in principle" for the demand—although he stated that one should rather speak of a "contribution of solidarity" than an equalization of burdens—but he refrained from making any concrete pledges. A few days earlier, in preparation for the trip, Kohl had actually discussed a proposal of his interior minister, Wolfgang Schäuble, to offer Modrow immediate establishment of a currency and economic union between the FRG and the GDR. Schäuble had argued that the Federal Republic should not hesitate "to take quick, long steps" in order "to direct the revolution [in the GDR] into the right channels." Otherwise, the number of aspiring resettlers would grow.[199] But most participants in the round, among them Seiters, Teltschik, Duisberg, and other staff members of the Chancellery, had felt that the time was not yet ripe for such a far-reaching initiative. Thus Kohl had arrived in Dresden without a firm proposal and was now forced to be evasive.

Modrow, however, later accused the chancellor of not having kept his promises. Neither the "contribution" of solidarity nor the compensation for the advanced visa-free traveling regulation was ever paid, he claimed; negotiations on a contractual community never took place; and soon Kohl also had lost interest in him as a responsible interlocutor.[200]

To some extent, Modrow's bitterness was justified. The GDR government did try to follow up the Kohl-Modrow talks by preparing a draft for a "Treaty on Cooperation and Good Neighborhood Between the German Democratic Republic and the Federal Republic of Germany," which was dated January 17, 1990, and submitted to Chancellery Minister Seiters on January 25.[201] But Kohl actually changed course after Dresden for reasons that had little to do with the East German prime minister personally or the substance of his policy.

Kohl's turn was actually triggered by a rally at the ruin of the Frauenkirche after his meeting with Modrow in the late afternoon of December 19. Here tens of thousands of East German citizens had gathered in a sea of black-red-and-gold flags, mostly without the GDR emblem, to hear the West German. Kohl's address was cautious and moderate, although he conjured up the "unity of our nation," which, he said, remained his political goal.[202] But the crowd cheered with frenetic applause at nearly every sentence of the chancellor, chanting "Deutschland, Deutschland," "Helmut, Helmut," and "We are one people" time and again. It was a deep emotional experience that left a lasting impression on all members of the West German delegation, similar to what Minister President Späth and his aides had experienced a week earlier. Kohl himself, who was also affected by the emotions, concluded his speech by proclaiming: "God bless our German fatherland."[203]

Back at the Hotel Bellevue, the chancellor stressed positively on West German television that there had been no riots or chaos. The people of the GDR understood that "we need time, must have patience and will have to undertake many small steps." The contractual community would be established by April 1990; the first free elections in the GDR would take place the month thereafter.[204] The memorable day ended with a meeting between Kohl and bishops of the Evangelical Church of the GDR and a dinner with GDR artists, one of whom stated that 1989 was a year in which "reality had surpassed fantasy."[205]

There was in fact a "new togetherness, strengthened cooperation and new common ground" in relations between the two German states, as Kohl declared before the Bundesrat (the upper house of the Federal parliament) upon his return to Bonn; "new horizons" were opening up for all Germans, and the prospect of German unification gradually took shape.[206] It soon became clear, however, that the unification process would have its problems. A controversy about the formal recognition of the Oder-Neisse line as the western boundary of Poland brought back memories of the past and aroused political concern internationally, although the debate was caused more by domestic political shuffles in the Federal Republic than by revived disagreement between Warsaw and Bonn.

As there had been some discussion about the issue earlier in December, Federal president Richard von Weizsäcker, who had been one of the few CDU politicians supporting the Eastern treaties of Willy Brandt's SPD-FDP government in the early 1970s, used the opportunity of his annual Christmas address to speak of the inviolability of the Polish border, stating that "Even when none of us can speak for all of Germany, we can and want to—in fact, we are obligated—to speak clearly and distinctly for ourselves. This means that we clearly state that the Polish western border will not change, not now and not in the future."[207]

The chairman of the Association of Expellees, Herbert Czaja, a member of the CDU faction of the Bundestag, reacted immediately to the statement by saying that von Weizsäcker did not have the right "to arrogantly determine the future of Germany and the home of the Eastern German expellees."[208] In view of the dispute, Bundestag president Rita Süssmuth proposed on December 29 that both German states should issue a joint declaration on the continued existence of the Polish border in order to calm Polish fears. This suggestion was rejected by the chancellor, however, who claimed that it was "not acceptable at the present moment." The border discussion was "not relevant," Kohl said, as the GDR did not now have a freely elected government on the one hand, and on the other, the Bundestag had passed a resolution on the Polish border on November 8, 1989, in which the "great majority" of the deputies had stated that the Germans "would not now or in the future dispute the Polish western border."[209]

On January 25, a new idea was introduced when Foreign Minister Genscher and his colleagues, Roland Dumas of France and Gianni De Michelis of Italy, at a Vienna meeting of the 35 participating states of the Conference on Security and Cooperation in Europe, proposed to link the question of the German-Polish border with the general structure of European stability. Genscher said that he completely agreed with Dumas and De Michelis that a CSCE summit was "urgently needed in view of the drastic developments in East and Central Europe." European stability could only come from "the already existing framework, that of the CSCE."[210]

Mikhail Gorbachev apparently also felt that a solution of the German question could be reached only if it was accompanied by European guarantees. Prior to a meeting with Modrow in Moscow on January 30, the Soviet leader declared that no one challenged "in principle" the unification of Germany:

> Basically, no one casts any doubt upon it. However, the development of events in the world, in the German Democratic Republic and the Soviet Union, requires profound assessment and an analytical approach to a solution of the issue, which is an important aspect of European and world politics. It is essential to act responsibly and not seek a solution to this important issue in the streets.[211]

Now the unification of Germany no longer seemed to be a question of principle but merely a tactical matter of how and when—despite the differences that remained. Or, as Gorbachev told an East German television reporter just before the meeting with Modrow, "Time itself is having an impact on the process and lending dynamism to it."[212]

THE ELECTION OF MARCH 18, 1990

In early February, while the communist leadership in the Kremlin began to yield its "leading role" and opposition movements in Eastern Europe were only beginning to coalesce into political forces, politics in eastern Germany were in effect usurped by West Germans. The political invasion was part of a profound shift that began in January when the authority of the East German state dwindled quickly in the face of an expanding exodus and growing expectation of unity. In view of the continued flow of about 2,000 East German resettlers to the Federal Republic daily, unification was widely regarded as the only possible solution. A public opinion poll taken jointly by the Leipzig-based Central Institute for Youth Research and the West German National Market Research Institute in early February found that 75 percent of East Germans questioned were now in favor of unification—27 percentage points more than in November 1989.[213]

Nowhere was the new mood more evident than in the political race toward the GDR's first free parliamentary elections on March 18, 1990. The elections had originally been scheduled for May 6, but due to the rapidly deteriorating political and economic situation, the Modrow government and the opposition leaders at the Round Table panel had decided on January 28 to move the date ahead. This was not without risk, however, as the opposition parties and groups were only beginning to shape up and still lacked profile, while it was uncertain whether the SED—now labeled the Party of Democratic Socialism (PDS)—would benefit from the advanced elections.

The former state party had declined continuously, along with the Modrow government, but was still far superior to the political amateurs of the opposition groups in terms of organization, party discipline, and political experience, even if its membership was down to 890,000 from 2.4 million by late January.[214] In addition, the relatively large number—more than 50—of new political movements and parties created the danger that the elections might lead to a fragmentation of GDR politics or even to "ungovernability" at a time when leadership was most needed.[215]

New Forum was a particularly good example of the weaknesses of idealistic forces in the realm of party politics.[216] It had been formed by an "initiative group" of some 30 people led by Bärbel Bohley and Jens Reich on the weekend of September 9-10, 1989, well before the East German revolution. Their idea was that a new, humane, and socialist East Germany could rise from the people and that the task of the movement was to elicit the people's will without encumbering it with structures or preconceptions. New Forum had been based on a concept that—while bold and defiant under the communists—was now regarded by many as quaint and obsolete.[217] Sebastian Pflugbeil, who represented New Forum in the Modrow government as a minister without portfolio, later said the opening of the Berlin Wall on November 9 had been the beginning of the end of the movement's hopes. "Our motivation from the beginning was to break the chains and be free to set our own course," he explained. Instead, the tumbling of the Wall had cleared the way for a takeover by West Germany's powerful businessmen and political parties. The people had "lost their heads and followed their stomachs." Shifting from dejection to gallows humor, he concluded, "We will have to find a new population."[218]

Other citizen movements, such as Democracy Now and the Initiative for Peace and Human Rights, suffered from similar motivation gaps and conceptual deficiencies. Democracy Now, with its roots in the Evangelical Church of the GDR, had also been established in September 1989, in an "Appeal for Intervention" signed by Hans-Jürgen Fischbeck, Ludwig Mehlhorn, Wolfgang Ullmann, and Konrad Weiss, among others, in East Berlin.[219] But the movement dated back to August 13, 1986. Curate Reinhard Lampe had staged a solitary protest against the building of the Berlin Wall 25 years previously. The council of the Bartholomew Church in East Berlin declared its solidarity with him after his subsequent imprisonment. Thereafter a working group had been established within the church to discuss political issues and formulate political position papers. On August 13, 1989, three years after Lampe's individual protest, more than 300 people had met at the Confession Parish in East Berlin and agreed that it was time now "to call into being an opposition movement for the democratic renewal of the GDR" and that a memorandum of incorporation should be worked out during the next month.[220] This memorandum, eventually dated September 12, stated that "a democratic reshuffle of the GDR" was necessary, to be achieved by "a state based upon a fundamental consensus of the society" and a transition from state-owned property to a "socialization of the means of production"—in other words, the eventual realization of genuine socialism.[221]

The Initiative for Peace and Human Rights (IFM), on the other hand, was an organization of a different kind.[222] It was not an immediate product of the revolution of 1989, but instead originated in the international peace movement. It had been formed as early as January 1986 as the first independent GDR opposition group to promote disarmament and support political dissidents. In its structure, the IFM was almost a duplicate of comparable movements in the West, such as the Alternative List in West Berlin and the Green Party in West Germany, with whom it maintained close working relations. In the campaign for the election on March 18, the IFM ran on a joint party ticket with New Forum and Democracy Now as "Alliance 90."[223]

The main weakness of New Forum, Democracy Now, and the IFM was their lack of effective vertical party organization. All three movements had been founded as citizens' action committees. They had created a horizontal network of "base groups" that operated more or less independently, without a firm party platform and strict party regulations. The background of such striving for maximum leverage and plurality was of course the experience of nearly six decades of Nazi and communist dictatorship. *Basisdemokratie* was the magic term for an alternative concept of political government that most adherents of the initiative groups—many of them intellectuals, artists, church members, and former dissidents—regarded as ideal to replace the SED regime. The question was, however, whether a majority of the GDR citizens would support another experiment after 40 years of communist experimentation or would want the proven concepts promised by the political professionals of the West and their East German counterparts.

The Social Democratic Party (SDP), founded on the day of the 40th anniversary of the GDR (October 7, 1989) by 43 dissidents—among them dramatist Ibrahim Böhme and Pastor Markus Meckel—in Schwante, a small village near Oranienburg, seemed to represent an example of a well-tried and sound concept.[224] The East German Social Democrats not only carried the banner of a major German party with a long historical tradition, but they also received early support from their sister party, the powerful West German SPD. A joint "contact committee" was established, and West German Bundestag SPD deputies Gert Weisskirchen and Dietrich Stobbe traveled to the GDR as the vanguard of legions of SPD politicians and political experts to assist their new East German comrades in setting up an effective party apparatus. The SPD's advertising agency handled the campaign for the March elections in East Germany free of charge. East Berlin was selected for a meeting of the Socialist International to provide a broader perspective as well as additional reputation for the eastern Social Democrats. With West German backing, Böhme negotiated the advanced date of the elections with Prime Minister Modrow.[225] Most important, however, the venerable former West German chancellor Willy Brandt became the honorary chairman of the East German party and was now campaigning in the GDR; posters portrayed him over his oft-quoted formula for reunification, "What belongs together, will grow together." Thus the Social Democrats in the East could be confident of receiving a major share of the votes, and most observers expected them to win the election and form the new government.

On the conservative side, the West German CDU was much slower off the mark in supporting its East German counterpart. The main problem was that for 40 years the eastern Christian Democratic Party had been an ally of the communists as one of the "bloc parties" maintained as window dressing by the SED regime. Its last chairman, Gerald Götting, had been arrested after the revolution for fraud. His successor, Lothar de Maizière, who had been nominated chairman on November 11, 1989, insisted that the party had fully reformed, especially after a meeting of its executive board on November 20-21 in Burgscheidungen and a special party convention on December 15 in Berlin. But the taint of the past did not disappear so quickly, and West German Christian Democrats long remained reluctant to be seen with some of the old-guard leaders.[226]

Nevertheless, however, Secretary General Volker Rühe of the CDU was commissioned on November 15, 1989, to conduct "informal talks" with the new leadership of the GDR party. But when de Maizière declared in an interview with the West German tabloid *Bild am Sonntag* on November 19 that he looked upon "socialism as one of the most beautiful visions of human thinking" and that the unification of Germany was not "the issue of the hour" but a consideration that "perhaps our children or grandchildren may think about," CDU leaders in Bonn saw their skepticism about the changes within the eastern CDU more than confirmed.[227]

Another matter of concern among western Christian Democrats was the fact that the CDU had participated actively in the Modrow government and, on January 19, 1990, even decided to continue to do so, claiming that it did not want to "further destabilize the situation in the country."[228] Kohl in particular was outraged, privately criticizing de Maizière's tactics sharply.[229] Not surprisingly, Kohl kept his public distance from the chairman of the eastern sister party and waited for other conservative movements in the GDR to be founded, such as Democratic Awakening (DA) and the German Social Union (DSU), before he finally decided to lend his support.

Democratic Awakening had its origin in a political citizens movement that dated back to a meeting of nine members of religious, peace, and human rights groups on August 21-22, 1989, in Dresden. Its foundation was made public on September 14 by Pastor Edelbert Richter from Erfurt, who told a West German newspaper that the DA remained close to "certain social principles of socialism" and that "rightist ideas" were "excluded."[230] In fact, at the beginning the conceptual differences between the DA and other citizens' movements, such as New Forum or Democracy Now, were minimal. When the DA was formally established at its first party convention in Leipzig on December 16, 1989, however, representatives of two main streams contended for platform positions and the majority of the delegates. The Christian and ecologically oriented faction centered around Friedrich Schorlemmer, a pastor from Wittenberg, while the Christian-conservative faction grouped around Wolfgang Schnur, a lawyer from Rostock, and Berlin pastor Rainer Eppelmann, who supported a party structure based on the model of the West German CDU. After an internal struggle, the DA rejected further socialist experiments and looked forward to German unity within the boundaries of 1989.[231]

The DSU was also founded in Leipzig, but it came into being rather late, on January 20, 1990, as a merger movement of a variety of liberal, conservative, and Christian-social groups mainly in the south of the GDR. The German Social Union and its chairman, Hans-Wilhelm Ebeling, were heavily supported by the Bavarian CSU, and demanded "Freedom instead of Socialism" in order to provide an unmistakable alternative to any socialist policies.[232]

The strength of the DA, DSU, and CDU East was difficult to determine, but after the elections were scheduled for March 18, the western CDU was concerned that the division of the conservative forces would provide for a sweeping victory by the SPD. The date of the election had in fact been moved ahead not only because of the threat of the GDR's imminent economic collapse, but also because of political speculation by the PDS and SPD that they would benefit from an early vote, as their functioning party machines were likely to prevail over the still-struggling conservative organizations.

On February 2, therefore, Kohl met with de Maizière in West Berlin to consider an election alliance of the eastern CDU with the Democratic Awakening and the German Social Union. In another meeting on February 5, Kohl, Rühe, and Seiters then reached agreement with de Maizière, Schnur, and Ebeling to establish the "Alliance for Germany" to campaign jointly for the election.[233] Kohl, who attended the meeting at the Federal government's guest house in West Berlin in his function as chairman of the FRG's Christian Democrats, said afterward that he welcomed the decision by the West German CDU to support the alliance, adding that he planned to take part in the GDR election campaign and would appear at six campaign rallies.[234] CSU secretary general Erwin Huber also welcomed the formation of the alliance, but said that the CSU would adhere to its partnership with the DSU.

Not unlike the conservatives, the West German liberal FDP also cobbled together an East German coalition—the Alliance of Free Democrats—on February 12, whereas the Greens gave support to a variety of environmental and left-wing groups, among them the Green League, the Green Party in the GDR, and the Unified Left.[235] On the far right, however, West German involvement was contained early, when the participation of a growing number of neo-Nazis in the Monday evening demonstrations in the autumn of 1989 aroused concern. The GDR parliament also acted swiftly when the West German right-wing Republikaner tried to gain support among East German nationalists and to rummage in the blue-collar discontent of such cities as Leipzig. The Republican Party was banned, and Franz Schönhuber, its founder, was barred from entering the GDR.

But except for the Republicans, West German leaders who only recently had renounced any "tutelage" over Eastern affairs were now in effect taking charge of East German politics.[236] Even West German tax money—DM7.5 million—was spent for the East German election campaign. The money was channeled largely through foundations affiliated with West German parties. Walter Priesnitz, state secretary in the Ministry for Intra-German Relations, reported in Bonn that the three foundations affiliated with the CDU and CSU had received a total of some DM4.5 million—more than all 19 of the home-grown East German parties combined. Foundations affiliated with the FDP and the SPD were allocated DM1.5 million each.[237]

On March 18, some 12.2 million eligible voters in the GDR could choose among 19 competing parties and five joint slates representing an additional 14 parties. The joint slates ranged from the conservative Alliance for Germany to a coalition of Greens and feminists. The voters were to elect representatives to the 400-seat GDR parliament, the Volkskammer. A party needed only .25 percent of the ballots cast, not 5 percent as in the Federal Republic, to be eligible for representation in the legislature.

Early in the campaign, the SPD took a commanding lead. A public opinion poll taken in the first week of February found that if elections were held then, the SPD would win 54 percent, the PDS (the former communists) 12 percent, and the CDU 11 percent.[238] This was early in the race, however, and Chancellor Kohl's campaign had not yet started. It began on February 6, only one day after the formation of the Alliance for Germany, when the Federal government declared in Bonn that it had just created a cabinet-level "Committee on Unity" to chart the way toward a single Germany. And at a cabinet meeting on February 7, Finance Minister Theo Waigel and Economic Minister Helmut Haussmann, as well as the president of the German Bundesbank (the Federal Republic's central bank), Otto Pöhl, agreed that the Federal Republic should enter "immediately" into talks with the GDR on the creation of a currency union between the two German states and concurrent economic reform.[239]

West German SPD leader Vogel soon realized that meant a hasty race of the East Germans toward "good money" and even political unification, both of which now seemed to be associated with the Alliance for Germany, backed by the Federal government and Chancellor Kohl. As a result, the East German Social Democrats would suffer the fate of financial have-nots and be defeated by the voters as a party that could promise neither quick economic recovery nor the swift realization of German unity as part of abolishing the SED regime.

In a debate in the Bundestag on February 15, Vogel therefore attacked Kohl's proposed strategy for immediate progress toward monetary union, stating that "what is at stake here is not the absorption of East Germany or a territory without government"—intimating that this was Kohl's goal. "What we face here," Vogel declared, "is uniting with a people that has won its freedom by itself."[240] GDR prime minister Modrow followed suit by telling the East German parliament on February 20 that the GDR was "a good piece of Germany, on which one can build and must build in the future." Unification was not, Modrow said, "a matter of material values alone," and he warned "emphatically against leaving the solution of the national question of the Germans to the Deutsche mark alone."[241]

Modrow actually had every reason to be annoyed. The week before, while visiting Bonn, he had been taken aback by Kohl's attitude. The chancellor had refused to grant East Germany a desired aid package valued at about DM15 billion (about US$9 billion), but he had offered to make the West German currency the coin of both states instead and join the two in an economic union. Modrow had rejected this, although he knew that the East German economy could not survive very long without massive West German support, since it was expected that by the end of February the flow of refugees for the first two months of the year would exceed 100,000. The total for all of 1989 had been 383,000. Lothar de Maizière and Hans-Wilhelm Ebeling had already stated bluntly in almost identical words in interviews with the West German news magazine *Der Spiegel* that a collapse of the GDR could no longer be excluded.[242]

Kohl, however, gambled on this fear as well as on his promise to bring help—after the elections. At his first campaign appearance in the GDR on February 20, the chancellor listed the aid Bonn had provided to East Germany so far. Speaking in front of more than 100,000 people in the square under the Gothic cathedral of Erfurt—a city of only 220,000 but a strong bastion of the Alliance for Germany—Kohl said he was not willing to invest several billions more if it could not be guaranteed that this money would reach the people. But, the chancellor continued, thousands of West German business leaders stood poised to bring investments and jobs to East Germany, and that once conditions were right they would "build up a booming country in the shortest of times."[243] The masses cheered in a sea of West German flags. When a few hundred leftist demonstrators broke into raucous taunts, throaty chants of "Reds out! Reds out!" drowned them out.

The picture repeated itself several times before March 13-14, when Kohl made his last two appearances at campaign rallies in the GDR, addressing crowds of 100,000 in Cottbus and 300,000 in Leipzig. It turned out to be the right strategy. On election day, 48.1 percent of the votes were cast for the parties of the Alliance for Germany, 21.8 percent for the SPD, 16.3 percent for the PDS, 5.3 percent for the Alliance of Free Democrats, and 8.5 percent for others, among them Alliance 90—that is, New Forum, Democracy Now, and the Initiative for Peace and Human Rights combined—which received only 2.91 percent of the votes.

The outcome of the election was a resounding call for quick unification and a market economy as well as a clear rejection of any form of socialism. Even the Social Democrats seem to have suffered from their socialist past and their allegedly continued closeness to socialist ideas. Yet the election was also a result of the persuasive promises by Kohl and his CDU and CSU colleagues, who had told the East Germans that only the Christian conservatives could provide the money needed to revive the country's suffering economy and to establish a unified Germany without undue delay.[244] In fact, the large vote for the Alliance for Germany or, more precisely, for the parties backed by the CDU/CSU-FDP coalition in Bonn was "in effect a death sentence for the German Democratic Republic and an endorsement of absorption, as quickly as possible, into big, rich West Germany."[245]

The Process of
German Unification

Four months after the opening of the Berlin Wall, the election of an East German parliament dominated by West German-backed political parties was yet another milestone in the race for German unification.[1] It marked the collapse of communist power in the GDR and prompted West Germans to assume an ever more dominant role in East German politics and economics. The vote provided the basis for a government under the leadership of the chairman of the East German CDU, Lothar de Maizière. Much more than that, however, it was a personal triumph for West German chancellor Helmut Kohl, who swung the full weight of his own Christian Democratic Party behind a powerful pro-unity campaign in the GDR.[2]

In fact, since Kohl, not de Maizière, had been the driving force behind the victory, the vote extended his influence over East Germany and sped up his program of swift currency and economic union, with subsequent political union to follow. And de Maizière—a slight, reluctant, soft-spoken 50-year-old political amateur whose speech was hampered by shyness and a lisp—was not the man to stand in his way. On the contrary, the primary function of de Maizière's government would be to prepare its own dissolution and the absorption of the GDR into the Federal Republic.[3]

Therefore, although the exact timetable and the precise conditions for unification were still then unknown, the first free parliamentary election in the history of the GDR was also likely to be its last. If it was true, as one French paper noted and almost everybody acknowledged, that "last year the East Germans voted with their feet; now they voted with their stomachs," drastic action had to be taken. Even the leader of the East German SPD, Ibrahim Böhme, agreed that "in East Germany the people have voted for a quick path to unity."[4] Consequently, de Maizière sought to establish "a coalition as broad as possible" to achieve the two-thirds majority needed to change the constitution and clear the way for unification.[5]

Immediately after the election, de Maizière outlined the priorities of the policy that he, as the new prime minister of the GDR, intended to pursue in the months to come:

- to reach quick agreement with Bonn on how to bring about a currency, economic, and social union between the two German states;

- to hasten the replacement of the 15 GDR regions under strong central administration by five largely autonomous states (Länder), similar to West Germany's subdivisions, to ease the eventual direct accession of East Germany to West Germany;

- to advance unification within broader European unity by paying attention to the interests of Germany's neighbors, to the four victors of World War II, and to the 35-nation Conference on Security and Cooperation (CSCE);

- to be loyal to existing treaties; and

- to fully remove the Berlin Wall and the border fortifications between East and West Germany.[6]

Thus, instead of focusing on improving conditions within the GDR, de Maizière apparently sought to merge East Germany with the Federal Republic as quickly as possible to let the problems be resolved from the outside. It was a strategy that happened to coincide with Chancellor Kohl's policy, but it did throw the East German government instantly on the mercy of decisions from Bonn.

The Federal government acted swiftly. After a special session of the cabinet on March 20, the government announced that the currency union with the GDR would be possible by July 1, while at the same time Bonn would abolish provisions providing emergency accommodations and financial aid to GDR resettlers who so far had been eligible for a broad range of benefits, from payments and temporary shelter, to special help finding a job or housing. Officials in Bonn felt that access to West German marks would give East Germans quick and tangible evidence of movement toward unity and would lessen their urge to move to the West and decrease the stream of resettlers. In explaining this policy, Interior Minister Wolfgang Schäuble noted that the goal was to give East Germans hope for the future and to induce them to stay in their home regions.[7]

The issue of resettlers was, in fact, the most urgent problem for the two German governments in speeding up the unification process. Within less than three months, from January 1 until March 21, 1990, a total of 145,601

East Germans had entered the Federal Republic, compared with 343,854 in all of 1989. The GDR could not bear the exodus, and the FRG found the influx hard to accept. The sheer number of refugees—more than 2,200 daily in March 1990—shook the GDR economy and strained West German social services to their limits.[8] But the problem was not just economic. A poll commissioned by West German television in mid-March 1990 showed that public opinion had turned sharply against the migrants, as only 13 percent of West Germans and 33 percent of East Germans now sympathized with them. With the gates wide open and the Wall practically down—the "refugees" were no longer perceived as persecuted victims escaping from tangible repression but as profiteers yearning for quick Western money. At the same time, the poll also indicated that 82 percent in the West and 91 percent in the East were in favor of German unity.[9]

The combination of economic problems and public opinion made it seem only logical to seek a solution in unification, especially as the vast majority of the people in the GDR apparently wanted unity as well as a market economy and prosperity. Whether the further influx of resettlers could be stopped would depend on the degree to which the concrete hopes and personal expectations of GDR citizens, who also had cast their vote for the chancellor in Bonn, were going to be fulfilled. The question was whether the effectiveness of help, which could come only from the West, would be noticeable early enough to satisfy people who had already waited for so long. Would the terms of the agreement be acceptable to the Germans in both East and West? And, finally, would Germany's neighbors and the four victorious powers of World War II accommodate themselves to German unification, which in the past had been an obstacle, rather than a tool, to European peace and stability?

COMING TO TERMS WITH THE INEVITABLE

Thinking and planning for the merger of the two German states began in late January and early February 1990. Chancellor Kohl had been convinced since his visit to Dresden in December 1989 that unification was likely, indeed inevitable. Others had remained rather opposed to the idea of a unified Germany. This was particularly true for the people of the Soviet Union, where bad memories of the past mixed with uneasiness about the future of the Soviet empire in Eastern Europe if East Germany was lost. Yet the rapid deterioration of the situation in the GDR forced everyone, including the Soviet leadership, to adjust to new conditions that could be neither ignored nor denied.

Once again it was Nikolai Portugalov who marked the change. Portugalov had already contributed significantly to the launching of Kohl's ten-point proposal in November 1989. Now he declared in a sensational interview with the West German tabloid *Bild* on January 24 that "if the people of the GDR want reunification, it will come." The Soviet Union, Portugalov was quoted as having said, would "not oppose such a decision." And, even more clearly: "We will not intervene."[10]

In Bonn, Kohl and his advisors interpreted Portugalov's statement as an unmistakable sign of a fundamental turn in the Soviet attitude toward German unification. A *Pravda* article the previous day about George F. Kennan's proposal of a three-year moratorium regarding the German question also indicated increasing Soviet flexibility. Thus Kohl agreed on January 24, the same day as Portugalov's interview was published, to a "special food sale" to the Soviet Union of more than 100,000 tons of meat, 20,000 tons of butter, 15,000 tons of milk powder, and 5,000 tons of cheese at a "friendship price" subsidized by DM220 million from the Federal budget.[11]

The following day, Chancellery Minister Seiters met in East Berlin with Modrow, who painted a gloomy picture of the situation in the GDR. State authority was rapidly disintegrating, Modrow said, strikes were spreading, and the public was becoming increasingly aggressive. The East German prime minister asked for an early beginning of negotiations with the Federal Republic about a "contractual community," massive financial aid, and industrial cooperation, to prevent imminent collapse.[12]

On January 28, Modrow agreed with the Round Table to advance the date of the GDR elections to March 18. On January 29, Modrow stepped before the Volkskammer, where he repeated and confirmed in public what he had already told Seiters in private. Modrow later admitted in his memoirs that at this point in late January 1990 it had become clear to him "to combine the stabilization of the GDR with the gradual unification of the two German states."[13] Immediately after his speech in the Volkskammer, he left for Moscow, where he was scheduled to meet with Gorbachev on January 30, with the "German Question" obviously now on top of the agenda.

Modrow had prepared his visit to the Soviet capital in several conversations with Soviet ambassador Kochemasov. As a result, a paper entitled "For Germany, United Fatherland" had been worked out. The draft, proposing an initiative for the gradual unification of Germany with Berlin as its capital, was polished during the flight to Moscow and translated into Russian overnight. The plan called for the formation of a confederation with joint institutions and a gradual transfer of sovereignty to these bodies. The proposal also required that the GDR and the Federal Republic be "militarily neutral."[14]

The background of this initiative was a mix of frustration and hope. In November 1989, when Modrow had presented his proposal for a contractual community between the two German states, the East German prime minister had still been convinced that there would be a socialist future for the GDR. After his talks with Kohl in Dresden, however, he had not received any indication from Bonn that the Federal government was seriously interested in continuing the dialogue; on the contrary, not even the draft of January 17 for a Treaty on Cooperation and Good Neighborhood had prompted any response from Kohl or his aides. Meanwhile, the GDR economy was declining at an alarming rate, and the other CMEA countries, including the Soviet Union, were not in position to assist their East German comrades. Thus Modrow had concluded that he had to come forward with a new proposal for the settlement of the German question.

Now, on the morning of January 30, the plan became the subject of negotiations with Gorbachev in his office, not in the Kremlin, but in the building of the Central Committee of the CPSU. At the meeting Prime Minister Nikolai Ryzhkov, Foreign Minister Eduard Shevardnadze, and the head of the Central Committee's International Department, Valentin Falin, were also present.[15]

At the beginning of the talks, Gorbachev indicated he assumed that on March 18 a majority of the East Germans would vote for continued existence of the GDR and that the SPD had the best chances to win the elections. Modrow gave a more realistic assessment of the developments in his country. He described the facts and processes that had made it inevitable to move up the date of the election, and he left no doubt that only his proposed initiative for a gradual unification of the two German states could help stabilize the situation. Gorbachev agreed. Similar measures had already been considered by his own government, he said. German unification could no longer be ruled out as "a possibility in the future." The Soviet Union would respect the right of the German people to self-determination. It would be necessary, however, to enter into deliberations with the United States, Great Britain, and France—if possible, at the highest level—to develop a Four Power formula for the changes that would occur and to find a solution that would take into account the interests of the GDR as well.[16]

The Federal government in Bonn followed the events in Moscow closely. The first detailed account of the Gorbachev-Modrow talks was given by the Moscow correspondent of ADN, the East German news agency, who described Gorbachev's position accurately. The ADN report was confirmed by Modrow himself at a press conference a few hours later, when the East German prime minister stated that "the unification of the two German states is the perspective that lies before us."[17]

Chancellor Kohl and his advisors were thrilled. The Soviet leader now seemed prepared to accept the idea of eventual German unification, at least in principle, while Modrow had indicated once again that he no longer saw any alternative to a German confederation, or even full-fledged unification, to prevent instability and chaos in his country.[18] At a cabinet meeting the following day, January 31, Kohl called Gorbachev's and Modrow's statements "encouraging," reflecting the historical developments that had occurred in the past few months in the GDR and inner-German relations. Kohl stressed that these developments could not have been initiated without Gorbachev's reform policies. Now, due to the new course in Moscow, German unity could come earlier than anyone had expected. Therefore it would be necessary to establish working groups to prepare for the implementation of German unification instantly.[19]

Immediately following the cabinet session, an "Arbeitsgruppe Deutschlandpolitik" was constituted in the Chancellery to meet regularly, about twice a week, in order to coordinate the activities of the various branches of the government regarding unification. Its first task was to lay groundwork for a cabinet-level "Committee on German Unity," to be chaired by the chancellor himself. The committee would consist of interministerial working groups, with permanent as well as nonpermanent members, and would pursue the goal of hammering out the nuts and bolts of German unification in its national and international dimensions.

Yet there was little time for careful consideration and long-term planning. The chancellor was scheduled to meet with Modrow at the World Economic Forum in Davos, Switzerland, on February 3, where he would also have to give a speech on the future architecture of Europe, including the implications of a new Deutschlandpolitik. Meanwhile, Foreign Minister Genscher responded to the question of German neutrality that had been raised again in Moscow by Gorbachev and Modrow. Genscher asserted in a television interview on January 31 that attempts to extend the integrated NATO structure to include the GDR "would most certainly block the way for German unification." German unity could not occur if Soviet security interests were not observed.[20] At the same time, Genscher emphasized that the Federal Republic's continued membership in NATO was important for the stability of Europe. But the military alliances would take on a more political character and eventually evolve into "cooperative security structures for all of Europe." Genscher predicted "not a withdrawal from the alliance, but rather . . . a turn of the alliances from confrontation to cooperation."[21]

When Modrow explained his plan to the international press corps in East Berlin on February 1, journalists focused almost exclusively on the issue of military neutrality. Modrow stressed that his thoughts constituted merely an "offer for a dialogue," but he insisted that the border between the GDR and the FRG would "cease to be dividing lines of the two military blocs with all resulting consequences" if a confederation was established.[22] A spokesperson for the Federal government in Bonn commented spontaneously that Modrow's plan contained "essential elements" of Chancellor Kohl's ten-point proposal for a German confederation announced in November. Later in the day, however, Kohl, Genscher, and numerous other representatives of the CDU/CSU, FDP, and even the SPD rejected the notion of a neutral Germany, among them West Berlin mayor Walter Momper (SPD), who said the plan reminded him of Soviet proposals for German neutrality in the 1950s. He expressed his doubts "whether such plans correspond to current times."[23]

To what extent the question of alliances and military security would become an issue of debate in the months ahead was also made clear when leading politicians of the CDU and CSU quickly voiced their opposition to Genscher's proposal of not expanding NATO territory eastward into "the part of Germany at present forming the GDR." Willy Wimmer, the defense policy spokesman for the CDU/CSU faction in the Bundestag, said that NATO membership would guarantee Moscow that Germany was anchored in an association of states oriented to stability.[24]

Just prior to Kohl's departure for Davos on the afternoon of February 2, Soviet ambassador Kvitsinsky delivered a personal message from Gorbachev. The Soviet president agreed with "a contractual community as a step on the way toward a confederation of the two German states" and invited the chancellor to come to Moscow for confidential talks on February 9. Kohl gladly accepted the invitation but, after a brief look at his calendar, asked to set February 10-11 for the appointment.[25]

The next day in Davos, Modrow informed Kohl that the decline of the GDR was accelerating daily. Until the end of 1989 everything had still been relatively stable. But now even government authority at the local level was eroding. An early merging of the two German states was therefore inevitable. Money was a factor as well; Modrow said DM15 billion would be required at once to prevent financial disaster in March. Beyond that, making the D-mark the sole currency in the GDR was also a possibility.[26]

Brent Scowcroft and Robert Blackwill of the US National Security Council, who attended a Wehrkunde conference in Munich on the weekend of February 3-4 on basic changes of the strategic situation in Europe, were deeply impressed by the tempo of German developments, sensing that after the election on March 18 German unity could become reality very quickly. Gorbachev had already informed the US government about his forthcoming talks with Kohl, and Soviet foreign minister Eduard Shevardnadze was going to see Secretary of State Baker immediately prior to Gorbachev's meeting with the chancellor.

During a conversation between Scowcroft and Blackwill with Horst Teltschik at the Hotel Bayerischer Hof on the evening of February 3, the German and the Americans agreed to maintain the closest consultations possible; Kohl also would be informed about Baker's talk with Shevardnadze. The US officials left no doubt that their administration would support the German unity efforts and that Washington would resist any Soviet attempts to use the unification issue as an instrument for either bribery or blackmail, or a combination of both, for instance by turning the envisaged CSCE summit into a semipeace conference.[27]

On Monday, February 5, the German press was full of reports about the dramatic situation in the GDR. Modrow and CDU-East leader Lothar de Maizière declared that a collapse could no longer be excluded.[28] In an interview with Radio Suisse, a shaken Modrow had even agreed to a unification of Germany without neutrality. Meanwhile, the Arbeitsgruppe Deutschlandpolitik had met twice in the Chancellery that day to discuss various scenarios that seemed feasible after the March 18 election. They included an immediate incorporation of the GDR into the Federal Republic on the basis of Article 23 of the Basic Law without the previous formation of a new GDR government, as well as accession on the basis of Article 146 after negotiations with a new government. In addition, the idea of economic and monetary union was considered. The participants agreed that after Kohl's talk with Gorbachev and consultations with the Western allies, especially President Bush, an operational concept for the unification process had to be worked out as quickly as possible.[29]

The following day, Chancellor Kohl informed the CDU-CSU faction in the Bundestag that he intended "to enter immediately into negotiations with the GDR on a monetary union and economic reform." The parliamentarians were completely surprised. Even Bundestag members had difficulties keeping abreast of the developments. Yet they accepted the idea, despite some concern that such a move might endanger the stability of the West German D-mark and undercut East Germany's own efforts to heal its economy.

Kohl's proposal, which had been approved by the cabinet on February 7 after some discussion, especially with the president of the independent Bundesbank, Karl Otto Pöhl, was designed mainly to contain the flow of people from the East and stave off the economic collapse of the GDR. But for the chancellor the economic and financial matters were no more than a minor aspect of a truly historic opportunity: the unification of Germany after

45 years of division. Therefore it was anything but an accident that the cabinet combined its decision of February 7 on a monetary and economic union between the FRG and GDR with the establishment of the "Committee on German Unity" that had been prepared by the Arbeitsgruppe Deutschlandpolitik since January 31. The committee would be chaired by Kohl himself and include working groups headed by cabinet ministers to deal with the issues of the currency union, economic reform, the adaptation of social regulations, and foreign and security policies. In addition, Chancellery Minister Seiters underscored Bonn's intention to begin talks on "confederative cooperation" with the GDR immediately following the elections on March 18.[30]

Thus the stage was set for the final round on coming to terms with the inevitable. On the eve of Kohl's meeting with Gorbachev, Horst Teltschik used a background briefing with the press to speak of East Germany's imminent collapse. The briefing was on "deep background," meaning that the official's name could not be made public. But next morning Teltschik's name was reported by all major papers. According to the *Süddeutsche Zeitung*, Teltschik's tactic was to paint the gloomiest possible picture of affairs in East Germany so that Kohl could convince the Soviets that only rapid union would forestall chaos.[31] In other words, Teltschik was assumed to have been deliberately alarmist to prepare the ground for Kohl's talks in Moscow and to accelerate the pace of union.[32]

When Kohl and Genscher arrived at Moscow's Vnukovo II airport on February 10, the Federal Republic's ambassador to the Soviet Union, Klaus Blech, passed on a letter from James Baker. The US secretary of state had promised to inform Kohl about his most recent talks with the Soviet leadership before the chancellor and foreign minister entered into negotiations with the Soviets.

Gorbachev and Shevardnadze also felt that the unification of Germany was unavoidable, Baker reported in his letter. They had concerns, however, about possible instability and insecurity in Europe as a result of the unification. Moreover, they complained about a lack of firm German resolve to recognize the existing borders in the future. Baker had responded, according to his own words, by arguing that unification had in fact become inevitable, that the process would evolve very quickly after the elections on March 18, and that it was therefore necessary to separate the internal aspects from the external factors. Regarding those external factors, negotiations among the Four Powers were not appropriate means as the Germans would not accept them. A two-plus-four arrangement was the only realistic formula. If the two German governments agreed, talks could begin soon after the elections. Gorbachev had called this proposal "conceivable," Baker wrote, but had not made any commitment. Concerning the membership of a united Germany in NATO, the Soviet leader had told the US secretary of state that he was ready "to think about any possible solution," but that a NATO extension would not be acceptable.[33] Kohl and Genscher were visibly relieved by this very helpful and precise communication.

At 4:00 P.M. Gorbachev and Kohl met at the Kremlin, accompanied only by their personal advisors, Anatoly Chernayev and Horst Teltschik and two interpreters. Genscher and Shevardnadze discussed separately the planned CSCE summit, disarmament issues, and the transformation of the military alliances. For Kohl and Gorbachev, however, there was only one topic: the future of the German question.

The chancellor described developments since the opening of the Wall and declared that the unification of Germany was now imminent. Although he preferred to have more time, the process was irresistible and unstoppable; unification would include the Federal Republic, the GDR, and Berlin. He said there was no cause for mistrust concerning the Oder-Neisse border. He acknowledged, however, that the problem of alliance membership was more difficult. Neutralization of Germany would be "unacceptable and a historical stupidity," as Germany's post-1918 isolation and Schaukelpolitik had shown, Kohl stated. He would be prepared, however, to take the security interests of the Soviet Union into account and could therefore imagine not extending NATO to the territory of the GDR.[34]

After Kohl had ended, Gorbachev first asked what time frame the chancellor had in mind. Kohl responded that he had no answer to that question. At the end of December he would have spoken of years, but now people were voting with their feet. If he did not react, chaos could occur.

Then Gorbachev raised several other questions regarding the Oder-Neisse border, the future military status of Germany, and the issue of German unity in the process of European integration. Eventually the Soviet leader leaned over the table and spoke quietly. There were no differences of opinion, he said, between the Soviet Union, the Federal Republic of Germany, and the GDR about unity and the people's right to strive for it; the people had to know themselves in what direction they wanted to go; the Germans in both East and West had already proven that they had drawn their lesson from history; no war would start on German soil again.[35]

Thereafter, the atmosphere of the dialogue, which lasted for two and a half hours, became increasingly relaxed. Everyone in the room was aware that a breakthrough had been achieved. Gorbachev had agreed, at least in principle, to nothing less than the unification of Germany. Even if security considerations, the military status of a united Germany, and the border question with

Poland remained unsolved, the fact was undisputed that Germany was growing together and would soon be a united country again.

At the end of his conversation with Kohl, Gorbachev repeated his statement on German self-determination, and he did so once again when the two foreign ministers joined their chiefs. Later that night at a joint dinner, the atmosphere was cheerful, almost exuberant. Not without sarcasm, Valentin Falin said sneeringly to Vadim Sagladin that they could both retire now that the German question had been solved.

The following day the Soviet news agency TASS reported:

> Gorbachev stated—and the Chancellor agreed with him—there were at present no differences of opinion between the USSR, the FRG and the GDR that the Germans must decide about the question of the unity of the German nation themselves and must make their choice, in what forms of government, at what time, at which tempo and under what circumstances they want to realize their unification.[36]

In Germany, on Monday, February 12, Josef Riedmiller of the *Süddeutsche Zeitung* wrote about Kohl's trip to Gorbachev that "on Saturday in Moscow the Soviet state and party chief handed over the key to the solution of the German question to his guest Helmut Kohl."[37] The chancellor himself, preparing for another meeting with Modrow on February 13 in Bonn, declared he had returned from Moscow with a "green light" for the unification of Germany. Gorbachev had promised unequivocally to respect the German people's decision and had said they must determine the time and path toward unity themselves. Kohl thanked Gorbachev "for having made this historical result possible," adding that it was "a good day for Germany."[38]

It was also a good day for Kohl, as the turn in Soviet Deutschlandpolitik gave him maximum leverage in his dealings with Modrow. During their December meeting in Dresden, the East German prime minister still had had cards to play. Now, with the new election date set for March 18 and Moscow's acquiescence in unification, Modrow represented a lame-duck administration in tatters and had few defenses against the West German chancellor, who had taken to speaking for both Germanys and who had started an all-out drive for swift monetary and political unification.[39] The East German prime minister himself was totally aware of his weakness and did not expect any "concrete results." But it was too late to cancel the meeting, which had been agreed upon in December with elections then scheduled to be in May. Now it was an "odd situation," as Modrow remarked in his memoirs, of negotiations among political adversaries in the middle of an election campaign.[40]

On the eve of Modrow's trip to Bonn, the government spokesman in East Berlin, Wolfgang Meyer, noted with chagrin that Kohl had never contacted Modrow about his plans for unity.[41] In particular, the Federal government had shown no intention of releasing the DM15 billion the chancellor had pledged to East Germany in December. In Bonn, on the other hand, aides to Kohl said privately that Modrow had no illusions "that his time is up." The chancellor himself felt it necessary to lay the political groundwork for March 18 under the banner of German unity and did not want to assist the Modrow regime in any form. He did not, for example, proclaim joint national responsibility with the East German prime minister; he did not say that both German states felt an obligation to preserve peace and stability in Europe and to promote détente, as he had done with Erich Honecker during Honecker's visit in Bonn and Wiebelskirchen in 1987.[42]

Thus on February 13, Modrow and his company of 17 cabinet ministers were received by Kohl with condescension, arrogance, and disregard.[43] In the course of the day, Kohl telephoned repeatedly to Genscher in Ottawa, who was participating in an "open skies" conference of the NATO and Warsaw Pact foreign ministers and on the side was trying to arrange urgent talks of the two Germanys with the four victorious powers from World War II—the United States, the Soviet Union, Great Britain, and France—about the external aspects of German unification. In view of such international dimensions, the presence of the East German lame-duck delegation in Bonn was obviously regarded as secondary.

During the talks with Kohl, Modrow presented a paper on the position of the Round Table, referring to a "mutually complicated situation that is characterized by rapid destabilization" and demanding again a "solidarity contribution" of DM10-15 billion. The prime minister himself spoke of the GDR's impending insolvency. The chancellor, however, remained unimpressed and showed little interest in assisting Modrow's communist government. He merely pointed out that Bonn had approved technical aid from the Federal Post Office as well as some DM5-6 billion in aid and credits in a supplementary budget for 1990 to provide for the basic needs of Germans in the GDR. This demonstrated, Kohl said, that Bonn had committed itself to enabling East Germans to "stay in their home region and help forge the new economic beginning there."[44]

More important, however, the chancellor pointed to the dramatic situation in the GDR, with presumably more than 100,000 resettlers in February alone, and proposed to begin with talks among experts about a monetary and economic union as early as the following week as a first concrete step toward unification. Gorbachev had already agreed to two-plus-four negotiations about the external aspects of unification, Kohl said. Now it was up to the Germans to do their homework. The chancellor then seized the opportunity to cite Gorbachev's declaration on German unity again, adding that "under no circumstances" should the new attitude of the Soviet Union be construed "as a warrant for a national solo attempt."[45]

Modrow and some of the ministers accompanying him expressed disappointment with Bonn's rejection of the GDR's request for emergency aid. Yet they accepted the idea of preliminary talks on a monetary and economic union. Although aides to the chancellor privately admitted that Kohl had proposed these talks only because he did not want to treat Modrow as a "trustee in bankruptcy" and so there would be some "first steps" taken in the form of a commission on monetary union, the East Germans, confronted with financial insolvency, economic chaos, and political turmoil, simply had no choice.[46] Thus the critique of the opposition SPD in Bonn, comparing the chancellor with a "patronizing rich uncle who keeps his pockets closed," was as understandable morally as it was irrelevant politically.[47]

ESTABLISHING THE ECONOMIC AND MONETARY UNION

The decision to begin with talks for the establishment of a currency union between the two German states was based on the developments that began in the summer of 1989. The mass exodus of East Germans to West Germany and the rapid deterioration of the GDR had made quick steps toward economic recovery imperative. Yet the immediate impulse for Chancellor Kohl to take the initiative did not come until the late evening of February 1, 1990, when Minister President Lothar Späth of Baden-Württemberg, who had just returned from another visit in East Germany, telephoned the chancellor from Stuttgart that the GDR was "finished" and that Modrow saw "no way out anymore."[48]

The following day, Kohl deliberated with his personal advisors and several ministers in the Chancellery on a possible solution. Much to everyone's surprise, Finance Minister Theo Waigel, who in the previous week had stated that the D-mark could be introduced in East Germany only after the GDR economy underwent a long adjustment, now demanded the immediate creation of a currency union. Bonn should "go on the political offensive," Waigel said. All plans for a gradual unification had "turned into garbage."[49]

When Kohl met with Modrow at the World Economic Forum in Davos the next day (February 3), the East German basically confirmed the alarming news that Späth already had communicated. The time to begin talks on the establishment of a currency union had actually come. On February 6, the chancellor called publicly for such talks to give new hope to the East Germans and convince them not to resettle in the West. Extending the D-mark to the GDR would allow East Germans to buy the goods they wanted and help to rebuild their country. In addition, it would encourage East German enterprises to step up production and make the country more attractive to Western investors.

Bundesbank head Karl Otto Pöhl later admitted that he had been "unpleasantly surprised" by Kohl's proposal; the Bundesbank would have preferred a step-by-step process that might have taken years.[50] Even worse, however, Pöhl had discussed the matter with the chancellor and the finance minister the previous day and had received no word that such a far-reaching proposal was intended.[51] Thus on February 6, when the chancellor made his proposal, Pöhl was still skeptical about the possibility of a quick arrangement of a monetary union. After a meeting with East German state bank head Horst Kaminsky in East Berlin, Pöhl said the idea of introducing the D-mark as the currency of the GDR was "fanciful." He had observed that such a step would "surely take awhile" and that the GDR would first have to strengthen its currency and build an efficient economy. Both bankers emphasized that they considered a monetary union between the two German states to be "improbable and not feasible" in the short run.[52]

Obviously, Pöhl had been caught off guard by the chancellor. The next day, February 7, when the cabinet in Bonn decided—in addition to forming the Committee on German Unity—to offer the GDR the establishment of a currency union between the two German states, Pöhl, who was present at the meeting, also acquiesced. It was above all a political move. Finance Minister Waigel, who announced the decision after the meeting, called Bonn's offer to allow the adoption of the D-mark as the official currency in the GDR a "very decisive signal in the direction of the unity of Germany." He cited the crisis in the GDR and the continuing flow of some 2,000 East German resettlers daily into the Federal Republic as justification.[53] The head of the FDP faction in the Bundestag, Wolfgang Mischnick, told the cabinet that the situation was even more serious than the chancellor had pointed out. No one could even be sure that the Modrow government would hold out until March 18. "The D-mark," Mischnick said, "is the only perspective."[54] The cabinet consented. The faster, the better; sooner or later, the Federal Republic would have to take over the deadbeat GDR anyway. In view of such strong political pressure, the Bundesbank could only withdraw its reservations and give in.

Economics Minister Haussmann noted that if agreement on the union was reached, he expected a quick transfer of several billion D-marks into the GDR and "a new intra-German economic miracle." But he also cited complete freedom of commercial activity, recognition of private property, unlimited rights of investment, and tax and price reforms as prerequisites for a currency union. In addition, the GDR would have to accept the Bundesbank as an autonomous institution for securing monetary stability. More critically, the East Germans would need to restructure their economy, ending price subsidies and closing unproductive factories, which therefore could mean the loss of jobs in the GDR.[55]

The most important factor, however, was time—or rather, the lack of it in a rapidly developing East German scenario of economic downturns, mass exodus, and political destabilization. The newly formed Committee on German Unity, on which the Bundesbank also had a voice, therefore began working on a plan for a single German currency and a package of sweeping changes in the GDR's economy immediately.[56] And experts inside and outside the government intensified their discussion about the implications of the envisaged measures.

Most experts agreed that the crucial factor would be the rate at which the East German mark was to be exchanged for the West German mark. But some also expressed concern that the move toward a single currency would lead to a sharp rise in unemployment in the GDR and to a burst of inflation, an increase in interest rates, and larger budget deficits in West Germany. An analysis by the Deutsche Bank Group concluded on February 12:

> The unexpected swiftness of the prospect for currency union and its attendant uncertainty has given rise to market expectations of higher inflation and larger budget deficits. On balance, we think that the risk of inflationary tendencies and larger budget expenditures is real and will remain with us throughout the transitional period. However, from a logical standpoint, this scenario does not have to be the only outcome. A lot will depend on the rapid improvement of productivity in East Germany and more robust economic growth in both parts of the country, which will facilitate the economic integration process.[57]

Obviously, the decision for a monetary union between the two German states was largely a leap into the unknown. There were no precedents for comparison, since a monetary union was generally seen as the last stage of political and economic integration. Chancellor Kohl, however, had been forced by the events "to put the economic cart before the political horse."[58]

Nevertheless, the quickly established working groups in the Chancellery and in the ministries of finance, economics, and labor tried to solve the task of merging the two enormously disparate German economies and preparing for the extension of the D-mark as an all-German currency in record time.

Their goal, according to a Chancellery official, was to have "elaborated elements of the operation at hand" when Prime Minister Modrow visited Bonn in mid-February.[59]

The results virtually amounted to a complete Federal Republic takeover of the GDR. Bonn offered to accept responsibility for the GDR economy, monetary stability, unemployment, pensions, welfare, and the infrastructure, but requested that the entire West German economic order be introduced in East Germany as well. The adaptation of the GDR to the Federal system was to be sealed in a state treaty on the "establishment of a united economic and social area" in which the West German law and West German government would prevail. Thereafter, even budget decisions of the GDR parliament would be dependent upon West German consent.[60]

Thus the framework of the economic and monetary union had already been worked out when the East German delegation arrived in Bonn on February 13. Room for discussion was therefore limited, as GDR economic minister Christa Luft soon realized. She had long rejected the calls for a rapid currency union and was still seeking a multibillion-dollar aid package from West Germany instead. During the negotiations with Kohl, Waigel, and Haussmann, she now continued to insist that immediate financial aid of between DM10 and DM15 billion was more necessary to shore up the battered GDR economy than a monetary union, which would be successful only over the long term. When her request was rejected, she felt affronted.

In her memoirs, she later regretted that "the noble subject 'German unity' was thrown before the greedy animal 'election campaign.'"[61] Actually, however, events had long overtaken Professor Luft, a Marxist economist and former dean of the Hochschule für Ökonomie in East Berlin—an SED elite university. She had "hesitated too long and thought too short," the West German newsmagazine Der Spiegel noted, and was now taught a lesson by the reality of economic forces and political power play.[62]

Prime Minister Modrow, on the other hand, demonstrated greater realism when he agreed in principle to the creation of a currency union and an economic community, preliminary stages to the establishment of a united Germany. He also accepted the formation of a commission of experts, which would begin preparatory talks as soon as possible. At a joint press conference with Modrow, Kohl asserted that the introduction of the D-mark as the currency of the GDR and the conversion of the East German planned economy to a market economy was an "unusual, even revolutionary answer" to the new situation in the GDR. With the D-mark, the Federal Republic was employing its "strongest economic asset," Kohl said, adding that Bonn also wanted to ensure that Germans in the GDR were socially secure. Citing the large West German export surplus—some DM130 billion in 1989—and the country's capital export of DM100 billion annually, the chancellor maintained that the redirecting of only a small portion of these funds to the GDR could signify a strong impetus for the economy there.[63]

Simultaneously, the Economics Ministry in Bonn announced that the Federal government's extensive credit program to support business start-ups, environmental protection, and economic aid in the GDR could begin shortly. Some DM6 billion would be made available and administered through the European Recovery Plan until 1993 for such projects, with DM1.2 billion available already in 1990. A third of the total amount would come out of the Federal budget, and Bonn would finance the rest through the capital markets. For repayments, GDR-marks were to be exchanged at the East German central bank for D-marks at an exchange rate of 2.4:1.[64]

The following day, Modrow spoke with West German business leaders and agreed with the head of the Federation of German Industry (BDI), Tyll Necker, that an economic and monetary union was a single issue that could not be separated. Necker assured the GDR prime minister of West German industry's willingness to make concrete proposals for pilot projects, but he rejected unconditional financial aid. The president of the Federation of German Banks, Wolfgang Röller, said that the monetary union had to be introduced as quickly as possible, calling it the most important measure for building confidence. He also described as essential the admission of private banks in the GDR.[65]

A few days later, on February 20, Chancellor Kohl met with representatives of business and labor to ask for their support for the establishment of a monetary union and economic reforms in the GDR. After the meeting, the chancellor noted that industry, the retail sector, the trades, and banks had already initiated numerous talks, cooperation plans, and joint ventures and had undertaken concrete projects. He said that he was impressed with the willingness of the private sector to become active in the GDR.[66] President Necker of the BDI asserted that the planned monetary union would lead to a rejuvenation of the GDR and give its citizens reasons for staying; support for the union would therefore be "an excellent investment in the future." Necker again rejected unconditional emergency aid for the GDR and large-scale transfer of purchasing power, and he described as "completely unjustified" the anxiety in the GDR about the introduction of the social market economy.[67]

The Federation of German Trade Unions (DGB), on the other hand, supported the East German call for emergency aid from the Federal Republic. Although Franz Steinkühler of the Metal Trade Union had practically declared on February 9 that the GDR was finished, the head of the DGB,

Ernst Breit, said that emergency aid could be a new start, leading to tangible improvement and showing the people in the GDR "that there exist concrete prospects for them."[68] In addition, Breit called on the Federal government to assist the GDR in modernizing its infrastructure and in environmental protection, but he rejected incentives for private investments, saying that these would occur anyhow. He also predicted that West Germans would come under considerable financial strain, and that this would increase after the monetary union and national unity. He observed, however, "that German unity is worth such a burden."[69]

On the same day that the chancellor met with the business and labor representatives, the joint commission charged with working out concrete steps toward the envisaged economic and monetary union between the two German states started its deliberations in East Berlin. "We agree that we want to work swiftly," the state secretary in the West German Finance Ministry, Horst Köhler, said after initial talks with the head of the East German delegation, Minister without Portfolio Walter Romberg. The East German minister declared that social questions were at the top of his delegation's agenda, saying "there are many people in the GDR who would like clear answers." Köhler indicated that the commission would begin negotiations by taking stock of the issues under consideration. This would include the compilation of data in order to be able to resolve questions as they arose.[70]

The commission then formed subcommittees dealing with currency, economic reform, finance, and social matters. It met again behind closed doors on March 5 and March 13, reaching "progress in individual points," according to the West German Finance Ministry. Meanwhile a working group of the Bundesbank headed by Claus Köhler had prepared a submission on the details of a currency union. The paper was discussed by experts from Bonn, East Berlin, and the West German central bank at the Bundesbank building in Frankfurt's Wilhelm Epstein Street on March 2. It laid down what would happen on Day X (presumably July 1), how the conversion would be arranged, and how the "Joint Currency Area" (JCA) should be organized.[71]

Chancellery Minister Seiters noted, however, that all such discussions, including the deliberations of the intra-German monetary commission, were essentially theoretical until the East German election on March 18. Only thereafter, with the formation of a freely elected new East German government, could Bonn and East Berlin continue consultations and "come to a decision at a not yet determined date."[72]

Yet on March 13, Kohl pledged at a campaign rally in Cottbus to convert the savings accounts of small savers at a favorable exchange rate of 1:1. On the following day, he urged the cabinet to agree, thus giving the East Germans the impression that the parties representing the West German government, unlike the opposition Social Democrats, were inclined to live up to their decades-long promises of solidarity with their fellow countrymen in the East. Kohl had actually been pressed to make the announcement after an opinion poll on March 12 had predicted that the SPD would win a clear majority of 44 percent, while the Eastern CDU was lagging far behind with only 20 percent. Even worse, on the same day, the rumors were confirmed that Wolfgang Schnur, the leader of the Democratic Awakening and a prominent leader of the "Alliance for Germany," had been an "unofficial co-worker" of the GDR Ministry For State security—a revelation that would force Schnur to resign as head of the DA on March 14. Schnur's Stasi file had been examined by the Office of the District Attorney and Rainer Eppelmann, a board member of the DA.[73]

Thus Kohl's announcement, only five days before the election, of a 1:1 conversion of savings accounts can be understood as a last-minute attempt to upset the predicted outcome of the vote and to counter the impact of the Schnur affair. The chancellor brought his authority, and the financial power of the Federal Republic, into play to help his party win the election.

Whether the results would have been any different without his announcement cannot be known. But the election became a personal triumph for Kohl and provided a strong basis for the rapid implementation of the monetary and economic union that had been worked out in the days and weeks before. Now the GDR really was "finished," as Lothar Späth had prophesied on February 1, and the new GDR government of Prime Minister Lothar de Maizière was nothing more than a transitional regime—with the goal of achieving unification and unity as quickly as possible.[74]

Only two days after the election, West German interior minister Wolfgang Schäuble declared after a cabinet meeting that the currency union would be feasible by July and that at the same time the Federal Republic would abolish provisions for emergency accommodations and financial aid to GDR resettlers. The provisions, which had been in force since 1950, provided East Germans settling in the Federal Republic with payments of DM200 each in stopgap aid and low interest rates on credits as well as other social benefits. Schäuble said the cabinet was preparing itself for the introduction of the D-mark in the GDR by the start of the parliamentary recess at the beginning of July. The goal of the policy was to give East Germans hope for the future and to induce them to stay in their home regions.[75]

Before the East German election, the Bundesrat (the representation of the federal Länder) had already called for the immediate repeal of the provisions on March 16. Several of the West German state prime ministers described unbearable conditions in the resettlers' overcrowded temporary quarters. In particular, Saarland prime minister Oskar Lafontaine had asserted that the situation could not tolerate further delays and had demanded an end of payments to East German pensioners resettling in the West, cancellation of all other payments for the accommodations and integration of the resettlers, and an investing of the savings in the GDR.[76] After being named on March 19 by the SPD executive committee as the party's candidate for chancellor in the Bundestag elections scheduled for December 2, 1990, Lafontaine also appealed for a "cautious transition" to a currency union with the GDR, which required "careful preparation," he said.[77]

In this respect, Lafontaine was in full accordance with most of the financial experts of the Federal Republic. The savings deposits of GDR-marks alone that would have to be converted totalled DM162 billion. In addition, the economic situation of the GDR was very bleak indeed. A "Consolidated Balance-Sheet of the GDR Credit System as to December 31, 1989" by the East German state bank—classified "Top Secret"—exceeded even the worst expectations. The GDR's foreign debts totaled more than DM34 billion, and with credit expansion, state bank lending to state enterprises surpassed DM200 billion.[78] This meant that about 60 percent of the operations of GDR companies were being financed with borrowed money.

In view of such figures, the West German government also knew how difficult and problematic implementing a quick monetary union would be. Converting every East German savings deposit and financial claim at par would cost the Bundesbank some DM160 billion and pump up the money supply by 16 percent, while most of the East German companies, overburdened by their debt repayments in D-marks, would go bankrupt, creating unemployment and forcing the Federal government to intervene and provide stabilizing measures in order to prevent social unrest. As a result, inflation would heat up, the West German budget deficit would rise, and heavy government borrowing would drive up interest rates.[79]

Was Kohl's political promise to convert GDR-marks into D-marks at a ratio of 1:1 financially reasonable, or even technically feasible? The commentator of the *Augsburger Allgemeine* noted that:

> Apart from the fact that a general exchange of one-for-one would turn the hard Deutsche Mark into a soft currency and would heat up inflation, even the two-for-one rate is an expensive present, because the exchange rate on the free currency market is 4:1. That is the exchange rate which forms the base for intra-German business. And there is good reason for this: GDR goods, with less being produced by relatively more people, cost more to make and rarely come up to Western standards. For this reason they have

been, and will have to be, made available more cheaply. At a 1:1 rate there would no longer be any competitive capability. Factory after factory would have to close, or wages would have to be drastically lowered. Wages would then approach the social assistance level, there would be no motivation to work, and qualified people would look for better paid jobs in the West.[80]

In a letter to Chancellor Kohl, the Bundesbank board of governors thus recommended a general exchange rate of two GDR-marks for one D-mark. Its president, Karl Otto Pöhl, added on March 31 that the Bundesbank also suggested that personal savings of up to 2,000 GDR-marks be exchangeable at a rate of 1:1. He underscored that this unanimous recommendation to the Federal government was made while keeping in mind the economic competitiveness of the GDR. Pöhl observed that this represented an overall outline, which also took into account maintaining price stability in the Federal Republic. In his view, the suggested exchange rate actually meant an upward evaluation of the GDR-mark, while a 1:1 exchange rate would put too much strain on the Federal Republic, as all East German debts would then have to be paid back at that rate.[81] On April 4, Bundesbank vice president Helmut Schlesinger affirmed Pöhl, saying that the board had considered in its recommendation that the GDR debt was very high, with its banking system showing liabilities of DM460 billion, more than twice the amount of savings and circulating cash. A one-for-one rate might lead to a price-wage spiral, Schlesinger said, which the central bank could then counter only "by firmly applying monetary brakes, with consequences for economic growth and employment."[82]

Despite its firm data basis, however, the Bundesbank's recommendation sparked sharp criticism and protest in both German states. In Bonn, the opposition Social Democrats and the Greens accused government leaders of cheating the citizens of the GDR by going back on promises they made during the East German election campaign, and in East Berlin acting prime minister Hans Modrow as well as the designated new prime minister, Lothar de Maizière, called on the chancellor to come out in favor of a 1:1 exchange rate, while the board of the GDR state bank insisted on a 1:1 rate for all savings and income.[83]

The Federal government responded by saying that it had taken note of the Bundesbank recommendations and would examine them carefully but had not come to any decisions as yet, which could occur only after talks and agreement with a newly formed government in East Berlin. The schedule was to present the new government, immediately after Easter (April 15-16), with a draft of a treaty on an economic and currency union that would obligate the GDR to dismantle barriers caused by its planned economy, institute the West German mark under conditions set by the Federal Republic's central bank, and put a completely new tax system and a budget law into effect. During a cabinet meeting on April 4, the chancellor insisted that the negotiations on the economic union should be concluded by May 1, well in time for the local elections in the GDR on May 6. Everybody in the room agreed, however, that the real difficulties with the GDR would begin only after the currency union, when unemployment would rise very quickly.[84]

The chancellor himself publicly reaffirmed his goal of implementing the currency union by the summer. In an interview, Kohl predicted that if negotiations with the GDR went "relatively smoothly," it was very conceivable that "our countrymen will already have the D-mark in hand when they set out on their summer vacations." The chancellor told East Germans that he would keep his word and that Bonn would make an effort to have a 1:1 exchange rate for GDR- and D-marks for "normal savers" in the GDR.[85]

Kohl was convinced that a quick and permanent improvement of living conditions in East Germany through economic reconstruction was politically necessary for German unity to be achieved. He was also optimistic about the financial feasibility of his unification policy. This optimism was largely based on the assumption that, according to a joint report of the five leading West German economic research institutes, German economic development in 1990 and 1991 would be marked by continued stability and additional growth. The estimates of the institutes assumed 3.75 percent economic growth in 1990, and near 4 percent in 1991, with significantly reduced unemployment as an immediate result of the "unification boom" and no more than 3 percent inflation. They also expected that the growing economy would provide sufficient revenues to enable the FRG to finance economic reforms in the GDR in such areas as pensions, modernization of the infrastructure, and the clean-up of the environment.[86]

The chancellor's position was further supported by the increasing commitment of West German business in East Germany. Immediately following the announcement of an intra-German monetary union and the election in the GDR, many West German companies from all industries declared their intention of setting up joint ventures, establishing new subsidiaries with East German collective combines, or founding their own subsidiaries in the GDR. According to a count by the National Association of Chambers of Commerce in Cologne, some 1,100 such declarations of intent were agreed upon by the end of March in the automobile industry, machine building and factory installation, electronics, retail, and service industries.

Another indication that the economic development in the GDR was moving rapidly in a new direction was the transformation of state-owned enterprises into stock corporations. On April 5, VEB Kombinat Elektromaschinenbau in

Dresden became the first East German industrial combine to take that step. The new holding had stock capital of 500 billion GDR-marks, which was held wholly by a trustee agency set up to oversee the change. Despite such signs of hope, however, the five West German economic research institutes—the same centers whose data had provided for the chancellor's optimism—agreed with the Bundesbank against the conversion of the two German currencies at a general exchange rate of 1:1. According to the joint spring report of the institutes, "this apparent gift would lead in reality to the loss of many jobs in the GDR." The institutes suggested instead that only a sum of about 2,000 GDR-marks in personal savings should be exchanged at a one-to-one rate. Except for these 2,000 DM/GDR-marks, the savings could be turned into bonds, the report said, so that the East German demand for consumer goods would not outstrip the supply and thus raise the risks of inflation in the Federal Republic. GDR firms, on the other hand, needed to have their debts canceled if they were not to go bankrupt, and East German wages should be negotiated freely on a firm-to-firm basis.[87]

Thus the Federal government was under pressure from both East and West. On Sunday evening, April 22, Chancellor Kohl asked members of the cabinet and representatives of the Bundesbank to join him for talks in Bonn. In view of the events in the Baltic states, where the dispute between Lithuania and the Soviet central government over the issue of independence threatened to turn violent, Kohl stated that a period of "hoar-frost" could not be excluded. Time was running out; quick decisions were therefore necessary. If the East Germans would move too slowly, the chancellor said, he was prepared "to put the cart in front of their door."[88]

Kohl's determination to go ahead as fast as possible was boosted on April 19, when the Soviet chargé d'affaires in Bonn told his German counterpart in the Foreign Ministry that the envisaged treaty on a monetary, economic, and social union of the two Germanys would affect basic positions and interests of the Soviet Union, endanger international obligations of the GDR, and touch upon rights of the Four Powers.[89] Although the démarche was no more than a low-level diplomatic intervention in a "nonpaper form," obviously designed to remind the Germans that the Soviets expected that the Federal Republic would assume responsibility for the GDR's commitments, the move also could be interpreted as proof of the considerable attention the Soviets were paying to the question of economic unification in Germany. And without a quick decision on the issue, the danger of Soviet interference would probably increase even further.

Thus at the April 22 meeting, the Bundesbank, the Federal government, and representatives of the governing coalition of the CDU/CSU and FDP agreed on the basic outlines of a draft treaty with the GDR. The compromise set a 1:1 rate for the exchange of East German marks to D-mark for wages, salaries, and pensions, as well as for cash and savings up to 4,000 East German marks per person. Any amount over the 4,000 GDR-mark limit would be exchanged by East Germans at a rate of 2:1. The draft treaty also provided for the adaptation of GDR pensions to the West German pension system, paying retirees 70 percent of average net earnings after 45 years of employment. This represented a major increase to East Germany's 2.7 million retirees, since most GDR pensions would be higher than those formerly paid in GDR-marks. The draft did not include compensation payments for the elimination of subsidies and the implementation of a price reform in the GDR, however. Both the government and the coalition parties were in agreement that future wage policies would be of "great importance" for the competitiveness of companies in the GDR.[90]

A meeting between Chancellor Kohl and Prime Minister de Maizière to begin formal negotiations on the treaty was arranged by telephone for April 24. Since the proposal was "broadly in line" with the demands of East Germany's new coalition government, no major dispute was expected. Obviously, Bonn had decided "that the political necessity of a generous offer to the East Germans outweighed the risks of inflation," Ferdinand Protzman commented for *The New York Times,* adding that "Bonn's offer would appear to be a major advance toward the unification of East Germany and West Germany."[91]

So it was. During the meeting between Kohl and de Maizière in Bonn— the first since the East German CDU chairman had been named GDR prime minister on April 12—the two heads of government merely confirmed that the economic, social, and currency union between the FRG and GDR should go into effect on July 2. Experts from East and West Germany would begin negotiating the details the next day in East Berlin. Bonn's delegation would be led by Hans Tietmeyer, a Bundesbank director on temporary leave from his bank duties now acting as personal advisor to Chancellor Kohl on the monetary and economic union, and the East German delegation headed by Günther Krause, a state secretary in Prime Minister de Maizière's office.[92]

Yet there was very limited leeway for negotiations, although the East German SPD in de Maizière's coalition government indicated it would bargain for even better terms than those offered. The SPD-East saw problems especially with wages on the one-to-one basis without subsidies for prices. De Maizière himself noted he did not believe that the Federal government was holding more bargaining chips, but he did agree with his coalition partner that East Germany should insist on compensation payments to cushion the transition from the heavily state-subsidized GDR price system to market prices.[93]

Opinion polls in the Federal Republic showed, however, that only 19 percent of West Germans favored putting the general rate for the monetary union at one to one. Finance Minister Waigel confirmed that Bonn's offer was "at the upper limit" and that one had "to see clearly that the measure of what is economically feasible in West Germany has to be drawn into account."[94] Once again Waigel could refer to the Bundesbank, which remained critical regarding the planned currency union and saw the move as a test of German monetary stability. The central bank continued to stress the importance of limiting the risks stemming from a possible excess of money in the GDR, as the conversion would create approximately DM118 billion in new cash or liquidity assets, which would support a demand for goods and services with a nominal value of about DM236 to 240 billion in the DM2.3 trillion economy of West Germany.

On May 2, the Tietmeyer-Krause commission reached agreement that all salaries and wages, rents, pensions, scholarship funds, and certain social services would be converted at a rate of 1:1 when the currency union took effect in the GDR after July 1. The salary and wage level paid on May 1, 1990, was set as the amount to be exchanged. GDR pensions would be adapted to the system in the Federal Republic, meaning that with the currency reform most East German pensions would increase compared with their present level. For the exchange of cash and saving accounts, a three-tiered formula was established: Children up to 14 years of age would be able to exchange 2,000 GDR-marks at the rate of 1:1; people between 15 and 59, 4,000 marks; and persons over 60 years of age, 6,000 marks. Any amounts above those limits would be exchanged at a rate of 2:1. The commission also agreed that the official rate until the implementation of the currency union would be 2:1 instead of the 3:1 rate valid since the beginning of 1990.[95]

Thus the ground for the economic unification of Germany seemed to be prepared. Even the Soviet leaders were reacting more positively now, after de Maizière had assured them during a visit to Moscow at the end of April that a unified Germany would honor the GDR's trade obligations vis-à-vis the Soviet Union.[96] But several problems still remained to be solved among the Germans themselves: the financial adjustment between the "old" and "new" federal states (Länder) of a unified Germany, details of the social union, and, above all, the question of property rights and land ownership—the "decisive point" of the negotiations, according to CDU general secretary Volker Rühe. Rühe's firmness was strongly supported by Otto Count Lambsdorff, the party chairman of the FDP, who stated that there could be no currency union "without a clear recognition of private property and the introduction of a market economy."[97]

Despite such difficulties, however, the Federal government's timetable provided for cabinet consultations on the draft of the agreement to be completed by May 18 and for the first reading of the bill to be held on May 22 in the Bundestag. This tight schedule put additional pressure on the East German government to give in to the Western demands. Thus Tietmeyer could report at a meeting of the CDU party group in the Bundestag on May 8 that the GDR was likely to permit West Germans to purchase land in the GDR under certain conditions and that the negotiations therefore could be concluded by May 12.[98]

The Tietmeyer-Krause commission actually finished its work shortly before midnight on the predicted date. But various problems of the agricultural and industrial restructuring of the GDR and the issue of property rights had to be separated from the treaty and covered in subsequent agreements. One of the stickiest issues, the question of how to settle the claims of former owners of properties in East Germany and how to dispose of state-owned properties, including land and farms, was thus set aside to ensure that the currency union could take effect by the July 2 deadline demanded by Chancellor Kohl.[99]

An agreement was reached, however, between the Federal government and the 11 West German states on a package of financial support for the GDR and a unified Germany in the transitional period until 1994. The agreement of May 16 called for the creation of a DM155 billion "German Unity Fund," out of which the GDR was to receive DM22 billion in the second half of 1990 and DM35 billion in 1991. During the following three years, DM28 billion, DM20 billion, and DM10 billion, respectively, would flow to the GDR to help finance GDR budget deficits. According to Western estimates, these would come to DM31 billion for the second half of 1990 and to DM52 billion in 1991 alone. The GDR itself was expected to finance one-third of the deficits annually by borrowing.[100]

In all, Bonn was to contribute DM67.5 billion to the fund, some DM20 billion of which would come from savings incurred when the costs of German division, such as West Berlin aid and subsidies for regions near the intra-German border, were eliminated. The other DM95 billion would come from capital markets, with Bonn, the federal states, and local governments equally dividing the repayment of the principal and interest payments. A repayment period of between 20 and 30 years was expected, depending on interest rate developments.[101]

On May 17, West German finance minister Theo Waigel and his GDR counterpart, Walter Romberg, met for concluding talks on details of the Unity Fund before they eventually signed the "Treaty on the Establishment of a

Monetary, Economic and Social Union Between the Federal Republic of Germany and the German Democratic Republic"—a document that consisted of the state treaty itself, its appendixes, and several protocols—on the desk of West Germany's first chancellor, Konrad Adenauer, in the Schaumburg Palace in Bonn on May 18, 1990.[102] Chancellor Kohl and Prime Minister de Maizière attended the ceremony, which was held in the same room where the Basic Treaty—the first major treaty between East and West Germany—had been signed on November 8, 1972. "What we are experiencing is the moment in which the free and united Germany is born," Kohl said in a speech before the signing. "Germany continues to grow together. State unity has moved closer. What has to be done now is to rapidly complete it." De Maizière added that "the actual realization of German unity is beginning. The monetary, economic and social union makes the unification process irreversible."[103]

The centerpiece of the treaty was the establishment of the social market economy and the conversion of East German marks to D-mark in the GDR on July 1. Bonn and the GDR declared in the preamble of the agreement their desire "to introduce the social market economy into the GDR as the basis for the further economic and social development with social balances and safeguards and responsibility toward the environment, and thus to lastingly improve the living and working conditions of its population." The treaty also stated that the unification of the two German states could occur "forthwith" and that the GDR could join the Federal Republic in accordance with Article 23 of the Basic Law. The GDR would guarantee private property, the free establishment of prices, and the dismantling of state monopolies. It also pledged to abolish state subsidies and use the newly available funds to finance economic restructuring. The GDR would also adopt the Federal Republic's model for retirement, health, accident, and social insurance. Bonn, in turn, agreed to help balance the deficit-plagued GDR state budget for a transitional period and would temporarily subsidize the establishment of a new East German system of social benefits, which meant in effect that the GDR would lose its sovereignty in monetary matters to the Federal Republic's central bank once the D-mark became the official currency.[104]

This state treaty, which required ratification by the two German parliaments, was not undisputed, however. Herta Däubler-Gmelin, a deputy chairperson of the West German SPD, accused Chancellor Kohl of increasing the burdens and risks of unity for citizens in both parts of Germany by "hectic and wrong tactics."[105] And the executive committee of the SPD passed a resolution on May 21 to oppose the treaty until certain measures were added to provide greater social security for GDR citizens, better protection of GDR firms during the transition to a market economy, and stronger environmental

protection measures. The committee thus called for a reopening of negotiations to supplement or amend the treaty. Otherwise it threatened to block ratification in the Bundesrat, where the SPD, although in the opposition in the
Bundestag, had a majority because of recent state parliamentary election vic-
tories in North Rhine-Westphalia and Lower Saxony.[106]

In contrast to its Western sister party, the SPD in the GDR expressed support for the treaty, but protests and demonstrations by teachers, textile workers,
and farmers indicated that many East Germans expected high unemployment
to be the price of German unification. Economists predicted that many inefficient East German factories would close in the next year, unable to compete
in the free market. The number of people who registered for unemployment
had already risen from 38,313 in March 1990 to 64,948 in April 1990.
Economists now estimated that between 500,000 and 2 million East German
workers would lose their jobs by the end of 1991. The GDR minister of labor,
Regine Hildebrandt (SPD), therefore stated in an interview that she expected
"the worst."[107]

During the first reading of the treaty in the Bundestag on May 23, Finance
Minister Waigel appealed to the SPD not to gamble away the chance for
German unity. No one knows, he said, whether the reforms in the East bloc
would last and how long the "new thinking" of Soviet president Mikhail
Gorbachev would continue. SPD deputy Ingrid Matthäus-Maier, on the other
hand, stressed that the SPD had the "duty" to seek an arrangement that
reflected the will of the people of the GDR, although her party did not want
to obstruct the treaty now under consideration. She said that Chancellor Kohl
had misused the unity process to further "interests of power and party politics." The SPD's candidate for chancellor, Saarland prime minister Oskar
Lafontaine, who was recovering from wounds suffered in an assassination
attempt on April 25 in Cologne, declared in a magazine interview that most
people considered the pace of German unification to be "overly hasty, pre-
cipitous and thus wrong."[108]

In the end, however, the differences between the Federal government and
the opposition SPD were resolved. On May 29, the two sides agreed to form
groups to discuss environmental issues, measures for preventing the misuse
of the currency exchange, and aid for structural changes in the GDR economy. They also concurred that particular attention should be paid to the
problem of possible mass unemployment in the GDR. After concluding the
negotiations with the Federal government, the SPD finally decided to
endorse the treaty, although the text was left largely unchanged and although
Finance Minister Waigel rejected the use of additional funds for further measures to promote structural changes in the GDR economy. He argued suc-

cessfully that, as a result of the abundance of measures already agreed upon, "the available financial framework" was "exhausted."[109] The treaty was then ratified by the parliaments of the two German states on June 21-22 and went into effect on July 1.

ON THE ROAD TO OTTAWA

The economic unification of Germany had been negotiated and arranged largely by the Germans themselves, with little, indeed almost no, interference from outside. Yet the fact was that the establishment of a monetary, economic, and social union was only part of an extraordinary complex development. The larger question of the political and military unification of Germany aroused uneasiness and suspicion worldwide and caused leaders in both East and West to consider bringing the German unification process under some form of international control.

As early as November 14, 1989, only five days after the opening of the Berlin Wall, French president François Mitterrand called for a meeting of the 12 leaders of the European Community "to discuss the recent developments in the situation in Europe" in order to retain "some control over those changes," as French officials and analysts said in Paris.[110] After Chancellor Kohl had presented his ten-point confederation plan of November 28, Mitterrand told a group of selected French journalists that he regarded the unification of Germany as "a legal and political impossibility."[111] During a detailed talk with Foreign Minister Genscher, he maintained that a reunited Germany "as a force in its own right, uncontrolled," was unbearable for Europe; never again should there be a situation like in 1913, before the outbreak of the First World War.[112]

Mitterrand's longtime confidant Régis Debray even threatened to revive "the old Franco-Russian entente" if a reunited Germany developed too much weight.[113] And former French foreign minister Jean François-Ponçet expressed most clearly an anxiety widespread in France and other countries of Europe when he alluded to the resurrection of an "economic and political hegemony of a nation of 80 million inhabitants becoming the industrial colossus of Europe," should the two Germanys be reunited.[114]

Others also voiced their concern. British prime minister Margaret Thatcher cautioned that the growing together of the Germans "must not be rash." Italy's prime minister Giulio Andreotti spoke of a "wrong timing" of the Kohl plan. And in the Soviet Union, Mikhail Gorbachev warned "not to blow into the flames" of the reform process in Eastern Europe, while Foreign

Minister Shevardnadze said there was no country in Europe that would not view a reunited Germany as a threat to the stability of the postwar order.[115] The United States, on the other hand, reacted more positively. At a NATO Council meeting in Brussels on December 3-4 following US-Soviet summit conference at Malta, President Bush supported Germany's desire for unity, adding, however, that the unification of Germany must not disturb Washington's new constructive relationship with Moscow. Referring to Kohl's confederation plan, Bush said that "certain models" should not anticipate strict self-determination. The unification process had to be pursued in the framework of German obligations toward NATO and the EC, and it also had to take into account the rights and responsibilities of the Four Powers.[116] US secretary of state Baker, who had been "upset" when he had first heard about Kohl's solo attempt, primarily insisted that a united Germany must remain a member of NATO and that "there should be no deal of neutralism for unity."[117]

The mix of skepticism and support was repeated. While the French foreign minister Roland Dumas carefully avoided the term "German unity" in the French National Assembly on December 12, he did warn against "new fears and tensions in Europe after the lifting of the Iron Curtain" and insisted on the "inviolability of the Polish western border." On the same day in a speech at the Berlin Press Club, James Baker tried to develop elements of "a new architecture for a new age" to support German unity.[118] As early as December 15, however, all members of the North Atlantic Alliance, including France, eventually agreed to back up German unification by accepting the formula "to work for a state of peace in Europe in which the German nation will recover its unity in free self-determination."[119] With this decision, the allies adhered as much to their historical reunification promise as they yielded to the contemporary pressure of uncontrollable events and the combined resoluteness of US and West German policies.

The new course stood its first test only a week later, when President Mitterrand visited the GDR and conceded publicly that it was up to the Germans themselves to decide about their striving for unity. The idea of a contractual community was a "pragmatic approach," Mitterrand said, so long as peace and balance in Europe were maintained and the borders remained "inviolable."[120] The president's reorientation had probably also been influenced by meeting with Gorbachev in Kiev on December 6, where he had been told by the Soviet leader that it was "counterproductive to humiliate Germany." The Germans were "entitled to unity," and the time had come "to prepare the framework for a united Germany."[121]

Yet Mitterrand's East Berlin speech was an expression of an overt duplicity concerning German unification. Although the president endorsed German unification publicly, he remained cautious internally. While he obviously realized that he could not prevent German unification, he nevertheless sought to influence the development indirectly, via the negotiations of the Four Powers. In a communication to Kohl, Mitterrand insisted that Germany's neighbors and the Four Powers had a "right of say" and pronounced his readiness to negotiate with the Germans a remodeling of the Quadripartite Agreement on Berlin.[122] Franz Pfeffer, Bonn's ambassador in Paris, noted in a telegram to the Foreign Office that Mitterrand was convinced that the unification of Germany was inevitable but that he wished to direct it "into orderly channels"; many officials in the bureaucracy even tried "to act as a brake."[123] Memories of the past, national psychological resentments, and the fear of a dramatic shift of economic and political power made it obviously difficult to welcome German unification as a step in overcoming the partition of Europe and as realization of a longtime goal of Western policies.

The dichotomy of the French attitude became obvious again during a "private" meeting between Mitterrand and Kohl on January 4, 1990, at the president's country seat in Latché in the Gascogne. Mitterrand declared that two problems were interrelated, the Soviet and the German. The nationalistic elements in the Soviet Union would not yield to the German question. Gorbachev's fate would depend on it. Therefore the unification of Germany should not lead to a stiffening of the situation in the Soviet Union. Yet the greatest obstacle, Mitterrand said, was the membership of the two German states in different military pacts and the "threat of a neutralization of Germany." Thus the German and European unification should be attempted simultaneously.[124]

When Kohl responded that the Franco-German alliance, the traditionally close personal relationship between the German chancellor and the French president, and their joint commitment toward the EC would continue to be the cornerstones of his policy, Mitterrand's answer ("I shall adhere to that!") indicated how significant these elements were to him at this particular moment.[125]

For Kohl, French support for his policy was critically important. So was backing from Washington and cooperation with Moscow. Therefore he reacted instantly when, on January 8, Soviet ambassador Kvitsinsky transmitted a request by Foreign Minister Shevardnadze for food aid. With no delay, Kohl called Minister of Agriculture Ignaz Kiechle to check how much meat could be delivered in the shortest possible time. After Kiechle's response an hour later that he could provide 120,000 tons within four to six weeks, the chancellor asked immediately to prepare a national plan as well as an EC program—with priority to the national plan. The effect of German help would not only safeguard Gorbachev's position, Kohl argued, but would improve the climate for German unification as well.[126]

Yet the chancellor protested vehemently when Moscow's ambassador in Washington, Yuri Dubinin, informed Secretary of State Baker on January 10 that the Soviet Union wished to hold an early Four Power meeting regarding the proposed contractual community between the Federal Republic and the GDR. "We don't need four midwives," Kohl commented, and advised Foreign Minister Genscher to let his three Western power colleagues know that Germany's right of self-determination was at stake and that any response to the Soviet Union should occur only after closest consultation with Bonn.[127] The chancellor obviously had not forgotten the December 11, 1989, meeting, requested by the Soviets, of the ambassadors of the Four Powers in the Allied Control Council in Berlin, which had given the negative impression of reviving the former World War II coalition. Any such connection of the present situation with the unfortunate past, Kohl maintained, would inevitably discriminate against the new Germany and obstruct the settlement of current issues.[128]

The chancellor could actually afford to take such a position, as the Soviet government was rapidly running out of options. A confidential West German analysis on the state of affairs in the Soviet Union at the beginning of 1990, submitted to Kohl on January 16, estimated that Gorbachev was confronted with increasingly severe problems. The economic and social conditions in the Soviet Union continued to deteriorate; between 60 million and 100 million citizens were living close to, or below, the subsistence level; and the mood in the army and among the security forces was worsening dangerously. Thus Gorbachev's recent remark that "in the case of German unification, there will be a two-line announcement that a marshal has taken over my position" was interpreted in Bonn as a threat aimed not only at Germany.[129]

The drama of the situation was underlined the same day by another Soviet entreaty for help from Bonn. This time Kvitsinsky presented a long list of specific demands for the food aid program, and his request was more urgent than the one a week earlier. Kohl's policy advisors therefore agreed at a meeting in the Chancellery on January 17 that the Federal Republic should make "concrete proposals for comprehensive cooperation, even in the security field," and give the assurances that Moscow needed for the time after German unification.[130]

Meanwhile, the discussion in the Soviet Union was evolving as well. Influential members of the foreign policy establishment, such as Vadim Sagladin, Nikolai Portugalov, and Foreign Minister Shevardnadze, indicated privately and publicly that they—in contrast to Valentin Falin or Gorbachev's right-wing opponent, Yegor Ligachev—gradually had gotten used to the idea of German unification. Shevardnadze in particular tried to develop the framework for a uniting Europe in which the German question could be linked to the reform processes in Eastern Europe. A "European agenda," Shevardnadze argued in an *Izvestiia* article on January 22, could possibly be an acceptable way to make Germany "the core of European security."[131] Portugalov's already mentioned interview with the West German tabloid *Bild* two days later was yet another indication of the new Soviet flexibility.

Bonn reacted with chagrin and anger when British prime minister Margaret Thatcher, abandoning her prior reticence, told *The Wall Street Journal* in late January that the unification of Germany might pose "enormous problems" for Gorbachev if it came too quickly and that German unity could be realized only if all other obligations were taken into account. Otherwise, it would be destabilizing and "exceedingly unfair" toward Gorbachev. Kohl and Genscher should subordinate their "narrow nationalistic goals" to the long-term needs of Europe; it would be necessary to "drum this far-sighted vision into their heads."[132]

The chancellor was taken aback. Thatcher had never before uttered such criticism, privately or otherwise. And now such a broadside, of all places even in an American newspaper, could not remain unchallenged, the chancellor said. He asked Horst Teltschik to inform British ambassador Christopher Mallaby that he regarded the prime minister's remarks as "extraordinary unfriendly."[133]

Yet the developments in Germany left little time for grudges and resentment. On January 28, with thousands of East Germans still migrating to the West every day, leaving an economy on the verge of collapse, the Round Table in East Berlin and the GDR government agreed to advance the election date scheduled for May 6 to March 18. In Washington, this decision confirmed the view that the East German authorities were increasingly unable to maintain the internal stability of the GDR and that therefore the perspective of a unified Germany was no longer a mere possibility but a near certainty that required an immediate response.

Thus far, the US administration had been convinced that the unification process would unfold gradually and that no serious moves were necessary until the election in May. Now, with the situation changed so dramatically, President Bush began instantly—still on Sunday, January 28—to consult with his national security advisor, Brent Scowcroft, the deputy advisor, Robert M. Gates, and Robert Blackwill, the NSC director for European and Soviet affairs. The same day, Secretary of State Baker conferred with his key aides, including department counselor Robert Zoellick, director of policy planning Dennis B. Ross, and Raymond Seitz, assistant secretary of state for European Affairs. Thanks to Baker's closeness to Bush, Scowcroft's talents as a brilliant staff officer, and Blackwill's unremitting mediatorship, the three US officials became key players in managing German unification policy.[134]

Dennis Ross's Policy Planning Staff eventually produced a version of the plan that later became known as the "two-plus-four" concept. Under this formula, the two Germanys would first negotiate their economic, political, and legal unification; after that, the United States, Britain, France, and the Soviet Union would discuss with the two Germanys the external aspects of the unification process, among them guarantees for borders, the size of a unified German army, its membership in alliances, and security arrangements for Germany's neighbors.[135]

On January 29, Baker seized the opportunity to discuss the idea with British foreign secretary Douglas Hurd, who happened to be in Washington at the time. Hurd supported the two-plus-four concept, even if he had to admit that his government's first preference was "four-plus-zero"—that is, the four Allied powers getting together to discuss the fate of Germany without the Germans. But such negotiations, he declared realistically, would not be accepted by Bonn.[136]

Two days later, on February 1, Zoelleck and Ross presented the four-plus-zero plan for the first time to a German, Frank Elbe, Genscher's right-hand man in the Foreign Ministry.[137] Elbe immediately informed his boss, who met with Baker on February 2 and promptly rejected "four-plus-zero" categorically—as Hurd had predicted. The German foreign minister was also opposed to a "2-plus-15" arrangement—the two Germanys and the 15 other members of NATO—or a forum of the 35 members of the Conference on Security and Cooperation in Europe deciding Germany's future. But he liked the two-plus-four idea, although he wanted to make sure that it was two plus four, not four plus two. The two Germanys should first determine the nature of their unification on their own, before dealing with the other powers on external issues. The Federal Republic and the GDR would then also be prepared to take a common position on German policy and jointly present "the German matter" at the planned CSCE summit meeting later in the year, Genscher said. He expressed satisfaction with the US decision to support the convening of the CSCE summit only after an agreement was reached at the Vienna negotiations on the reduction of conventional military forces in Europe, which had gone on between the NATO and Warsaw Pact countries since March 1989. An agreement in Vienna could be achieved by June or July and the CSCE summit held by October or November, the West German foreign minister predicted.[138]

Genscher's approach to anchor German unification in a set of international arrangements was confirmed by Chancellor Kohl in a speech to the World Economic Forum in Davos, Switzerland, on February 3. Kohl emphasized that German unity could take place only by free self-determination, within the framework of the CSCE and on a foundation of the negotiations on disarmament and arms control. The use of such a framework would be the best way to take the security interests of other countries in both East and West into account, Kohl said. The chancellor rejected the idea of German neutrality, however, calling it "contrary to the logic of the process of pan-European unification." "A united Germany in the heart of Europe should not have any special status which would isolate it," Kohl declared. The Federal Republic "unswervingly" supported NATO and would "remain firmly anchored in the European Community."[139]

Noting that the prospect of a united Germany aroused misgivings among some people in East and West, the chancellor also pointed out that the Federal Republic had proven itself to be a "stable, free and democratic state based on the rule of law and social justice" over the previous 40 years and had been a "predictable and reliable ally." Bonn had "from the beginning placed its national objective—the freedom and unity of all Germans—into the larger European framework" and had been a "resolute champion" of European union and the CSCE process and an advocate of disarmament and arms control. That would not change. The unified Germany would also be "a trustworthy partner in the task of building a peaceful order in Europe." In fact, Europe would be "every German's future."[140]

By stressing the stabilizing aspects of an international framework for the German unification process, Kohl and Genscher tried to dispell concerns that a united Germany could one day return to former aspirations of expansionism and hegemony. German support of the US two-plus-four idea was as much part of this approach as the German agreement to negotiations on various levels was instrumental to the success of the American concept.

The extent to which Bonn's reassurance policy was really working, however, remained to be seen. Secretary Baker began a trip to Eastern Europe and the Soviet Union on February 5 to further boost the two-plus-four idea. During a brief layover next morning at Shannon Airport, Ireland, where he met at 5:00 A.M. with French foreign minister Dumas for a one-hour talk scheduled at the last minute, Baker found out that the French too supported the US formula. Like his British counterpart Douglas Hurd a week before, Dumas stated that the French government also would have preferred four-plus-zero. But in view of the strong German position, he would sign on to two-plus-four as well.[141]

In Moscow, President Gorbachev's response proved to be less decisive. When informed about the US concept by Baker at the huge table in the Kremlin's Catherine Hall on February 7, he indicated that he shared the British and French preference for four-plus-zero, but refused to accept two-plus-four at the time. Thus Baker left Moscow for Bulgaria and Romania without a clear Soviet answer. Before he departed, however, he drafted the three-page "For-Your-Eyes-Only" letter to Chancellor Kohl, laying out his own arguments as well as Gorbachev's reactions, that Klaus Blech handed over on February 10.[142]

Kohl already had been informed about the French and British approval of the US plan. Now he learned from Baker's letter that Gorbachev had called this proposal "conceivable" but had not been willing yet to commit himself to the plan.[143]

Thus equipped with information about the positions of the various governments, the chancellor underlined in his own talk with Gorbachev Baker's point that the two-plus-four concept was "a good idea." On the other hand, Kohl said, he could not agree to a conference of the Four Powers on Germany—causing the Soviet leader to proclaim: "Nothing without the Chancellor."[144] Kohl and Gorbachev concurred, however, that the unification of Germany should be "embedded" in the pan-European architecture and the overall process of East-West relations.

At a press conference after the meeting with Gorbachev, Kohl proclaimed himself optimistic about the two-plus-four formula. Both German governments would meet after the March 18 elections to reach an agreement on unity, the chancellor said. They would then confer on the matter with the Four Powers before dealing with it at the planned CSCE summit in the autumn. Kohl admitted that there were still differences of opinion between Bonn and Moscow with regard to possible German neutrality. Moscow had noted, however, that for the Federal Republic, such a status was out of the question. Both sides agreed that the membership of the two German states in different military alliances would have to be discussed in close coordination with the US, Great Britain, and France and that a solution would have to be found jointly.[145]

Foreign Minister Genscher, who accompanied Kohl to Moscow, also indicated after talks with Shevardnadze that the Federal Republic was seeking a conference of the two German states with the four victorious Allied powers to discuss the consequences of German unity for Europe and the question of the alliances. The meetings would be held as soon as possible after the East German elections. The results would be put to the CSCE, whose members included virtually all European nations, the United States, and Canada.[146]

The discussion on the two-plus-four issue was expected to continue at a conference of the NATO and Warsaw Pact foreign ministers in Ottawa on Tuesday, February 13. The meeting had been convoked to negotiate an "open skies" agreement (under which each of the two alliances would each allow reconnaissance flights over its territory by the other) and would provide an ideal opportunity for backstage arrangements, as all key players from both East and West—Baker, Genscher, Hurd, Dumas, and Shevardnadze—would be present.

The US, German, British, French and Soviet foreign ministers, who were supposed to be discussing the open skies proposal, in fact spent much of their time in Ottawa focusing on the two-plus-four question; most of their colleagues from the other NATO and Warsaw Pact countries did not have a clue as to what they were dealing with. The proposed language of the envisaged two-plus-four arrangement was hammered out during an early-morning breakfast among Baker, Hurd, Dumas, and Genscher at the West German embassy in Ottawa. From that breakfast, the foreign ministers drove back to a full session of the conference. There Baker walked over to Shevardnadze with a piece of paper in his hand and whispered the text the Western allies had just agreed upon, reading from the paper written in his own longhand. The translator scribbled it all down in Russian for Shevardnadze, who merely responded that he would have to call Gorbachev.[147]

Two hours later, Shevardnadze and Baker met again in a private conference room. The Soviet foreign minister informed his American colleague that Gorbachev supported the idea but that he needed some changes in the text. Meanwhile, President Bush, who was aware that Kohl and Genscher occasionally did not tell each other what they were doing, conducted his own telephone diplomacy from Washington, speaking twice with the chancellor to personally make certain that Kohl approved of the deal Genscher was striking with Baker and the other foreign ministers at Ottawa. Only after the chancellor had told the president that he agreed did Bush give Baker his green light.[148]

The new language was approved after intense consultations among the six governments involved, and the two-plus-four announcement was released. Members of the press received the news before most of the NATO and Warsaw Pact ministers. The Dutch, Italians, and Belgians were particularly incensed. They were told, however, "in no uncertain terms," as one US administration official said, "that this was a matter for the Allied powers with legal rights in Germany and nobody else."[149]

THE "TWO-PLUS-FOUR" NEGOTIATIONS

The Ottawa declaration of February 13, 1990, stated that the four victorious powers from World War II—the United States, the Soviet Union, Great Britain, and France—and the two Germanys would jointly work out "the external aspects of the establishment of German unity, including questions of the security of neighboring states."[150] The foreign ministers of all six countries would meet on the matter, and preliminary discussions of their political directors would begin soon.[151]

West German foreign minister Hans-Dietrich Genscher noted in addition that the declaration marked the first time that the Four Powers had supported the phrase "establishment of German unity," which originated in the Federal Republic's Basic Law. "That is something other than a confederation," he said.[152]

Genscher also declared that the representatives of NATO and the Warsaw Pact at the Ottawa conference had agreed to Bonn's proposals for the convening of a CSCE summit meeting later in the year and for the continuation without interruption of negotiations in Vienna after the successful conclusion of a first agreement there on conventional disarmament. This would have "far-reaching effects" on the strength of the Federal Republic's armed forces if the indigenous armed forces of countries with foreign troops of NATO and the Warsaw Pact on their soil were included, Genscher said. Negotiations after "Vienna I" should continue immediately so that disarmament would keep pace with the political changes in Europe.[153]

By emphasizing a possible limitation of the size of the German Bundeswehr, Genscher referred to one of several important questions that the two-plus-four would have to deal with during their negotiations. Other issues were the future military status of a united Germany; the withdrawal of the 380,000 Soviet troops stationed in East Germany; security assurances for Germany's neighbors, possibly in the "European framework" of the CSCE; the final recognition of the Oder-Neisse as the western border of Poland; and the dissolution of Four Power rights and the establishment of German sovereignty.

Neutrality or NATO Membership?

The discussion on the future military status of Germany had been intense even before Ottawa: Should a united Germany become neutral or remain a member of NATO? Would any forces be deployed on the territory of what was still the GDR? And what would be the overall troop level in the united country? The US administration adhered to the principle that the unification process should occur "in the context of Germany's continued commitment to NATO"[154]—whatever that meant—while the Soviet leadership agreed with the concept of GDR prime minister Modrow that a united German "fatherland" should be neutral and not be a member of either NATO or the Warsaw Pact.[155] In between the two positions, West German foreign minister Genscher had proposed in a speech at the Evangelic Academy in Tutzing, Bavaria, on January 31 that a united Germany should remain in NATO, but that NATO troops would not be stationed on East German territory once the GDR and the Federal Republic were merged, so that the West would not gain a military advantage from German unification.[156]

Yet all these positions appeared to be in flux, as most governments previously had dealt with German unification only in the abstract and had not considered any specific concept in detail. The American thinking also was still open to new proposals at this time, although Secretary of State Baker had been rather firm in his Berlin speech on December 12 in formulating certain criteria under which the United States would back unification, including the provision that Germany remain a member of NATO and the West European institutions. In this respect, the Genscher plan of January 31 had been characterized in Washington as "a very positive contribution" and a "pretty good effort" to bridge the differences between the Eastern and Western approach to the problem, whereas Soviet and East German demands for a neutral Germany were rejected categorically.[157]

The US position was supported by West European as well as several East European governments. They also preferred a united Germany to be firmly anchored in some alliance structure, largely because they were wary of a neutral Germany emerging as an economic and political powerhouse in the center of the continent. Czechoslovak president Vaclav Havel specifically told Baker on February 6 in Prague that he opposed a neutral Germany and that he would so tell Gorbachev as well when he met the Soviet president later in the month.[158] Poland's foreign minister, Krzysztof Skubiszewski, also shared this view when he remarked during a meeting with Chancellor Kohl in Bonn on February 7: "I cannot win anything from neutrality. For us Poles, the binding of Germany is imperative."[159]

But in Ottawa, it was still too early to solve the question, as the Soviets were not ready yet to agree to a united Germany integrated in the West. Foreign Minister Shevardnadze accepted German unification as inevitable but tried to evade the issue of continued NATO membership by referring to a "European solution."[160] Europe should move quickly to demilitarize itself and lock a greater Germany into a new "pan-European" political structure for its own safety, Shevardnadze said, adding that:

> No one doubts the right of Germans to self-determination. But Germany's neighbors, the European states, are entitled to guarantees that a united Germany, if and when established, will not be a threat to them, that it will not seek to revise European borders and that it will not see a rebirth of Nazism and Fascism.[161]

The Soviet foreign minister warned against rushing German unification, saying it should not be "a political game of rapid chess with a five-minute time limit for each move," and asked the 35 nations of the Conference on Security and Cooperation in Europe to devise "political approaches to the new trends in Europe."[162]

The CSCE idea was also endorsed by some Western foreign ministers. The British foreign secretary, Douglas Hurd, said in Ottawa that "as the Warsaw Pact disintegrates, the East Europeans need somewhere to go. NATO and the European Community are not suitable, but a strengthened CSCE seems right." Similarly, Genscher called for the creation of "pan-European institutions to foster the coalescence of Europe within the CSCE framework," including bodies to guarantee human rights, protect the environment, and resolve conflicts. And Italian foreign minister Gianni De Michelis even circulated proposals for a "second Helsinki Act" that would create a single European security system with provisions that would gradually become legally binding on the nations that signed.[163]

Yet the retreat to the CSCE scheme as a new security structure spanning both NATO and the Warsaw Pact was more a long-term vision than a short-term solution. As long as such a structure did not exist, Germany was likely to remain a member of the North Atlantic Alliance, with its army firmly tied to NATO's command system. The real question therefore was how the Soviet Union could be convinced that a united Germany within NATO would be safer than a united Germany outside the alliance, and what guarantees could be given that an even more powerful NATO would not misuse its additional strength to endanger the security of the East.

After the Ottawa meeting, most Western foreign policy experts agreed that the Kremlin would not insist on neutrality for a united Germany, though in public it said it would.[164] As early as on February 15, an "authoritative Communist Party official" in Moscow conceded that demilitarized neutrality for a reunited Germany was no longer the Soviet bottom line. "We have lost our ability to exploit German domestic politics," he admitted. "We no longer have time for a long-term foreign policy strategy."[165]

As Czechoslovakia, Hungary, and Poland were all eager to see the Soviet forces leave their countries soon, the pressure on the Soviet Union was actually mounting to reach an agreement with the West on troop withdrawals from Central Europe as quickly as possible. In addition, the Soviet leadership was no longer confronted with the collapse of the Soviet empire in East Germany and Eastern Europe alone, but was increasingly experiencing the disintegration of the Soviet Union itself. After the Central Committee of the CPSU had voted on February 7 to change Article 6 of the Soviet Union's constitution to give up the party's constitutional monopoly on power, criticism of the party had already become surprisingly open. Uncontrolled mass demonstrations had begun to rock the streets of Moscow; in Azerbaijan, Tadzhikistan, and Armenia, ethnic strife and bloodshed occurred.[166] It seemed questionable, therefore, whether the Soviet leadership would be able to maintain its position that a reunited Germany could not be part of NATO, as Gorbachev had also told East German prime minister Modrow in a telephone conversation on February 12, one day before Modrow's visit to Bonn.[167]

In the Federal Republic, in any case, speakers for both the parties of the governing coalition and the opposition SPD confirmed during a foreign policy debate in the Bundestag on February 15 that they rejected neutrality or demilitarization for a future united Germany. Chancellor Kohl in particular warned against any attempts to take a "special German path," stating that the history of the 20th century showed that nothing was "more detrimental to the stability of Europe than a Germany swaying between the two worlds, between East and West." Just the opposite was true, Kohl said. Germany in a firm alliance with free democracies and in increasing political and economic integration in the EC would be "the indispensable factor for stability which Europe needs in its midst." Therefore Germany should remain anchored in NATO and the EC, the chancellor stressed, adding that he was in accordance with President Bush that no NATO installations or troops should be stationed on the soil of what was still the GDR.[168]

Such agreement did not exist with regard to another important question, however: the definite recognition of the Oder-Neisse line as the western boundary of Poland.

The Border Question with Poland

The issue had come up as early as the summer of 1989, when the right-wing Republican Party gained 7.5 percent of the votes in local elections in West Berlin and 7.1 percent in the election for the European Parliament (its best result, 14.6 percent, was in Bavaria). To prevent further such successes, conservative politicians argued that the former German territories east of the Oder and Neisse rivers would have to be included if the German question were on the agenda again in the process of the transformation of Europe. This argument, however, elicited a clarifying statement by Foreign Minister Genscher, who, obviously afraid that a new discussion on the Oder-Neisse line would be detrimental to the international position of the Federal Republic, had told the United Nations in September 1989 that the Polish people should know "that its right to live within secure borderlines will not be put in question by us Germans through territorial claims, either now or in the future."[169]

The Bundestag also took up the issue, passing a resolution on November 8 approving of Genscher's statement, even using the foreign minister's own wording.[170] Chancellor Kohl, on the other hand, failed to repeat the guarantee during his official visit to Poland one day later. He remained consistent during the following weeks and months in defending his idea that the decision on the finality of Poland's western border was not an issue for the West German parliament and government, but rather for a parliament and government representing all of Germany.[171]

Even after Ottawa, the chancellor declined to state unequivocally that the Oder-Neisse line would be permanent and that a reunited Germany would renounce any claims to prewar German territory now under Polish control. In a long telephone conversation with Polish prime minister Tadeusz Mazowiecki on February 23, as well as after weekend talks at Camp David with President Bush on February 24-25, Kohl repeatedly stressed that he had no intention of demanding any changes in the existing borders. But he also said that he could not make binding commitments about the German-Polish boundary either, since this could only be done by "a freely elected all-German Government and a freely elected all-German Parliament."[172]

President Bush and his administration, though unhappy about Kohl's evasiveness, could only accept the chancellor's position. They realized that his ambiguity on the issue was driven not by ideological attachment to the former German territories of Silesia, Pomerania, and East Prussia but by domestic political concerns regarding the upcoming national election on December 2; a considerable number of voters, particularly those whose families had been expelled from the areas east of the Oder-Neisse line, might be attracted to the Republican Party if he appeared to sign away these lands too quickly. "Our assessment is that Kohl personally understands full well that the Polish-German border cannot be changed and will not," one US official said after the Kohl-Bush meeting. "He is a man who is facing a close election and is concerned that if he adopts a totally unambiguous stance, he is going to have some critical votes siphoned off."[173]

In Poland, however, Kohl's continuous policy of avoiding a clear-cut statement on the border issue provoked criticism from the media and caused the government in Warsaw to launch a concerted diplomatic drive for a place at the conference table of the two-plus-four negotiations. The campaign, described by government spokeswoman Malgorzata Niezabitowska as "extraordinary measures," started on February 21 with a proposal by Prime Minister Mazowiecki to negotiate and initial a treaty with the two German states guaranteeing secure borders immediately after the East German elections on March 18. The treaty "corresponding to a peace treaty" should then be signed and ratified by the united German governmental and parliamentary bodies after unification. In addition, Mazowiecki wrote a letter to the Four Powers, asking for Poland to receive "an own voice and an own place" at the two-plus-four negotiations, and he devoted an entire news conference to the issue.[174] Eventually, President Jaruzelski also became involved in the campaign when he met with the Soviet ambassador Vladimir I. Brovikov and coined the slogan "Nothing about us without us."[175]

In the Federal Republic, Mazowiecki's suggestion for a German-Polish declaration of will was supported by the opposition Social Democrats and by Foreign Minister Genscher, who said that such a declaration was "not only feasible, but necessary." However, Genscher rejected the prime minister's demand for Polish participation in the two-plus-four talks.[176] Other leaders in both East and West also put pressure on Kohl to modify his position. In the United States, for example, several Democratic Senators insisted that it was time for the chancellor "to put the border issue to rest once and for all."[177]

But although the chancellor expressed "much understanding for the Polish wishes" at a cabinet meeting on February 28, he said he was unable to meet the expectations for legal reasons. If anything, he could only agree to joint resolutions of the Bundestag and the new East German parliament after March 18 to reassure Poland that Germany would make no territorial claims on it now or in the future.[178] Kohl's stubbornness therefore appeared to be infinite, although privately he admitted that in view of the external and internal constraints he would have "to move further," even if he did not want to do so.[179]

Foreign Minister Genscher and FDP chairman Lambsdorff now publicly distanced themselves from the chancellor's position on the issue, while SPD chairman Vogel said Kohl's equivocation was "increasingly damaging to German interests." French foreign minister Dumas lamented that there were "moments where silence is full of ambiguity."[180] As a result of such "international pressure scenery"—to use Kohl's own characterization of the situation, which he regarded to be primarily an expression of general uneasiness about German unification—the government coalition in Bonn eventually agreed to a joint resolution on the Oder-Neisse question in the Bundestag on March 8. Kohl strongly supported the text and was extremely satisfied when the resolution passed with only five abstentions and no negative votes.[181]

While Prime Minister Thatcher spontaneously called the resolution "a highly statesmanlike step" that would be very useful, President Mitterrand said the French position required guarantees that went considerably beyond the declaration. He insisted on the conclusion of a German-Polish border treaty "before the expected unification of the two German states" and agreed with President Jaruzelski and Prime Minister Mazowiecki during their visit to Paris on March 10 that Poland also should participate in the two-plus-four negotiations.[182]

The new Franco-Polish alliance did not prove to be very effective. Only one day later, the West German government was informed by US senator Richard Lugar of Indiana that the Senate had withdrawn a resolution on the Polish border that would have been directed against the Federal Republic but had become meaningless after the Bundestag resolution on the issue. Senator Lugar also suggested that the Polish government was forcing Germany's friends to choose between Poland and the Federal Republic. If so, in the case of the United States, the choice was clear.[183]

In addition, Chancellor Kohl, at first disturbed about Mitterrand's attitude, quickly took the offensive himself. In two long telephone calls with the president of the Commission of the European Community, Jacques Delors, on March 13 and with Mitterrand on March 14, the chancellor announced that he was now going to accelerate the unification process and that he expected the allies "not to hide if a storm comes up." Simultaneously, Horst Teltschik called James Baker in the State Department and Robert Blackwill in the White House to inform the US administration that the Federal Republic was opposed to Poland's participation in the two-plus-four negotiations and that no formal German-Polish treaty on the border issue was possible before unification. After detailed consultations with the French government, Kohl talked with President Bush on March 17 to make sure that Bonn and Washington were speaking the same language and would pursue the same tactics. No dissent occurred.[184]

The outcome of the March 18 election in the GDR further strengthened the chancellor's position. When President Bush congratulated Kohl on his party's victory, he also let him know that he would tell Mazowiecki in Washington the following day that he trusted the West German government and that the Polish prime minister should do the same.[185] The Poles soon concluded that their demand to participate fully in the two-plus-four negotiations could no longer be realized. On March 26, Foreign Minister Skubiszewski agreed with Genscher that the Oder-Neisse border was a German-Polish matter and that therefore a settlement by the Four Powers was inappropriate. In addition, Poland dropped its insistence on a two-plus-four meeting in Warsaw.[186]

Security Guarantees within NATO

The election in the GDR caused the governments in Paris and Moscow to modify their policy too. The French, obviously worried that the Federal Republic might waver in its commitment to the EC, now even pressed the

West Germans to swallow the GDR as quickly as possible and again focus attention on European integration. Foreign Minister Dumas noted that it would be best for "East Germany's provinces" to be incorporated in the Federal Republic to avoid "the complicated negotiation of absorbing a thirteenth state into the community." The EC should act to prevent the process of integration from becoming bogged down as a result of German unification, Dumas said.[187] And Mitterrand's foreign policy advisor, Jacques Attali, informed Kohl that the French were now working "at high pressure" on an EC initiative to promote a European Political Union in order to embed German unification into the integration of Europe.[188]

Meanwhile, Soviet foreign policy experts indicated that Moscow eventually would compromise on its demand that a united Germany be neutral. President Gorbachev had still flatly rejected the idea of a united Germany's NATO membership in an interview on West German television as late as March 8, saying that "we will not agree to that. This is absolutely ruled out."[189] Only one day after the East German election, however, the CPSU Central Committee advisor on German affairs, Nikolai Portugalov, declared that NATO membership for a united Germany was "unacceptable right now," but that this was only Moscow's "starting position in the two-plus-four negotiations."[190] Vyacheslav I. Dashichev, a senior associate of the main Soviet research institute dealing with Eastern Europe, even went a step further when he stated in an interview with the West German daily *Die Welt* on March 20: "You have to bind a united Germany into the framework of NATO. . . . There is the image of a cannon not being fixed to the deck of a ship, and some people compare a neutral Germany to such a cannon."[191]

Portugalov's and Dashichev's statements reflected a major weakening of the Soviet position after a meeting of the Warsaw Pact foreign ministers in Prague on March 17. Gyüla Horn of Hungary, Jiri Dienstbier of Czechoslovakia, and Krzysztof Skubiszewski of Poland candidly expressed their opinion that they would not be opposed to NATO membership of a united Germany. And the election of March 18 in the GDR had provided for an additional "very substantial push" in that direction, Secretary of State Baker said after talks with Genscher and Shevardnadze at the Namibian independence ceremonies in Windhoek on March 22. Moscow now seemed to be searching for security guarantees on the basis of Germany's continued integration in the NATO structure, and the West could be confident of achieving its goal of keeping Germany in the alliance.[192]

It therefore was all the more surprising when, on the following day, in an address at a meeting of the Western European Union in Luxembourg, Genscher called on NATO and the Warsaw Pact to "establish cooperative security structures aimed at strengthening military security" and then to "transform these cooperative structures into an interlocking system of mutual collective security."[193] With these statements, Genscher went far beyond his January 31 proposal not to extend the NATO structure into East Germany. His new initiative questioned the alliances as such—at least in their present form. Commentators immediately interpreted it as a signal for the dissolution of the Warsaw Pact and NATO alike.

Chancellor Kohl was furious. He instantly let his foreign minister know that he did not share his views and that he would not allow the Federal government to be committed by statements that he could not support.[194]

There was in fact more behind this controversy than misleading language resulting from "visionary thinking." True, Genscher was as determined to maintain Germany's ties with the West as Kohl.[195] But the real question was whether Moscow could be convinced that continued German membership in NATO would neither violate Soviet security interests in the short run nor exclude reforms of the security structure in the long term. In this respect, Genscher was far less uncompromising than Kohl. His attempt at developing a common East-West security philosophy apart from the existing alliances was intended to provide a face-saving solution to address general Soviet security concerns, thus corresponding favorably with Shevardnadze's plan to strengthen the security aspects of the CSCE.[196]

The search for security guarantees prompted another visit by Portugalov to Bonn. On March 28, he indicated that the statements he had to make had been reconciled with Gorbachev's advisor Anatoly Chernayev—which had not always been the case in the past—and thus represented the official view of the Soviet leadership. Portugalov frankly declared that it would be necessary to obtain written guarantees on Germany's future military status and that a united Germany within NATO would not be directed against the Soviet Union. Therefore, it was imperative for Moscow to find out if the Federal Republic would remain part of NATO's integrated military structure and what would happen with the tactical nuclear weapons now deployed in West Germany. The Soviet Union proceeded from the assumption that a united Germany would continue to renounce weapons of mass destruction and adhere to the Non-Proliferation Treaty (NPT). In addition, the size of the German army would have to be reduced.[197]

Portugalov's statements indicated that the leadership in Moscow was now actually looking for solutions on the basis of continued German membership in NATO and that the position of the Soviet Union on the security issue had become very flexible indeed. As a matter of fact, Portugalov did not even mention the term "neutrality" this time.

In preparation for the first round of the two-plus-four negotiations on May 5 in Bonn, Chancellor Kohl therefore felt strong enough to specify the German demands with regard to the alliance question. In a meeting with Foreign Minister Genscher and Defense Minister Gerhard Stoltenberg on April 2, Kohl insisted that

1. Articles 5 and 6 of the NATO Treaty, the so-called protection clauses, should be valid for the whole of a united Germany.
2. A date should be fixed for the withdrawal of the Soviet forces from East Germany.
3. Bundeswehr troops should be stationed in all of Germany, and conscription also should be applied to the entire country.[198]

Simultaneously, Boris Meissner, a senior German expert on the Soviet Union, suggested offering Moscow a comprehensive bilateral treaty on cooperation and the renunciation of force. Negotiations on the issue would begin shortly, well before German unification, to demonstrate that Germany would continue to consider the key relevance of German-Soviet relations and would remain an important Soviet partner.

On April 23, Kohl explained the idea to Ambassador Kvitsinsky. He intended to work out a "charter of cooperation with the Soviet Union in the sense of the great historical tradition," the chancellor said. Preparations could start immediately. In the course of the negotiations, the obligations of the GDR toward the Soviet Union should also be "worked up" and then be included into a "far-reaching perspective" of German-Soviet cooperation after unification. Looking forward, Kohl said that by the time he left the Chancellery he would like to have reached two goals: that the train toward European integration should have become unstoppable by then and that the best possible relations should have been established between Germany and the Soviet Union.[199]

Kvitsinsky indulged in euphoria, too. Ever since he had come to Germany, it had been his dream to create something between Germany and the Soviet Union "in the sense of Bismarck," he said. The treaty Kohl now proposed was absolutely compatible with the thinking of President Gorbachev. At the two-plus-four negotiations, the Soviet Union was mainly interested in a reduction of the size of the German army, a corresponding decrease in the forces of the Four Powers, and addressing the issue of US nuclear weapons on German territory. But all this, as well as the question of the Polish western border, could be settled at the forthcoming negotiations. It could all be done.[200] No word again about the neutralization of Germany, no exclusion of German NATO membership.[201]

Thus the perspective of a unified Germany in NATO appeared to be almost a certainty as the first ministerial meeting of the two-plus-four on May 5 in Bonn neared, where the talks would quickly come down to the Soviets asking the Western powers what economic and security incentives they would grant Moscow in return for the expeditious withdrawal of the 380,000 Soviet troops from East Germany. The Soviets were not expected to try to prevent German unification altogether—it was far too late for that—but they could drag their feet until they were satisfied that arrangements for a united Germany would be militarily and politically acceptable. The question therefore, as a US administration official said, was how to "make it digestible for the Soviets" to accept the "inevitable outcome sooner rather than later."[202]

The idea in Washington was to present a package of initiatives that would be discussed only informally in the two-plus-four talks and then delegated to the relevant negotiating forums, where they would actually be addressed: For example, the Soviets and Germans would:

1. Work out a troop reduction arrangement for the German forces as part of the Conventional Forces in Europe (CFE) talks in Vienna, while the Soviets would be allowed to maintain their troops in East Germany for a fixed transition period, as would the Western powers in Berlin.

2. The united Germany would reaffirm East and West Germany's promises never to obtain nuclear, chemical, or biological weapons and would formally confirm the Oder-Neisse line as its eastern border with Poland.

3. Negotiations would begin soon to eliminate all or most US- and Soviet-controlled short-range nuclear missiles, and perhaps artillery shells with nuclear warheads, from Germany and Eastern Europe.

4. West Germany would reassure the Soviets that all of the contracts they had with East German industries would be assumed by a united Germany, and Bonn also would strongly hint to Moscow that if it played along on two-plus-four, generous economic aid would follow, including help to subsidize the cost of maintaining Soviet troops in East Germany for the transitional period.

5. Finally, the CSCE would be given an expanded and formalized role for conflict resolution and intra-European dialogue for its member states, so that after a united Germany joined NATO—and the Warsaw Pact faded away—the Soviets and East Europeans would remain structurally integrated in a common institution.[203]

When the North Atlantic Council gathered in Brussels for its regular spring session on May 3, NATO secretary general Manfred Wörner said there was unanimous accord that a united Germany should be a full member of NATO.

NATO's military forces, though, would not be expanded into the territory that was currently East Germany, limiting the immediate negative military consequences German unification and membership in NATO would have for the Soviet Union. Soviet troops would be allowed to remain in East Germany after unification for an unspecified transitional period to ease Moscow's security concerns. On the other hand, Wörner said, Germany should not be subjected to "discriminatory regulations" that restricted its armed forces over and above any reductions negotiated at the Vienna conventional arms talks. Any concerns the Soviets or other Europeans felt about the size of the German army could be addressed in NATO-Warsaw Pact conventional arms talks, and not by singling Germany out for special treatment.[204]

The NATO ministers also approved President Bush's decisions to cancel plans for the deployment of a new generation of more accurate and powerful short-range "Lance" missiles and newer artillery in Germany and to advance the timetable for opening negotiations with the Soviet Union about reducing or eliminating short-range nuclear armaments in both parts of Europe.[205] In addition, the ministers expected that a united Germany would renounce the possession of nuclear, chemical, and biological weapons, as both East and West Germany already had done individually. They also slated for discussion at the upcoming London NATO summit meeting ways of transforming the NATO military alliance into a more political organization, thus furthering the acceptability of united German membership to its neighbors in both East and West. President Bush and Prime Minister Thatcher had already agreed to such an "early NATO summit" during their talks in Bermuda the previous month. At the summit meeting, the all-German NATO membership, the conventional and nuclear US presence in Europe and the future strategy of the alliance also would be discussed.[206] Summarizing the logic of NATO's strategy on Europe and Germany, US secretary of state Baker now added after the meeting at the alliance's headquarters in Brussels that it was crucial "there be no image of winners and losers in this process."[207]

The US administration was afraid, however, that NATO might relinquish its primacy as the West's binding political and military force. "We do want to remain a European power," a senior administration official said in Washington on May 3,

> but the question is how do you do that when the only institutional voice of the United States right now in Europe is NATO. As the importance or the salience of the military role of NATO declines, will NATO tend to atrophy as a vehicle for discussion of political issues that affect the Atlantic community? That is what the United States is looking out for now.[208]

President Bush's new arms proposals and the planned NATO summit were thus US attempts to manage the transition in Europe without a decline of America's position. The decision to forgo the modernization of short-range nuclear missiles and nuclear artillery systems stationed in Germany was of particular significance in this respect. While it could be understood as a concession to the Soviet Union, it also helped to ease relations with Bonn, for the Germans had already rejected US plans for sending new nuclear weapons. Insisting on pushing the plan therefore would have been likely to undercut Washington's ties with Bonn and diminish its role in the German unification process.[209]

Accordingly, the July 5-6 NATO summit in London was designed to solve major problems deriving from the dramatic changes in Europe and especially in Germany. Secretary General Wörner stated in this respect after a council meeting of the alliance in Brussels on May 3:

> Today's special meeting begins a series over the next two months which allow us to define the future tasks of our alliance, develop ideas for a future security structure of Europe, prepare membership of a united Germany in NATO and adjust our alliance policies and strategies to changing circumstances. This will be a very decisive moment in the history of our alliance.[210]

Essentially four subjects were expected to be considered in this "series" of deliberations within the alliance: how NATO's political role could be enhanced; what conventional forces the alliance would need, given the Soviet pullback and the anticipated results of arms control negotiations; what European-based nuclear weapons NATO should keep; and how exactly the CSCE could be strengthened to reinforce NATO. "We have no intention of shifting the balance in Europe to the detriment of the Soviet Union," Wörner maintained. On the contrary, NATO clearly wanted "to respect and take into account the legitimate security interests of the Soviet Union."[211]

The whole plan was aimed in part at easing Soviet opposition to continued German membership in NATO. President Bush and Prime Minister Thatcher, bowing to the inevitable, had agreed at a meeting in Bermuda that Germany would not have any limitations on its sovereignty. This "unrestricted control" was an additional argument why many European governments, including the one in Moscow, felt that NATO had to be retained. Since German unification was happening "not in a Europe that's growing together, but a Europe in which one power has suddenly collapsed, leaving chaos in its wake," a Western diplomat in Bonn concluded that "this is when we need as much stability as we can get, and NATO and the European Community are the only structured sources of stability that exist in Europe."[212]

NATO and EC representatives therefore continued to be involved in the German unification process. In this respect, the role played by the president of the EC Commission, Jacques Delors, is particularly worth mentioning. Although not attended by the fanfare of the two-plus-four negotiations themselves, the EC's short-term incorporation of a dilapidated East German economy—in rapid time as the process of unification exploded—and long-term vision of Germany ensconced in political, economic, and monetary union were important contributions toward minimizing the destabilizing effects of unification. EC representatives also were involved in the negotiation of the internal German treaties in the summer and autumn of 1990. It does not seem unlikely, therefore, that the Soviet acceptance of continued German membership in NATO also was made possible in part by the assurance of continued political and economic control over Germany through the mechanisms of the EC.

D-Mark for the Soviet Union

The negotiations of the first two-plus-four conference in Bonn on May 5, 1990, had been prepared by the political directors of the respective foreign ministries during two meetings in Bonn and Berlin on March 14 and April 16. Four "issue areas" were defined for the talks: the borders of a future Germany (which all six participants agreed would surround the territory of West Germany, East Germany, and Berlin—"no more, no less"); political and military matters; problems relating to Berlin; and a final international settlement and replacement of the rights and responsibilities of the Four Powers.

The Soviet Union initially had asked to include a fifth point, a "peace treaty." The head of the West German delegation, Dieter Kastrup, had resisted the demand on the grounds that negotiations on this point would have to involve the many other nations that had formally declared war on the Third Reich and could easily turn into a humiliating exercise for Germany. Poland, however, would be invited to join in when the conference focused on the Oder-Neisse line.[213]

In a series of private meetings on the eve of the foreign ministers' conference, Chancellor Kohl met again with Secretary of State Baker and Foreign Minister Shevardnadze. Kohl and Baker agreed that the NATO "special summit" would convene immediately prior to the CPSU's planned party convention in the summer. If the NATO summit introduced the envisaged reforms, it could back up Gorbachev's position and become a milestone on the path toward the solution of the external aspects of German unification.[214]

In his talk with Shevardnadze, Kohl stressed the importance of economic relations between Germany and the Soviet Union. The Federal Republic would have to take on a "special responsibility" in this respect, the chancellor declared, adding that he would personally take care of the issue. Shevardnadze informed Kohl that President Gorbachev would be ready to meet him soon, probably in July, outside Moscow. Kvitsinsky's report on the German proposal for a "General Treaty" on bilateral cooperation had been accepted "with great interest." It had come "right on time," the Soviet foreign minister said. Now he had been asked by President Gorbachev and Prime Minister Ryzhkov to transmit a request for a new loan. The Soviet Union would be glad if the Federal Republic could be helpful. A compromise regarding the question of German NATO membership was not excluded.[215]

By the time Shevardnadze left, Kohl had decided that he would try to assist Gorbachev with the money. He was convinced that after the food aid program in January a new round of quick support for the Soviet Union could further improve the climate of Soviet-German relations and provide the basis for a solution of the difficult political problems in the two-plus-four process. With no delay, he asked Hilmar Kopper of the Deutsche Bank and Wolfgang Röller of the Dresdner Bank (who was also the chairman of the German Association of Banks) to check if a new loan for the Soviet Union could be arranged shortly. But Kohl said that the action had to be kept secret, and Kopper and Röller should move under the seal of secrecy.[216]

The next day, May 5, when the six foreign ministers gathered for their first two-plus-four meeting, Soviet ambassador Kvitsinsky presented a memorandum to Horst Teltschik at the Chancellery on behalf of Shevardnadze concerning the request for loans amounting to DM20 billion at a term of five to seven years. State guarantees by Western governments would counter rumors that the Soviet Union was insolvent and encourage banks to grant it new credits.

On May 8, the chancellor received Röller and Kopper and explained the Soviet wishes to them. Röller confirmed that the economic and financial crisis in the Soviet Union had led to a situation in which deliveries remained unpaid and liabilities were not met. Kopper agreed. The Soviet Union was losing credibility with the international financial markets. A liquidity crisis was building up, with no solution possible by private business. Thus the Federal government had to put together an international initiative for joint countermeasures, Kopper said.[217]

Kohl realized that this would become the first major test of the Federal Republic's growing responsibility in the international arena. The Soviet Union was moving rapidly to a state of confusion, and there was a serious danger that it could crumble by the July CPSU party congress. Although Gorbachev's formal power had never been greater than it was at that point (he had ascended to the presidency on March 15), the genuine economic and political implosion from below threatened his position.[218] The Soviet leader, who a year before had been celebrated as a heroic figure in the European revolution of 1989, was now viewed with pity by Western observers as an enormously capable man devoured by the very revolution that he had set in motion.[219]

In any case, there were two uncertain months before the party congress could clarify perestroika's political prospects more definitely. During this time, financial support to ease Moscow's solvency crisis was essential for securing Gorbachev's position and overcoming the obstacles to a conventional arms limitation treaty and German unification as well. Kohl therefore agreed with Röller and Kopper that the two bankers would travel with Horst Teltschik on a secret "special mission" to Moscow for exploratory talks on the issue.

Teltschik then called Kvitsinsky to ask for an appointment with Prime Minister Ryzhkov and, should the occasion arise, with President Gorbachev. The mission was to demonstrate the readiness of the Federal Republic to respond to Moscow's request as fast as possible, Teltschik said.

Within 24 hours, Kvitsinsky reported back that Teltschik, Kopper, and Röller were expected in Moscow on Sunday, May 13. They would see Ryzhkov and maybe Gorbachev as well, presumably on Monday. The decision to receive the Germans at such a short notice had been taken on May 9 during the Soviet army victory parade on Red Square. Gorbachev was very satisfied with the talk between Kohl and Shevardnadze and hoped that the "problem under consideration" could be solved quickly.[220]

The trip on May 13 was organized by Kohl's personal secretary, Juliane Weber, and kept so secret that even the pilot of the special Bundeswehr plane did not know the destination until directly before takeoff. In Moscow, the small German delegation was welcomed by Kvitsinsky, just installed as deputy foreign minister. On May 14, Teltschik, Kopper, and Röller met with Prime Minister Ryzhkov, Foreign Minister Shevardnadze, and President Gorbachev, as well as with Deputy Prime Minister Stepan Sitarian and the head of the Foreign Trade Bank, Yuri Moskovsky. The Soviets asked for DM1.5 billion promptly to ensure their solvency, and long-term credits of between DM10 and DM15 billion on concessionary terms (a redemption scheme of five free years and 10 to 15 years for repayment).

Teltschik, who had been told by Chancellor Kohl before departure not to miss this chance of a lifetime for German unity, replied that the Federal Republic was ready to be helpful to whatever extent possible, including acceptance of the East German responsibilities vis-à-vis the Soviet Union. Such support, however, should be part of a "package" to solve the German question. Gorbachev agreed. A bilateral treaty between the Soviet Union and the Federal Republic could become a "cornerstone of the European Home," he said. As far as the security question was concerned, it would be necessary, however, to avoid the impression among the people of the Soviet Union that their security might be impaired. A solution, although difficult, was possible.[221] Gorbachev also agreed to meet with Chancellor Kohl after the CPSU party convention in July, possibly in the Caucasus.

When Teltschik, Kopper, and Röller returned to the airport, they still found it difficult to believe that they had actually been able to talk to all relevant Soviet leaders that day. The fact that they had all been available to the German delegation indicated how serious the problems of the Soviet Union were and how much Moscow was expecting from the Federal Republic. It had also turned out that the chancellor's recent initiatives with regard to the Soviet Union—the proposal for concluding a bilateral treaty and the offer for financial assistance—had been the right moves at the right time to promote a final settlement of the German question. Now the unification of Germany apparently was close at hand.

Agreement in the Caucasus

Meanwhile, the talks of the first full ministerial two-plus-four conference at the Foreign Office in Bonn on May 5 had been concluded. The foreign ministers had presented their opening speeches and then focused mainly on the agenda and the sites for the next meetings. Soviet foreign minister Shevardnadze, however, had used his opening statement to stress again that German membership in NATO was unacceptable and that the gloomy chapters of German-Soviet history were still remembered by the people in the Soviet Union:

> The population of our country, which sustained such frightening losses in the last war, cannot accept the idea of including [a unified] Germany in NATO. . . . We are dealing here with an issue of special importance to Soviet people, to our whole society. If an attempt is made to push us into a corner on matters touching our security, it will lead to a situation—I will say it candidly—in which our political flexibility would be severely curtailed, because emotions would boil up inside the country, shades of the past would rise to the surface, national complexes with roots in the tragic pages of our history would be revived.[222]

But Shevardnadze also emphasized that the differences between the Soviet Union and the Western powers "need not be dramatized," as they were "usual for the negotiating process."

Then the Soviet foreign minister put forward a proposal that had already been launched by the Soviets on February 10, when Chancellor Kohl had met with Gorbachev in Moscow. The Soviet Union would no longer insist that the military status of a united Germany be defined before East and West Germany could merge; a solution to the issue might even be put off for a few years.[223]

It was a proposal for decoupling the external aspects of German unification from the internal unification process. Genscher had welcomed the idea on May 5 as a "historic turnaround" that cleared the way for rapid German unification. Kohl, however, opposed it on the grounds that it would be a "fatal development" to reunite Germany quickly while postponing a decision on whether or not the new country would belong to NATO.[224] The discord did not result in a major irritation between Kohl and Genscher again, however. Genscher swiftly changed his position when he realized the difference with Kohl and asked a spokesman to declare that he was "open to consideration of what is behind the Shevardnadze proposal." But he said that he agreed with Kohl that Germany should emerge from the two-plus-four talks with full sovereignty and without any open questions about alliances.[225]

Another revealing aspect of the meeting in Bonn was the fact that the East German delegation, though physically present at the conference table, was hardly involved in the decision-making process as such. "Four plus two: that equals five" was a joke often heard among observers of the talks, who accepted one Germany as a political, if not yet a diplomatic, fact. The new East German government and Foreign Minister Markus Meckel were *quantités négligeables* in the power game between East and West.[226] Chancellor Kohl had even warned US secretary of state Baker that the position taken by Meckel, who was toying with the idea of neutralizing the GDR and a unified Germany, would "prevent the GDR from being at the forefront of the supporters of a German NATO membership." But he was sure that the East Germans were backing him, not Meckel, on this issue, especially since Poland, Hungary, and Czechoslovakia also had come out in favor of continued German membership in NATO.[227]

In any case, the Western leaders made little effort to coordinate their measures with the government in East Berlin. A draft submitted by the GDR Foreign Ministry at the political directors' level at the two-plus-four negotiations on June 9 regarding the text for a final settlement was accepted only with astonishment and concern. As the text dealt not only with the NATO membership of Germany but with matters affecting the security of states that did not even participate in the two-plus-four process, the document was quickly dismissed as yet another example of diplomatic unawareness and lack of political instincts on the part of the new GDR leadership.[228]

Kohl and Genscher, on the other hand, knowing about the Western backing for their policy, were increasingly optimistic that the remaining problems could be solved to their liking. As early as the day after the two-plus-four session in May, the chancellor asserted that there were "no more hurdles along the way to the realization of the right of all Germans to self-determination."[229] Genscher agreed. In a policy statement before the Bundestag on May 10, he declared that the "long-cherished yearning of the Germans for peaceful unification" was "coming to fruition." He quoted Eduard Shevardnadze's words at the Bonn meeting that the process of unification was "under way" and that one must not "lag behind the events." This remark by the Soviet foreign minister proved, Genscher argued, that the Soviet Union was "interested in swiftly settling the external aspects" of German unity.[230]

The fact that the Soviet Union had changed its attitude so drastically was to a large extent due to the unwavering US backing of the West German position. During a meeting with President Bush in Washington on May 17, Chancellor Kohl therefore expressed thanks to the US administration for its "magnificent support from the outset" on Germany's path toward unity. Kohl also reaffirmed that a united Germany would make use of its right to belong to the alliance of its choice, which "is and will always be the North Atlantic Alliance."[231]

There were differences between Kohl and Bush as well, though not public ones. Both agreed that the United States would have to maintain its presence in Europe and share responsibility for shaping the future of the continent. Both called for reinforcing NATO's traditional political profile, for the intensification of cooperation between the United States and the European Community, and for expanding the CSCE into a system of assured human rights, guaranteed security, and comprehensive cooperation for all 35 member countries. However, when Kohl reported that Gorbachev was asking for financial aid and that the Federal government was prepared to guarantee a loan of DM5 billion, Bush referred only to Lithuania, saying the situation there made it extremely difficult for him to support Gorbachev economically and financially; Kohl meanwhile insisted that it was in the common interest of the West to enable Gorbachev to continue his reform policy. A successor was unlikely to be better. Thus it was important that the United States contributed to support the Soviet leader. The Lithuanians had his sympathy, Kohl declared. Yet they must not be allowed to determine the West policy.[232]

Upon his return to Bonn, the chancellor continued to work on the aid program for the Soviet Union. In the early morning of May 21, he received the bankers Röller and Kopper again. Help was urgent, Kohl said. He felt like a farmer who had to get his harvest in the barn as quickly as possible before a thunderstorm. Time was not working in Germany's favor. Nevertheless, the message to Gorbachev should be unmistakable. The loan would be given only if it was clear beforehand that the two-plus-four negotiations would be concluded successfully.[233]

Later in the day, Teltschik informed the Soviet chargé d'affaires, Leonid Ussychenko, about Kohl's position. On the following day, Kohl himself wrote a letter to Gorbachev, in which he offered the DM5 billion loan and expressed his expectation that a two-plus-four decision could still be reached in 1990. A comprehensive treaty on cooperation would also be possible. As far as the question of long-term credits was concerned, Kohl referred to a "joint effort of all Western industrial nations," saying that he had already discussed the issue with President Bush. He forgot to mention, however, that Bush had been rather evasive on the matter.[234]

On June 1, Kohl met with Kopper and Röller once more, this time in the Dresdner Bank building in Frankfurt. They confirmed that they were "capable to act" within a few hours. The contract was eventually signed in Moscow on June 18 and guaranteed by the Federal government in Bonn at the beginning of July. As early as July 13, Finance Minister Waigel informed the chancellor that the DM5 billion had been fully absorbed, which he interpreted as proof of the tense financial situation of the Soviet Union.

Moscow's relief about the loan was demonstrated by Foreign Minister Shevardnadze during a meeting with Genscher in Geneva on May 23, only one day after Kohl's letter to Gorbachev. Now the other questions could be solved as well, Shevardnadze declared euphorically. Most important were the CFE negotiations in Vienna, where a ceiling for military forces in a united Germany could be agreed upon. Genscher, who later characterized his five-and-one-half-hour discussion with Shevardnadze as "productive" and said progress had been made on a number of issues, responded instantly that the East German National People's Army (NVA) would be dissolved completely, while the West German Bundeswehr should be downgraded to 350,000 troops.[235]

Yet Genscher had failed to coordinate his offer with either Chancellor Kohl or Defense Minister Gerhard Stoltenberg and thus could hardly have been surprised when Stoltenberg proposed different figures at a meeting of the Bundestag Defense Committee on May 29. The defense minister suggested that the wartime strength of the Federal armed forces be reduced from 1.34 million to approximately 950,000 troops, while the peacetime strength could be cut from 495,000 to 400,000 after an agreement on conventional disarmament in Vienna.[236]

Stoltenberg agreed with Genscher, however, that changes in the military posture in Europe were conditional on the German unification process. At a conference of the NATO Defense Planning Committee on May 22-23 in Brussels, Stoltenberg appealed to his NATO colleagues to work constructively for the conclusion of a treaty on conventional disarmament in Europe during the current year. The implementation of such a treaty, together with further confidence-building measures, would "practically eliminate the possibility of a surprise attack on NATO as a whole" and lead to "a dramatic improvement of our mutual security," the ministers declared, who also called for lowering the degree of readiness of NATO forces and for a rethinking of the long-standing NATO strategies of forward defense and flexible response. The number of maneuvers should be reduced and military spending plans reevaluated.[237]

Similarly, Chancellor Kohl argued in a speech at the disarmament conference of the Inter-Parliamentary Union on May 25 in Bonn that, although the transatlantic security system was "vital" for the Germans and for Europe and although a united Germany should become a member of NATO, the North Atlantic Treaty Organization, which was adapting its strategy to the changed situation, did not want to reap "one-sided advantages" from the developments in Central and Eastern Europe.[238] Genscher still went a step further in his argument. During a ceremony on May 26 at Georgetown University in Washington, D.C., he maintained that the loss of ideological foundations for the East-West conflict made it necessary to change the armaments, strategy, and structure of the alliance systems alike. Once again, the West German foreign minister called for a strengthening of NATO's political role and for the creation of cooperative security structures for Europe as a whole.[239]

Such thinking was remarkably close to arguments Shevardnadze had put forward in a letter to Genscher the day before. There was a "necessity for the transformation of the existing alliances in Europe to predominantly political organizations and their gradual substitution by all-European structures," the Soviet foreign minister wrote—thus closing in on the Western position that would make it possible eventually for the Soviet Union to accept not only the unification of Germany, but the NATO membership of a unified Germany as well.[240]

In an *Izvestiia* article a few days later, Shevardnadze indicated that the West was now already "seriously interested" in taking Soviet security concerns into account by implementing "political and practical reforms of NATO" and developing "initiatives in the area of all-European security."[241] Observers therefore immediately suspected that the Soviet leadership was now trying to pave the way toward a compromise on the German question—regardless of a continuous routine of occasionally tough rhetoric by one or another representative from Moscow.

But there was little the Soviets could do anyway, when even the French president made it clear to Gorbachev during a visit to the Soviet Union on May 26 that continued West German membership in NATO was inevitable and that ideas of a united Germany in both alliances or a "French solution"—that is, a membership in the political organization of NATO without participation in the military integration—were all unacceptable. The constraints of Soviet political tactics were further illustrated by the fact that the West German defense minister, Gerhard Stoltenberg, and the GDR minister for defense and disarmament, Rainer Eppelmann, signed an agreement on May 28 in the East German city of Strausberg, stating that the Federal Armed Forces and the National People's Army of the GDR would establish official relations as of June 1. There was little the Soviets could do to prevent or delay a development that was close to becoming an established fact.

The Western governments, on the other hand, skillfully exploited the Soviet dilemma: Kohl tempted with hard currency; Genscher outlined visions of a new Europe; the French supported Poles and Germans alike; Thatcher played tough; and the Americans were backing the chancellor, who promised during a visit to Washington on May 17 that he would never sacrifice NATO and the US presence in Europe—not even for German unity. Besides, the West was ready to make a solution of the external aspects of the German question more palatable for the Soviets by seeking progress in three decisive areas: in the process of the CSCE, in the disarmament negotiations, especially in Vienna, and in the economic and financial cooperation between East and West.

At the summit meeting between Bush and Gorbachev from May 31 through June 3 in Washington, the Soviet president indicated for the first time that he might even accept that a united Germany remain a member of NATO. He agreed with Bush that "the matter of alliance membership is, in accordance with the Helsinki Final Act, a matter for the Germans to decide."[242] The two leaders discussed a nine-point plan designed by Washington and Bonn to induce the Kremlin to accept the presence of a united Germany in NATO, which had first been presented to Shevardnadze by Baker in Moscow in mid-May. The carrot was to make Germany's membership in the alliance so nonthreatening in military terms and so economically beneficial to the Soviet Union that it would eventually acquiesce. The stick was of course the gathering momentum of German unification and the broad European and American support for unified Germany's membership in NATO, which made the diplomatic costs to Moscow of seeking to block German unification almost prohibitive.[243]

Virtually all elements of the plan had already been discussed in public: (1) the commitment of a united Germany not to develop nuclear, chemical, or biological weapons; (2) the limitation of the size of the united Germany's armed forces; (3) the reduction of NATO's short-range nuclear weapons in Europe; (4) the reorientation of NATO's military strategy and force structure; (5) NATO's renunciation of stationing alliance troops in East Germany; (6) Germany's renunciation of claims not only to Polish territory but also to former German areas now in the Soviet Union, such as East Prussia; (7) the allowance for Soviet forces to remain in East Germany for a transition period, with expenses paid by the German government; (8) the expansion of the CSCE into a pan-European organization; and (9) Germany's offer of a variety of trade, lending, and commercial arrangements to help the Soviet Union succeed in its economic reform program.

Gorbachev "clearly appreciated" the nine points, a State Department official later said, but he also wanted some "intangible things." This was particularly true with regard to the future of NATO, the official added: "The nine points are telling him that NATO will eventually change, but that's a pig in a poke for him. He wants to see something now, have something to point to, to prove that NATO is no longer the Cold War menace but just a grouping of Western states which want constructive relations with the East."[244] President Bush himself was also confident after the Washington conference that Gorbachev might agree soon to a solution of the German question. Yet this would happen only, he told Chancellor Kohl in a telegram on June 4, if Soviet security concerns were sufficiently respected in both the Vienna negotiations on limitation of conventional forces and at the NATO special summit in London in early July.[245]

When the NATO foreign ministers gathered for their regular spring session of the North Atlantic Council on June 7-8 in Turnberry, a small Scottish coastal resort, they were therefore supposed to lay the basis for a redefinition of the alliance's mission from a military pact to an anchor of stability and collective security in Europe at a time of dramatic change.[246] How far this change had proceeded already was underlined by the fact that the foreign ministers of the Warsaw Pact were meeting at the same time in Moscow, where they pronounced an end to the notion of the West as an "ideological enemy" and agreed to study ways of transforming the pact into a democratic alliance of independent states with "beneficial links" to NATO.[247] Secretary of State Baker declared in this respect in Turnberry:

> With the clear and present military danger from one source waning, surely the alliance can look beyond the narrower task of preventing war to the broader one of building the peace. Moving in this direction does not require a revolution in our thinking. It just requires that we adapt to new realities and build upon our proven collective defense structure a broader notion of secu-

rity. . . . The way to build the peace is to reassure the Central and Eastern Europeans and the Soviets that they will not be left out of the new Europe.[248]

British prime minister Thatcher, who also addressed the meeting, stated that in view of the countries of Eastern Europe "reaching out to the West," the Western nations should no longer think of them as "potential enemies or as part of a wider threat to our way of life," but as "friends in need of help, wanting to return to their rightful place in Europe." Politically, Thatcher concluded, NATO no longer had "a clear front line." Yet as long as the Soviet Union remained a well-armed superpower, and as long as threats of instability hang over Europe, NATO should continue to maintain its deterrents. "You don't cancel your home insurance policy just because there have been fewer burglaries on your street in the last 12 months," the prime minister said.[249]

The question therefore was what exactly the reorientation of NATO meant—would, for instance, the redefining of its strategy and military structure affect the idea of deploying an advanced tactical air-to-surface missile (TASM)? Whereas President Bush had indicated that the United States still planned to go ahead with the TASM program as a long-term alternative to the canceled modernization of NATO's short-range Lance missile system, an aide to Foreign Minister Genscher left no doubt in Turnberry that Bonn was not going to negotiate an increase in nuclear forces. "This is not the time to speak about new nuclear weapons that could reach the Soviet Union from Germany," he said. "That is ridiculous."[250]

The policy of the Federal Republic was actually moving in the opposite direction in order to ensure Moscow's support for German unification at a time when the Soviet leadership seemed both threatened and ready to compromise. After Gorbachev thanked Chancellor Kohl in a letter of June 11 for his support "to overcome some temporary problems that occurred during the present phase of the Soviet economic reform" and declared that a settlement of the external aspects of German unity was now possible, Kohl immediately responded by announcing talks with the EC and the Group of Seven (G7) on an unconditional loan for the Soviet Union.[251] Gorbachev then wrote back on June 15, inviting the chancellor to visit the Soviet Union between July 15 and 20.

At the same time, Foreign Minister Genscher met twice with his Soviet counterpart, in Brest on June 11 and Münster on June 18, to intensify the work on the two-plus-four arrangement. The selection of the Soviet border city Brest as a meeting place was a particularly symbolic act. It was the site where the Brest-Litovsk Treaty had been signed in 1918 and where Eduard Shevardnadze's brother Akaki, a sergeant in the Red Army, had been killed in the first days after the German invasion of the Soviet Union on June 22,

1941. Now, 49 years later, in June 1990, the Soviet and German foreign ministers reached out for reconciliation. Eduard Shevardnadze himself referred to that symbolism when he remarked:

> This was an extraordinarily important meeting. The choice of the place has a symbolic significance on one hand—the memory of some aspects of our common past—and on the other hand, which is most important, it is a demonstration of our will to finally draw a line under the past and to open a new chapter.[252]

Their negotiations focused mainly on two areas: how to "change" the alliances from military pacts to political instruments and how German-Soviet relations would develop after unification. Bonn intended to present a package solution by the second half of July, with proposals for CSCE institutions, a positive declaration of the NATO summit, ceilings for the forces of a united Germany, loan arrangements for the Soviet Union, and a preliminary draft with elements of a bilateral basic treaty between Bonn and Moscow.[253] Genscher thus tried to shape the framework for a general restructuring of the relationship.

The Soviet's primary concern, on the other hand, was the military situation. On June 12, Gorbachev publicly agreed for the first time in a report to the Soviet parliament on his talks with President Bush in Washington that West German troops could remain in NATO while East Germany retained "associated membership" in the Warsaw Pact. The united Germany *in toto* should "honor all obligations" inherited from the two Germanys, Gorbachev said.[254] On June 18, Shevardnadze handed over a memorandum to Genscher during their Münster meeting on "contractual relations" between the two alliances. Obviously, the idea of associated membership in combination with the envisaged cooperation between the two military pacts was considered a vehicle to make the integration of a unified Germany in NATO acceptable for the Soviet Union.

But the Federal government in Bonn was determined to retain exclusive NATO membership without the possibility of Soviet interference. Gorbachev's suggestion and Shevardnadze's memorandum were therefore rejected, just as the previously proposed neutral Germany, joint membership for Germany in both alliances, and the dismantling of the alliances had been. The new shift in the Kremlin's attitude was interpreted merely as yet another indication that the Soviet leaders were slowly reconciling themselves to the idea that a unified Germany would be in NATO, provided that Moscow's political, economic, and security concerns were met.[255]

In this respect, Bush wrote in a letter to Kohl on June 21 that the forthcoming NATO summit in London should provide a clear message to Gorbachev that NATO was going to change. Kohl agreed strongly, and he also welcomed Bush's proposals for a declaration on the continuation of the CFE negotiations in Vienna in the 1990s with far-reaching reductions of conventional forces and for a statement on a revision of the "flexible response" strategy and forward defense.[256]

The Federal Republic itself helped improve the political climate of the negotiations by compromising on two questions beforehand. In talks with the Soviet Union on the financing of the "Western Group of Soviet Forces" in the GDR, Foreign Minister Genscher suggested on June 19 retaining the existing treaty of the GDR with the Soviet Union and paying DM1.4 billion in 1990 for stationing of the Soviet forces in East Germany. And, even more important, the parliaments of the two German states adopted a matching resolution on June 21—only one day before the second two-plus-four conference was held in Berlin—guaranteeing the Oder-Neisse line as Poland's western border and calling on a unified Germany to finally confirm the border in a treaty.[257]

The Berlin two-plus-four meeting was noteworthy because it began with the removal of "Checkpoint Charlie" by crane before the eyes of the foreign ministers from the United States, Britain, France, the Soviet Union, and the two Germanys. The checkpoint, a beige-painted metal shack built on the western side of Friedrichstrasse shortly after the Berlin Wall was erected in 1961, had been the only crossing point between East and West Berlin for non-German vehicles and pedestrians until November 1989. It had also been the scene of a tense confrontation between Soviet and American tanks in October 1961 and of successful and unsuccessful attempts by East Germans to escape to the West.[258]

Apart from the removal of this famous symbol of the Cold War, the two-plus-four meeting in Berlin was dominated by discussions on an unexpected Soviet draft of "Basic Principles for a Concluding Settlement with Germany." In the new proposal, Shevardnadze said the final document should include measures to reduce the size of the future German army within three years to 200,000 or 250,000 troops and to shape it in such a way that it would be "incapable of offensive operations"; Allied troops would maintain their positions in Germany during the transition period. The Soviet foreign minister also suggested that Germany remain under the regime of the Four Powers for another five years and be bound during this time by all international treaties signed by West and East Germany, including those involving NATO and the Warsaw Pact.[259]

GDR foreign minister Meckel immediately endorsed the Soviet proposal, failing to consult with Genscher. The Western delegations rejected the new

Soviet ideas categorically. Genscher was particularly straightforward, arguing that on unification day Germany should be "fully sovereign" and not be "singularized or discriminated by any conditions or burdened with open questions."[260] Baker said the Soviet plan would "restrict German sovereignty and would do so for some years."[261]

Shevardnadze himself, however, emphasized repeatedly that Moscow was not seeking to block progress toward German unity and that he expected to have a final agreement that would resolve all aspects of German unity by the end of the year. Obviously, he had undertaken his initiative at least in part for domestic consumption, as a congress of the Russian Republic's Communist Party was in progress, a CPSU congress was expected to take place in the first week of July, and the day of the Berlin two-plus-four meeting—June 22— was the 49th anniversary of Nazi Germany's invasion of the Soviet Union.[262]

In addition, much of the progress toward German unity would depend on the forthcoming NATO conference in London. Shevardnadze himself declared in Berlin that his statements were not the "ultimate truth" and that the Soviet leadership was waiting for the outcome of the NATO meeting. He also accepted a tentative agreement "on the interim outline of the elements of a final settlement," which all participants of the Berlin conference expected to be finished by the CSCE summit scheduled for November 7, 1990.

The London NATO conference of July 5-6 was mainly prepared in Washington. Several departments of the US administration had cooperated to put together the draft "London Declaration: The North Atlantic Alliance in Transition," which generally found much support, particularly in Bonn and Paris. Only British prime minister Thatcher objected to the text, which she felt went too far.[263] On the other hand, the West Germans would have been prepared to go even further, especially with regard to the number of troops of a united Germany, which had not been explicitly mentioned in the text out of concerns about "singularizing" the Germans in the document.

But the question of the size of the future German army had already been discussed by Genscher and Shevardnadze during several of their ten meetings since the beginning of 1990. Shevardnadze had most recently brought up the issue at the Berlin two-plus-four conference in June. On July 2, West German defense minister Stoltenberg presented an internal government paper in which he agreed to a Bundeswehr ceiling of 370,000 land and air forces plus 25,000 naval units if the conventional ceilings would generally be lowered at the CFE negotiations in Vienna. In this respect he differed with Genscher, however, who said that "any figure above 350,000" was "too high." Presumably, Genscher had made a personal arrangement with Shevardnadze to aim at the 350,000 level. Thus Chancellor Kohl saw himself forced to intercede in the dispute, which had meanwhile become public, saying that 370,000 might be attainable, but that he would not be opposed to 350,000 if all other questions could be solved.[264]

In any case, the NATO summit in London was unaffected by the inner-governmental controversy in the Federal Republic. The London Declaration of July 6 was supported by Genscher as well as Stoltenberg, not to mention the chancellor. It stated that Europe had entered "a new, auspicious era" and that with the unification of Germany, the division of Europe could be over-come. Therefore, NATO was turning to the countries of Central and Eastern Europe and "offered them its hand in friendship." NATO would "remain a defensive alliance" and "never, under any circumstances first use force." The Warsaw Pact was invited to adopt a joint declaration on the renunciation of force, and all its member governments were additionally invited to establish permanent diplomatic relations with NATO.[265]

Regarding military issues, the declaration requested a fundamental shift in the size and structure of conventional forces in Europe as well as negotia-tions between the United States and the Soviet Union on the reduction of short-range nuclear forces. NATO would revise its plans for defense and arms control and work out a new military strategy, away from forward defense and flexible response and diminishing the role of nuclear weapons. The CSCE process, on the other hand, would be enhanced and strengthened, with regular summit meetings, a CSCE secretariat, the establishment of a center for conflict resolution, and a parliamentary assembly consisting of representatives of all CSCE member states.[266]

In Moscow, the London Declaration was received not only with consent but with relief. NATO secretary general Wörner, who had been invited to the Soviet Union earlier in the year, visited Moscow on July 14, a week after the London meeting. He realized that the Soviet leadership was assessing the con-tent of the document "very positively and nearly without criticism." An impor-tant factor had also been the timing of the initiative. The news from London had reached the Soviet capital in the midst of difficult deliberations at the 28th Party Congress of the CPSU (July 2-13). There the delegates had decided about the future course of the Soviet Union and thus about the political fate of Gorbachev, Shevardnadze, and the reform program, and the London Declaration was welcomed as a "concession from the other side." In view of the growing internal opposition, Shevardnadze later noted in his memoirs, the declaration had been helpful to the extent that "it may have saved my policy. . . . Otherwise, it would have been impossible for us to succeed in our own country."[267]

For Germany, the declaration was an important step forward in the process of unification. Before London and until the party congress, Gorbachev had been under enormous pressure from conservatives not to give in on Germany. At the party congress, "generals and party bureaucrats, led by the right-winger Yegor Ligachev," still "put up a fierce resistance against the loss of the Western bastion of the socialist camp," Shevardnadze told the West German news magazine *Der Spiegel* in 1991. The foreign minister had defended his policy by arguing that there was only one alternative: to block the development by using the 500,000 Soviet troops stationed in the GDR. Everybody knew what that would mean. Gorbachev had backed him up, asking "Do you want to have tanks again?" and "Shall we teach them again how to live?"[268]

Gorbachev and Shevardnadze eventually had won the battle for peace in Germany, and on July 10 Gorbachev was also confirmed with a clear majority as general secretary of the CPSU. After the party congress, his position was strengthened enough that he could go ahead to resolve the German question with new emphasis. The London Declaration provided the necessary alibi. But the key motive was economic.

Chancellor Kohl meanwhile had kept his promise to do whatever possible to help Gorbachev financially, bilaterally as well as multilaterally. After the announcement on June 22 that the West German government would guarantee the bank credit of DM5 billion that had been under consideration for some time, Kohl had put strong pressure on his EC colleagues at a Dublin meeting of the leaders of the European Community on June 26 to endorse a German appeal for short-term credits and long-term economic aid to the Soviet Union. The German loan was the largest single credit that the Soviet Union had ever received from Western banks. But much more was needed. The Soviet Union's hard-currency debt alone was estimated at US $64-65 billion in mid-1990. The EC Commission was therefore instructed to cooperate with the International Monetary Fund, the World Bank, and the European Bank for Reconstruction and Development in working out plans with the Soviet government for economic aid to the Soviet Union. The decision did not commit the 12 EC countries to pledging specific amounts, but it confronted the United States, Japan, and the other members of the G7, who were scheduled to meet for a world economic summit on July 9-11 in Houston, Texas, with momentum and a growing sense of urgency about the need to help Gorbachev.[269]

Japan and the United States had been particularly reluctant to give substantial economic aid to the Soviet Union. Tokyo was insisting on a prior solution of the Kuril Islands question. Washington criticized Moscow's policy toward the Baltic states and was afraid that financial aid would indirectly subsidize the Soviet military, as US defense secretary Richard Cheney said on June 25. Now the EC endorsement of multilateral cooperation set new standards, which made it more difficult for the United States and Japan to keep aloof at the meeting in Houston.

Chancellor Kohl traveled to Texas via Rome, where he saw the German soccer team win the world championship on July 8. On the following day in Houston, he urged the G7 to focus extensively on the situation in Eastern Europe and to provide aid to the Soviet Union, which would benefit Gorbachev, who was still struggling for his political future at the 28th Party Congress.[270] The world economic leaders did not make concrete promises but did welcome the political transformation and economic reforms in the former communist countries. They also backed up the decision from Dublin to give the EC Commission a mandate for the lead role in preparing a study on the Soviet economy and providing recommendations for reforms and possible criteria for Western help.[271]

Kohl was still at the hotel in Houston when he received an invitation from an obviously grateful Mikhail Gorbachev to visit his hometown, Stavropol, in the Caucasus. The chancellor was satisfied. At this point he knew that his forthcoming trip to the Soviet Union would not fail. The personal invitation was a mark of confidence and a signal that further progress in the process of German unification could be expected.

The trip to the Soviet Union began late on the afternoon of July 14 aboard a Bundeswehr Boeing 707 at Cologne-Bonn airport. During the flight to Moscow, Kohl picked a quarrel with Genscher regarding the size of the armed forces in a united Germany, when he insisted on a ceiling of 400,000, while Genscher still urged 350,000, including the navy. Kohl even accused Genscher and the FDP, above all Jürgen Möllemann, of aspiring to a professional army—an idea anathema to Germans, who had once seen a professional army stand opposed to the Weimar Republic—by their attempt of radically downgrading the number of troops.[272]

In Moscow, the German delegation was welcomed at Vnukovo II airport by Shevardnadze and Kvitsinsky, who then accompanied Kohl and his entourage to their residence at Ulitsa Kosygina No. 38 on the Lenin Hills. Shortly before they arrived at their destination, Shevardnadze ordered the cars to stop at the site where Napoleon was said to have looked down at the burning Moscow in 1812. Now the city gleamed in a sea of lights. It had rained during the day but had cleared up, and the wet roofs and roads reflected the dim shine of countless streetlamps under a cloudless night sky.

Next morning Kohl and Teltschik drove with interpreter Andreas Weiss to the guest house of the Soviet Foreign Ministry—the former city palace of a rich Russian merchant—on Moscow's Aleksei Tolstoy Street. There they were escorted to the first floor, where Gorbachev was waiting already with Chernayev and interpreter Ivan Kurpakov. Thus, only six people were present during the private conversation that followed. The Soviet president quickly got to the point. Bismarck once had said that one had to seize the mantle of history. Well, Gorbachev declared, these were historical times, and opportunities were to be seized. A situation was evolving that would lead the Soviet Union and Germany together again. If both countries had been living apart in the past, they now would have to meet anew. The Soviet Union's relationship with Germany would be of equal importance with the normalization of relations with the United States. This would serve Europe, too.

When Kohl interjected that three points were important now—the withdrawal of Soviet forces from the GDR, the membership of a united Germany in NATO, and the future ceiling of the armed forces of a unified Germany—Gorbachev paused for a moment. Then he quietly and earnestly conceded that Germany could remain a member of NATO if the scope of the alliance was not extended to the territory of the GDR as long as Soviet forces were stationed there. Yet the Four Power regime in Germany could be terminated at once, after the two-plus-four document became effective. It would only be necessary to conclude a separate treaty on the presence of Soviet forces in East Germany "for a duration of three to four years."[273]

Kohl listened carefully and then repeated all of Gorbachev's statements to make sure that there was no misunderstanding, while Teltschik took hurried notes. It was a historical moment indeed. The breakthrough had been achieved. The framework of a solution to the German question was established. Germany would soon be a unified country again. Only the details of the settlement remained to be worked out.

The conversation between Kohl and Gorbachev ended after nearly two hours. Then the group of six was joined by the foreign and finance ministers, but neither the Soviet president nor the German chancellor mentioned the agreement that had just been reached. The two leaders and their aides wanted no information to leak before the time had come to make the understanding known to the public.

After lunch, the delegations departed for Stavropol—a city of 200,000 at the foothills of the Caucasus, some 1,600 kilometers south of Moscow. From there, the group was transported by helicopters to Arkhiz, up in the mountains, where the concluding talks would be held in Gorbachev's hunting lodge in the narrow valley of the Selemchuk River. On arrival in the late afternoon of July 15, the delegations first gathered for a walk to the roaring river in cardigans and casual shirts and trousers. Gorbachev climbed down the steep bank to the crystal-clear water, stretched out his hand to Kohl, and asked him to follow suit. The pictures quickly went around the world: Germans and Soviets at ease.

The formal negotiations began next morning, July 16, at the same long table where both delegations had had their breakfast. Agreement was reached soon that the two-plus-four negotiations should lead to a document relating to international law. The united Germany would encompass the Federal Republic, the GDR, and Berlin, provided that the united Germany would renounce weapons of mass destruction, that the military structure of NATO would not be extended to the territory of the GDR, and that a separate treaty would be concluded on the temporary stationing of Soviet forces in East Germany.

At this point, Genscher remarked that the two-plus-four document must include the right of the Germans, according to the Helsinki Final Act, to join an alliance of their choice, which apparently meant full membership in NATO. The reaction of Gorbachev, who had of course answered the question already in his private conversation with Kohl the day before, was of "delightful consistency," Teltschik noted in his diary.[274] If Germany was fully sovereign, the Soviet president now also told the German foreign minister, this would be "self-evident." He would ask only that NATO not be mentioned explicitly.

The members of the West German delegation were as surprised as they were pleased about what they had just heard. But the Soviet participants were visibly stunned as Gorbachev now made official the Soviet acceptance of the membership of a united Germany in the Western alliance.

Subsequently, the details of the arrangement were worked out. The presence of Soviet forces in East Germany would be settled in a separate treaty and would be linked to the Western commitment not to extend the NATO structures to the territory of what was now the GDR as long as Soviet troops were stationed there. Nonintegrated units of the Bundeswehr could, however, be deployed in East Germany at once, and forces of the Four Powers would remain in Berlin during the transitional period. Nuclear weapons of NATO, on the other hand, would not be transferred to the territory of the GDR even after the withdrawal of Soviet troops, which meant in effect that East Germany would become a nuclear-free zone. But the protection guarantees of Article 5 and 6 of the NATO Treaty would immediately apply to Germany as a whole, including the territory of the GDR.

Regarding how long Soviet troops were expected to remain in East Germany, Gorbachev now spoke of five to seven years, but was reminded by Kohl that on the day before he had mentioned three to four years—which would be "more realistic," the chancellor said, who also promised support for the reeducation and housing of the returning soldiers. Gorbachev responded favorably.

Then the negotiations turned to the question of economic cooperation. Deputy Prime Minister Sitarian as well as President Gorbachev argued that the obligations of the GDR vis-à-vis the Soviet Union were considerable. The stationing costs of the Soviet forces in the GDR, which amounted to the equivalent of 6 million tons of oil per year, represented a particular problem. These costs would even increase after unification. A settlement was necessary in order to avoid "uneasiness among the soldiers that might spread to the entire army." On the other hand, the Federal Republic could seize great economic opportunities in the Soviet Union. The Soviets did not fear becoming dependent on Germany, nor should the Germans be afraid.

Kohl responded that the Soviet Union was the most important partner of the Germans in the East. The bilateral treaty on Soviet-German cooperation should introduce a new quality in the relationship between the two countries to break the "vicious circle of the recent past." Thus he would continue to work for Western support of Gorbachev's reform policy, the chancellor said, as he had just done in Dublin and Houston.

At last, the two delegations agreed without further discussion that the future ceiling of the armed forces of a united Germany would be 370,000.[275] And the Soviet side accepted the Federal government's position rejecting Polish demands for postponing Germany's sovereignty until after the conclusion of a German-Polish border treaty and of making the borders between Poland and Germany a "principal component" of a general peace settlement for Europe.[276] Finally, Kohl invited Gorbachev and his wife, Raissa, to a return visit in the Federal Republic and his hometown Ludwigshafen, stating with satisfaction that in the past three to four months they had covered a long way. On that note, the four-hour talks ended.

From a German viewpoint, the results were truly sensational. Many positions that had already been lost in the internal debate—for instance, between Foreign Minister Genscher and Defense Minister Stoltenberg—or had been given up in precipitate statements by rash East and West German politicians commenting on possible options in the unification process had now been recovered; Germany would be united. Germany would be fully sovereign. Germany would be a member of NATO. German troops would be stationed in all of Germany. And the security guarantees of Article 5 and 6 of the North Atlantic Treaty would apply immediately to Germany as a whole, once the two-plus-four final document became effective.[277]

From a Soviet perspective, however, the course and outcome of the Caucasus meeting looked quite different. When Shevardnadze joined Genscher aboard one of the helicopters that transported the delegations to Mineral'nye Vody, where the official press conference was held, the atmosphere was still businesslike. The two foreign ministers already spoke about the next two-plus-four meeting that was going to take place in Paris the following day, and Genscher tried to get Shevardnadze's support on the difficult Polish question. But when the Soviet foreign minister left Mineral'nye Vody in his own plane for Paris a short time later, he was subjected instantly to a "painstaking interrogation" by his aides and the Soviet journalists aboard who wanted to know why all questions had been solved with such "lightning speed."[278]

In his response, Shevardnadze rejected the notion of too much hurry and referred to the various steps that had made the turn possible. But at last, he said, the development had been inevitable since there was the danger of a dead end:

> We are not capable of stopping Germany's unification, except by force. But that would amount to a catastrophe. If we refused to participate in the process [of German unification], we would lose a lot. We would not create the basis for a new relationship with Germany and would impair the all-European situation.[279]

After the decision in the Caucasus, the German unification process moved very quickly. On July 17, at the third round of the two-plus-four conference with temporary Polish participation, the Polish demands were met inasmuch as the six foreign ministers concurred that the definite recognition of the Polish western border would be included in the final document relating to international law.[280] During the summer, the Moscow and Arkhiz agreements were put into contracts. All treaties between Germany and the Soviet Union were negotiated bilaterally; the GDR government was informed in just enough time that it could concur. Trilateral talks were held only on questions concerning the cooperation of GDR companies with Soviet firms.

A major problem arose in late August, when Shevardnadze informed Genscher that the Soviet troop withdrawal would not be possible "technically" within three to four years, but only in five to seven years at the earliest. Besides, the reduction would depend on the "volume of the German material and financial support."[281] Shevardnadze's letter was followed up by a visit of Deputy Foreign Minister Kvitsinsky to the Chancellery on August 28, where he demanded that the Federal Republic pay for the transport costs of the troop withdrawal as well as for new housing for the returning soldiers in the Soviet Union and for the stay of the troops that remained in the GDR for the transitional period. Otherwise there might be an uprising in the Soviet army, he said.[282]

Chancellor Kohl, Foreign Minister Genscher, Finance Minister Waigel, and Economic Minister Haussmann agreed on August 29 that the Federal

Republic should be "generous" in aiding the housing program but "tough" with regard to stationing costs. Their financial calculations were made even more complicated on the following day, however, when President Bush also requested money from Bonn to support the United States in regard to the costs for the economic embargo and the deployment of American troops against Iraq.[283]

A week later, on September 5, Soviet ambassador Vladislav Terekhov presented a specific list of the Soviet financial demands: DM3.5 billion for stationing costs from 1990 until 1994; DM3 billion for transportation; DM11.5 billion for the construction of 72,000 apartments, including the necessary infrastructure, such as kindergartens, shops, pharmacies, and so on; DM500 million for education programs and advanced training; and up to DM17.5 billion for Soviet real estate and property in the GDR.[284]

In a telephone conversation with Gorbachev on Friday, September 7, Kohl offered the Soviet Union DM8 billion—everything included. But the Soviet president merely responded that this figure would "lead nowhere." The housing program alone swallowed up DM11 billion. Added to this were the transportation and stationing costs. The situation was dramatic, Gorbachev said. He suggested a call again on Monday, September 10.

During the return call, Kohl proposed DM11 to 12 billion. Gorbachev expressed his hope that the Federal Republic would be able to raise DM15 to 16 billion. Because of the economic reform he was in a difficult situation. If DM15 billion could not be settled upon, everything had to be considered again from the beginning. Kohl then presented a compromise that the state secretary in the Finance Ministry, Horst Köhler, had put in his pocket: In addition to the DM12 billion proposed earlier, the Federal Republic could provide a non-interest-bearing loan of DM3 billion. Negotiations on the loan could begin as early as tomorrow. Gorbachev was relieved: The German experts were to come to Moscow immediately.[285]

A few hours later Kvitsinsky called from the Soviet capital to inform the Federal government that Gorbachev had just given instructions to conclude the negotiations on the German-Soviet treaty on the following day. The rush was indeed necessary, as the foreign ministers of the two-plus-four were scheduled to meet for their fourth session on September 12 in Moscow. It was supposed to be the final two-plus-four conference, where the concluding settlement would be signed.

On the eve of September 12, however, there was one last hitch when the British demanded inclusion of a passage in the text of the final document stating that the ban on NATO forces to be deployed in East Germany should not apply to "small military activities, such as participation in maneuvers."[286]

When Shevardnadze learned about the request, he immediately let his Western colleagues know that if they adopted the addition the planned two-plus-four meeting would be canceled. In other words, there would be no treaty, and the Western powers would bear the responsibility.[287]

Early the next morning, the proposal was withdrawn and the "Treaty on the Concluding Settlement with Regard to Germany" could be signed.[288] The two-plus-four negotiations, which had begun on May 5 in Bonn, were concluded with a six-page document that amounted to a "major diplomatic triumph for Bonn and a historic concession by Moscow."[289] It settled the external aspects of German unification and terminated the rights and responsibilities of the Four Powers in Berlin and in Germany as a whole. For the transition period, the Allies agreed to suspend their remaining occupation rights on October 3, the Day of German Unity, after the 35 CSCE countries could welcome the accord at a meeting of their foreign ministers on October 1 in New York.

Finally, the German-Soviet "Treaty on Good Neighborhood, Partnership and Cooperation" was initialed on September 13 and, like the other treaties and agreements pertaining to the unification of Germany, put into effect by the all-German government and the all-German parliament after October 3.[290]

THE TREATY ON GERMAN UNITY

With the establishment of the economic and monetary union and the successful conclusion of the two-plus-four negotiations, two very important aspects of the German unification process had been settled. A third element was the definition of a legal framework for merging the two Germanys and the formulation of a new, modified, or adopted internal order for the enlarged Federal Republic.[291]

Discussion of the constitutional and legal implications of the unification of Germany began in earnest in late January 1990. The decision of the Round Table in East Berlin on January 28 to advance the East German election from May to March was prompt, and it was followed almost immediately by Gorbachev's remark during Hans Modrow's visit to Moscow that the Soviet Union was "not principally opposed to a unification of the two German states." When Modrow presented his confederation plan for Germany on February 1, it was only logical that the planning for a united Germany would have to catch up with the events.

On February 7, Bonn installed its "Committee on German Unity" with six working groups, among them a group on "State Structures and Public Order" headed by Interior Minister Wolfgang Schäuble, and a group on "Legal

Questions, Particularly Legal Adjustment" led by Justice Minister Hans Engelhard. Some 140 new positions for additional government personnel were established at once to deal with the immensely complicated matters. The first and foremost debate was over the two legal approaches to unification: via either Article 23 of the Basic Law, saying that the constitution would apply in any German state that acceded to it, or Article 146, which declared that the Basic Law ceased to be in force once the German people adopted a new constitution by a "free decision."[292]

The route of direct accession, regarded as both fast and easy, was supported by most departments of the Federal government, as Engelhard told the Committee on German Unity on February 14.[293] Bringing East Germany into an expanded Federal Republic would maintain a tried and tested system that had already shaped a prosperous and democratic state, the advocates of an Article 23 accession argued. Moreover, it would assist and facilitate the rapid implementation of the monetary and economic union option that had been proposed by Chancellor Kohl on February 6.[294]

The preparation of a new constitution, on the other hand, would be more time-consuming and probably controversial, but it offered the chance of formulating a new text in which ideas and demands from both parts of Germany, East and West, could be considered. The Article 146 approach was therefore supported by some East and West German Social Democrats, who maintained that Bonn could not simply "annex" the GDR, and by most leaders of the East German civil movements, who felt steamrollered by the political professionals from Bonn.[295] Bärbel Bohley, for instance, complained that she had "the feeling that we are being occupied." And Markus Meckel of the Eastern SPD said many GDR citizens were afraid of being unable to compete in the capitalist system.[296] An opinion poll by the Wickert Institute published on February 26, however, showed that 89.9 percent of the West Germans and 84.1 percent of the East Germans preferred to adopt the Basic Law as the constitution of the united Germany, and that most of them further believed it should be taken over intact.[297]

A ten-page discussion paper, prepared in late February in the interior ministry, outlined the two options and their variants at length. Interior Minister Schäuble had established a special German Unity staff that was to become the core drafting group of the unification treaty, which started its work with some 20 members led by Klaus-Dieter Schnapauff. Other members of the ministry, above all the state secretaries Franz Kroppenstedt and Hans-Heinrich Neusel, and the head of the constitutional department, Ministerial Director Eduard Schiffer, contributed to the working staff whenever their expertise was needed.

On March 1, Schäuble presented the discussion paper at a meeting of the State Structures and Public Order working group with the leaders of the government and senate chancelleries of the West German states. His preference was clear—a quick accession on the basis of Article 23—although the Central Round Table in East Berlin had agreed at its first session the previous December "to begin at once with the preparation of the draft of a new constitution" and had voted only the previous week explicitly against accession according to Article 23.[298] Schäuble was skeptical, however, whether Prime Minister Modrow and his government or the Round Table still represented the majority will of the GDR population. The *plébiscite de tous les jours*—the continuing exodus of about 2,000 East Germans from East to West every day—seemed to prove that the opposite was true, and the elections of March 18 would demonstrate what the East Germans were really striving for.[299]

Schäuble therefore had instructed Schnapauff and his team to be prepared for the fastest possible development. Even unification immediately after the East German election could not be excluded if one of the GDR states, or the entire country, voted to join the Federal Republic at once; according to constitutional experts, the government in Bonn would have no legal means of blocking them. In any case, Schäuble had convinced himself early in 1990 that unification would come sooner rather than later and that the unity of Germany would have been realized before the end of the year.[300]

The East German SPD, on the other hand, called for a council of legislators of the two German states to prepare a new constitution. The proposal was put forward at the end of a four-day congress in Leipzig on February 25, where the Social Democrats agreed on a "Schedule for German Unity." The council would meet in parallel to the two-plus-four negotiations on the external aspects of German unification and present its draft by the summer, when the five reconstituted states in East Germany would hold elections. Then a new constitution could be voted on, and at the start of 1991 a new all-German parliament could be elected, replacing both the West German and the East German chambers.[301]

In view of the decision of the Round Table to reject an accession according to Article 23 and the SPD proposal to write a new constitution, Robert Leicht, a prominent writer with the weekly journal *Die Zeit* in Hamburg, commented in an article on March 2 "that the effort of thinking about a wholly new constitution would be tantamount to reinventing the wheel, and who knows if the wheel would not be worse the second time?"[302] Moreover, Leicht wrote, the Basic Law bound West Germany to western democracy, and there was "no reason to snap this intellectual bond or to relativize it."[303]

The Article 23 approach was also supported by some hundred constitutional law experts on March 27 in Bonn. Meanwhile, however, the unambiguous vote by the citizens of the GDR on March 18 to tackle the question of German unity expeditiously provided additional impetus. The experts stated in their declaration that the possibility for the German Democratic Republic to join the Federal Republic as provided for in Article 23 kept "open wide room for maneuvering, for careful transition, for a just settlement of interests, if necessary for a step-by-step enactment of the Basic Law."[304] The "most successful constitution in German history" had brought the Germans of the Federal Republic "free and stable democracy, guarantees of human dignity and human rights, prosperity and social security based on the rule of law"—values the "peaceful revolution" in the GDR also stood for, the experts said. They also stressed that the economic, currency, and social union between the two German states could not be achieved without a unified constitution. Joining the Federal Republic would mean immediate membership in the European Community and would "preserve reliability in domestic and foreign policy." The process of drawing up a new constitution, on the other hand, could lead to uncertainty "with dangers for the internal stability and for the trust of the community of peoples."[305]

Such arguments had to be taken seriously, and the parties of the new coalition government in the GDR—the CDU, DSU, Democratic Awakening, the Liberals, the German Forum Party (DFP), the League of Free Democrats (BFD), the FDP, and the SPD—therefore agreed on April 12 to seek unification via Article 23. Despite an "unofficial" letter by Soviet ambassador Kochemasov to the GDR prime minister on April 16 stating that the Soviet Union could not accept the application of Article 23 since it would dissolve East Germany's obligations vis-à-vis the Soviets and the other allies, the new GDR government under de Maizière was determined to go ahead with German unification as fast as possible. Actually, it had no choice. The government declaration of April 19 indicated its favor of a quick accession according to Article 23.

For Schäuble, the issue was no longer an open question either when the "Alliance for Germany" scored a landslide victory in the East German election. Even before the coalition agreement was signed in East Berlin on April 12, he arranged the first interdepartmental conference on the preparation of a "Bill on the Introduction of Federal Law in the GDR (First Transition Bill)" in the Interior Ministry in Bonn on April 4.[306] Soon thereafter, on April 18, he met with his new East German counterpart, Peter-Michael Diestel, to settle practical questions.

The two ministers agreed to abolish most controls at the intra-German border by the summer; formalities for travelers between the two German states would be ended as soon as possible and shifted instead to the outer borders of the Federal Republic and the GDR. They established working groups for formulating joint border policies on combating terrorism and drugs, and they announced that police and fire department personnel as well as catastrophe and civil defense experts would be exchanged. In addition, Schäuble said that the West German Federal Intelligence Service would cease activities in the GDR because of the changed political situation; Diestel for his part pledged that the GDR's disbanded Ministry for State Security would not continue or resume its earlier espionage activities against the Federal Republic.[307]

The justice ministers from Bonn and East Berlin also began working toward the harmonization of the legal systems of the two German states. Hans Engelhard and his GDR counterpart, Kurt Wünsche, agreed during a meeting in Bonn on May 9 on a five-point plan to increase their cooperation. On the previous day, during a Bundesrat symposium entitled "Legal Ways Toward German Unity," Wünsche already had acknowledged that the laws of the Federal Republic should take precedence over those of the GDR.[308]

The measures now agreed upon between Wünsche and Engelhard included plans to dispatch five West German justice officials to the GDR ministry to serve as expert advisors in certain legal fields and to work on the reorganization of the GDR judicial system. A number of West German judges would also be sent to the GDR to serve as advisors, perform judicial services, and help set up new administrative, financial, and social jurisdictions in the GDR. In addition, Engelhard and Wünsche expressed the need for the further simplification and improvement of legal services between the two Germanys before unification and proposed partnerships between the legal administrative bodies in the East and West German Länder (federal states).[309]

At this point, however, it was still not clear when the unification process would be complete. When Shevardnadze met with Chancellor Kohl on the eve of the two-plus-four conference on May 4 in Bonn, Kohl told him that he expected German unity to be established "by December 31, 1992."[310] But after Shevardnadze's ambiguous statement on May 5 that Moscow no longer insisted on a clear definition of the military status of Germany before East and West Germany could merge—implying that the pressure for unification was mounting—Kohl concluded that "the question as for the timing of all-German elections rises anew." Even a date in 1990 was not unthinkable anymore, he said.[311]

During the "coalition round" on May 15, when the final text of the state treaty on the economic and currency union was agreed upon, the leaders of the parties of the governing coalition of CDU/CSU and FDP also unanimously voiced their approval for scheduling the all-German election "by the end of the Bundestag's current legislative session"—that is, December 2, 1990, or on January 13, 1991, at the latest—and called on the parliament of the GDR to take steps so that joint elections could be held as soon as possible.[312] Kohl also was optimistic that the opposition SPD and Greens, who were critical of the coalition's present stance and still rejected all-German elections at such an early date, would not dare block the unification process. The fact that the SPD East and those West German states that were led by SPD governments had already agreed to the DM115 billion "German Unity Fund" was, in the chancellor's view, a distinct sign of the readiness of the opposition eventually to consent to a policy of rapid unification.[313]

Klaus-Dieter Schnapauff's special staff in the Interior Ministry therefore hurried to conclude its work on a paper called "Basic Structures of a State Treaty for the Establishment of German Unity." On May 29, Schäuble presented it to the parliamentary state secretary, Günther Krause, in Prime Minister de Maizière's office.[314] The text was continuously refined in close consultations with Krause and his staff until it evolved into a draft entitled "Elements of a Settlement to be Reached for the Establishment of German Unity," in essence a blueprint for the treaty eventually signed on August 31.

Krause, on the other hand, on May 29 presented no more than a brief, five-page note entitled "Germany's Unity." But the sketchy paper—with subchapters on the Basic Law, economics, finances, domestic affairs, foreign affairs, legal matters, and schools/universities—candidly expressed the expectations as well as fears of the 16 million East Germans as they were plunging into another world.[315] One week later, on June 8, Schäuble and Krause met again, now accompanied by Chancellery Minister Seiters and the minister in the GDR prime minister's office, Klaus Reichenbach, for preliminary talks on the second, unity treaty, which followed the first state treaty on the economic, monetary, and social union.

As a result of the initial talks, a "Joint Government Declaration on Open Property Questions" was passed on June 15, 1990. It dealt with businesses and private property nationalized after the founding of the GDR in 1949 that the governments in Bonn and East Berlin expected to be reprivatized in the form of a "socially tolerable equalization of different interests."[316] Yet the question was "explosive," as the parliamentary state secretary in the Ministry for Intra-German Relations, Ottfried Hennig, had cautioned as early as April.[317] The protection of private property was guaranteed in the West German constitution, and the guarantees also applied to GDR citizens who had acquired property in good faith without considering the legality of their government's actions in originally nationalizing it. But the existing legal framework did not cover finalizing the present ownership situation in the

GDR, nor did it permit the reestablishment of ownership conditions of the year 1945, Hennig told the Bundestag Committee on Intra-German Affairs. In other words, a new legal basis would have to be found to settle the disputes that were expected. Hennig had noted, however, that he saw little chance for those individuals whose property and assets had been nationalized between the end of World War II and the establishment of the GDR, as these measures had been undertaken by the Soviet occupying power and were legally binding.[318] But in all other cases "return of property rather than compensation" would be the guiding principle of the settlement.

This situation was still unchanged when the formal negotiations on the second state treaty began on July 6, in East Berlin, with delegations from the two central governments as well as representatives of the Länder governments—that is, including members of parties that were in opposition to the Federal government in Bonn—and the EC Commission from Brussels.[319] In the meantime, border controls between the two Germanys had been lifted. And with the new freedom, old claims had come to the fore. West German owners had started to examine their former property in the East; the new users had begun to fear that they might be thrown out of house and home; and the first lawsuits had already been filed.[320] Prime Minister de Maizière, who personally welcomed the negotiations' participants on July 6, said during the opening session that the issue of property rights, which had been left open in the state treaty on the economic, monetary, and social union, now had to be fixed "impeccably, with a binding mandate to the future common legislature to find a solution."[321]

In addition, the East German prime minister said the negotiations should be concluded quickly, possibly by the end of August. Then the treaty—which would receive the name "Treaty on German Unity" to underline its special significance—could be ratified by the Bundestag and Volkskammer in September, before all-German parliamentary elections were held. Yet the accession of the GDR would become effective only after the election in order to avoid a "political vacuum" wherein the interests of the GDR population would not be represented.

The election itself would be held separately in the Federal Republic and the GDR, de Maizière stressed. If the new all-German parliament was elected on the basis of a common election law, including the usual 5 percent clause, only the traditional parties with well-equipped organizations would succeed; the small civil movements that had emerged during the East German revolution of 1989 would have no chance. Therefore, an election law should be passed that would guarantee a fair representation of the new political groupings in the all-German parliament.

Finally, de Maizière turned to the marks of the new state: What would be its name? What colors and symbols would decorate its flag? What melody would be played as the national anthem, and which text would be sung? What city would be chosen as capital of the united Germany?

The prime minister maintained that the answers to such questions were important for the identification of the citizens with their new state. Possible alternatives would need to be discussed quickly. The name of the new state, for instance, could be either "Deutsche Bundesrepublik" (German Federal Republic) or "Bund Deutscher Länder" (Federation of German States); its capital might be the newly united city of Berlin, for decades a symbol of division and East-West confrontation but now a possible cornerstone of peace and East-West cooperation. As far as the national anthem was concerned, de Maizière said he could agree to the West German melody—written by the Austrian Joseph Haydn—but that it should be combined with the text of the GDR hymn by Johannes R. Becher, "Auferstanden aus Ruinen" (Risen from Ruins), rather than Hoffmann von Fallersleben's "Einigkeit and Recht and Freiheit" (Unity and Right and Freedom) sung by the West Germans. (As an experienced violinist, he had already tested the combination of Becher's text with Haydn's music, and it had worked out fine.) Only the decision about the colors of the national flag was difficult and required further thought, the prime minister declared.[322]

Schäuble later noted that he had conceived de Maizière's suggestions with a "different degree of seriousness." To change the name of the Federal Republic had of course been out of the question from the start. If the name did not exist already, he had told the prime minister, "it would have to be invented." Regarding the flag and the national anthem, he could not imagine compromises either. But the question of the future capital of a united Germany as well as the electoral procedure and the property issue required careful consideration, and solutions would have to be acceptable for the citizens of both parts of Germany.[323]

On the afternoon of July 6, when State Secretary Günther Krause took over as head of the East German negotiating team, the talks went more smoothly. Krause and Schäuble were at one in hoping to accomplish German unity as quickly as possible, and had already agreed on May 29 to aim at December 2 as the appropriate date for all-German elections.[324] Unlike de Maizière, Krause never gave the impression that he intended to save much from the old GDR to pull over into the new state. On the contrary, he often complained about the prime minister, who was "asking too many people for advice," had "too much regard for the Social Democrats," and was "constantly showing consideration for the Soviets," who might be concerned about the speed of developments in Germany. The differences escalated into open conflict behind the scenes at the end of July, when Krause told de Maizière by telephone that "if we do not make headway now, I will no longer take part." Well into August he kept up his threat to return to his university post as a professor for computer science in Wismar and forget about politics if the situation did not improve.

But for Schäuble, Krause was indispensable—not despite but because of his personal disposition. Without Krause, everything would have been more difficult, complicated, and, above all, time-consuming. Therefore Schäuble brought all his influence to bear to convince Krause that it was necessary to stay on. The close cooperation between the two actually contributed significantly to the relative smoothness in the enormously complex legal transition of a communist dictatorship to a democratic constitutional state in the former GDR.

On July 6, for instance, Schäuble and Krause came to terms on the schedule for the future course of the negotiations so quickly that the note-taker had difficulties keeping track with the details of the agreement. Only one major difference occurred. The East Berlin government still proceeded on the assumption that in principle GDR laws would continue to be valid. Otherwise, the unanimity was so complete that instructions could be given the same day to the various departments of the respective governments to prepare talking papers and drafts for the individual parts of the envisaged treaty.

On July 30, Schäuble and Krause also agreed to a "conceptual framework" for an all-German election treaty, as required by a decision of the East German Volkskammer on July 22. The decision had rejected Prime Minister de Maizière's earlier request for separate elections in both German states and caused a heated discussion on whether the West German 5 percent clause should be applied to all of Germany or modified in a new election law to be worked out between the two German governments. A compromise was found in a draft formulated by the head of the electoral law department in the West German Interior Ministry, Counselor Irmgard von Rottenburg, to apply the 5 percent clause in all of Germany but to allow "ticket combinations" of parties and political groupings in order to improve their chances of getting across the 5 percent hurdle. The draft was eventually agreed upon by Schäuble and Krause on July 30, and the treaty was signed by the two negotiators on August 3.[325]

On the same day, August 3, Prime Minister de Maizière announced after a meeting with Chancellor Kohl at Lake Wolfgang in Austria that he intended to step before the Volkskammer the following week and propose the unification of Germany as early as October 14. The situation in the GDR was dramatic, de Maizière argued. The state of the economy made "acceleration of the German unification train" inevitable. The problems of the "mastering of 40 years of socialist mismanagement" were greater than had been expected. Now he hoped that an early accession—and advanced all-German elections—would provide new investments, jobs, and economic security.[326]

Schäuble disagreed. He was concerned that the Constitutional Court of the Federal Republic would reject the advanced elections and insist on compliance with the regular schedule. The interior minister therefore called upon the chancellor at midnight on August 3 to change his mind. Kohl promised "to think the matter over again" and stated next morning that the SPD should agree to amend the Basic Law in order to make all-German elections on October 14 possible. As he had expected, the SPD rejected the proposal on August 8, and the elections eventually were held as planned on December 2.

Meanwhile, the negotiations on the unification treaty proceeded routinely. The second round of the talks took place in East Berlin on August 1. Five days later, a first draft of the treaty was finished. On August 20, the delegations met at the Federal Ministry of Transportation in Bonn-Bad Godesberg's Kennedyallee for their third round of talks, which lasted until August 24. While these negotiations were still continuing, the People's Chamber in East Berlin passed a basic decision in the early-morning hours of August 23, declaring "the accession of the German Democratic Republic to the jurisdiction of the Basic Law of the Federal Republic of Germany according to Article 23 of the Basic Law with effect from October 3, 1990."[327]

This meant that the GDR would accede to the Federal Republic before all-German elections would be held—contrary to Prime Minister de Maizière's former position not to relinquish the GDR until the people of East Germany were represented fully in an all-German parliament. Yet after the agreement between Kohl and Gorbachev in the Caucasus and the imminent signing of the two-plus-four treaty at the forthcoming conference on September 12 in Moscow, the decision of the GDR parliament to render East Germany "to the jurisdiction of the Basic Law" as early as October 3 was the final step toward German unity. The negotiations on the unification treaty were therefore conducted both with greater urgency than before and more optimism and a clear perspective of their outcome.

The fourth and final round of the negotiations, which took place on the Rhine again, began on August 30 and concluded with the initialing of the treaty at 2:08 A.M. on August 31. Later in the day, after only a few hours of sleep, Schäuble and Krause then signed the treaty at the Crown Prince's Palace in East Berlin. It was passed by the Bundestag and Volkskammer on September 20 and went into effect on September 29. Meanwhile, on September 24, the GDR minister of defense and disarmament, Rainer Eppelmann, also had signed an agreement on the withdrawal of the GDR from the Warsaw Treaty Organization as of October 3. The Allied Kommandatura held its final session in Berlin on October 2. And on October 3 at 0:00 hours, Germany was a united country again.

The enlarged Bundestag, which now also included 144 deputies of the former GDR, met for its first session on October 4 at the Reichstag in Berlin. On October 14, regional elections were held in the new Länder of East Germany. And on December 2, the first all-German parliamentary election took place, together with elections for the Berlin House of Representatives. The new Bundestag convened on December 20, and Helmut Kohl was reelected by it as chancellor on January 17, 1991, for another four-year term.

Implications of
German Unification

Spectacular midnight fireworks over the old Reichstag in Berlin heralded the unification of Germany on October 3, 1990. Hundreds of thousands of people greeted the newly united country on the streets of its capital at the Spree River. Yet the celebration was a public festival, not an expression of nationalistic exultation. The official speakers all stressed the European dimension of the German unification process and the necessity of opening a new chapter in the history of the European continent. None of them argued that the new Germany should use its enlarged power to return to a Reich-style policy of trying to dominate Europe and intimidate the world. The Germans seemed to have made peace with their neighbors, and the neighbors seemed to have made peace with them.

Long before the unification of Germany had become a reality, Foreign Minister Hans-Dietrich Genscher had in fact declared that the Federal government wished "to make the destiny of Germany part of the destiny of Europe." Speaking at a meeting of the Human Rights Dimension of the Conference on Security and Cooperation in Europe on June 5, 1990, in Copenhagen, Genscher cited Thomas Mann's statement: "We want a European Germany and not a German Europe."[1] Now, on October 3, Chancellor Helmut Kohl confirmed in a "Message to All Governments of the World" that Germany, with its newly achieved national unity, wanted to "serve the peace in the world and promote the integration of Europe."[2] And President Richard von Weizsäcker asserted during the Day of Unity state ceremony in Berlin's Philharmonic Hall that German unification was "part of a pan-European historical process aimed at the freedom of all people and a new peace order on our continent."[3]

The perception of a postunification Germany firmly anchored within the stable framework of "pan-Europeanism" was certainly the most favored scenario among Germans and non-Germans alike. The question was, however, whether a scenario of reduced tensions between national interests, increased European integration, and flourishing freedom and democracy was also very realistic.

There was another perception of Germany after unification, one that worried many observers. Envisaging a return to nationalistic eruptions at home and a Bismarckian foreign policy abroad, some wondered if Germany would dislodge its anchor with the West as it rediscovered the old ties with the Soviet Union and the East. Would it earnestly try to play the old game of becoming a middleman between East and West again, or play the East against the West for its own advantage? Might it have forgotten the tragic lessons of German and European 19th- and 20th-century history and repeat the mistakes of the past?

Possible answers to such questions must take into account the new structural complexity of the world, in which the European order has largely been redefined. The collapse of the Soviet empire, the liberalization of the nations of Eastern Europe from Soviet-dominated—or, in the case of Albania, China-influenced—communism, and the unification of Germany are the key elements of revolutionary change. The emergence of the new order has been accompanied not only by the usual amount of uncertainty in the abstract, but also by widespread, deep insecurity and the potential of military conflict and even war, as the developments in the former Yugoslavia and the disintegrated Soviet Union have already shown.[4]

In this respect, the unification of Germany is of particular significance. The united Germany is located in the center of Europe, next to the developing but still struggling market economies and emerging new democracies of East-Central Europe and close to the conflict zones of the former Soviet Union and the Balkans. Germany therefore cannot escape the effects of the transformation of the East European order; it will have to participate in the transition there from repressive dictatorships and state-planned economies to pluralistic democracies and free-market management. At the same time, the united Germany will remain firmly tied to the Western nations and will have to play its role in the development of the European Community and the Atlantic Alliance.

In any event, Germany will no longer be able to sail in the lee of world politics, as was the case during four decades of US-Soviet predominance. Germany must now search for and find a new role for itself in almost every respect.[5] What could be the elements of this new role? Will the policy of the newly united Germany be characterized by inward-oriented parochialism, or by outward-directed power and arrogance? Will the enlarged and fully sovereign Germany pursue a rather unselfish course of European integration, or will it be tempted to establish a "Fourth Reich"—thus resuming or varying the tradition of the First Reich from 800 until 1806, the Second from 1871 until 1918, and the Third from 1933 until 1945? And what are the immediate as well as long-term political, military, and economic implications of German unification as such?

In short, what can Europe and the world expect from a country that has stirred so much controversy for so long and that nevertheless has been placed by the forces of history at the center of the dramatic changes since the revolution of 1989? Even shorter, whither Germany in the "new architecture" of the international order in Europe and beyond?

ASCENDANCE OF A FOURTH REICH?

It seems only logical that the size, power, and influence of the newly united Germany implies that Germany's new role will a priori be burdened with historical recriminations as well as current demands.[6] Regardless of the substance of its policy, Germany will be suspected of at least secretly pursuing the course of a "Fourth Reich." At the same time, countries from both East and West as well as from the North and the South will ask for its political, economic, and probably even military assistance.

During the 1991 Gulf War, the Germans received some firsthand experience of what leadership, or the calling into international responsibility, means in terms of being courted and condemned, applauded and criticized, supported and opposed—often simultaneously. While warnings against another erratic German Nationalrausch (lust for nationalism) still prevailed, the Western allies expected a greater German commitment to the anti-Saddam Hussein front.[7] When the government in Bonn pointed out that Germany's constitution prohibited out-of-area military cooperation, even within collective security regimes of the United Nations, the Germans were accused of "escaping international responsibility by hiding behind this amorphous provision of the Basic Law."[8] And when the Federal government subsequently decided to at least help finance the war by taking over a major share of its costs, Bonn was accused of "checkbook diplomacy."[9]

The situation was not without irony. Before the Gulf War, the predominant fear had been that a united Germany would return to the ways of Bismarck. Now the resounding complaint was that the Germans were looking toward Switzerland as a model for their united country. Hardly anyone was reflecting on what the international reaction might have been if the Germans had enthusiastically welcomed the war in the desert, if the German government had hurriedly deployed several Bundeswehr divisions to the Iraqi border and dispatched an armada of destroyers to the Gulf, or if a bull-like Chancellor Kohl had preferred gunboat diplomacy over a policy of moderation. Thus the dilemma of German politics between historical constraints and current requirements became apparent.

The irritation about Germany's enigmatic wavering during the Gulf War was increased by the fact that as a result of the collapse of the Soviet empire, the emancipation of Eastern Europe, and the fading predominance of the United States in the European theater, the whole "European equation" was changing.[10] Actually, the augmented strength of Germany had been caused only partly by the unification of the country itself; to a much broader degree, it was due to complex structural transformations of the international order in general that made Germany "indeed once again the ascendent state in Europe—and the only one to emerge from the Cold War clearly much stronger."[11] With its newly established unity, geographical location in the middle of a continent, and traditional role as Europe's central power, Germany seemed bound to play a key role in the shaping of a "New European Order."

Yet during the time of the Gulf War, Germany was still immersed in its own unification and had not even begun searching for a new role. Although it was commonly observed that the Federal government could not simply sustain its post-World War II foreign policy posture in an international environment that had changed so drastically, the formulation of a new policy tailored to its own exigencies while also compatible with the legitimate expectations of the international community could be achieved only gradually. Moreover, the slowing—and sometimes regressing—of the reforms in Eastern Europe, the violent disintegration of Yugoslavia, and the pauperization of Russia and the other members of the Commonwealth of Independent States, as well as the problems of financing the absorption of the five East German Länder and advancing the integration of Western Europe, further obfuscated the elucidation on views in Bonn of a new German foreign policy in the post-Cold War era.[12]

Even at this early time, however, it was apparent that Germany's future would hardly be characterized by a return to patterns of the past. The political balancing act that the German Reich had performed during the Wilhelmine period under Chancellor Bismarck and his successors between 1871 and 1918 and during the Weimar Republic from 1918 until 1933—let alone the nationalist-racist course under Hitler—was neither sensible nor feasible in the international environment on the threshold of the twenty-first century. Whereas the unification of the Reich in 1871 had led to isolation throughout the late nineteenth and early twentieth centuries with disastrous results, the unification of Germany in 1990 was achieved on the basis of firm and continuous institutional ties to the West and with the acceptance of its neighbors all around. The former Reich had been established by war and had lived—or to some extent also may have been forced to live—in opposition to the existing order, with disputes over borders and clashes over diverging national interests. The united Germany of 1990 not only relinquished any historical or legal claims to former German territories, but had been created via negotiations in the two-plus-four process and thus from the outset constituted an integral part of the international community.[13] Daniel Hamilton argues therefore that:

> Kaiser Wilhelm's Germany was encircled; Helmut Kohl's Germany is enmeshed in a dense web of overlapping institutions, and is in the forefront of efforts to deepen and extend this network of linkages throughout Europe. On the whole, German leaders still believe that they will be able to advance German interests more effectively through the policies of the Atlantic, European and international institutions in which Germany is embedded, than through direct and unilateral German action.[14]

Maintaining Germany's ties with multilateral institutions was not just a matter of belief, however, but a concern of national interest. Both a seesaw Schaukelpolitik between East and West and the attempt to establish a position of hegemony had proven to be fatal mistakes. The Federal Republic's close association with the West after World War II, on the other hand, had brought about economic prosperity and political stability. A change of course and the return to a nationalistic policy outside the well-tried institutions thus was highly unlikely, indeed out of the question.[15]

The idea of turning the Federal Republic into a Fourth Reich after unification remained the dream of only a few. The rise of nationalism in Germany—as well as in most other countries of Europe, especially in the East, for that matter—at the beginning of the 1990s was actually less the result of an attractive new ideology or the expression of an inner wish of a major portion of the people than an upshot of the collapse of communism and an effect of social and economic turmoil in the aftermath of the revolution of 1989.

In Eastern Europe, the initial outburst of nationalist passions was largely a consequence of the disappearance of longtime Soviet control and suppression; in Western Europe, the collapse of communism led to the fading of a common "enemy image" as an integrating factor of society.[16] In addition, the dramatic structural changes that caused high unemployment and deep social insecurity provoked mass migration (facilitated by the removal of borders) and, in turn, increased hostility against foreigners. Yet the people who voted for right-wing parties often did so merely to express their protest against the passivity of the traditional political establishment, which they found unable to cope with the mounting problems in a rapidly changing world.[17]

Regarding Germany, however, the new nationalism of the 1990s was often confused with the excessive nationalism of the past. The question was raised as to whether there was, in view of the history of the German Reich in the late 19th and early 20th centuries, a "resurgent German militarism" that might come to the forefront again as a result of new German unity, the development of a new German pride, and the search for a new German identity. Angela Stent, associate professor of government at Georgetown University, noted in this respect though that

> those who fear a resurgent German militarism should remember that in the first half of the 1980s the United States was primarily concerned with an excess of pacifism and antinuclear sentiment in Germany. If the experience of postwar West Germany is any guide, the new German nationalism will not be aggressive, but rather directed toward peaceful, all-European goals.[18]

Although the situation in East Germany—with the formation of numerous right-wing, antiforeigner, anti-Semitic, and militaristic circles—was less certain, Professor Stent stated that the numbers of these groups had remained small. She concluded that the movements were unlikely to find much support in a united Germany unless a worldwide recession had a major impact on the German economy.[19]

Actually, the new German nationalism, combined with neo-Nazi tendencies and aggressive militarism, which had been feared throughout the unification process in 1990, did not become a lasting political factor after unification—despite an epidemic of attacks by radical youths, skinheads, and neo-Nazis against foreigners from 1991 to 1993. Yet the official German policy, though concerned about the increasing public outrage against the liberal German asylum laws and the perceived beginning of a new "migration of nations," continued to be oriented toward European integration, and the overwhelming majority of the German people also seemed to be inclined to support that goal further.

Moreover, the triumph of unification was largely ascribed to the success of the German Ostpolitik of the 1970s and 1980s and was thus embedded in the framework of European reconciliation and détente rather than in the view of a competitive East-West struggle in which the West eventually had scored a decisive victory over the East. This "Europeanization" of the German question helped make the unification of Germany more palatable to its neighbors. It also eased difficulties about coming to terms with the past, both Nazi and Stasi. The debate over how unique the Nazi terror had been, compared for instance with the crimes of Stalinism, was now followed by painful revelations and a heated internal discussion about the mechanism and practices of the East German secret police.[20]

The European dimension of German unification had already been stressed by Foreign Minister Genscher at the first two-plus-four conference in Bonn on May 5, 1990, where he had said that rather than creating new problems for Europe, the unification of Germany would "play a part in ensuring a new and lasting stability." Moreover, Genscher had added, the German government considered "the transformation of this insight of European history into a policy for Germany and for a gradually uniting Europe to be Germany's European mission as we approach the end of this century."[21]

European integration had in fact been a central element of the foreign policy of the Federal Republic ever since its foundation in 1949. The European idea had offered both a way of welcoming Germany back into the community of civilized states and an ersatz identity for the deflected national feelings of the German people. But the Germans, unlike nations whose relationship toward their own history was less broken and who thus saw a lesser need to seek refuge in the idea of integration, viewed European unification also as a way to overcome the unrestrained forces of nationalism. Meshing the two parts of Europe in an all-European "peace order," rather than restoring the unity of the German nation-state, had thus been a primary goal of German politics.[22] Due to its geographical position in Europe as "the East of the West, but also the West of the center,"[23] Germany had even seemed to be predestined to "repair the bridge between Eastern and Western Europe."[24] Consequently, the policy of West European integration and the concept of East-West détente had been supplemented by a vision of pan-European cooperation.[25]

When Gorbachev's philosophy of a "common European home" and the East European revolution of 1989 had eventually let pan-European utopianism evolve into a concrete perspective, the German politicians saw themselves already at the vanguard of all-European integration and believed the unification of Germany to be only an intermediate step toward the unification of Europe. Germany should fulfill its "European mission," as Foreign Minister Genscher had said, to complete the task that it had begun with integration in the West by turning now to the East.[26] Fear that Germany's commitment to Europe might weaken after regaining unity and sovereignty quickly dissolved in the wake of new initiatives aimed at creating a "European Union," as was agreed upon in the Maastricht Treaty of February 7, 1992.[27]

In fact, the goal of integrating Europe remained central to German foreign policy after unification. Continued German support for strengthening West

European institutions and the search for ways of extending the boundaries of the European Community eastward were principal matters of German national interest. This remained true even when the political and economic implications of the unification process and the effects of the dramatic changes in Eastern Europe began to strain the resources and leadership of the newly united country. More, rather than less, emphasis was therefore put on the idea of European integration. The key German role in moving along European unification demonstrated its determination to create a new European order based on integration and reconciliation while avoiding a return to nationalistic exuberance and hostility in the name of misread patriotism.

EMPHASIS ON EUROPE: WEST AND EAST

Despite the country's well-practiced European vocation, Germany was anything but prepared to play a major role on the stage of world politics when the country was united again on October 3, 1990. As a result of two military, moral, and economic catastrophes in recent history and after 40 years of relative passivity since 1945, the German nation appeared to be suffering from an endemic aversion to exercising military power and took sides in international conflicts only as a "civilian force."[28] Additionally, in the wake of unification, Germany was caught up in uniting internally and seemed to have neither the time nor the attention to find a new role externally. The German government practiced a costly checkbook diplomacy instead, yet with fewer political benefits than the expenses should have warranted, such as during the Gulf War of 1991.[29]

Meanwhile the reorientation of German foreign policy has progressed, and it becomes increasingly clear that Germany's focus has shifted from playing the limited role of a junior partner in the West against the communist East to assuming a key position in the remodeling of Europe after the end of the Cold War. This does not imply that existing ties with NATO or the EC are threatened, but the new German emphasis on both Western and Eastern Europe provides for wider responsibility and greater influence. As Robert Gerald Livingston has noted, "Russian power has now receded once again from Eastern Europe. And as so often happened in the past, German power is replacing it there. . . . With unification, Germany resumes its historical role as a Central European power, whose interests in the East are every bit as important as those in the West."[30]

The two chosen arenas of Germany's primary interest, Eastern Europe and the EC, are therefore likely to dominate German foreign policy in the time to come. The EC—despite all its deficiencies—continues to be of principal importance, as it is the only organization that can provide the framework for a policy eventually aimed at all-European integration. Neither the military alliance of NATO nor the conference forum of the CSCE can fulfill this task. Only the political and economic network of the EC seems to be a proper starting point for the European unification process.

In November 1989, shortly after the opening of the borders between East and West Germany, experts warned that as a result of the rapprochement of the two Germanys the efforts to unify the internal markets of the member countries of the EC would "not be derailed, but . . . slowed."[31] For West Germany, the development in the East would take priority over the process of integrating with its Western partners and would also hasten the debate over the status of Austria, Turkey, Hungary, and other countries seeking a special status with the European Community. As a result, the European economic region was going to expand—possibly with the effect that the deepening of integration would suffer, if not be sacrificed.

Former West German chancellor Helmut Schmidt also stated after the last GDR election in March 1990 that the speed of European unification could be "a little hampered" by rapid German unification and that the EC's project to create a single internal market by 1993 might have to be postponed.[32] At the same time, a leading European industrialist, Jacques Calvet, chairman of the Peugeot car company, even urged the European Community to halt the political and economic integration exercise and stop the process of opening its internal market since the changes in Eastern Europe had made the future too uncertain. "It would be wild madness to continue calmly writing pieces of paper and making directives. Directives to do what? What is the common future? I don't know," Calvet told the Italian newspaper *La Repubblica,* adding that he had never believed in the opening of the internal market anyway and that his conviction had been "strengthened by the slowness with which they have gone along this path."[33]

West German chancellor Kohl, on the other hand, stressed time and again that the German unification process should be embedded in a stable European framework and, moreover, that the unification of Germany should act as a catalyst, accelerating European integration on the path toward political union. For instance, in a policy statement to the Bundestag on May 10, 1990, Kohl said that furthering the process of European unity required strengthening the European Parliament's powers of jurisdiction and control, intensification of the unity and cohesion of the EC in all areas, development of a joint security policy, and execution of the work of EC institutions with greater efficiency. Specifically, the chancellor referred to the EC summit that had been held in Dublin the previous month, where he had emphasized that his government did not want to solve the German problem at the expense of other EC countries. Kohl then told the Bundestag:

> Our aim must be German and European unity. It would be very harmful to Europe's future if the structurally weak EC countries were now to lag behind in their development instead of progressing on the way to structural adjustment because there is now a chance for greater freedom in Central, Eastern and Southeastern Europe, and of course also in the GDR. We want both to exert a positive influence on the developments in Central, Eastern and Southeastern Europe and to accomplish German unity with everything this entails—and we also want to avoid a further widening of the gap in the development of the individual EC countries. What is needed instead is a gradual harmonization of developments.[34]

In Dublin, Kohl and French president Mitterrand also had an initial discussion on key elements of further European integration within the framework of two parallel intergovernmental conferences scheduled to coincide with the EC summit in Rome the following December. The two conferences involved economic and monetary union on the basis of the decisions taken in Strasbourg in December 1989, as well as political union, which in the German view had from the outset been the fundamental objective of the Rome treaties establishing the European Economic Community in 1957. At the same time, Kohl urged completion of the single European market by December 31, 1992, as scheduled.[35]

Yet differences of opinion remained as to what end the concept of European integration would eventually lead. While the French government believed that the unification of Germany gave even greater urgency to political union as the best way of anchoring a single German state to the community, British prime minister Margaret Thatcher already objected to the Community's agenda for economic and monetary union and made it clear that transfer of greater political authority to the EC and its executive body, the European Commission, was unacceptable to her. A single European government—as part of a Federation of European States—therefore continued to be no more than a distant dream.[36]

The EC special summit in Dublin nevertheless gave significant momentum toward greater unity, with the long-term objective remaining the creation of an economic and political unit capable of competing successfully with both the United States and Japan. Overriding British objections, the Community heads of government endorsed a plan to achieve "economic and monetary union," including the creation of a common currency—the so-called European Currency Unit (ECU)—and regional central bank (Eurofed) after the single market went into effect in 1993. East Germany would automatically join the Community when it was absorbed by the Federal Republic, while other Eastern European countries would be offered loose association agreements rather than membership.[37]

The decision to "deepen" rather than "widen" the Community corresponded with the prevailing German view that the EC could fulfill its task of becoming the hub of the new Europe only if at first the integration of Western Europe was brought to a successful end. The accession of some or all European states, leading eventually to a community stretching from the Atlantic to the Baltics and the Ukraine, was therefore pragmatically recognized as impracticable for the foreseeable future. The Maastricht Treaty of February 7, 1992, therefore envisaged the foundation of a European Currency Institute in January 1994 as a transitional step toward the establishment of a European Central Bank and the creation of a common currency by January 1, 1999. Regarding the expansion of the Community, however, it was only said that any European state whose system of government was based on democratic principles could apply for membership; no commitment was made to decide on the enlargement quickly.[38] On the other hand, agreements were concluded with the Czech and Slovak Federal Republic (CSFR), Poland, Hungary, and Romania as a transitional stage, likely to lead to EC membership eventually. Agreement was also reached with the European Free Trade Association (EFTA) to establish a "European Economic Area."

Yet even the creation of central EC financial institutions and the vision of a political union were controversial among the members of the community. Germany, which for a long time had "sublimated its nationalism in the Europe of the EC" and had viewed the community as "an ersatz for a lost Fatherland," found it increasingly difficult to bring its commitment to Western Europe in line with the political and economic burden in the East.[39] The British, who had insisted on an "opting-out" clause in the Maastricht Treaty anyway, could hardly envision a full economic and monetary union before the year 2000, and more likely not within 15 to 20 years. And the Danes even voted against the treaty in a referendum on June 2, 1992, before revising their decision on May 18, 1993.[40]

Despite growing difficulties, however, the basic idea of the European Community as the framework for all-European cooperation has not been questioned by any European government thus far. In fact, there seems to be no realistic alternative if Europe does not want to return to a system of nation-states—with at best a functioning "balance of power," or competing nationalism and ugly militarism, possibly with the gloomy perspective of a continuation of the European Civil War that marked European history during the first half of the twentieth century, at worst.[41] Regarding Germany, there is particularly good reason to hold on to the EC, whose Common Market took almost 53 percent of Germany's exports in 1991 (as compared with only 6 percent going to the United States) and whose political backing lends the German voice greater force.[42] Moreover, the post-1989 institutionalization developments in the EC were directly related to Germany's own attempts, and those of its neighbors, to embed the unified Germany in European structures.

One reason to slow down the process of European economic and monetary union, however, could be that rushing into it would make it more difficult for Eastern European countries to join the EC. In this respect, the united Germany is performing a delicate balancing act. On the one hand, the German government has assigned clear priority to deepening the integration among the present members of the EC over any schemes to widen the Community to countries that do not seem economically prepared for membership.[43] On the other hand, Germany is afraid of mass migration from Eastern Europe if the people in the former eastern bloc are excluded from the West European welfare zone indefinitely and, after losing hope, decide to leave their homelands and move westward.

The flow of "economic refugees" has already started—mainly from Romania —and could easily grow to unacceptable proportions if the EC tries to seal itself off the East. Estimates about possible numbers of economic migrants from Eastern to Western Europe vary from 30 million to as many as 120 million people. Scholars believe that a large number of the 390 million citizens of the former communist bloc in Eastern Europe and the Soviet Union must be regarded as potential migrants.[44] The prospect of EC membership for at least the new Czech Republic, Slovakia, Hungary, Poland, Romania, and the Baltic states in the not-too-distant future could ease the migration problem, as this would have a positive effect both economically and psychologically in the countries directly concerned, as well as in their neighboring states, which would then retain their hope to soon join the Community, too. Germany therefore supports association agreements and even EC membership for Central, East, and Southeast European countries to give them access to EC— and, particularly, German—markets, which is crucial to the reconstruction and future prosperity of the former communist economies. And the potential problem is magnified by the very real movements of "political refugees," such as those fleeing violent conflict in ex-Yugoslavia.

The extent to which Germany feels vulnerable to instability in the East is also demonstrated by the fact that German private investment and state grants, credits, or credit guarantees to Eastern Europe outstrip the aid of all other Western countries combined. While American, British, French, or

Japanese firms and governments were slow in committing themselves to investments in Eastern Europe (except in Hungary), the Germans moved in massively. In 1990, German firms accounted for some 59 percent of the acquisitions and 38 percent of the joint ventures made by foreigners in Eastern Europe and the Soviet Union; France, with 13 percent of the acquisitions and 18 percent of the joint ventures, and the United States, with only 3 percent and 14 percent, respectively, were a distant second and third, while Japan was not even in the picture.[45] In 1991, Germany provided more than DM75 billion in grants, credits, and loans to the former Soviet Union, and another DM30 billion to the East and Central European countries of the former East bloc. According to a very droll Czech joke, "the only thing worse than being dominated by the German economy is—not being dominated by it."[46]

In turn, Germany is bound to play a decisive role in the future of Eastern Europe, which may not become entirely a "sphere of German influence" but will certainly be a second focus of attention, next to the EC, of German foreign policy. It also can be expected that the German government will try to combine the two—that is, to act in Eastern Europe as a representative of the EC, thus avoiding resemblance to the policies of former German regimes, and to use the funds of the Community to satisfy Eastern Europe's longer-term financial needs, which have been estimated at around $1.37 trillion, an amount too high for German resources alone to take care of.[47]

Yet for Germany, the East European problem is not just compounded by memories of the past and burdened with the need for massive capital investment. The dismal economic situation in Eastern Europe also has a direct impact on the state of the industry in the former GDR. Until 1989, about 80 percent of total East German trade had been with the East. In 1991, the figure declined by some 60 percent, thus affecting 850,000 jobs in East Germany directly and another 500,000 indirectly.[48] In other words, the collapse of the East German industry was caused not only by its own inefficiency and lack of competitiveness and by the implementation of the German Economic and Monetary Union, but by the simultaneous breakdown of its East European trading partners as well. The Deutsche Bank has estimated that it will take years to restore any significant import capacity in the East and that even then Western exports to Eastern Europe will hardly reach more than a meager 7 percent.[49]

Despite such bleak economic outlooks and other pitfalls, from a German point of view Eastern Europe is too close to be neglected. The German government therefore will try to promote West European integration along with a strong push for the inclusion of Eastern Europe, arguing that without complementing the integration efforts in the West with corresponding measures in the East the process of European integration could not succeed at all.

SECURITY WITHIN NATO, THE WEU, AND THE CSCE

The end of the Cold War and the collapse of the Soviet empire (with the subsequent withdrawal of Soviet forces from Central and Eastern Europe, including East Germany) have presented new challenges for all.[50] Apart from redirecting its foreign policy in general, Germany therefore is required more specifically to redefine its security interests and formulate a new postunification security policy.

Although the old Federal Republic saw itself largely as a "civilian" power, and despite the fact that the vast majority of German political analysts and the public favor a continuation of the civilian role for the united Germany as well, the Gulf War of 1991, the fighting in former Yugoslavia, and the emergency situation in Somalia caused an intense debate about new responsibilities after unification, including German participation in the peacekeeping and peace-making missions of the United Nations.[51] The discussion was marked by general disillusionment about the "new beginning" after 1989 and the disenchantment of the new "era of peace." After the Soviet threat vanished, new conflicts emerged instead. With them came actual warfare, which had been virtually unknown in Europe during the time of a nuclear "balance of terror." Violent nationalism, bloody ethnic conflicts, and hostile border disputes had been swept under the rug of superpower hegemony. The new situation—with greater openness but with less stability—demanded a new security system to respond to the challenges and dangers of the post-Cold War period and to provide peace and stability in a period of change and adjustment.[52] And Germany, it was agreed in the debate even within the SPD, clearly has to take sides, not only in the form of humanitarian relief operations but also in committing itself to the solution of problems, perhaps including the use of force.

Yet in the German view, the future security system should not be a completely new one. Throughout the process of unification, the government in Bonn maintained its position that NATO and the German membership in the Atlantic Alliance would remain the cornerstones of European security. In speeches before the American Council on Germany in New York on June 5, 1990, and at commencement ceremonies at Harvard University two days later, Chancellor Kohl emphasized the importance of preserving German-American friendship and the transatlantic partnership for the future of Europe.

Friendship and partnership with the United States, Kohl said in New York, were of "vital importance" for the Germans. It would soon become clear to all of Europe that "a united Germany as a member of the Western defense alliance will increase the security of everyone concerned and, as such, will become a cornerstone of a stable European peace order." Firm ties also would be upheld between the North American democracies and Europe through the process of CSCE, as this was the only basis also endorsed by the East for legitimate and lasting involvement of the United States and Canada in the construction of the future Europe. However, the CSCE would not replace NATO, the chancellor stated categorically.[53] At Harvard, where he was awarded an honorary doctorate, Kohl advocated that Europe and the United States combine their resources and that German-American friendship should be "a decisive prerequisite for Europe and America managing to cope in unison with the tasks of the future."[54]

Yet the premises of international security have changed so drastically since 1989 that the existing order is ill at ease. As long as a bipolar super-structure determined to a large extent the formulation of individual foreign and security policies, the security system was "rigid, albeit predictable," Peter Volten has noted. With the total collapse of the Soviet Union, this system came to an end. As a consequence, the "rationale for a common language, either superimposed on satellites or arrived at after endless debate, is gone in the East and contested in the West."[55]

The new order, therefore, will have to take into account that the disappearance of the disciplinary effect of the East-West conflict will lead to a nationalization of the foreign and security policy of individual countries on the basis of nationally perceived interests, influenced both by geostrategic considerations and domestic moods and preferences.[56] However, it is also true, on the other hand, that no single nation, not even a superpower, can build a new world order by itself.[57] That is why, in the German case, although the Atlantic Alliance may "slip to second or third rank"—behind the focus on Eastern Europe and the EC—the German government nevertheless will "adhere to multilateralism, devote itself to stability, and apply the lessons and techniques learned in the West over 40 years to diplomacy with the post-communist East."[58]

Within this framework NATO, the EC, West European Union (as the military arm of a common European defense force), and the CSCE are most likely to constitute the main pillars of the future German security policy.[59] The basic idea is to establish a system of interlocking institutions that complement each other and provide a whole set of political, economic, and security management tools that no single institution would possess on its own. From a German point of view, such multilateralism bears the advantage of not only allowing Germany to maintain a lower profile than would be the case if it acted as an individual power, but also of making the most cost-effective use of limited resources.[60]

Yet in military security, NATO remains at the core of German politics. The alliance embodies the transatlantic partnership and could be replaced only partly, if at all, by the membership of the United States and Canada in the

CSCE. The integrated military structure of NATO provides a solid underpinning for strategic unity and indivisibility of European and American security, which are complementary, not competitive. NATO, though also contested to a certain extent after the end of the Cold War, is still an important element of the American-European dialogue, the only organization that can guarantee the security of its member states. The new uncertainties, conflicts, and wars in the aftermath of the revolution of 1989 have only underlined the necessity of not being rash in changing or dissolving institutions that have proven to be effective and useful.[61]

In addition, NATO may well be needed in establishing the new European order, as it is capable of providing a framework for consultation as well as action. The transformation of the former Soviet empire and the development of legitimate political regimes with fixed territories and respected borders is an extremely complicated and sometimes painful process. It has the potential to turn violent in many instances in an unforeseeable future; the catastrophe in Yugoslavia may just be "a foretaste of what may happen elsewhere."[62] Crisis management and conflict resolution, therefore, will be major tasks in the years to come. In the past, NATO has proven to be effective as an insurance policy against external aggression and as a harmonizing instrument among its member states. Now the alliance could make an important contribution in drawing the democracies of Central and Eastern Europe and the states of the former Soviet Union into the new Europe by helping them to overcome the difficulties of transition and to be secure.[63]

The establishment of the North Atlantic Cooperation Council (NACC), inaugurated in December 1991 in Brussels, was an important step to raise the alliance's liaison relationships with the countries of Central and Eastern Europe to a qualitative new level in recognition of the democratic progress they had made. The invitation to these nations, including the three newly independent Baltic states, to join the NATO allies in an institutionalized framework of consultations was more than a symbolic gesture and may evolve soon into a primary security forum of a future Euro-Atlantic community. All nations from Vancouver to Vladivostok could be represented, because the alliance achieved consensus in January 1992 that it would also invite the new states on the territory of the former Soviet Union to join the NACC and participate in all NATO's enhanced liaison activities as soon as they were recognized by the allies.[64] Germany strongly supported the creation of the NACC, which it regards to be a substantial contribution to the reconstruction of political order in Eastern Europe and, in the longer term, a reasonable accompanying measure to the inclusion of countries such as the Czech Republic, Slovakia, Hungary, and Poland into the EC.[65]

The NATO liaison work plan is aimed at helping the new governments in Eastern Europe remodel their armed forces. It contains a variety of activities, including visits and exchanges, fellowships for the study of democratic institutions, opening up of Western science programs to Eastern participation, and, above all, multiple military contacts through, for instance, training the officers of Eastern countries in NATO colleges. In addition, the NACC is discussing conventional and nuclear arms control issues, including proliferation and a whole new generation of confidence- and security-building measures, covering all kinds of military activities, budgets, military doctrines, and training, among others. NATO is also providing expertise on the safe, controlled destruction of nuclear weapons, particularly the elimination of all ground-launched short-range nuclear forces, compliance with the Nuclear Non-Proliferation Treaty, and export controls on the transfer of nuclear and chemical weapons technologies to third parties. The alliance also is facilitating the exchange of information and experience on verification and the conversion of defense industries to civilian use.[66] All such steps will tighten the new bonds between East and West and encourage the Eastern countries to associate themselves with the Western alliance, thus promoting a new security identity in the Euro-Atlantic community.

The second pillar of the new security order in Europe, as seen from a German viewpoint, is the CSCE. The new CSCE institutions established in November 1990 at the Paris summit, such as a Conflict Prevention Center in Prague, a Secretariat, an Office of Free Elections, and an enhanced mechanism for political consultations, could make the CSCE process more permanent and assertive in ensuring compliance with the Helsinki Final Act of 1975 and the Charter of Paris of 1990. The decision of March 1992 to suspend the rule of unanimity in the CSCE in certain circumstances to allow measures to be taken against states violating the Helsinki accord or the Paris charter was another step in the CSCE's evolution into a security forum with the tools to implement its principles and decisions. NATO, in turn, at its Rome summit in November 1991 adopted specific initiatives to reinforce the CSCE emergency mechanism by giving a more authoritative role to both the Committee of Senior Officials (the CSCE "permanent executive") and the Conflict Prevention Center, and by suggesting that more means be given to implement CSCE decisions. As a result, NATO and the CSCE could reinforce each other and develop into a dual structure of European security.[67]

At the July 1992 CSCE summit meeting in Helsinki, the idea of developing a system of interlocking institutions was pursued further. A "Helsinki Declaration," issued on July 10, reaffirmed the centrality of human rights and democratic institutions to the search for peace in Europe. It holds all participating states accountable for their actions and makes clear that the fulfillment of CSCE commitments by one state is a matter "of direct and legitimate concern to all participating states."[68] A second document entitled "Helsinki Decisions," which also was signed on July 10, then complemented decisions taken by NATO at the London and Rome summits and by the European Community at the Maastricht meeting. They give the CSCE the means to join with these organizations and others in an interlocking European and transatlantic structure that could serve as a new foundation for peace in Europe.

The 12 chapters of Helsinki Decisions try to set up more coherent structures to enable the CSCE to better organize for the tasks ahead. Included are new, more effective groupings, such as the "troika" and ad hoc steering groups, enhanced authority for the chairman-in-office, and clearer provisions for fact-finding missions. In addition, a clear structure was established to strengthen the CSCE's ability to prevent and manage crises, including early warning and prevention, political management of crises, use of instruments of conflict prevention and crisis management, and CSCE peacekeeping.

The detailed new security provisions give the CSCE for the first time an orderly set of procedures with which to pursue its goals of preventing and managing crises:

The early warning phase concentrates on human rights and democratic institution building as the most important long-term preventative steps. The Office of Democratic Institutions and Human Rights in Warsaw assumes a major role in this phase, as does the new High Commissioner on National Minorities.

The political management phase focuses on consultations by the Committee of Senior Officials (CSO) and political steps to encourage an end to a crisis.

The third phase brings in specific instruments, such as fact-finding, rapporteur missions and mechanisms for peaceful settlement of disputes. An important step forward is also the agreement to commence negotiations of a comprehensive structure for peaceful settlement of disputes, including directed conciliation.

If a crisis persists, the final phase then envisages formal peacekeeping operations in support of a political solution, either by CSCE countries directly or with the assistance of international organizations such as NATO and WEU.[69]

Together, these new structures add weight to the political decisions taken in CSCE bodies. It is thus a natural complement to NATO and the EC, and could be particularly useful in helping to integrate the newly independent Eastern European states into the democratic world and in providing a vehicle for consultation and early warning about local crises that may emerge.[70]

The civil war in Yugoslavia has demonstrated, however, how difficult the implementation of any such security scheme will be under the new circumstances of the post-1989 period. While the NATO alliance hesitated to use its superior force in a conflict with the potential for prolonged partisan warfare, the new CSCE mechanism for conflict resolution missed its first test at proving itself, and EC emissaries also had difficulties reaching a compromise between the hostile parties representing the various ethnic groups and nationalities. In any case, the Yugoslavian experience and, more generally, the security anarchy in parts of Europe after the collapse of the Soviet Union call for an operational concept of effective crisis management and a new security order stretching across the previous East-West borders. Such anarchy demands appropriate responses, which neither the Western institutions alone nor the pan-European CSCE scheme seem to provide.

Germany, on the other hand, demonstrated a new, formerly unknown foreign policy "assertiveness" in the Balkans and seemed to have learned a lesson from the Gulf War of 1991. The early recognition of Croatia and Slovenia on December 23, 1991, and the forceful condemnation of Serbian aggression in Bosnia and Herzegovina represented a change of style and leadership that could mark the beginning of a more active German role in the future. The turning point was underlined by the resignation of German foreign minister Hans-Dietrich Genscher on May 18, 1992, who had been in office since 1974. His successor, Klaus Kinkel, and the new defense minister, Volker Rühe, who replaced Gerhard Stoltenberg, quickly announced their readiness to take Germany's increased responsibilities into account and accept not only German civilian obligations, but military tasks within multilateral organizations as well.[71] The question remains, however, whether Germany will eventually also be ready to support the use of force, or use force itself if necessary, to stop carnage, either on the basis of NATO-WEU decisions or within the framework of UN peacekeeping or peace-making missions. Such policies could also imply, in the not-too-distant future, permanent membership of the UN Security Council.[72]

Another question is the extent to which the European Community will develop a military arm.[73] From a German viewpoint, it seems only logical to further diffuse—that is, to continue to "multilateralize"—necessary European efforts in the military sphere in order to avoid German solo attempts. The creation of a Franco-German corps as the nucleus of a future European army in May 1992 was a step in that direction.[74] The WEU provides another option as a possible instrument of a European security identity. Germany and France have already agreed on the future arrangement that after 1996 the WEU will become part of the EC. Until then, Chancellor Kohl regards the

WEU as the "European pillar in NATO."[75] The alliance, for its part, has meanwhile established regular contacts with the WEU to harmonize the work of the two organizations and has agreed to allow the WEU to rely on NATO assets and logistics for its operations and also use NATO procedures. The alliance's new strategy, with its emphasis on more multinational units, also aims to promote greater European integration within the alliance and, for instance, to allow the possibility of a NATO-WEU joint deployment of the Rapid Reaction Forces of its member countries.

Despite such cooperation and mutual goodwill, however, and despite the fact that after ratification of the Maastricht Treaty for most member states the WEU will be the defense arm of the EC, it does not seem very likely that the WEU can become a functioning military organization very quickly. It therefore will be necessary for the foreseeable future to maintain the system of interlocking institutions, thus combining the efforts of NATO, the CSCE, and the EC-WEU. If, on the other hand, NATO itself develops into a pan-European security institution, binding commitments among allies could be diluted and the ability of NATO to translate common purposes into action might be constrained.[76]

Thus a merger of NATO and the CSCE and the creation of a collective security structure from Vancouver to Vladivostok can be envisaged only in the long term. Such a structure cannot rely on political commitments and legal procedures alone, but also must be based on common values, the practice of close cooperation, and, above all, a demonstrable capacity to uphold the security of all its members even in the most difficult circumstances.[77] If NATO wants to remain a functioning alliance, effective in providing stability and the hard core of security that contains potential conflicts and prevents any relapse into the balance-of-power politics of the past, it has to maintain its present status, possibly enlarged by the inclusion of some Central or East Central European states, until developments in Eastern Europe and the former Soviet Union make new considerations feasible. As only a functioning NATO can assist the transformation of the European order, thus the key to a stable Europe is to make the relationship between NATO, the WEU, and the CSCE more and more operational and to remain in principle open to the countries in Eastern Europe and the former Soviet Union, many of which, including Russia, have expressed interest in ultimately joining the alliance.[78]

From a German viewpoint, however, restructuring the security order in Europe is not the primary task. The German government agrees with most experts that the post-Cold War definition of security has changed. Successful economic reconstruction of Eastern Europe, as well as the creation of legitimate political government, legal security, and cultural freedom, will therefore contribute more significantly to peace in the region than any military intervention, however sophisticated that action could be. This view indicates a shift from military to socioeconomic thinking and also reflects internal constraints and external demands in the formulation of German foreign and security policy that stem from the huge burden the German economy is bearing as a consequence of unification and the collapse of communism in the East. As Eckart Arnold has noted:

> Germany will not be stronger but weaker for quite a time. Difficult shifts in German foreign policy do not therefore arise—as widely expected—from additional economic power. On the contrary, a potential lack of political stability and weakness at its economic base are the real problems of German policy, undermining its capacity for compromise abroad.[79]

An account of the costs and benefits of German unification will show to what extent the financial stability of Germany is threatened and why the economic implications of unification affect German foreign and security policy.

ECONOMIC COSTS AND BENEFITS

In February 1990, with the Wall down and the talks on the German Economic and Monetary Union (GEMU) under way, West Berlin's governing mayor, Walter Momper, described the proposed absorption of the GDR into the Federal Republic as an "anschluss of poverty." West German economist Reiner Kuhn, on the other hand, predicted "an explosion of economic activity in the East." And Thomas Kielinger, editor-in-chief of Bonn's *Rheinischer Merkur*, even declared that Germany was "poised to become the predominant industrial power in Europe, if not the world."[80]

Apparently, opinions about the economic implications of German unification were still largely divided at that time. Whereas many in the West feared that the integration of a collapsing society with a rust-belt economy and an infrastructure that was said to be "all scrap" would probably cost more—in financial terms—than it was worth, others proved to be abundantly optimistic about the economic outlook for a united Germany. Estimates of the sums required to bring East Germany up to West German standards ranged from DM500 billion to DM1.1 trillion (US$300 billion to $650 billion). Social services alone would cost Bonn an extra DM10 billion ($6 billion) a year, as the restructuring of the East German economy would leave some 1.4 million people unemployed initially.[81] But East Germany, with more than 16 million inhabitants and a disciplined, well-educated work force of 9 million, was also known as the wealthiest among the state-planned economies of the East bloc. People asked why this industrial heartland of prewar Germany with the Leipzig-Dresden-Chemnitz triangle should not resume its traditional role as an economic powerhouse in the center of Europe.

Moreover, the amounts needed to rebuild the East German industry seemed to be easily available, as West German business ran the biggest trade surplus in the world, with $81 billion in 1989 alone (compared with a US deficit of $108 billion), and thus had sufficient cash to spare. In addition, the growth rate of the West German economy, another important resource for the modernization of East Germany, was estimated for the decade of the 1990s at 3.2 percent a year (compared with 2 percent for the United States). Moreover, as new markets opened up in Eastern Europe, the Germans would be in a privileged position. Their location was ideal, and their manufacturing was already weighted toward products the East would need most: machinery and industrial systems, chemicals and high-tech materials, and top-quality consumer goods. In the long run, therefore, unification could be expected to provide for a major boom in the German economy—perhaps leading to another Wirtschaftswunder (economic miracle) in the end.

Yet merging the two German economies was a matter of unprecedented complexity, posing economic problems unknown to scientists and politicians alike. With GEMU, enacted on July 1, 1990, East Germany adopted the currency, laws, and regulations of the free market economy as understood and practiced in the Federal Republic. All ideas of allowing East Germany three to four years for adjustment and avoiding a "jump into the cold water" were rapidly overtaken by events.[82] Only at that late date did the inefficiencies of the socialist command economy became fully evident. East Germany, after 40 years of communist misrule, proved to be "a Potemkin economy or worse—a corrupt, inefficient, industrial invalid that was hemorrhaging its human resources to the West."[83]

The GDR's centrally planned, semiautarkic economy—with full employment, free medical care, low-cost housing, free education, and price controls—had performed well in comparison with the other socialist countries of Eastern Europe; in a few select fields, such as porcelain and printing machinery, its enterprises had even been able to compete on Western markets and, for example, to sell sophisticated high-quality equipment in the United States. But the average East German firm was only one-third as productive as its Western counterpart, rarely produced goods of any marketability in the West (nor in the East once a choice was offered), often caused tremendous damage to the environment, and had accumulated large debts. Technology and productivity had in fact remained so far behind the Western average that after the true state of the country's industry was established in 1990, few people continued to believe the East German claim to the tenth highest gross national product (GNP) per capita in the world.[84]

It became evident that most state enterprises in the GDR had operated at a loss, requiring huge state subsidies. These subsidies, in turn, had produced large budget deficits—some $70 billion in 1989 alone. In addition, East German investment had been cut back sharply in the 1980s to preserve cash needed in part to service a $20 billion foreign debt. The small amount still available had been spent largely on microelectronics and robotics—potential export industries. As a result, in 1989 about 21 percent of industrial machinery in East Germany was more than 20 years old, compared with only 5 percent in West Germany; 29 percent was 11 to 20 years old.[85]

The opening of the GDR economy to the world market, combined with the transition from a centrally planned to a social market economy, brought about the ultimate collapse of the rickety East German system. GEMU's introduction of the D-mark in the East on an almost par basis, which admittedly grossly overvalued the East German economic output, dealt an additional crippling blow to the Eastern competitiveness. Relatively quick wage gains further increased production costs to the disadvantage of Eastern firms, compounding the difficulties faced by East German companies in competing in the global marketplace. Consequently, GDR industrial production began to decline sharply at the end of 1989, then plummeted after the introduction of GEMU. While 110,000 new businesses were established in 1990—with the highest concentration in restaurants and bars—significant portions of East German industry shut down and were likely to disappear as reconstruction proceeded. By the end of 1990, GNP had fallen by 18.5 percent, although the trend in new enterprise development continued, with an additional 142,000 in 1991.[86]

Consumer goods producers and farmers were among the hardest hit first as East German consumers abandoned their own country's products for the better-quality, or sometimes merely better-packaged, products from the West. Capital goods producers fared little better, as investment ground to a halt or went toward acquiring more sophisticated machinery from the West. In some cases, West German and foreign firms entered and virtually displaced Eastern firms throughout entire sectors. As an example, the state-owned banking monopoly all but disappeared when various West German commercial and banking associations entered the market, leaving behind only the shells of a few former GDR state banks to hold the mountains of former GDR commercial debt. Similar replacement of Eastern industries with efficient Western firms occurred in car manufacturing, the insurance business, and food processing.[87]

To manage the adaption of the East German economy to the new political and economic conditions, the Treuhandanstalt (Trust Agency) was established by East Germany's last semi-communist government under Prime Minister Hans Modrow in March 1990.[88] The agency acquired control over most of East Germany's corporate assets but saw itself as an instrument of industrial policy in a still quasi-socialist state. Only after the democratic election on March 18 did privatization become a clearer priority, and many of the senior officials of the communist regime, who had formed the core of the management, were replaced. The agency now grew quickly to an organization with 3,000 staff split between the Berlin headquarters and 15 regional offices throughout East Germany.[89]

On June 17, 1990, a trusteeship was passed by the government of Prime Minister Lothar de Maizière. Aimed at the swift privatization of East German industry plus 25 billion square hectares of real estate, 17.2 billion square hectares of farmland, and 19.6 billion square hectares of forest, the trusteeship now transferred all state-owned enterprises and property to the Treuhandanstalt and laid down that on the day of GEMU all enterprises should be converted into West German-style corporations. The Trusteeship and the Treuhandanstalt Charter, published shortly thereafter, formed the legal basis for the Treuhandanstalt's operations as an independent entity, constituted in public law. Since GEMU, it has reported to the Finance Ministry in Bonn.[90]

Since June 1990, the organization's objectives have been to privatize (principally through 100 percent sales), to restructure (with a view to privatizing), or to close the companies in its control when necessary. Additionally, the Treuhandanstalt was charged with breaking up the 127 central and 95 regional Kombinate (combines)—large vertically integrated conglomerates. In the GDR, the giants had exercised monopoly control of their market segments, been highly autarkic in their trading patterns, and had boasted their own supply companies, schools, and social services. As a result, instead of the approximately 8,000 original industrial companies, the trust agency eventually owned 12,993. All were supposed to be sold.

At the end of the 1980s, the combines had accounted for nearly 100 percent of the industrial goods production of the GDR.[91] On the other hand, there had been practically no small or medium-size business in East Germany, such as had formed the backbone of the economy in West Germany. Accordingly, the share of private property in companies and land in East Germany was a mere 4.6 percent. Only 2 percent of East Germans were independent or self-employed, most of them in the craft sector. And nearly all of the arable land belonged to so-called Genossenschaften (cooperatives).[92]

The privatization of companies and land was an extremely complicated and controversial process, hampered by political, legal, and economic difficulties. Above all, the unresolved "ownership problem" and the fact that immediately after the currency union East German companies lost most of their domestic and East bloc customers—due to superior Western goods and the East bloc's shortage of hard currency—initially sidetracked the Treuhandanstalt's executives into keeping the shellshocked East German companies afloat. A total of DM20 billion in liquidity credit was handed out in the first three months after GEMU merely to ensure that the companies could pay their wages. All companies received 40 percent of what they had requested in liquidity support.[93]

To prevent unemployment from increasing too rapidly, the Federal government also hurriedly introduced a system of short-time working under which the state paid 70 percent of the wages of workers who worked only part time, or in some cases not at all ("Kurzarbeit null"), yet remained on a company's payroll and received a top-up payment (to 90 percent of the full wage) from the company itself. This system was extended until the end of 1991.

The ownership question, caused by the Federal government's decision to return East German land, property, or business expropriated by either the Nazis or the communists, attracted more than a million claims. As a result, there was uncertainty for new business, and only a few hundred companies were privatized before the end of 1990. At the beginning of 1991, when the Federal government eventually decided that, in most cases, new investment had priority over restitution and no new investor needed to fear that a former owner could lay claim to a factory or plot of land after it had been sold, the privatization figure began to rise sharply. Within three years of its establishment, the Treuhandanstalt was able to privatize—either fully or in part—12,581 of the 12,993 industrial companies and nearly all of the 20,000 shops and service outlets initially under its control.[94]

The key component of East Germany's recovery was of course new investment. The capital stock in East Germany on a per capita basis had always been only one-third that in the West; two-thirds of the capital stock was "economically obsolete," according to a 1991 study on the economic aspects of German unification.[95] The data indicated both that the demand for investment was enormous and that rebuilding the derelict East German economy would be costly beyond imagination. Thus the policy of unification, which had been so successful diplomatically, could very well be on its way to become a fiasco financially.[96]

In sober figures, the American investment bank J. P. Morgan calculated that the development of the former GDR might require as much as DM1.5

trillion in private and public investment before the year 2000. Similarly, the International Monetary Fund believed that Germany's eastern section would need some DM120 billion annually in private capital alone to catch up with Western standards. Yet within the first year after GEMU, until July 31, 1991, the private sector had pledged no more than DM67.8 billion in new investment, actually investing less than DM13 billion.[97] By the end of May 1992, nearly two years following GEMU, the figure of pledged new investment had grown to DM138.5 billion, but still only 1,167,000 jobs were guaranteed by the new investors.[98]

Even generous government incentives contained in a package of interventionist measures passed by the Federal government in March 1991 could not improve the situation significantly. The "Upswing East" program allowed the government to provide for potentially more than 50 percent of funds invested in the new German Länder. Small and medium-size businesses were especially favored. The intention was to create a large development zone with a high growth future and a booming center in Berlin, the new capital.

In all, some DM170 billion of public money was injected into East Germany in income support, corporate subsidies, and infrastructure investment in 1991, and DM218 billion in 1992.[99] This meant that there was enough cash to satisfy some of the pent-up demand for consumer and investment goods even prior to the expected "takeoff." About one-third of the public money that was spent, however, went directly into current consumption: short-time work, unemployment benefits, and increased pensions, among others. As a result, most East Germans were better off than before, although the price of many basic goods had risen and rent and heating subsidies were being reduced. A Bundesbank report in 1991 estimated that the average East German household had assets of DM20,000.[100]

The cash inflow may also have contributed to prevent widely predicted mass unrest as factories closed and unemployment rose to double-digit percentage points throughout the former GDR. The real questions were whether and how long the size of the West German assistance could be sustained and if the volume of the program would suffice to transform East Germany into a modern market society in the available time span.

The reasons why the private sector did not invest as much as had originally been expected were numerous. Investments were impeded by an inefficient public administration at the local and state level, an immature property and real estate market, a shortage of public infrastructure and unresolved liability for corporate debt, and environmental damage amassed under the former GDR regime. Foreign governments also complained about the "sometimes ambivalent treatment of potential foreign investors by the . . . Treuhandanstalt."[101]

Stuttgart's mayor Manfred Rommel, commenting on the bureaucratic difficulties delaying new investments, ironically declared that "even a rebuilding of the Wall is out of the question now as it would take at least eight years to get a building permit."[102]

In addition, the initially low wages were raised so quickly in East Germany —by 50 percent in 1990 and 1991, regardless of the continuing productivity gap—that even West German companies increasingly preferred to invest in Portugal or even the Czech Republic rather than in the former GDR. The Federal government's—and above all Chancellor Kohl's—hope that German companies management decisions would be influenced more by national sentiments than by profit considerations turned out to be false. Moreover, by the time wages in East Germany have completely caught up to the West German levels (predicted to be as early as 1995), the advantage of low production costs will be gone entirely and the investment climate will deteriorate even further.[103]

Many firms therefore apparently decided that it was easier and more profitable to produce in the West and export to the East, rather than to produce and sell in the East, or even to produce in the East and export to the West. Consequently, East German industry declined dramatically. By the end of 1991, food processing was down -13.3 percent; the chemical industry, -14 percent; car manufacturing, -22.3 percent; the textile industry, -32.8 percent; machine building, -37.9 percent; electronics, -54.7 percent; the computer industry, -71.4 percent; and the optical industry, -88.0 percent. Only the building sector was booming—with construction and restoration paid for largely by public money.[104]

But the lion's share of initial investment had to come from the public sector anyway—from the Federal government and the taxpayer—if progress was to be achieved at all. Even the privatization process was not possible without public funding. Otherwise, the many deadbeat GDR firms could not be sold. For each D-mark that the private sector paid for acquiring a privatized company, three D-marks of public money had to be spent in order to discharge old debts or clear up existing environmental damage. In other words, each privatization success increased the Treuhandanstalt deficit. Experts in the Finance Ministry in Bonn estimated that the trust agency would account for a total deficit of at least DM400 billion by the time it concluded its work, probably at the end of 1994.[105]

Large sums of public money also were necessary to improve the infrastructure of East Germany. The Ministry of Transportation spent DM15 billion for the repair and renewal of roads and waterways and pushed through special measures that sharply reduced the planning period usually required to build a major road. The Environment Ministry allocated DM5 billion for the first phase of an environmental clean-up of East Germany that will take many years to complete, while West Germany's stringent emission control laws are being phased in only gradually.[106] And the Postal Ministry planned to invest as much as DM55 billion until 1995 on improving the telecommunications system of East Germany.[107]

Yet this was only the beginning. According to a report by international consultants McKinsey & Company in April 1991, DM100 to DM250 billion will be necessary in the area of transportation alone to bring East Germany up to the Western level. The total investment to reach equality between East and West Germany, the report says, will amount to DM1.5 to 2 trillion. In this process, a reduction of the East German labor force from 9.25 million employees on September 30, 1989, to about 5 million in 1993 was inevitable, lifting the unemployment rate up to 40 percent in some areas.[108]

Despite all efforts, however, the differences between the economic conditions of the two parts of Germany could not be reduced during the first two years after unification. Moreover, the trend of unequal economic development in the two regions even continued. While West Germany experienced an economic boom of strength and perhaps duration unrivaled by any expansion in the country for over 30 years, East Germany showed all signs of a dramatic economic contraction accompanying the process of structural adjustment from a command to a free market economy. Whereas West German GNP continued to grow by 4.5 percent in 1990 and 3.1 percent in 1991, the East German economy declined by 18.5 percent in 1990 and some 25 percent in 1991. Labor market developments were similarly divergent, with unemployment shrinking in the West and growing rapidly in the East.[109]

Then the huge transfers from West Germany into East Germany also began to put strains on German fiscal and monetary policy, as did resurgent developments in Eastern Europe and the Commonwealth of Independent States. It should be noted in this respect that, apart from the assistance to the former GDR, West Germany also accounted for 57 percent—DM74 billion—of the DM130 billion in economic aid given to the former Soviet Union by the Western industrial nations from September 1990 through January 1992 (compared with only DM4.1 billion from Japan, for instance).[110] As a result, German public debt grew to an estimated DM1.3 trillion in 1992. In 1991, new debt amounted to as much as 3.7 percent of GNP and thus even exceeded the 3.5 percent rate of the United States.[111]

To limit borrowing requirements, the Federal government implemented a package of tax increases on July 1, 1991, that included higher consumption taxes on oil products and other goods and services as well as a surcharge on income taxes. Thus Federal revenues were boosted by some DM18 billion in 1991 and DM30 billion in 1992, but consumer price inflation accelerated sharply, to over 4 percent (March 1992: 4.3 percent). Additional tax hikes were announced in 1993, including another increase of the gasoline tax (effective January 1, 1994) and a "solidarity tribute" taken from all salaries in the western part of the country for investments in the east. Also, EC harmonization efforts have led to a rise in Germany's standard value-added tax rate by at least 1 percentage point from 1992's 14 percent rate.[112]

The positive effects of unification on West German households, on the other hand, should not be overlooked either. East Germans purchased many West German products after unification. Retail sales in West Berlin rose 50 percent year over year in 1990 due to the surge in demand from East German consumers. Investment in the West German retail sector also increased around 20 percent to meet increased demand. Altogether, some economists estimated that the demand from East Germany has contributed up to one-half of West Germany's growth since July 1990. Another indicator of the "unification effect" was the large number (more than 350,000) of East German "commuters," who lived in East Germany but worked in the West.[113]

Generally, however, the economic costs of unification far outweighed the economic benefits during the first three years after the introduction of GEMU. While the West was paying in hard currency, the East suffered from mass unemployment and structural adjustment problems. The initial optimism shared by many politicians and financial experts alike that economic unity could be achieved easily, quickly, and free of charge apparently was misguided. Economic unification will be achieved in the end, but the process is much more complicated, will take much longer, and is much more expensive than had originally been expected. Above all, it will require huge amounts of public money so long as the private investment "takeoff" lacks momentum. Public money, however, will have to be raised by borrowing in the capital markets as well as by extended tax increases and burden sharing by states, communities, and individual citizens. It is an illusion to believe that the enormous task of rebuilding East Germany and the other countries of the former communist East bloc is possible without sacrifices from everyone.[114]

The truth of the matter is that higher taxes, inflation, public sector deficits, and higher interest rates are the consequences, in fact the price, of German and European unification. Yet since there never has been, and still is not, a realistic political alternative, the price has to be accepted as a necessity with which both East and West will have to cope. Moreover, the price does not even seem to be too high, compared with the benefits of political freedom that have been achieved as a result of the European revolution of 1989.

THE NEW ARCHITECTURE OF EUROPE

In view of the dramatic changes that have occurred since 1989, the whole political, economic, social, and military setting of Europe has come under review.
Eastern Europe has eventually returned to Europe, and Europe itself is in the
process of trying to find a new identity (albeit one built on its past), define its
borders and develop new strategies and instruments for a better future.[115]
   In other words, the end of the Cold War is not, as Francis Fukuyama once
suggested, "The End of History."[116] The opposite is true. The realities in Europe
after the end of the East-West struggle and division—the unification of
Germany, the collapse of the Soviet Union, and the liberation of Eastern
Europe from Soviet-dominated communism, but also the reemergence of the
nation-state, ethnic violence, and border disputes—have opened an entirely
new chapter in the books of European history. The present stage marks a revolution of political, economic, and military structures as much as it witnesses
a "revolution of civilizations" unfolding, in which the East meets the West
and the West meets the East.[117]
   The extent to which the term "revolution" is justified in describing what is
happening in Europe today is another issue. The events in the East have little
to do with the old notion of insurrection and violence or the concept of left
and right. And while the revolutions of 1789, 1848, and 1917 were driven by
utopia—a new ideal for the future—the revolution of 1989 was motivated by
ideological skepticism, pragmatism, and the yearning for a decent life now.[118]
The demise of communism therefore constituted a revolution in the sense of
an overthrow of a political and social regime, including violence in at least
some instances, but without a new utopia filling the ideological vacuum.
Scattered ideas and small ideological pieces float around instead: liberalism,
capitalism, parliamentary democracy, free market economy, nationalism, and
ethnicism, among others. As we are abandoning the Europe of Yalta, we
might end up in seeing again the Europe of Sarajevo.
   It is also true that within three years after the lifting of the Iron Curtain in
Hungary, Czechoslovakia, and Germany, new barriers are going up in Europe.
Economic deprivation, ethnic upheaval, and social dislocation are causing
migration out of poverty and desperation from the East as well as from the
South, which in turn leads to the closing of borders in a free Europe where
boundaries were supposed to have lost their divisive character.[119] And the
wars in former Yugoslavia and Moldova, demonstrating that Europe is no
island of stability and that peace is not for granted, have made the governments of Europe uneasy and less certain about political mechanisms and
capabilities. During a conference of the Aspen Institute Berlin in March
1992 on the situation in Yugoslavia, a journalist from Bosnia-Herzegovina

commented that it was ironic that the discussion was taking place in a united Berlin where the Wall separating East from West had been pulled down by the forces of freedom, while in his home republic new walls were being erected every day by antidemocratic elements—another of the new realities in the Europe after 1989.[120]

Yet our vision must look beyond the chaos of postrevolutionary disturbances if we want to outline ideas about the architecture of a New Europe for the post-Cold War era. With the European revolution of 1989, the Enlightenment ideals of the 18th century, for too long associated mainly with Western Europe and the United States only, can now again be applied to Eastern Europe as well. They still compete, as they already did in the 19th and early 20th centuries, with the forces of nationalism that are casting shadows over the new democracies in the East and risk creating new divisions of Europe, particularly in multiethnic societies. But the rediscovery of classical values upon which the liberated people of Eastern Europe can build pluralistic societies, democratic governments, and free market economies should offer sufficient inspiration to cope with the new dangers from old enmities.[121]

The reemergence of East European nation-states after decades of alleged communist internationalism is perhaps the most striking phenomenon today. While the evolution of the nation-state in Western Europe over the past 40 years has led to voluntary transfers of state functions from the nationalist to the supranationalist level, developments in Central and Eastern Europe seem to be moving in the opposite direction. With the collapse of communism, ethnicity has become a powerful political force, threatening to erect new divisions between countries and, even more acutely, sometimes within them. Whether the "Europe of Regions" can be extended to the East remains to be seen. The Visegrad Cooperation among Poland, Hungary, and the Czech and Slovak republics and the exploration of ties among northern states that rim the Baltic and of southern states on the Black Sea could easily be disrupted by nationalist differences. The interest of these states in associating themselves with such Western institutions as the IMF, EC, Organization for Economic Cooperation and Development, or NATO, on the other hand, is evidence of a tendency toward international cooperation, even if this cooperation at first may take place only within the framework of intergovernmental organizations in which nation-states will not surrender their sovereignty to some higher authority.[122]

The idea of nation-states is actually not bad as such; unlike in Germany, nationalism is not a "dirty word" in, say, Britain or France. In fact, nation-states can provide identity. Yet they also can suppress identity if the right to self-determination is subjected to majority rule, and the application of self-determination may cause conflict or even war—as in former Yugoslavia and several other countries of Eastern Europe—if different ethnic or religious groups refuse to live together peacefully within the borders of an existing state.

Therefore nation-states and the right to self-determination may contradict each other in several ways. A fundamental challenge for democracies in modern history has thus been to encompass, represent, and transcend ethnic ties on the basis of common, indeed universal, values. An important step in that direction was undertaken with the integration of Western Europe after World War II, although the specific future of its structure and institutions were hardly ever outlined. Even Jean Monnet, who gave so much inspiration and guidance to the rise of the European movement, wrote at the close of his life that "one day this process will lead us to the United States of Europe; but I see no point in trying to imagine today what political form it will take, as the words we are quarreling about are not exact: federation or confederation. . . . No one can say."[123]

Today, no one can say if the East European turmoil will have an effect on Western European integration—apart from a migration from Eastern nations that has already begun for economic reasons. What is necessary, however, is a concept for a dynamic process of all-European integration. The system of "interlocking institutions," consisting mainly of the European Community, NATO, and the CSCE, could provide the organizational framework for such a process at the outset. The Helsinki II decisions, described in the previous chapter, provide an example of how the system might work. The idea is, of course, to transcend, à la the post-World War II integration of Western Europe, old territorial disputes, irredentist claims, and ethnic grievances to prevent localized disputes from becoming a source for serious conflict both within and among the states.

The EC may have failed in achieving many of its goals. But it has been extremely successful in overcoming traditional hostilities among the nations of Western Europe, not the least the so-called Erbfeindschaft ("congenital hatred") between Germany and France. If we are to ensure comparable levels of peace and prosperity for Europe as a whole, structures comparable to those in the West should be introduced in the East. They should be aimed at shaping and developing interdependence and at promoting a new "common" sense—resulting not from a new ideology but from the pragmatic conviction of the necessity for cooperation.[124]

The second element of a new order in Europe will have to be economic reconstruction and development. Without prosperity, no new order can survive. If it is true that the supreme motive for the revolution of 1989 has been the quest for a better life, including material goods, rather than the realization of an idealistic dream, then the demands of the people need to be addressed soon to avoid new frustration and the collapse of democratic order into authoritarian rule. The EC is not capable of accepting patronage over all of the emerging "archaic mininationalisms" of Eastern Europe, from Slovenia and Croatia to Slovakia and the Baltics.[125] But the Community can provide active economic support on a very pragmatic day-to-day basis. Instead of pointing at such distant goals as full EC membership for everyone, which is not realizable at the moment, concrete steps are needed: a solution for the serious debt burden, which amounts to some $30 billion in Poland, $20 billion in Hungary, and $17.4 billion in former Yugoslavia; the opening of the West European market for East European goods, especially in the sensitive sectors of textiles and agriculture; and a gradual association of the East European states with the Community, including ever more intense cooperation.[126]

Yet the countries of the EC cannot focus on Eastern Europe alone, but must make every effort to create or maintain competitive high-tech economies on their own. As Konrad Seitz has stated correctly, Western Europe's "economic future does not lie in the East, but must be gained and secured in the successful competition with the most developed nations of the world, i.e., Japan and America."[127] This means that the economic dividing line between the two parts of Europe that has replaced the political and ideological division of the two parts of Europe will continue to exist and will remain an unfortunate reality for a rather lengthy period of time. However, the East will not benefit from a demise of the West. Thus the economic scenario of the new Europe will be a complex mix of West-West, East-West, and East-East relationships combining the slowed-down modernization of the West with pent-up modernization of the East.[128]

The economic reconstruction tasks in the East are in fact gigantic, but they are additionally burdened with a complete and unprecedented restructuring of the political and military order. Therefore the new architecture of Europe not only requires models of economic modernization, but asks for a new policy and security framework as well. NATO, the CSCE, and the EC will contribute to develop the appropriate mechanisms, yet it would be naive to assume that they can do so easily. Quick technocratic solutions do not apply to a region that has been plagued with authoritarian repression, military conflict, and political instability for centuries and has just managed to escape the stranglehold of communism. In a situation where human as well as material resources, and even nature, have been either crippled or destroyed to a large extent, normalcy cannot return quickly. New political, economic, and social elites will have to be educated and trained, and the management of a market economy as well as the practicing of political democracy is as much a matter of experience as of knowledge.[129]

Despite such rich potential for obstacles and pitfalls, however, there is a fair chance for meeting the challenge of extending the Euro-Atlantic community eastward—to the benefit of both East and West. The historical opportunity that exists can be exploited to advantage if the Eastern countries resist the temptation of basing their future exclusively on the idea of nation-states; if the EC becomes a responsible leader contributing forcefully to the reconstruction and development of Eastern Europe both politically and economically; if the CSCE evolves into an instrument of effective all-European cooperation, conflict prevention, and crisis management; and if NATO and the WEU remain sturdy cornerstones of the West and begin to initiate cooperative structures of security for Europe as a whole.

■ C O N C L U S I O N ■

This book has tried to describe the unification of Germany in 1989-90 as part of a European revolution that changed many of the premises of world politics. It has attempted to analyze the implications of both the German and European events and to draw conclusions for the future. The results are encouraging as well as disillusioning: The century ahead holds both unmatched promises and unprecedented risks and challenges.

The new united Germany, to be sure, was born not out of revived nationalism but of political and economic necessity. The process of German unification began with Hungary's dismantling of the Iron Curtain with Austria in May 1989. Subsequently, massive waves of refugee East Germans fled to the West, while others demonstrated against the SED regime in the streets of Leipzig and elsewhere. It was only after the opening of the Berlin Wall on November 9, 1989, and the formation of a new East German government under Prime Minister Hans Modrow that West German chancellor Helmut Kohl came forward with a "Ten-Point Proposal"—ironically upon Soviet initiative—envisaging a German confederation but hardly mentioning the possibility of German unification.

Unification, therefore, was not the result of West German resoluteness and determination. Nor was it caused by Soviet diplomatic clumsiness or Hungarian treachery on the issue of socialist borders. The true causes of unification lay in the inefficiency of the East German regime, its lack of competitiveness, financial bankruptcy, and inability to adapt to the requirements of a technologically advanced society. The people who left their homeland to go west—mostly young, and usually with children—had lost patience and did not want to wait for another generation to reach Western standards. Moreover, the détente policy of the 1970s and 1980s had offered them better insight into the realities of both Western pluralism and Eastern party-monocracy, further reducing the legitimacy of socialism. And finally, the need for Abgrenzung (delimitation) had blown the apparatus of state security out of proportion and created an atmosphere of surveillance and persecution that an ever-increasing number of East Germans were no longer be prepared to accept.

Yet the main cause for unification was eventually economic. When Prime Minister Modrow visited Soviet president Mikhail Gorbachev in Moscow at the end of January 1990, he knew—and said so behind closed doors—that the GDR was finished. Insurmountable economic difficulties and a hopeless financial situation made a bail out by West Germany inevitable, as the Soviet Union was facing a catastrophe itself and thus was unable to come to the aid of its East

German comrades. The rest was a matter of negotiations in the framework of the two-plus-four process, during which the West German government—with the support of its Western partners—insisted on maximum leverage and continued membership of the united Germany in the Western alliance.

The new Germany that eventually emerged from this process thus remained embedded in the network of Western integration and was firmly tied to Western institutions and procedures. That is why the united Germany of 1990 can hardly be compared with the united Germany of 1871. While the former German Reich was isolated and in many respects hostile to the existing European order, the newly united Federal Republic of Germany was the product of a developing new order in the post-Cold War era. In addition, the amount of interdependence that had been established between Germany and its partners in the EC since the 1950s could only lead to the conclusion that neither the Germans nor their neighbors in Western Europe were interested in questioning the achievements of Western integration. In other words, the unification of Germany per se would not have changed the orientation of German politics and altered the focus of its attention; it even might have led to a deepening of integration in the West to balance the effects of unification in the East.

The real revolution, therefore, did not happen in Germany, but in Eastern Europe. The collapse of the Soviet Union and the liberation of peoples from Soviet domination were the two most outstanding factors affecting the European order in general and the German role in particular. For Germany, new challenges in the East now complement the tasks in the West. Germany resumes its traditional place as a central power in Europe, a fact that forces upon the German leaders new responsibilities and demands.

Thus far, however, the German response has been moderate and predictable. The political elite of the Federal Republic seems inclined to continue proven practices of the past. The framework of German politics continues to consist of NATO, the EC, and the CSCE (though with a pan-European perspective and a new move toward German contributions, either civilian or military, to peacekeeping and peace-making missions of the UN and NATO-WEU). Except for the general notion that the increased potential for conflict and small wars in the post-Cold War era requires a hitherto unknown German readiness to commit itself to some form of military intervention, the traditional "civilian approach" of German foreign policy seems unchanged. Fears that the united Germany of 1990 might ascend to a "Fourth Reich" are therefore unfounded. The new Germany is likely to be as European and peaceful as the old Federal Republic between 1949 and 1990—despite the novelties resulting from the revolution of 1989 and the quest for a new European architecture in which Germany has its role to play.

■ N O T E S ■

CHAPTER I

1. See Paul M. Kennedy, *The Rise and Fall of the Great Powers: Economic Change and Military Conflict from 1500 to 2000* (New York, 1987).

2. David Calleo, *The German Problem Reconsidered: Germany and the World Order, 1870 to the Present* (Cambridge, 1978), p. 1. See also Gordon A. Craig, *Über die Deutschen* (Munich, 1982), pp. 268-69; Luigi Barzini, *The Impossible Europeans* (London, 1983), chap. 3.

3. Calleo, *The German Problem Reconsidered*, pp. 1-2.

4. See Andreas Hillgruber, *Deutsche Geschichte 1945-1982: Die "deutsche Frage" in der Weltpolitik*, 4th ed. (Stuttgart, 1983), pp. 11-12.

5. See Sebastian Haffner, *Preussen ohne Legende* (Hamburg, 1979), pp. 216-29; Rudolf von Thadden, *Fragen an Preussen: Zur Geschichte eines aufgehobenen Staates* (Munich, 1981), chap. 5.

6. Manfred Görtemaker, *Deutschland im 19. Jahrhundert: Entwicklungslinien* (Opladen, 1983), chap. 2.

7. See Hans-Dieter Dyroff, ed., *Der Wiener Kongress 1814-1815: Die Neuordnung Europas* (Munich, 1966); Karl Griewank, *Der Wiener Kongress und die europäische Restauration 1814-15*, 2nd ed. (Leipzig, 1954).

8. Metternich later justified his policy by arguing that only the restoration of legitimate governments had been able to create "a state of quietness" that ensured peace and a good future. See his letter to Baron von Binder, June 9, 1826, quoted in Werner Näf, ed., *Europapolitik zu Beginn des 19. Jahrhunderts: Quellen zur neueren Geschichte* (Bern, 1953), Vol. 2, p. 47.

9. See also Henry Kissinger, *A World Restored: Castlereagh, Metternich and the Problems of Peace, 1812-1822* (Boston, 1957).

10. Peter Burg, *Der Wiener Kongress: Der Deutsche Bund im europäischen Staatensystem* (Munich, 1984).

11. See Günter Wollstein, Das *"Grossdeutschland"* in der Paulskirche: Nationale Ziele in der bürgerlichen Revolution 1848-49 (Dusseldorf, 1977).

12. Metternich himself realized the national implications of his policy during the negotiations that led to the German Customs Union when he noted that it might be a first step toward political union in Germany, "yet under Prussian protection and with Prussian preponderance." See his June 1833 report to Kaiser Franz I in: Fürst Richard von Metternich-Winneburg, ed., Aus Metternichs nachgelassenen Papieren (Vienna, 1880), Vol. 5, p. 504.

13. Bismarck called this a "mathematical logic of facts." See his letter to Leopold von Gerlach of April 28, 1856, in: Otto von Bismarck, Die gesammelten Werke, Friedrichsruher edition (Berlin, 1924), Vol. 14/1, p. 441.

14. Lothar Gall, for instance, writes on page 503 of his voluminous biography on Bismarck, Der weisse Revolutionär (Frankfurt am Main, 1980), that Bismarck had stated immediately after 1871 that the enlarged Prussia which now had become the German Reich was definitely "saturated." It did not have any further demands and was merely interested in preserving the status quo. "Looking backward," Gall argues, "there can be no doubt that he was totally serious about that. As a matter of fact, he subsequently rejected categorically, occasionally even with sharpness, all opposing ideas and activities, for instance from German-ethnic circles in Eastern Middle Europe."

15. Bismarck defined the role of Germany in international relations earlier the same year in a speech at the Reichstag on February 19, stating that the German government desired no more than the role "of an honest broker who really wants to get the business accomplished." In: Lothar Gall, ed., Bismarck: Die grossen Reden (Berlin, 1981), p. 152.

16. Ludwig Dehio, Germany and World Politics in the Twentieth Century, (New York, 1959), p. 39. Similarly, Henry Kissinger has argued in his essay entitled "Bismarck, the White Revolutionary" that clumsy successors were unable to manage the inheritance of the ingenious first German chancellor, in: Daedalus (Summer 1968), pp. 888-922. See also Winfried Baumgart, Deutschland im Zeitalter des Imperialismus 1890-1914 (Stuttgart, 1982); Dirk Stegmann, Die Erben Bismarcks: Parteien und Verbände in der Spätphase des Wilhelminischen Deutschlands. Sammlungspolitik 1877-1918 (Cologne, 1970).

17. Calleo, The German Problem Reconsidered, p. 5.

18. See George L. Mosse, Die Nationalisierung der Massen: Politische Symbolik und Massenbewegung in Deutschland von den Napoleonischen Kriegen bis zum Dritten Reich (Berlin, 1976); Fritz Stern, Gold und Eisen: Bismarck und sein Bankier

Bleichröder (Berlin, 1978); and Sebastian Haffner, *Von Bismarck zu Hitler: Ein Rückblick* (Munich, 1987).

19. See James J. Sheehan, ed., *Imperial Germany* (New York, 1976).

20. Walter Hubatsch, *Die Ära Tirpitz: Studien zur deutschen Marinepolitik 1880-1918* (Göttingen, 1955).

21. Calleo, *The German Problem Reconsidered*, p. 21.

22. *Ibid.*

23. See H. W. Koch, ed., *The Origins of the First World War: Great Power Rivalry and German War Aims* (London, 1972).

24. Luigi Albertini, *The Origins of the War of 1914*, Vols. 1-3 (London, 1957), and Fritz Fischer, *Germany's Aims in the First World War* (New York, 1967). See also Fischer, *The War of Illusions* (New York, 1975).

25. Peter Gay, *Weimar Culture: The Outsider as Insider* (New York, 1970), p. 2.

26. *Ibid.*

27. See Alexander De Conde, *A History of American Foreign Policy* (New York, 1963), pp. 466-67.

28. *Ibid.*, p. 467.

29. The famous economist John Maynard Keynes, who had been a member of the British delegation, was so upset about the course of the negotiations that he not only left the conference early but immediately set to work on a book dealing with the disastrous implications of its outcome for the future. See John Maynard Keynes, *The Economic Consequences of the Peace* (New York, 1920).

30. See, for instance, Karl-Dietrich Bracher, *Die Auflösung der Weimarer Republik: Eine Studie zum Problem des Machtverfalls in der Demokratie* (Villingen, 1955); Karl Dietrich Erdmann and Hagen Schulze, eds., *Weimar: Selbstpreisgabe einer Demokratie; Eine Bilanz heute* (Dusseldorf, 1980).

31. Ernst Nolte, *Die Krise des liberalen Systems und die faschistischen Bewegungen* (Munich, 1968), p. 80.

32. Arthur Graf Gobineau, *Versuch über die Ungleichheit der Menschenrassen* (Stuttgart, 1939); Georges Vacher de Lapouge, *Essai sur l'inégalité des race*

humaines (1874); Houston Stewart Chamberlain, *Die Grundlagen des XIX. Jahrhunderts,* 2nd ed. (Munich, 1900). See also Georges Vacher de Lapouge, *L'Aryen: son role social,* 1st ed. (1899).

33. Ernst Nolte, *Der Faschismus in seiner Epoche: Die Action francaise. Der italienische Faschismus. Der Nationalsozialismus* (Munich, 1963), pp. 343-56.

34. See Gottfried Reinhold Treviranus, *Das Ende von Weimar: Heinrich Brüning und seine Zeit* (Dusseldorf, 1968), pp. 333-59; Karl-Dietrich Bracher, *The German Dictatorship* (New York, 1970).

35. Dehio, *Germany and World Politics,* p. 32.

36. Calleo, *The German Problem Reconsidered,* p. 86. In this respect Calleo writes that Hitler's regime, like most historical phenomenon, "did have many elements of continuity with the past. The links seem particularly clear in foreign policy. In his general geopolitical analysis, Hitler was similar in many respects not only to annexationists like Ludendorff, but also to Bethmann-Hollweg and Rathenau. All were concerned with what they saw as Germany's precarious position in the coming world of superstates."

37. Adolf Hitler, *Mein Kampf* (Munich, 1942), p. 741.

38. See Hans-Ulrich Thamer, *Verführung und Gewalt: Deutschland 1933-1945* (Berlin, 1986), chap. 8. Hitler's geopolitical ideas were laid out with great clarity already in his early writings, for instance in *Mein Kampf,* and varied remarkably little until his "Testament" of April 1945. See Hitler, *Mein Kampf; Hitler's Secret Book* (New York, 1961); *The Testament of Adolf Hitler,* edited by Francois Genoud (London, 1961).

39. For the reasoning behind Hitler's calculation, see Calleo, *The German Problem Reconsidered,* pp. 94-95.

40. See Sebastian Haffner, *Anmerkungen zu Hitler* (Munich, 1978), pp. 62-94. Haffner also notes that the immense success of Hitler's foreign policy was caused more by favorable circumstances than by the Führer's genius.

41. See Thamer, *Verführung und Gewalt,* chap. 9.

42. Winston Churchill, *The Second World War, Vol. III: The Grand Alliance* (London, 1950), Part 2, p. 469.

43. See Anthony Eden (Earl of Avon), *The Eden Memoirs: The Reckoning* (London, 1965); Llewelyn Woodward, *British Foreign Policy* (London, 1962), Vol. 2.

44. Department of State, *Post-War Foreign Policy Preparation* (Washington, DC, 1949), p. 558.

45. See R. J. Gannon, *The Cardinal Spellman Story* (New York, 1962), p. 223.

46. *Diplomatic Papers: The Conferences at Cairo and Tehran 1943* Foreign Relations of the United States (FRUS), (Washington, DC, 1961), p. 600.

47. Henry Morgenthau, Jr., *Germany Is Our Problem* (New York, 1945). See also Warren F. Kimball, *Swords or Ploughshares? The Morgenthau Plan for Defeated Nazi Germany 1943-1946* (Philadelphia, 1976).

48. John Foster Dulles, Memorandum, November 1944, in: *Selected Correspondence and Related Material 1944*, Box No. 25, Folder Re Post-War Planning, John Foster Dulles Papers, Seeley G. Mudd Manuscript Library, Princeton, NJ, p. 2.

49. See Diane Shaver Clemens, *Yalta* (Oxford, 1970). Regarding the US position, see Edward R. Stettinius, Jr., *Roosevelt and the Russians: The Yalta Conference* (Garden City, NY, 1949).

50. Stalin's speech of May 9, 1945, quoted from: J. Stalin, *Über den Grossen Vaterländischen Krieg der Sowjetunion* (Berlin, 1952), p. 221.

51. United States Department of State, *Documents on Germany 1944-1985* (Washington, DC, 1986), p. 55.

52. See Hermann Graml, *Die Alliierten und die Teilung Deutschlands: Konflikte und Entscheidungen 1941-1948* (Frankfurt, 1985); Mike Dennis, *The German Democratic Republic: Politics, Economics and Society* (London, 1988), p. 11.

53. Dennis, *The German Democratic Republic*, p. 11. See also Herbert Feis, *Between War and Peace: The Potsdam Conference* (Princeton, NJ, 1960), and Charles L. Mee, *Meeting at Potsdam* (New York, 1975).

54. See Edward J. Rozek, *Allied Wartime Diplomacy: A Pattern in Poland* (New York, 1958); Georg Bluhm, *Die Oder-Neisse-Grenze in der deutschen Aussenpolitik* (Freiburg, 1963).

55. US embassy London dispatch, transmitting PS-SHAEF(44)26, State Department archives, file 740.00119 (Germany).

56. James S. Sutterlin and David Klein, *Berlin: From Symbol of Confrontation to Keystone of Stability* (New York, 1989), p. 11.

57. George F. Kennan, *Memoirs 1925-1950* (Boston, 1967), p. 258.

58. Dennis, *The German Democratic Republic,* p. 12.

59. *Ibid.,* p. 19.

60. Address by Secretary of State Byrnes on United States Policy Regarding Germany, Stuttgart, September 6, 1946, in: *Documents on Germany, 1944-1985,* pp. 91-99. "The American people," Byrnes stated, "want to return the government of Germany to the German people. The American people want to help the German people to win their way back to an honorable place among the free and peace-loving nations of the world."

61. Special Message to the Congress on Greece and Turkey: The Truman Doctrine, March 12, 1947, *Public Papers of the Presidents of the United States: Harry S. Truman: Containing the Public Messages, Speeches, and Statements of the President: January 1 to December 31, 1947* (Washington, DC, 1963, pp. 176-80.

62. See John Gimbel, *The Origins of the Marshall Plan* (Stanford, 1974).

63. See Sutterlin and Klein, *Berlin,* pp. 26-37; Avi Shlaim, *The United States and the Berlin Blockade, 1948-1949: A Study in Crisis Decision-Making* (Berkeley, CA, 1989).

64. Four-Power Communiqué on Arrangements for Lifting the Berlin Blockade Effective May 12, New York, May 4, 1949, in: *Documents on Germany, 1944-1985,* p. 221.

65. Henry Krisch, *The German Democratic Republic: The Search for Identity* (Boulder, 1985), pp. 9-10; Dietrich Staritz, *Die Gründung der DDR. Von der sowjetischen Besatzungsherrschaft zum sozialistischen Staat* (Munich, 1984); Hermann Weber, *Geschichte der DDR* (Munich, 1985), chap. 2.

66. Hans-Peter Schwarz, "Das aussenpolitische Konzept Konrad Adenauers," in: Klaus Gotto et al., *Konrad Adenauer: Seine Deutschland- und Aussenpolitik 1945-1963* (Munich, 1975), pp. 105-27.

67. Hans-Peter Schwarz, *Adenauer. Der Aufstieg: 1876-1952* (Stuttgart, 1986), p. 212.

68. Arnulf Baring, *Aussenpolitik in Adenauers Kanzlerdemokratie: Bonns Beitrag zur Europäischen Verteidigungsgemeinschaft* (Munich, 1969), pp. 48-62; Hans-Peter Schwarz, *Die Ära Adenauer: Gründerjahre der Republik 1949-1957* (Stuttgart, 1981), pp. 55-61.

69. Randolph S. Churchill, *The Sinews of Peace: Post-War Speeches by W. S. Churchill* (Cambridge, 1949), pp. 198-99.

70. See James L. Richardson, *Germany and the Atlantic Alliance: The Interaction of Strategy and Politics* (Cambridge, MA, 1966), pp. 11-23; and, more recently, John A. Reed Jr., *Germany and NATO* (Washington, DC, 1987), pp. 34-35. Reed states that "Adenauer knew the value of German manpower and military skill to the Western Alliance. He also was aware that western military leaders wanted Germany in NATO and needed German troops for NATO's defense. ... The German Chancellor realized that the prospect of rearmament could be a powerful weapon for obtaining goals he had set for himself and the new Germany. In this respect, Adenauer clearly used NATO's military needs to Germany's advantage."

71. See Manfred Overesch, *Die Deutschen und die Deutsche Frage 1945-1955* (Hannover, 1985).

72. Regarding Adenauer's "policy of strength," see Bruno Bandulet, *Adenauer zwischen West und Ost: Alternativen der deutschen Aussenpolitik* (Munich, 1970); Anselm Doering-Manteuffel, *Die Bundesrepublik Deutschland in der Ära Adenauer: Aussenpolitik und innere Entwicklung 1949-1963* (Darmstadt, 1983), pp. 36-38 and 48-51.

73. Grundgesetz für die Bundesrepublik Deutschland, May 23, 1949, in: Ingo von Münich, ed., *Dokumente des geteilten Deutschland. Quellentexte zur Rechtslage des Deutschen Reiches, der Bundesrepublik Deutschland und der Deutschen Demokratischen Republik* (Stuttgart, 1976), p. 91.

74. Dieter Oberndörfer, "John Foster Dulles und Konrad Adenauer," in: *Konrad Adenauer und seine Zeit: Politik und Persönlichkeit des ersten Bundeskanzlers. Vol. II: Beiträge der Wissenschaft*, ed. by Dieter Blumenwitz et al. (Stuttgart, 1976), pp. 229-48.

75. Note From the Soviet Union to the United States Transmitting a Soviet Draft of a Peace Treaty with Germany, March 10, 1952, in: *Documents on Germany, 1944-1985*, pp. 361-64.

76. See Peter März, *Die Bundesrepublik zwischen Westintegration und Stalin-Noten: Zur deutschlandpolitischen Diskussion 1952 in der Bundesrepublik vor dem Hintergrund der westlichen und der sowjetischen Deutschlandpolitik* (Frankfurt am Main, 1982); Hans-Peter Schwarz, ed., *Die Legende von der verpassten Gelegenheit. Die Stalin-Note vom 10. März 1952* (Stuttgart, 1982); Rolf Steininger, *Eine vertane Chance: Die Stalin-Note vom 10. März 1952 und die Wiedervereinigung* (Berlin, 1985).

77. Lawrence L. Whetten, *Germany's Ostpolitik: Relations between the Federal Republic and the Warsaw Pact Countries* (London, 1971), p. 11.

78. *Ibid.*, pp. 11-12.

79. Klaus Gotto, "Adenauers Deutschland- und Ostpolitik 1954-1963," in: Gotto et al., *Konrad Adenauer,* pp. 156-286.

80. Sir Ivone A. Kirkpatrick, "German Unity," Memorandum, December 16, 1955, File WG 1071/G1374, Public Record Office.

81. *Ibid.*

82. Whetten, *Germany's Ostpolitik,* p. 12.

83. Hans-Peter Schwarz, *Die Ära Adenauer: Epochenwechsel 1957-1963* (Stuttgart, 1983), pp. 297-306.

84. See Erich Honecker, *Aus meinem Leben,* 14th ed. (Berlin, 1989), pp. 197-207.

85. Honoré M. Catudal, *Kennedy and the Berlin Wall Crisis: A Case Study in U.S. Decision Making* (Berlin, 1980).

86. Gilbert Ziebura, *Die deutsch-französischen Beziehungen seit 1945: Mythen und Realitäten* (Pfullingen, 1970); Alfred Grosser, *Affaires extérieures. La politique de la France 1944-1984* (Paris, 1984).

87. Karl Jaspers, *Lebensfragen der deutschen Politik* (Hamburg, 1963). A detailed account of German Ostpolitik is provided in William E. Griffith, *The Ostpolitik of the Federal Republik of Germany* (Cambridge, MA, 1978).

88. Willy Brandt, *Begegnungen und Einsichten: Die Jahre 1960-1975* (Hamburg, 1976), p. 101.

89. *Ibid.*, p. 102.

90. Joachim Nawrocki, *Relations Between the Two States in Germany: Trends, Prospects and Limitations* (Bonn, 1985), pp. 44-45.

91. Karl Kaiser, *German Foreign Policy in Transition: Bonn Between East and West* (London, 1968).

92. "Die Lage der Vertriebenen und das Verhältnis des deutschen Volkes zu seinen östlichen Nachbarn," Denkschrift der Evangelischen Kirche in Deutschland, October 14, 1965 (Hannover, 1965).

93. Whetten, *Germany's Ostpolitik,* p. 16.

94. Hans-Peter Schwarz, ed., *Konrad Adenauer: Reden 1917-1967. Eine Auswahl* (Stuttgart, 1975), p. 482.

95. Auswärtiges Amt, *Die Bemühungen der deutschen Regierung und ihrer Verbündeten um die Einheit Deutschlands 1955-1966* (Bonn, 1966).

96. Gerhard Schröder, "Germany Looks at Eastern Europe," *Foreign Affairs*, Vol. 44, No. 1 (October 1965), pp. 19-20.

97. Whetten, *Germany's Ostpolitik*, p. 18.

98. "Regierungserklärung von Bundeskanzler Kurt Georg Kiesinger vor dem Deutschen Bundestag," December 13, 1966, in: *Europa-Archiv*, Vol. 22, No. 1, (1967), pp. D15-19.

99. *Ibid.*

100. *Ibid.*; Nawrocki, *Relations Between the Two States*, p. 45.

101. "Bericht von Bundeskanzler Kurt Georg Kiesinger über die Lage der Nation im geteilten Deutschland," March 11, 1968, in: *Europa-Archiv*, Vol. 23, No. 19, (1968), pp. D456-58; Whetten, *Germany's Ostpolitk*, p. 20.

102. See Arnulf Baring, *Machtwechsel: Die Ära Brandt-Scheel* (Stuttgart, 1982), p. 238.

103. The rulings of the Federal Constitutional Court, the highest court in the Federal Republic, confirmed this view by stating on July 31, 1973: "The Basic Law . . . assumes that the German Reich survived the collapse of 1945 and did not cease to exist either as a result of the capitulation or as a result of the exercise of foreign government power in Germany by the Allied occupation forces." And, in another passage: "The German Reich continues to exist . . . and continues to be capable of legal acts, although for lack of organization, in particular for lack of institutions, it is unable to act as a single state." See "Urteil des Bundesverfassungsgerichts betreffend die Frage der Verfassungs-mässigkeit des Gesetzes zum Vertrag über die Grundlagen der Beziehungen zwischen der Bundesrepublik Deutschland und der Deutschen Demokratischen Republik vom 31. Juli 1973-2 BvF 1/73," in: Ingo von Munch, ed., *Dokumente des geteilten Deutschland: Quellentexte zur Rechtslage des Deutschen Reiches, der Bundesrepublik Deutschland und der Deutschen Demokratischen Republik.* (Stuttgart, 1974), Vol. 2, p. 358.

104. See Peter Bender, *Neue Ostpolitik: Vom Mauerbau bis zum Moskauer Vertrag* (Munich, 1986), pp. 123-29.

105. Willy Brandt, *Friedenspolitik in Europa* (Frankfurt, 1968), p. 189. Brandt predicted: "The farther road will be laborious. It will lead, as we see it, from the renunciation-of-force agreement to a guaranteed, balanced European security system, including both world powers, and eventually to a solid and just peace order for our continent which also means a solution of the German questions in accordance with the Germans themselves and their neighbors."

106. Bundesministerium für gesamtdeutsche Fragen, ed., *Dokumente zur Deutschlandpolitik*, Vol. 4/9 (Frankfurt, 1963), p. 572.

107. Brandt, *Friedenspolitik in Europa*, pp. 148-72.

108. "Budapester Appell der Teilnehmerstaaten des Warschauer Vertrages an alle europäischen Länder," March 17, 1969, in: *Sicherheit und friedliche Zusammenarbeit in Europa. Dokumente 1967-1971* (Berlin, 1973), pp. 86-90.

109. Whetten, *Germany's Ostpolitik*, p. 26.

110. "Rede des Ersten Sekretärs der Polnischen Vereinigten Arbeiterpartei, Wladyslaw Gomulka, auf einer Wahlkundgebung in Warschau," May 17, 1969, in: *Europa-Archiv*, Vol. 24, No. 13, (1969), pp. 313-20.

111. Andrzej J. Chilecki, ed., *Polnische Stimmen. Eine Dokumentation vom 13. Mai 1969 bis 25. April 1970* (Bonn, 1970), p. 19.

112. Peter Raina, *Gomulka: Politische Biographie* (Cologne, 1970), p. 184.

113. Brandt statement at a press conference on May 19, 1969, in: *Die Welt*, May 20, 1969.

114. *Pravda*, July 11, 1969.

115. *Süddeutsche Zeitung*, July 11, 1969.

116. See Baring, *Machtwechsel*, chap. 2, "Ein Bündnis für die Neue Ostpolitik," esp. pp. 197-201.

117. See Benno Zündorf, *Die Ostverträge: Die Verträge von Moskau, Warschau, Prag, das Berlin-Abkommen und die Verträge mit der DDR* (Munich, 1979), passim.

118. Roger Morgan, "West Germany's Foreign Policy Agenda," *The Washington Papers*, No. 54 (Washington, DC, 1978), pp. 19-31.

119. Baring, *Machtwechsel*, pp. 251-53; Bender, *Neue Ostpolitik*, p. 143.

Chapter 2

1. Nawrocki, *Relations Between the Two States*, p. 5.

2. Erich Honecker, Interview with British publisher Robert Maxwell, in: *Neues Deutschland*, February 7, 1981.

3. It should be noted in this respect, however, that the GDR had failed to gain full diplomatic recognition in the Basic Treaty, since "permanent representatives" were established instead of ambassadors, and Bonn's view of the "special nature" of relations was underscored by the insertion of a reference in the preamble to the two states' different view of the national question, the survival of a single German nation. On the other hand, the Federal Republic was committed by the Basic Treaty to the "inviolability of borders and respect for the territorial integrity and sovereignty of all states in Europe," including, of course, the GDR. See Dennis, *The German Democratic Republic*, p. 37.

4. *Ibid.*, pp. 38-39.

5. *Neues Deutschland*, September 14, 1970. See Dennis, *The German Democratic Republic*, pp. 37-38.

6. See Siegfried Kupper, "Politische Beziehungen zur Bundesrepublik Deutschland 1955-1977," in: Hans-Adolf Jacobsen, et al., eds., *Drei Jahrzehnte Aussenpolitik der DDR: Bestimmungsfaktoren, Instrumente, Aktionsfelder*, 2nd ed. (Munich, 1980), p. 438.

7. See Manfred Rexin, "Koexistenz auf deutsch. Aspekte der deutsch-deutschen Beziehungen 1970-1987," in: Gert-Joachim Glaessner, ed., *Die DDR in der Ära Honecker. Politik-Kultur-Gesellschaft* (Opladen, 1988), p. 47.

8. The complete text of Article 1 of the 1974 GDR constitution is translated as follows: "The German Democratic Republic is a Socialist State of workers and peasants. It is the political organization of the employed in city and country under the direction of the working class and its Marxist-Leninist party." In: *Gesetzblatt der DDR*, Teil I, Nr. 47, September 27, 1974, p. 432.

9. Ronald Asmus, "The GDR and the German Nation: Sole Heir or Socialist Sibling?" *International Affairs*, Vol. 60, No. 3 (1984), p. 403.

10. Egon Bahr, "Wandel durch Annäherung. Ein Diskussionsbeitrag in Tutzing, July 15, 1963," in: Karsten Schröder, *Egon Bahr. Mit einem Beitrag von Günter Grass* (Rastatt, 1988), pp. 325-30. There Bahr had stated: "We have said that the wall is a sign of weakness. One could also say, it was a sign of fear and the instinct

of self-preservation of the communist regime. The question is if there are not possibilities to gradually liberate the regime from those entirely justified worries to the extent that a loosening up of the borders and the wall becomes practicable, as the risks would be acceptable. That is a policy which could be reduced to the formula: Change through rapprochement."

11. Peter Bender, *Offensive Entspannung: Möglichkeiten für Deutschland* (Cologne, 1964).

12. Nawrocki, *Relations Between the Two States*, pp. 32-33. Of the about 5,000 refugees who kept leaving the GDR annually after 1961, only a few dozen risked life and limb in crossing the border security areas. Most GDR refugees managed to escape by other means, on trips abroad, hidden in cars or freight, or not returning from official missions, for instance as artists or athletes.

13. Dennis, *The German Democratic Republic*, p. 38.

14. National income, for instance, rose from 108.7 billion Ostmarks to 141.7 billion Ostmarks between 1970 and 1975. See Deutsches Institut für Wirtschaftsforschung, *Handbuch DDR-Wirtschaft* (Reinbek, 1977), p. 309.

15. For details see Gerd Meyer, *Die DDR-Machtelite in der Ära Honecker* (Tübingen, 1991).

16. *Gesetzblatt der DDR*, Teil I, November 5, 1973, p. 517. The new regulations went into effect on November 15, 1973.

17. Nawrocki, *Relations Between the Two States*, pp. 59-60.

18. *Ibid.*, p. 126.

19. Dennis, *The German Democratic Republic*, p. 39. See also Hermann Weber, *Geschichte der DDR* (Munich, 1985), pp. 455-59.

20. Dennis, *The German Democratic Republic*, pp. 40-41; Helga Haftendorn, *Sicherheit und Stabilität. Aussenbeziehungen der Bundesrepublik zwischen Ölkrise und NATO-Doppelbeschluss* (Munich, 1986).

21. Erich Honecker, "Rede in Gera, October 13, 1980," in Hermann Weber, ed., *DDR: Dokumente zur Geschichte der Deutschen Demokratischen Republik 1945-1985* (Munich, 1986), pp. 373-74.

22. *Neues Deutschland*, October 14, 1980. See also A. James McAdams, *East Germany and Detente: Building Authority after the Wall* (Cambridge, 1985), p. 171.

23. *Neues Deutschland*, p. 170. Against this background, Honecker was confident enough, as has already been mentioned, to raise the nationality question again (see note 2), stating proudly in a conversation with British publisher Robert Maxwell in February 1981: "As far as the German question is concerned, history has already decided. . . . Unlike in the FRG, where the bourgeois nation continues to exist and where the national question is determined by the irreconcilable class antagonism between the bourgeoisie and the working masses . . . in the German Democratic Republic, in the socialist German state, the socialist nation is developing." Honecker, *Aus meinem Leben*, p. 391. See also Antonia Grunenberg, "Zwei Deutschlands—zwei Identitäten? Über deutsche Identität in der Bundesrepublik Deutschland und der DDR," in: Glaessner, ed., *Die DDR in der Ära Honecker*, p. 99.

24. Dennis, *The German Democratic Republic*, p. 39.

25. Ernst Martin, *Zwischenbilanz: Deutschlandpolitik der 80er Jahre* (Stuttgart, 1986), chap. 2. See also Klaus Ehring and Martin Dallwitz, *Schwerter zu Pflugscharen. Friedensbewegung in der DDR* (Reinbek, 1982).

26. Jonathan Carr, *Helmut Schmidt* (Dusseldorf, 1985), pp. 214-20.

27. The deal was made possible through the personal initiative of one of the most conservative German politicans, Franz Josef Strauss, the chairman of the Bavarian CSU. This alliance between the West German right and the East German left indicated the depth that the inner-German relations had reached meanwhile. For details, see the chapter "Der Milliardenkredit und die Begegnungen mit Honecker" in the memoirs of Franz Josef Strauss, *Die Erinnerungen* (Berlin, 1989), pp. 470-98.

28. See, for instance, Günther Gaus, *Wo Deutschland liegt: Eine Ortsbestimmung* (Hamburg, 1983), pp. 269-71. Gaus was the Federal Republic's permanent representative in East Berlin from 1974 until 1981.

29. Dennis, *The German Democratic Republic*, p. 39. Another prominent example of the practice of expelling dissidents from the GDR was lyrist Reiner Kunze who later, after the collapse of the SED regime, published the official state security documents regarding his case. See *Deckname "Lyrik." Eine Dokumentation von Reiner Kunze* (Frankfurt, 1990). In fact, Biermann's expatriation was partly a result of his declaring his solidarity with Kunze. An analysis of the Biermann and Kunze case is provided by Manfred Jäger, "Das Ende einer Kulturpolitik. Die Fälle Kunze und Biermann," *Deutschland-Archiv*, Vol. 9 (1976), pp. 1233-39. See also Klaus Kleinschmidt, "Das grosse Schweigen. Zur kulturpolitischen Situation in der DDR nach dem Ausschluss von neun Schriftstellern," *Deutschland-Archiv*, Vol. 12 (1979), pp. 899-905.

30. Martin, *Zwischenbilanz*, pp. 55-57.

31. *Ibid.*, p. 98.

32. See Jerzy Holzer, *"Solidarität" Die Geschichte einer freien Gewerkschaft in Polen* (Munich, 1985), esp. chap. 5: "Der August-Sieg," pp. 110-34.

33. McAdams, *East Germany and Detente*, p. 167.

34. Andrzej Fils, "Crisis and Political Ritual in Postwar Poland," *Problems of Communism*, Vol. 37 (May-August 1988), pp. 43-54.

35. *Neues Deutschland*, September 4, 1980.

36. McAdams, *East Germany and Detente*, p. 169.

37. *Neues Deutschland*, October 17, 1980.

38. *Christian Science Monitor*, December 5, 1980; Helmut Fehr, "Politisches System und Interessenausgleich im 'real existierenden' Sozialismus. Zum Verhältnis von Staat und evangelischen Kirchen in der DDR," *Aus Politik und Zeitgeschichte*, Vol. B 27 (1986), pp. 35-45. See also Reinhard Henkys, ed., *Die evangelischen Kirchen in der DDR. Beiträge zu einer Bestandsaufnahme* (Munich, 1980).

39. *Neues Deutschland*, November 18, 1980.

40. McAdams, *East Germany and Detente*, p. 182.

41. Stefan Heym, for instance, stated at the conference that, contrary to Lenin's theory, "just wars" were no longer possible; the Soviet SS-20 were as unjust as the American Pershing missiles; and people who planned the use of such weapons were criminals on both sides. See *Berliner Begegnung zur Friedensförderung: Protokolle des Schriftstellertreffens am 13./14. Dezember 1981* (Darmstadt, 1982), p. 66. Günter de Bruyn said that the policy of the GDR would be inconsistent and harmful to itself if it welcomed the peace movement in the West but rejected peace efforts of independent groupings in its own country. If such movements were forced underground, valuable potential for peace would be lost, and the GDR government would lose its credibility. See Harald Kleinschmidt, "'Ich habe mir einen Traum erfüllt.' Zur Berliner Begegnung zur Friedensförderung," *Deutschland-Archiv*, Vol. 15, 1982, pp. 5-9.

42. See Ehring and Dallwitz, *Schwerter zu Pflugscharen*, pp. 69-87.

43. While the SED leadership now claimed that, in view of the aggressive intentions of imperialism, it would be an illusion to create peace without weapons,

even the official synods and representatives of the Evangelical Church in the GDR protested against the persecution of youths wearing the "Swords to Ploughshares" emblem. See Peter Borowsky, *Deutschland 1969-1982* (Hannover, 1987), p. 272; Ehring and Dallwitz, *Schwerter zu Pflugscharen*, p. 64.

44. Tad Szulc, "Poland's Path," *Foreign Policy*, No. 72 (Fall 1988), p. 221.

45. Regarding the role of the Catholic church in Polish history, see Georges Castellan, *Gott schütze Polen! Geschichte des polnischen Katholizismus 1795-1982* (Freiburg, 1983).

46. See Szulc, "Poland's Path" p. 222.

47. Rudolf L. Tökés, "Hungarian Reform Imperatives," *Problems of Communism*, Vol. 33 (September-October 1984), pp. 6-8.

48. Susan Tifft, "Facing the Cold Realities," *Time*, June 6, 1988, p. 18.

49. See Bela Csikos-Nagy, "Position and Future of the Hungarian Economy," *Volosag* (Budapest), Vol. 9 (1984), p. 91, and Imre Kovacs, "The Present and Future of the Hungarian Economy," *Figyelo* (Budapest), July 21, 1988, p. 3.

50. See also Ronald D. Asmus, "East Berlin and Moscow: The Documentation of a Dispute," Radio Free Europe-Radio Liberty, *RFE Occasional Papers* (Munich), No. 1 (1985).

51. Michael Stefanek and Ivan Hlivka, "The National and the International in the Policy of the CPCZ," *Rude Pravo* (Prague), April 30, 1984.

52. A. James McAdams, "The New Logic in Soviet-GDR Relations," *Problems of Communism*, Vol. 37 (September-October 1988), p. 51.

53. Honecker later admitted that Gorbachev's new policy came as a great surprise to the East German communists. See Reinhold Andert and Wolfgang Herzberg, *Der Sturz: Erich Honecker im Kreuzverhör* (Berlin, 1990), p. 61.

54. See Alexander Fischer, "Aussenpolitische Aktivität bei ungewisser sowjetischer Deutschland-Politik (bis 1955)," in: Jacobsen et al., eds., *Drei Jahrzehnte Aussenpolitik*, pp. 56-57.

55. See Michail Gorbatschow, *Perestroika: Die zweite russische Revolution. Eine neue Politik für Europa und die Welt* (Munich, 1987), pp. 73-78; Tom G. Palmer, "Why Socialism Collapsed in Eastern Europe," *Cato Policy Report*, Vol. 12, No. 5 (September/October 1990), pp. 6-13.

56. See Hannes Adomeit, "Gorbatschows Westpolitik. Gemeinsames Europäisches Haus oder atlantische Orientierung," SWP-AZ 2555 (Stiftung Wissenschaft und Politik, 1988); March Kramer, "Beyond the Brezhnev Doctrine: A New Era in Soviet-East European Relations," *International Security* (Winter 1989), pp. 25-67; F. Stephen Larrabee, "Beyond Yalta: The Challenge of Change in Eastern Europe" (draft manuscript), p. 17.

57. Charles Gati, "Gorbachev and Eastern Europe," *Foreign Affairs*, Vol. 65, No. 5 (Summer 1987), p. 968. See also F. Stephen Larrabee, "Eastern Europe: A Generational Change," *Foreign Policy*, No. 70 (Spring 1988), pp. 49-50.

58. Regarding the background of Gorbachev's policy toward the GDR and the impact of the Soviet Union on the German unification process, see Gerhard Wettig, "Die Rolle der UdSSR bei der Vereinigung Deutschlands," in: Konrad Löw, ed., *Ursachen und Verlauf der deutschen Revolution 1989* (Berlin, 1991), pp. 45-63.

59. Gati, "Gorbachev and Eastern Europe," p. 963.

60. F. Stephen Larrabee, "Instability and Change in East Germany," (draft manuscript, Ebenhausen, 1989), p. 3.

61. *Ibid.*, p. 4.

62. Aufruf des ZK der Kommunistischen Partei Deutschlands, June 11, 1945, in: *DDR Dokumente*, pp. 32-36. See also Anton Ackermann, "Gibt es einen besonderen deutschen Weg zum Sozialismus?" *Einheit: Monatsschrift zur Vorbereitung der Sozialistischen Einheitspartei*, Vol. 1 (February 1946), p. 31.

63. Interview with Kurt Hager in: *Der Stern*, April 9, 1987. Reprinted in: *Neues Deutschland*, April 10, 1987.

64. *Pravda*, April 11, 1987.

65. See, for instance, Otfried Pustejovsky, *In Prag kein Fenstersturz* (Munich, 1968); Radoslav Selucky, *Reformmodell CSSR: Entwurf einer sozialistischen Marktwirtschaft oder Gefahr für die Volksdemokratien?* (Reinbek, 1969); and, as a more recent account, Zdenek Mlynar, ed., *Der "Prager Frühling." Ein wissenschaftliches Symposion* (Cologne, 1983).

66. *Pravda*, November 3, 1987. Reprinted in *Europa-Archiv*, Vol. 42 (1987), pp. D673-80.

67. The Polish experience of December 1981 may have been the last example of effective use of the Brezhnev Doctrine, when massive Soviet forces were

assembled inside Poland and along the Polish borders, ready for military intervention to liquidate Solidarity within 24 hours, had General Jaruzelski not decided to order Polish security forces to crack down on the opposition movement themselves.

68. Gemeinsame jugoslawisch-sowjetische Erklärung, March 18, 1988, in: *Europa-Archiv,* Vol. 43 (1988), pp. D238-43.

69. Gorbachev's speech at the Parliamentary Assembly of the European Council in Strasbourg on July 6, 1989, in: *Europa-Archiv,* Vol. 44 (1989), p. D588.

70. *Ibid.,* pp. 589-90.

71. *The New York Times,* October 26, 1989.

72. Larrabee, "Instability and Change," p. 5. See also Jürgen Engert, "Honeckers Macht wird brüchig," *Rheinischer Merkur/Christ und Welt,* March 25, 1988, p. 3.

73. Alfred Kosing, "Zur Dialektik der weiteren Gestaltung der entwickelten sozialistischen Gesellschaft," *Deutsche Zeitschrift für Philosophie,* No. 7 (1988), pp. 577-87.

74. The psychological preconditions of change in the GDR in the 1980s have been analyzed by Dr. Hans-Joachim Maaz, director of the Psychotherapeutic Clinic of Halle. See Hans-Joachim Maaz, *Der Gefühlsstau: Ein Psychogramm der DDR* (Berlin, 1990), pp. 135-42.

75. Larrabee, "Instability and Change," p. 6.

76. George Schöpflin, Rudolf Tökés, and Iván Völgyes, "Leadership Change and Crisis in Hungary," *Problems of Communism,* Vol. 37, (September-October 1988), pp. 23-46; Szulc, "Poland's Path," pp. 210-29. In characteristic Hungarian piecemeal fashion, a special deal was struck with the aging Kádár, giving him the largely ceremonial post of party president. The deal also included provisions to prevent abuse of him as a scapegoat and to limit the turnover in the Central Committee. Leadership renewal, therefore, was not guaranteed under this plan, because many old conservatives continued to hold power in the Central Committee.

77. See, for instance, Dennis, *The German Democratic Republic,* p. 2, who stated in 1988 that "the GDR can no longer be written off as a satrapy of Moscow; it is an increasingly more valued junior partner of its Soviet ally and its leaders exhibit greater confidence in their dealings with their West German counterparts." See also McAdams, *East Germany and Detente,* p. 198, who noted in

1985 that "one might say that the GDR was able to become something much greater under Honecker's leadership than the relatively straightforward captive of its surroundings, the 'sick man' of modern Europe, that it may have seemed in the not so distant past."

78. Weber, DDR: Dokumente zur Geschichte, pp. 367-70.

79. Erich Honecker, "DDR—ein sauberer Staat," Speech before the SED Central Committee, December 15, 1965, in: DDR Dokumente, pp. 282-83.

80. Dennis, The German Democratic Republic, p. 174.

81. Bericht des Politbüros an die 9. Tagung des ZK der SED (East Berlin, 1973), pp. 62-63.

82. See Peter Lübbe, ed., Dokumente zur Kunst-, Literatur- und Kulturpolitik der SED 1975-1980 (Stuttgart, 1984), p. 460. Rudolf Bahro, whose book Die Alternative—an analysis of bureaucratic dictatorship—had just been published in the West, was arrested in August 1977 and sentenced to eight years in prison in June 1978, despite declarations of solidarity from such famous Western intellectuals as Heinrich Böll, among many others. See Rudolf Bahro, Die Alternative. Zur Kritik des real existierenden Sozialismus (Frankfurt, 1977).

83. Jürgen Fuchs, Vernehmungsprotokolle (Reinbek, 1980). See also Rudolf Bahro, Eine Dokumentation (Frankfurt, 1977), p. 107.

84. P. U. Hohendahl and P. Hermingshouse, ed., Literatur in der DDR in den siebziger Jahren (Frankfurt, 1983), p. 7.

85. See Pedro Ramet, "Church and Peace in the GDR," Problems of Communism, Vol. 33 (July-August 1984), p. 49. See also interview with Stefan Heym, in: Der Spiegel, May 31, 1982, p. 100.

86. Report on the conversation of Erich Honecker with the church leaders, March 6, 1978, in: DDR Dokumente, pp. 370-72. See also Ramet, "Church and Peace in the GDR," p. 178, and Henkys, Die evangelischen Kirschen, pp. 19-22. Regarding the "social relevance" of the churches, it should be noted in this respect that in the late 1970s, 54.5 percent of the GDR population (9.1 million people), belonged to a Christian religious body; 7.7 million East Germans were members of the Evangelical Church, 1.2 million were Catholics, and 200,000 were adherents of unaffiliated churches.

87. Henkys, Die evangelischen Kirschen, p. 25. In October 1983, however, Honecker confirmed the "legitimate interests of the churches" and stated

carefully that the government of the GDR would stick to the accord of March 1978. See Erich Honecker, Interview on Luther and the relationship between state and church in the GDR, October 6, 1983, in: *DDR Dokumente*, p. 389.

88. *Neues Deutschland*, February 12, 1985, p. 1.

89. Berliner Appell, in: Ehring and Dallwitz, *Schwerter zu Pflugscharen*, p. 227. See also Ramet, "Church and Peace in the GDR," p. 50, and Clemens Richter, "Aus christlicher Verantwortung? Die DDR-CDU zur Friedenserziehung und zum Wehrunterricht," *Deutschland-Archiv*, Vol. 12 (1979), p. 237. The Catholic Church, which had been very reluctant to make political statements until the late 1970s, now also began to protest against the militarization of GDR society. See Clemens Richter, "Veränderte Haltung der DDR-Katholiken," *Deutschland-Archiv*, Vol. 16 (1983), p. 454.

90. Ramet, "Church and Peace in the GDR," p. 51.

91. See Weber, *Geschichte der DDR*, pp. 454-55.

92. Ramet, "Church and Peace in the GDR, pp. 52-53.

93. In the 1980s, some 4,300 pastors were at work in the GDR's 7,200 Evangelical Church communities. Most of them participated actively in the protest movement or tried, at least, to provide cover and moral support. It is certainly fair to say that the Evangelical Church of the GDR, and particularly the pastors, provided the basis for the articulation of dissident ideas and opinions. In fact, the churches turned out to be more important in organizing the opposition than the intellectuals in the cultural community—not to mention the students and professors at the universities who remained essentially silent until the very last moment.

94. *Die Tageszeitung*, November 1, 1983, p. 9.

95. Ramet, "Church and Peace in the GDR," p. 54. See also Robert English, "Eastern Europe's Doves," *Foreign Policy*, No. 56 (Fall 1984), pp. 44-60.

96. The crisis was eventually resolved by assurances of the East German government that the 50 GDR citizens would get exit visas, but the Permanent Mission of the Federal Republic had to be closed temporarily.

97. Ramet, "Church and Peace in the GDR," p. 54; Dennis, *The German Democratic Republic*, p. 182.

98. Larrabee, "Instability and Change," p. 11. Regarding the relationship between the church and the opposition, see Jürgen Israel, ed., *Zur Freiheit berufen: Die Kirche in der DDR als Schutzraum der Opposition 1981-1989* (Berlin, 1991), passim.

99. *Report of the Central Committee of the Socialist Unity Party of Germany to the 11th Congress of the SED* (Dresden, 1986), p. 85.

100. "Neues Forum" was established at the weekend of September 9-10, 1989, by some 30 people, among them Bärbel Bohley and Professor Jens Reich, who signed the proclamation "Aufbruch 89—Neues Forum" pleading for political reform. Zeno and Sabine Zimmerling, eds., *Neue Chronik DDR*, Vol. 1 (Berlin, 1990), pp. 33-35.

101. Martin, *Zwischenbilanz*, pp. 97-100.

102. "Commissioner: Ethnic Germans Are a Plus," *The Week in Germany*, April 7, 1989, p. 7.

103. "Genscher for Economic Aid for Poland," *The Week in Germany*, April 21, 1989, p. 1.

104. *Ibid.*, p. 1.

105. Cordt Schnibben, "'Ich bin das Volk.' Wie Erich Honecker und sein Politbüro die Konterrevolution erlebten," *Der Spiegel*, April 16, 1990, p. 73.

106. Günter Schabowski, *Der Absturz* (Berlin, 1991), p. 221.

107. *Ibid.*, p. 222.

108. Schnibben, "'Ich bin das Volk,'" p. 77.

109. *Ibid.*

110. VVS-Nr. 0008, MfS-Nr. 38/89, "Massnahmen zur Zurückweisung und Unterbindung von Aktivitäten feindlicher, oppositioneller und anderer negativer Kräfte zur Diskreditierung der Ergebnisse der Kommunalwahlen am 7. Mai 1989, May 19, 1989," in: Armin Mitter and Stefan Wolle, eds., *Ich liebe euch doch alle! Befehle und Lageberichte des MfS Januar-November 1989* (Berlin, 1990), pp. 42-45. For details, see also Manfred Schell and Werner Kalinka, *Stasi und kein Ende. Die Personen und Fakten* (Frankfurt and Berlin, 1991), pp. 285-87.

111. "'Mal sehen, wo wir landen wollen.' Ein ehemaliger SED-Funktionär über Fälschungen bei der DDR-Kommunalwahl 1989," *Der Spiegel*, April 30, 1990, pp. 69-73. Harry Klapproth committed suicide one week after his testimony.

112. Andert and Herzberg, *Der Sturz*, p. 83.

113. See Günther Schabowski, *Das Politbüro: Ende eines Mythos. Eine Befragung*, ed. by Frank Sieren and Ludwig Koehne (Reinbek, 1990), pp. 60-62. See also Report of the Politburo to the 8th Plenum of the Central Committee, in: *Neues Deutschland*, June 23, 1989. Krenz later claimed that he had been ordered by Honecker to go to China. This was disputed by Honecker, however, who referred to Krenz's first words after his return from Beijing: "I am grateful that I could head this delegation. . . . I am enthusiastic about what I saw in China. All my talks with the leading people of the People's Republic of China have been positive." Quoted in Andert and Herzberg, *Der Sturz*, p. 95.

114. Regarding the tense relationship between Gorbachev and Honecker, see Schabowski, *Der Absturz*, pp. 213-17.

115. "Der 13. August 1961—seine Ursachen und Folgen," *Neues Deutschland*, August 12-13, 1989.

116. On August 16, the government of the Federal Republic informed the public about the exact numbers of GDR refugees in West German embassies in Eastern Europe: 171 in Budapest, 40 in Prague, 1 in Warsaw, and 116 in the permanent representation of the Federal Republic in East Berlin. For details, see *Neue Chronik DDR*, Vol. 1, p. 15.

117. Markus Wolf, *In eigenem Auftrag: Bekenntnisse und Einsichten* (Munich, 1991), pp. 155-57.

118. *Ibid.*, p. 158.

119. Egon Krenz, *Wenn Mauern fallen: Die friedliche Revolution: Vorgeschichte, Ablauf, Auswirkungen* (Vienna, 1990).

120. Schnibben, "'Ich bin das Volk,'" p. 87. See also a top-secret paper of the Ministry of State Security dealing with the same issue: MfS, ZAIG, 0/225, "Hinweise auf wesentliche motivbildende Faktoren im Zusammenhang mit Anträgen auf ständige Ausreise nach dem nichtsozialistischen Ausland und dem ungesetzlichen Verlassen der DDR," September 9, 1989, in: *Ich liebe euch doch alle! Befehle und Lageberichte des MfS*, pp. 141-47.

121. Schabowski, *Der Absturz*, pp. 226-27. Schabowski says that when Honecker informed the Politburo about his decision, the situation had been rather macabre: In the middle of a deadly crisis, when the fate of the entire regime was at stake, the 77-year-old Honecker, awaiting surgery, had nominated as his vice-regent a person who was seriously diabetic and had had both legs

amputated. The information that Honecker intentionally sent Krenz on vacation has been confirmed by Markus Wolf in a diary entry of September 5, 1989, in: Wolf, *In einem Auftrag*, p. 170.

122. On August 24, the Hungarian government also agreed to the departure of the 100 GDR refugees in the West German embassy in Budapest. See *Europa-Archiv*, Vol. 44 (1989), p. Z165.

123. Schabowski, *Der Absturz*, p. 222.

124. Schnibben, "'Ich bin bas Volk,'" pp. 87-90.

125. Schabowski, *Der Absturz*, p. 222.

126. Schnibben, "'Ich bin das Volk,'" pp. 87-90. A meeting between the foreign ministers of the GDR and Hungary, Fischer and Horn, on August 31 in East Berlin ended in complete disagreement. Horn stated explicitly that the Hungarian government would accept only "a settlement in accordance with the duties of my country with respect to international human rights and its humanitarian political practice." Radio Budapest, September 1, 1989. Quoted from: *Neue Chronik DDR*, Vol. 1, p. 19.

127. Schabowski, *Der Absturz*, pp. 228-29.

128. Schnibben, "'Ich bin das Volk,'" p. 90.

129. Schabowski, *Der Absturz*, p. 230. Today Schabowski is convinced that an opportunity was missed when the discussion in the Politburo was cut off. If the debate had continued, it might have been possible to isolate Honecker and Mittag and to arrange the changing of the guard four weeks earlier than actually happened. But, Schabowski says, following the Politburo meeting on September 5, "the leadership of the country, after a brief, publicly unnoticed outburst, fell back into speechlessness."

130. Horst Schäfer, correspondent of the official GDR news agency ADN, reported from Passau, West Germany, that the "provocation against the GDR was staff-like organized," as an "icy-nerved business with GDR citizens" and with "silverlings for Hungary." Schäfer's report was reprinted by *Neues Deutschland* the following day. See "Provokation gegen die DDR stabsmässig organisiert. Eiskaltes Geschäft mit DDR-Bürgern—Silberlinge für Ungarn," *Neues Deutschland*, September 12, 1989. See also Wolf, *In einem Auftrag*, p. 173, and Schabowski, *Der Absturz*, p. 223.

131. John Edwin Mroz, "Back Door Opens in the Iron Curtain," *Los Angeles Times*, September 15, 1989.

132. *Ibid.*

133. *The Week in Germany,* October 6, 1989, p. 1.

134. For details, see *Neue Chronik DDR,* Vol. 1, pp. 60-62.

135. See Claus Gennrich, "Schewardnadse hat die Regierung der DDR zum Einlenken bewegt—Telefonate mit Ost-Berlin nach Vorschlägen Genschers," *Frankfurter Allgemeine Zeitung,* October 2, 1989, p. 2.

136. Schabowski, *Der Absturz,* p. 234.

137. *Ibid.,* p. 235.

138. *Der Spiegel,* Vol. 43, No. 39, September 25, 1989.

139. *Ibid.*

140. Hans-Dietrich Genscher, "Speech at the 44th Session of the General Assembly of the United Nations", New York, September 27, 1989, *Statements & Speeches,* Vol. 12, No. 20, p. 2. Genscher felt, however, that by refusing reforms the GDR was "destabilizing and isolating itself," which in effect could lead to a "de-Europeanization" of its policy: "If the reform policy surrounding the GDR increasingly expands and spreads, a refusal to reform contains within itself the danger of such a de-Europeanization." See *Der Spiegel,* September 25, 1989.

141. Genscher, Speech, September 27, 1989, p. 2.

142. Theo Sommer, "Kleine Schritte oder grosse Luftsprünge?" *Die Zeit,* No. 39, September 29, 1989, p. 3.

143. *Ibid.*

144. *Augsburger Allgemeine,* October 2, 1989.

145. *Die Welt,* October 3, 1989.

146. Serge Schmemann, "East Germans Act to Stem Exodus," *International Herald Tribune,* October 4, 1989, p. 1. On October 4, again nearly 10,000 GDR refugees had gathered at the site of the FRG embassy in Prague. See *Neue Chronik DDR,* Vol. 1, p. 65.

147. Schmemann, "East Germans Act to End Exodus," p. 1.

148. *Ibid.,* p. 7.

CHAPTER 3

1. Hans Modrow, *Aufbruch und Ende* (Hamburg, 1991), p. 13.

2. For details, see Eckhard Bahr, *Sieben Tage im Oktober: Aufbruch in Dresden* (Leipzig, 1990), pp. 25-54. See also Zimmerling and Zimmerling, eds., *Neue Chronik DDR*, Vol. I, pp. 67-68.

3. See *Neues Deutschland*, October 5, 1989.

4. Detailed reporting of the events began in *Die Tageszeitung*, September 9, 1989.

5. See *Neue Chronik DDR*, Vol. I, pp. 18-40.

6. The declaration was signed by Democracy Now, Democratic Awakening, New Forum, the Group of Democratic Socialists, the Initiative for Peace and Human Rights, the Initiative for a Social-Democratic Party in the GDR, and representatives of several peace circles. See *Gemeinsame Erklärung*, October 4, 1989, in: *Ibid.*, pp. 71-72.

7. *Ibid.*, p. 73.

8. Schabowski, *Der Absturz*, p. 237.

9. Krenz, *Wenn Mauern fallen*, p. 32.

10. Schabowski, *Der Absturz*, p. 237. See also Hans Modrow, "Bilanz nach 150 Tagen," *Die Zeit*, April 13, 1990, p. 5.

11. At this point the question may be raised if the downfall of the SED regime constituted a "revolution" or merely a "collapse." After discussing the theoretical characteristics of a revolution, Professor Hannelore Horn concluded that the "upheaval between October 1989 and March 1990 can in effect be seen as a revolution resulting essentially from internal weakness. At the political level, the revolution achieved its aims; at the social level, however, it remained—of necessity—still incomplete." Hannelore Horn, "Collapse from Internal Weakness—The GDR from October 1989 to March 1990," in: Dieter Grosser, ed., *German Unification. The Unexpected Challenge* (Oxford, 1992), p. 68.

12. Ansprache des Generalsekretärs des ZK der KPdSU und Vorsitzenden des Obersten Präsidiums des Obersten Sowjets der UdSSR, Michail Gorbatschow, auf der Festveranstaltung zum 40. Jahrestag der Gründung der DDR in Ost-Berlin, October 6, 1989, in: *Europa-Archiv*, Vol. 44 (1989), pp. D581-86.

13. Ansprache des Generalsekretärs des ZK der SED und Vorsitzenden des Staatsrates der DDR, Erich Honecker, auf der Festveranstaltung zum 40. Jahrestag der Gründung der DDR in Ost-Berlin, October 6, 1989, in: *Ibid.,* pp. D573-81.

14. Schabowski, *Der Absturz,* p. 239.

15. *Ibid.,* p. 241, and Günter Mittag, *Um jeden Preis. Im Spannungsfeld zweier Systeme* (Berlin, 1991), p. 18. Mittag claims in his memoirs that he actually participated in the conversation between Gorbachev and Honecker. This has been disputed, however, by a TASS correspondent who states that he was waiting with Mittag in the anteroom for the two general secretaries to end their talks.

16. Stenographische Niederschrift des Treffens der Genossen des Politbüros des Zentralkomitees der SED mit dem Generalsekretär des ZK der KPdSU und Vorsitzenden des Obersten Sowjets der UdSSR, Genossen Michail Sergejewitsch Gorbatschow, am Sonnabend, dem 7. Oktober 1989 in *Berlin-Niederschönhausen* (Verbatim Protocol), October 7, 1989, pp. 9 and 12-13.

17. *Ibid.,* pp. 14-15 and 22.

18. *Ibid.,* p. 26.

19. Schabowski, *Der Absturz,* p. 242.

20. Krenz, *Wenn Mauern fallen,* p. 96.

21. See Hannes Bahrmann and Christoph Links, eds., *Wir sind das Volk: Die DDR zwischen 7. Oktober und 17. Dezember 1989: Eine Chronik* (Berlin, 1990), pp. 7-8.

22. *Ibid.,* pp. 8-9. Most of the violence occured near the Gethsemane Church at the Schönhauser Allee, where a "Mahnwache" (memorial watch) for political prisoners had been held since October 2. For details, see *Und diese verdammte Ohnmacht. Report der unabhängigen Untersuchungskommission zu den Ereignissen vom 7./8. Oktober 1989 in Berlin* (Berlin, 1991), pp. 15-25.

23. "Betroffenheit und Sorge der Bundesregierung über die Entwicklungen in der DDR," October 6-8, 1990, in: *Bulletin,* No. 103 (1990), p. 891. See also "Bonn: 40 Years GDR No Cause for Celebration," *The Week in Germany,* October 13, 1989, p. 1.

24. *Ibid.*

25. "Lambsdorff: Reform in GDR First Step toward Unity," *The Week in Germany,* October 13, 1989, p. 1.

26. "Perspektiven europäischer Sicherheit und transatlantischer Partnerschaft." Speech by Defense Minister Stoltenberg, October 10, 1989, in: *Bulletin,* No. 104 (1989), pp. 899-900.

27. *Süddeutsche Zeitung,* October 7, 1989.

28. Erich Mielke, telegram to the heads of all district administrations of the Ministry for State Security, October 8, 1989, in: MfS, Dokumentenverwaltung, No. 103625, VVS-Nr. 0008-70/89, quoted from: Armin Mitter and Stefan Wolle, eds., *Ich liebe euch doch alle!* (Berlin, 1990), p. 200.

29. *Ibid.,* p. 201.

30. Schabowski, *Der Absturz,* p. 245.

31. *Ibid.,* p. 247.

32. *Ibid.,* pp. 248-49; Krenz, *Wenn Mauern fallen,* pp. 203-4.

33. Bahrmann and Links, eds., *Wir sind das Volk,* pp. 11-12.

34. See Bahr, *Sieben Tage im Oktober,* pp. 130-34 and 158; Modrow, *Aufbruch und Ende,* p. 15.

35. The appeal stated that "we all need a free dialogue on the continuation of socialism in our country. Therefore the underwriters promise all citizens that this dialogue will be conducted not only in the district of Leipzig, but with our government as well." Quoted from: Zimmerling and Zimmerling, eds., *Neue Chronik DDR,* Vol. 1, p. 91.

36. Schabowski, *Der Absturz,* p. 251.

37. *Ibid.,* pp. 251-52. While the main subject of concern was the situation in Leipzig, other demonstrations were planned in Dresden and Magdeburg. For details, see the report of the Ministry for State Security, "Information über eine Demonstration und Zusammenkünfte oppositioneller Kräfte in Leipzig, Dresden und Magdeburg," undated, MfS, ZAIG, No. 452/89, quoted from: Mitter and and Wolle, eds., *Ich liebe euch doch alle!* pp. 216-19.

38. Bahrmann and Links, eds., *Wir sind das Volk,* pp. 17-19. For the three Dresden party secretaries, this outcome had not at all been clear at the beginning. In

November 1989, Jochen Pommert wrote in a letter to Schabowski that it had been a free decision of the three "to look for a possibility to avert very bad things from the citizens of the city and the whole country in an alarming situation," and that there had been "nobody who directed, authorized or even covered us." Quoted from: Schabowski, *Der Absturz*, p. 252.

39. At the time, Dashichev was chairman of a scientific-consultative council at the Soviet Foreign Minstry. For details, see Gerhard Wettig, "Die sowjetische Rolle beim Umsturz in der DDR und bei der Einleitung des deutschen Einigungsprozesses," in: Jürgen Elvert and Michael Salewski, eds., *Der Umbruch in Osteuropa* (Stuttgart, 1992).

40. See "Auf eiserne Art," *Der Spiegel*, No. 16 (1991), p. 41.

41. Schabowski, *Der Absturz*, pp. 254-55.

42. Mittag, *Um jeden Preis*, pp. 22-23. See also "Das geht so nicht weiter! Günter Mittag über seinen Sturz und seine Rolle als Sündenbock," in: *Der Spiegel*, No. 37 (1991), p. 84.

43. Schabowski, *Der Absturz*, p. 255.

44. "Erklärung des Politbüros: Sozialismus steht nicht zur Disposition," *Neues Deutschland*, October 12, 1989.

45. Modrow, *Aufbruch und Ende*, pp. 18-19.

46. *Ibid.*, p. 19.

47. Schabowski, *Der Absturz*, p. 257.

48. Krenz, *Wenn Mauern fallen*, p. 139.

49. Tisch was also a member of the Politburo. His distaste for Mittag resulted from personal dislike ("an intriguer") as well as from political differences. Tisch claimed that Mittag was gradually destroying the GDR economy and with it the trade unions.

50. Krenz, *Wenn Mauern fallen*, p. 143.

51. Schabowski, *Der Absturz*, p. 261.

52. *Ibid.*, p. 262.

53. *Ibid.*, p. 263.

54. The strategy of moderation was also reflected in internal directives of the Ministry for State Security. See Erich Mielke, Telegram, October 16, 1989, in: MfS, Dokumentenverwaltung, No. 103525, VVS-No. 76/89, quoted from: Mitter and and Wolle, eds., *Ich liebe euch doch alle!* pp. 227-28.

55. Andert and Herzberg, *Der Sturz*, p. 29.

56. Honecker later admitted that he had been "very surprised," but "as usual in my life, I mastered my feelings quickly." He realized that "everything had been prepared." *Ibid.*, pp. 30-31.

57. See Krenz, *Wenn Mauern fallen*, pp. 144-45, and Schabowski, *Der Absturz*, p. 268. Mielke's role is still not clear. During the Politburo session on October 17, he apparently threatened to make public compromising material he had collected about Honecker. See Karl Wilhelm Fricke, "Honeckers Sturz mit Mielkes Hilfe," *Deutschland-Archiv*, Vol. 21 (1991), pp. 5-7.

58. Andert and Herzberg, *Der Sturz*, pp. 32-33. Later in the evening at home, he told his wife: "You know, I am really relieved. I couldn't do it anymore."

59. Communiqué of the Ninth Plenum of the Central Committee of the SED, October 18, 1989, in: *Neues Deutschland*, October 19, 1989.

60. Modrow, *Aufbruch und Ende*, p. 20.

61. "Wende und ideologische Offensive. Rede des SED-Generalsekretärs Egon Krenz," *Neues Deutschland*, October 19, 1989. See also Zimmerling and Zimmerling, eds., *Neue Chronik DDR*, Vol. 1, pp. 139-150. In his memoirs, Krenz later noted that "due to lack of time, I read the same address that I had delivered to the Central Committee of the party." Krenz, *Wenn Mauern fallen*, p. 208.

62. Modrow, *Aufbruch und Ende*, p. 21.

63. Zimmerling and Zimmerling, eds., *Neue Chronik DDR*, Vol. 2, p. 28.

64. *Nürnberger Zeitung*, October 28, 1989.

65. *General-Anzeiger* (Bonn), October 30, 1989.

66. Zimmerling and Zimmerling, eds., *Neue Chronik DDR*, Vol. 2, p. 14; Bahrmann and Links, eds., *Wir sind das Volk*, p. 42.

67. Modrow, *Aufbruch und Ende*, p. 21.

68. Krenz, *Wenn Mauern fallen*, pp. 222-23.

69. "In grosser Offenheit haben wir über alles gesprochen," *Neues Deutschland*, November 2, 1989.

70. Zimmerling and Zimmerling, eds., *Neue Chronik DDR*, Vol. 2, p. 49.

71. *Ibid.*, p. 62.

72. The speeches of Christa Wolf, Christoph Hein, and Markus Wolf have been partly reprinted in: *Ibid.*, pp. 64-67. Markus Wolf has also published his diary entry of November 4; see Wolf, *In eigenem Auftrag*, pp. 221-24.

73. *Frankfurter Allgemeine Zeitung*, November 6, 1989, p. 1.

74. Schabowski, *Der Absturz*, p. 282.

75. Zimmerling and Zimmerling, eds., *Neue Chronik DDR*, Vol. 2, pp. 74-76. Regarding the background of Modrow's nomination as prime minister, see Karl-Heinz Arnold, *Die ersten hundert Tage des Hans Modrow* (Berlin, 1990), pp. 16-21.

76. See *Der Spiegel*, No. 40 (1989), p. 27.

77. *Neues Deutschland*, November 4, 1989.

78. "Bonn Welcomes Opening of GDR Border," *The Week in Germany*, November 10, 1989, p. 1.

79. Helmut Kohl, "Policy Declaration on the State of the Nation in a Divided Germany," November 8, 1989, in: *Bulletin*, No. 123 (1989), pp. 1058-59.

80. *Ibid.*, p. 1058.

81. *Ibid.*

82. *Die Welt*, November 4, 1989; *Handelsblatt*, November 6, 1989.

83. "Kohl Begins Visit to Poland," *The Week in Germany*, November 10, 1989, p. 2.

84. Deutscher Bundestag, 11. Wahlperiode, 173. Sitzung, November 8, 1989, in: *Verhandlungen des Deutschen Bundestages. Stenographische Berichte*, Vol. 151, pp. 13018-21.

85. Schabowski, *Das Politbüro*, p. 113.

86. Zimmerling and Zimmerling, eds., *Neue Chronik DDR*, Vol. 2, pp. 71-72.

87. Schabowski, *Der Absturz*, p. 303; Schabowski, *Das Politburo*, p. 135. Under the planned travel law, GDR citizens would have been forced to cross over the border into the Western world with no more than DM15 of hard currency.

88. Bahrmann and Links, eds., *Wir sind das Volk*, p. 83.

89. *Neues Deutschland*, November 8, 1989.

90. Schabowski, *Der Absturz*, p. 305.

91. *Ibid.*; Modrow, *Aufbruch und Ende*, pp. 24-25.

92. Schabowski, *Der Absturz*, p. 306.

93. Krenz had received the text from the minister of the interior, Dickel, during the meeting of the Central Committee for approval. After the placet of the Politburo, the draft was expected to be returned to the government. Then the submission would be passed by the cabinet members in a routine rotation procedure. See *Ibid.*, p. 307.

94. Bahrmann and Links, eds., *Wir sind das Volk*, p. 91.

95. Schabowski, *Der Absturz*, pp. 309-10.

96. *Ibid.*, p. 310. After the first shivers had passed a few days later, Krenz admitted that he had made a mistake during the night the Wall was opened. "We should have dived into the turmoil," he said. "They would have celebrated us as a wall storming-party." Regarding the situation at the border regiments, see David Mertens, "Alarm in Oranienburg, während Berlin feierte," *Berliner Morgenpost*, September 30, 1991, p. 1.

97. Modrow, *Aufbruch und Ende*, pp. 25-26.

98. *Der Tagesspiegel*, November 11, 1989.

99. "Ein historischer Tag für Berlin und Deutschland." Speech by Chancellor Kohl at the Schöneberger Rathaus in Berlin, November 10, 1989, in: *Bulletin*, No. 125 (1989), p. 1065.

100. Der Tagesspiegel, November 11, 1989; Frankfurter Allgemeine Zeitung, November 11, 1989.

101. Horst Teltschik, 329 Tage: Innenansichten der Einigung (Berlin, 1991), p. 19. See also Horst Teltschik, "De Bärn is g'schält," Der Spiegel, No. 39 (1991), p. 102.

102. Teltschik, 329 Tage, p. 23.

103. Eduard Shevardnadze, Interview with chief editor Fyodor Burlazki, in: Literaturnaia gazeta, April 1991.

104. "Auf eiserne Art. Moskaus Ex-Aussenminister Schewardnadse hat enthüllt, dass die deutsche Vereinigung gewaltsam verhindert werden sollte," Der Spiegel, No. 16 (1991), p. 41.

105. Ibid.

106. For a review of Modrow's term of office, see Walter Süss, "Bilanz einer Gratwanderung. Die kurze Amtszeit des Hans Modrow," Deutschland-Archiv, Vol. 24 (1991), pp. 596-608.

107. Schabowski, Der Absturz, p. 284.

108. In August 1989, during a visit to the Federal Republic, Modrow openly called Markus Wolf his "friend." He had known Wolf for years, since they had jointly taken a cure at a spa. Both agreed that Honecker's distancing from Gorbachev's course was not acceptable, and Wolf supported Modrow in his attempt to improve relations with Dresden's partner city, Leningrad, despite an internal directive from the SED leadership in East Berlin that party connections with Soviet communities should no longer be enforced.

109. See Markus Wolf, Die Troika (Berlin, 1989).

110. In 1988 Kryuchkov was appointed chairman of the KGB. In this position he later became involved in the attempted coup against President Gorbachev in August 1991.

111. See Gerhard Wettig, Changes in Soviet Policy Towards the West (London, 1991), p. 131. Wettig notes that the Soviet Union was even afraid of an uprising in the GDR and that, although "all the evidence supports Shevardnadze's claim that, despite its concern, the Kremlin had made no attempt to bring about a change of regime in the GDR...important feelers were extended via the foreign divisions of the security services of the GDR and the Soviet Union. It would appear that these tentative contacts centered around Markus Wolf,

head of the foreign division on the East German side until 1987, and his Soviet counterpart, Vladimir Kryuchkov." See also the appraisal given by Valentin Falin to the Soviet leadership in the summer of 1989: "Moskau befürchtet Aufstand in der DDR," *Die Welt*, September 15, 1989. The report was alledgedly based on secondary information by the Bundesnachrichtendienst (BND), the West German intelligence service.

112. Regarding Soviet tactics in this respect see Gerhard Wettig, *Sicherheit über alles: Krieg und Frieden in sowjetischer Sicht* (Cologne, 1986), especially chap. 3.

113. In August 1990, the Berlin newspaper *Der Morgen* published an article confirming speculations about Kryuchkov, Wolf, and Modrow. The report even claimed that they had played a significant role in the overthrow of Honecker: "One needs little imagination to realize that Markus Wolf with his traditional relations to the Soviet security ministry, which is now led by Kryuchkov and has become a prop of perestroika, has been the organizer of those anti-Honecker fronts that took the initiative from Dresden on October 8." See also Schabowski, *Der Absturz*, p. 285.

114. Wolf, *In eigenem Vertrag*, p. 223.

115. *Frankfurter Allgemeine Zeitung*, November 15, 1989.

116. *Ibid.* See also Henry Kamm, "Bonn Outlines Aid for East Germany," *The New York Times*, November 15, 1989, pp. A1 and A12.

117. "Bonn More Cautious Than Business in Aiding GDR," *The Week in Germany*, November 17, 1989, p. 5.

118. *Ibid.*, p. 5.

119. Serge Schmemann, "Reunification Next? Dizzying Pace of Change and Old Ties Make Unity Seem a Distant Aspiration," *The New York Times*, November 16, 1989, p. A20.

120. David Binder, "Grim State of East Germany's Economy Is Disclosed to Parliament," *The New York Times*, November 16, 1989, p. A20.

121. *Ibid.*

122. Modrow, *Aufbruch und Ende*, pp. 36-37.

123. *Ibid.*, p. 40.

124. Schabowski, *Das Politbüro*, p. 124.

125. Regierungserklärung des Vorsitzenden des Ministerrats der DDR, Hans Modrow, abgegeben vor der Volkskammer in Ost-Berlin, November 17, 1989, in: *Europa-Archiv*, Vol. 44 (1989), pp. D716-28.

126. "'Nur in den Grenzen von heute'—DDR-Ministerpräsident Hans Modrow über die Lage in seinem Land und die deutsch-deutsche Zukunft," *Der Spiegel*, December 4, 1989, p. 34.

127. *Ibid.*, p. 35.

128. *Ibid.*, p. 42.

129. The first meeting of the Round Table was held on December 7, 1989, at the Dietrich Bonhöffer House in Berlin. Present were delegates of the CDU, DBD (Democratic Farmer's Party), Democracy Now, Democratic Awakening, Green Party, Initiative for Peace and Human Rights, LDPD (Liberal Democratic Party), NDPD (National Democratic Party), New Forum, SDP (Social Democratic Party), SED, United Left, FDGB, and the Independent Women's Association. For details, see Zimmerling and Zimmerling, eds., *Neue Chronik DDR*, Vol. 3 (Berlin, 1990), pp. 57-61. An analysis of the Round Table's function in the transition period is provided in Walter Süss, "Mit Unwillen zur Macht. Der Runde Tisch in der DDR der Übergangszeit," *Deutschland-Archiv*, Vol. 21 (1991), pp. 470-78. On the developments and activities of the Round Table, see Uwe Thaysen, *Der Runde Tisch Oder: Wo blieb das Volk?* (Opladen, 1990).

130. Zimmerling and Zimmerling, eds., *Neue Chronik DDR*, Vol. 2, pp. 51-52.

131. Schabowski, *Der Absturz*, p. 313.

132. *Gesetzblatt der DDR*, Part I, No. 47, September 27, 1974, p. 434.

133. Schabowski, *Der Absturz*, p. 321.

134. Zimmerling and Zimmerling, eds., *Neue Chronik DDR*, Vol. 3, pp. 34-37. On November 27, Wolfgang Berghofer had already declared in an interview with the West German tabloid *Bild Zeitung* that he would be a candidate for the chairmanship of the party against Egon Krenz. See Krenz, *Wenn Mauern fallen*, p. 238.

135. Krenz, *Wenn Mauern fallen*, p. 242.

136. Wolf, *In eigenem Auftrag*, p. 291.

137. Gysi not only had earned a reputation as a defender of dissidents, as has already been mentioned, but his mysterious omnipresence in the GDR's "October revolution" and his active role at various rallies of the opposition gave him a prominent position among the new leading figures of East Germany as well. His father, Klaus Gysi, a diplomat, minister of culture, and state secretary for church affairs under Honecker, also had been a well-known public figure in the GDR.

138. Zimmerling and Zimmerling, eds., *Neue Chronik DDR*, Vol. 3, p. 71.

139. "Erst Mitleid, dann zuschlagen," *Der Spiegel*, January 15, 1990, pp. 19-28.

140. *Bild Zeitung*, January 22, 1990.

141. Serge Schmemann, "East German Party Purges Ex-Leaders," *The New York Times*, January 22, 1990, p. A7.

142. *Ibid.*

143. Wolf, *In eigenem Auftrag*, pp. 273-77.

144. Zimmerling and Zimmerling, eds., *Neue Chronik DDR*, Vol. 3, p. 52.

145. *Ibid.*, p. 55. At the end of the SED regime, the minister for state security, Erich Mielke, disposed of a budget of 3.6 billion marks, which amounted to 1.3 percent of the entire GDR state budget. The MfS had a full-time staff of 105,000 and between 1 and 2 million, and possibly between 3 and 4 million, "unofficial informants." See Schell and Kalinka, *Stasi und kein Ende*, pp. 48 and 114.

146. Zimmerling and Zimmerling, eds., *Neue Chronik DDR*, Vol. 3, p. 60. See also David Ulrich and Gill Schröter, *Das Ministerium für Staatssicherheit. Anatomie des Mielke-Imperiums* (Berlin, 1991), p. 178.

147. Modrow, *Aufbruch und Ende*, p. 34.

148. Telegram No. 249 2705 33e 74-89, December 7, 1989, quoted from: Anne Worst, *Das Ende eines Geheimdienstes. Oder: Wie lebendig ist die Stasi?* (Berlin, 1991), p. 26.

149. Fernschreiben über den Beschluss des Ministerrates zur unverzüglichen Vernichtung von MfS-Akten, December 7, 1989, quoted from: *Ibid.*, p. 28.

150. Beschluss des Ministerrates, No. 6/18.a/89 (Betrifft: Beschluss über die Bildung des Nachrichtendienstes der DDR und des Verfassungsschutzes der

DDR. Der beiliegende Beschluss wurde bestätigt. Gez. H. Modrow. Dieser Beschluss ist nach Realisierung zu verrichten), December 14, 1989, in: *Ministerrat der DDR,* Dienstsache 816/89.

151. Worst, *Das Ende eines Geheimdienstes,* p. 32. The date May 6, 1990, was set on December 7 by the Round Table for the first free parliamentary elections in the history of the GDR. The date was later moved up to March 18.

152. *Ibid.,* passim; Gill and Schröter, *Das Ministerium fur Staatssicherheit,* part 2, pp. 177-291.

153. See Joachim Gauck, *Die Stasi-Akten: Das unheimliche Erbe der DDR* (Reinbek, 1991).

154. Schmemann, "Reunification Next," p. A20.

155. Henry A. Kissinger, "Living With the Inevitable," *Newsweek,* December 4, 1989, p. 51.

156. *Der Tagesspiegel,* November 15, 1989.

157. Schmemann, "Reunification Next," p. A20.

158. "Genscher: Germans Will Not Go It Alone," *The Week in Germany,* November 17, 1989, p. 2.

159. Gemeinsame Erklärung, unterzeichnet vom Bundeskanzler der Bundesrepublik Deutschland, Helmut Kohl, und vom Ministerpräsidenten der Volksrepublik Polen, Tadeusz Mazowiecki, in Warschau, November 14, 1989, in: *Europa-Archiv,* Vol. 44 (1989), pp. D679-86.

160. Kohl's advisor Horst Teltschik, who joined the chancellor during his trip to Poland, noted in his diary on November 14 that a full reconciliation between Germans and Poles would not be possible as long as the "pressing problem" of the border question could not be resolved. The Poles felt, Teltschik noted, that Kohl was honest but did not understand why he could not speak more directly and "break the spell." See Teltschik, *329 Tage,* p. 30.

161. Bahrmann and Links, *Wir sind das Volk,* p. 105.

162. "Erklärung der Bundesregierung zum offiziellen Besuch des Bundeskanzlers in Polen und zur Lage in der DDR." Statement by Chancellor Kohl before the Bundestag, November 16, 1989, in: *Bulletin,* No. 129 (1989), p. 1108.

163. Teltschik, *329 Tage,* pp. 32-33.

164. *Ibid.*, p. 37.

165. *Ibid.*, pp. 42-43.

166. *Ibid.*, pp. 43-44. At a meeting with Gorbachev in Moscow on November 1, Egon Krenz had realized that the Soviet leader "even then did not attach eternal value to the status quo of the German question." Krenz, *Wenn Mauern fallen,* p. 150.

167. Zehn-Punkte-Programm zur Überwindung der Teilung Deutschlands und Europas, vorgelegt von Bundeskanzler Helmut Kohl in der Haushaltsdebatte des Deutschen Bundestages, November 28, 1989, in: *Europa-Archiv,* Vol. 44 (1989), pp. D731-32.

168. *Ibid.*, pp. D732-33.

169. *Ibid.*, p. D733.

170. *Ibid.*, pp. D733-34.

171. Deutscher Bundestag, 11. Wahlperiode, 177. Sitzung, November 28, 1989, in: *Verhandlungen des Deutschen Bundestages. Stenographische Berichte,* Vol. 151, pp. 13520-22.

172. "Bundestag Parties Voice Approval of Kohl Initiative," *The Week in Germany,* December 1, 1989, p. 2.

173. *Ibid.*

174. "Plan for Intra-German Financial Relations Proposed," *The Week in Germany,* December 1, 1989, p. 5. Also on November 29, when Haussmann presented his plan for the GDR, his party chairman, Otto Lambsdorff, an economist himself, stated in a newspaper interview that the GDR would need between DM400 billion and 500 billion in order to repair the damage done to it over 40 years. Such a sum could not come from a government budget, but would be "no problem" for private capital.

175. Kissinger, "Living With the Inevitable," p. 51.

176. "Kissinger Expects a United Germany," *The New York Times,* November 16, 1989, p. A21.

177. George F. Kennan, "This Is No Time for Talk Of German Reunification," *The Washington Post,* November 12, 1989.

178. *The New York Times,* November 16, 1989, p. A21.

179. *Ibid.*

180. *The New York Times,* December 5, 1989, p. A1.

181. "Baker Says Unification Isn't Just a German Issue," *The New York Times,* December 12, 1989, p. A16.

182. Rede des amerikanischen Außenministers, James A. Baker, vor dem Berliner Presseclub in West-Berlin, December 12, 1989, in: *Europa-Archiv,* Vol. 45 (1990), pp. D77-84.

183. "Baker Says Unification Isn't Just a German Issue," p. A16.

184. *The New York Times,* December 12, 1989, p. A16.

185. Allgemeiner Deutscher Nachrichtendienst (ADN) Report, December 11, 1989.

186. "Bonn Leader Softens Plan For Steps to German Unity," *The New York Times,* December 12, 1989, p. A16.

187. *Ibid.*

188. Serge Schmemann, "Bonn's Social Democrats Trying to Upstage Kohl on Reunification," *The New York Times,* December 12, 1989, p. A16.

189. Another opinion poll in the GDR, taken by the SED-influenced Institute for Sociology of the Academy for Social Sciences, indicated that at the end of November, 58.3 percent of the people in the Neubrandenburg district were still opposed to unification. As the results of this poll also "proved" that Modrow was the most popular political figure in the country and that the SED was regarded as the best organization to represent the interests of the people, the reliability of the Neubrandenburg poll, whose findings were in sharp contradiction to almost any eyewitness account, seems to be rather weak. Actually, the movement toward unification apparently was growing rapidly in late November and early December. See Zimmerling and Zimmerling, eds., *Neue Chronik DDR,* Vol. 3, p. 80.

190. *Frankfurter Rundschau,* December 19, 1989.

191. Tagung des Europäischen Rates der Staats- und Regierungschefs in Strassburg, December 8-9, 1989, in: *Europa-Archiv,* Vol. 45 (1990), p. D14.

192. Teltschik, *329 Tage*, p. 85.

193. Schiller's exact verse at the beginning of the Piccolomini section of Wallenstein reads as follows: "Spät kommt Ihr—Doch Ihr kommt! Der weite Weg, Graf Isolan, entschuldigt Euer Säumen."

194. Information based on a conversation with Hans-Peter Mengele, a former senior staff member of Späth's, October 1, 1991.

195. Teltschik, *329 Tage*, p. 86.

196. *Ibid.*, pp. 88-89.

197. See Gemeinsame Mitteilung über die Gespräche zwischen dem Bundeskanzler der Bundesrepublik Deutschland, Helmut Kohl, und dem Vorsitzenden des Ministerrats der Deutschen Demokratischen Republik, Hans Modrow, in Dresden, December 20, 1989, in: *Europa-Archiv*, Vol. 45 (1990), pp. D90-95.

198. Modrow, *Aufbruch und Ende*, pp. 97-98.

199. Wolfgang Schäuble, *Der Vertrag: Wie ich über die deutsche Einheit verhandelte* (Stuttgart, 1991), p. 21.

200. Modrow, *Aufbruch und Ende*, p. 99.

201. Entwurf des Vertrages über Zusammenarbeit und gute Nachbarschaft zwischen der Deutschen Demokratischen Republik und der Bundesrepublik Deutschland, January 17, 1990, in: *Ibid.*, Annex 4, pp. 170-83.

202. Speech by Chancellor Kohl at the Frauenkirche in Dresden, December 19, 1989, in: *Bulletin*, No. 150 (1989), p. 1262.

203. *Ibid.*

204. See Teltschik, *329 Tage*, p. 92.

205. *Ibid.*

206. Statement by Chancellor Kohl before the Bundesrat, December 21, 1989, in: *Bulletin*, No. 150 (1989), p. 1268.

207. Christmas Address by President Richard von Weizsäcker, December 24, 1989, in: *Bulletin*, No. 151 (1989), p. 1270.

208. See "Discussion Continues on the Oder-Neisse Line," *The Week in Germany*, January 5, 1990, p. 1.

209. *Ibid.*

210. "Bonn, Rome and Paris Call for CSCE Summit," *The Week in Germany*, January 26, 1990, p. 1.

211. TASS, January 30, 1990. Prime Minister Modrow, who later stated that he had discussed with Gorbachev "the question of uniting both German states in the framework of European interests and their conditions of historic, social and economic reality," also referred to the broader implications of unification: "The prospect is before us," he said. "But it is difficult to set time limits for us because it must be supported by the European people." See Francis X. Clines, "Wary Gorbachev Sees Momentum Toward Germans' Reunification," *The New York Times*, January 31, 1990, p. A11.

212. TASS, January 30, 1990.

213. *Frankfurter Allgemeine Zeitung*, February 2, 1990.

214. *Stuttgarter Nachrichten*, January 30, 1990.

215. Berndt Musiolek and Carola Wuttke, eds., *Parteien und politische Bewegungen im letzten Jahr der DDR (Oktober 1989 bis April 1990)* (Berlin, 1991), p. 56. See also Daniel Hamilton, "After the Revolution: The New Political Landscape in East Germany," *German Issues* (American Institute for Contemporary German Studies), Vol. 7 (1990), passim.

216. For details, see Marianne Schulz, "Neues Forum. Von der illegalen Opposition zur legalen Marginalität," in: Helmut Müller-Enbergs et al., eds., *Von der Illegalität ins Parlament: Werdegang und Konzept der neuen Bürgerbewegungen* (Berlin, 1991), pp. 11-104.

217. "'Wir werden immer mehr'—SPIEGEL-Interview mit der DDR-Oppositionellen Bärbel Bohley," *Der Spiegel*, October 2, 1989, pp. 25-26. Serge Schmemann, "Bonn's Politicians Invade East Germany," *The New York Times*, February 10, 1990, p. A10.

218. Henry Kamm, "Some East Germans See Their Hopes Eclipsed by Bonn's Ascendancy," *The New York Times*, February 28, 1990, p. A 12. Such frustration about the opening of the Wall, which marked the end of the socialist experiment in the GDR, was also expressed by Bärbel Bohley in a conversation with the author, December 5, 1991.

219. See Jan Wielgohs and Helmut Müller-Enbergs, "Die Bürgerbewegung Demokratie Jetzt. Vom innerkirchlichen Arbeitskreis zur politischen Opposition," in: Müller-Enberg et al., eds., *Von der Illegalität ins Parlament,* pp. 105-147. See also Bernhard Maleck and Wolfgang Ullmann: "Ich werde nicht schweigen," *Gespräche mit Wolfgang Ullmann* (Berlin, 1991), pp. 67-71.

220. Hans-Jürgen Fischbeck, "Kulturrevolutionäre Gedanken nach vorn—mit Rückspiegel," in: *Demokratie Jetzt,* Vol. 2, No. 34 (1990), No. 34, p. 2.

221. See Gründungsaufruf "Demokratie Jetzt," September 12, 1989, in: Zimmerling and Zimmerling, eds., *Neue Chronik DDR,* Vol. 1, pp. 36-40.

222. For details, see Wolfgang Templin and Reinhard Weisshuhn, "Initiative Frieden und Menschenrechte. Die erste unabhängige DDR-Oppositionsgruppe," in: Müller-Enbergs et al., eds., *Von der Illegalität ins Parlament,* pp. 148-165.

223. Musiolek and Wuttke, eds., *Parteien und politische Bewegungen,* pp. 46-47.

224. The original name of the party was SDP. At a delegate conference on January 12-14, 1990, the party was then renamed "SPD der DDR."

225. "'Wir sind alle beschädigt'—SPIEGEL-Reporter Hans-Joachim Noack über den DDR-Sozialdemokraten Ibrahim Böhme," *Der Spiegel,* February 12, 1990, pp. 102-4.

226. Musiolek and Wuttke, eds., *Parteien und politische Bewegungen,* pp. 28-29. The motto of the party convention with some 800 delegates was "Erneuerung und Zukunft" ("Renewal and Future"). See Zimmerling and Zimmerling, eds., *Neue Chronik DDR,* Vol. 3, pp. 89-90.

227. Teltschik, *329 Tage,* pp. 38-39.

228. Musiolek and Wuttke, eds., *Parteien und politische Bewegungen,* p. 29.

229. Kohl generally felt that the participation of the CDU in the Modrow government was a mistake. See Teltschik, *329 Tage,* p. 105.

230. *Die Tageszeitung,* September 16, 1989.

231. Musiolek and Wuttke, eds., *Parteien und politische Bewegungen,* p. 35. On January 5, 1990, Pastor Schorlemmer and other members of the left wing of the DA announced their resignations from the DA and their new affiliation with the SPD.

232. *Ibid.,* p. 39.

233. Declaration "Aus nationaler Verantwortung—eine Allianz für Deutschland," in: *Deutschland Union Dienst,* Vol. 44, No. 26, February 6, 1990, p. 1.

234. Kohl had actually not waited for the alliance to be established but had already, on January 29, canceled a trip to South America scheduled for March as a result of the new election date. See "Kohl to Campaign for GDR's 'Alliance for Germany,'" *The Week in Germany,* February 9, 1990, p. 2.

235. Musiolek and Wuttke, eds., *Parteien und politische Bewegungen,* pp. 42-45.

236. Schmemann, "Bonn's Politicians Invade East Germany," p. A1.

237. "West German Politicians Make Final GDR Campaign Stop," *The Week in Germany,* March 16, 1990, p. 1. Marc Fisher, "Party Allied to Kohl Tops Vote in East Germany," *Washington Post,* March 19, 1990, p. A 16.

238. Schmemann, "Bonn's Politicians Invade East Germany," p. A10.

239. Teltschik, *329 Tage,* pp. 130-31.

240. "Insults Fly in Bonn Parliament During Debate on Unification," *The New York Times,* February 16, 1990, p. A8.

241. Henry Kamm, "No Undue Haste to Unity, Irate East German Urges," *The New York Times,* February 21, 1990, p. A10.

242. "'Ein Kollaps ist nicht auszuschliessen'—Der Vorsitzende der Ost-CDU, Lothar de Maizière, über den Zustand der DDR," *Der Spiegel,* February 5, 1990, pp. 20-21. "'Ich fürchte den Kollaps'—SPIEGEL-Interview mit dem DSU-Vorsitzenden Hans-Wilhelm Ebeling über die Zukunft der DDR und seiner Partei," *Der Spiegel,* January 29, 1990, pp. 26-27.

243. Serge Schmemann, "Kohl Stumps as if Germanys Were One," *The New York Times,* February 21, 1990, p. A10.

244. Fisher, "Party Allied to Kohl Tops Vote in East Germany," p. A1. "East Germans Vote for Unity," *Financial Times,* March 19, 1990, p. 1.

245. Serge Schmemann, "Mandate for Unity 'as Soon as Possible,'" *The New York Times,* March 19, 1990, p. A1.

CHAPTER 4

1. The victory of the Alliance for Germany was all the more impressive as 93.38 percent of the eligible voters participated in the election.

2. See, for instance, the cover story "Kohl's Triumph" in: *Der Spiegel,* March 19, 1990.

3. Serge Schmemann, "An Uneager Leader—Lothar de Maizière," *The New York Times,* March 21, 1990, p. A16.

4. *Der Tagesspiegel,* March 19, 1990.

5. The Social Democrats initially refused to enter into a coalition with the DSU, which had taken strongly conservative views in the campaign and vigorously attacked the SPD, but later they agreed. See Henry Kamm, "German Losers Reject Victor's Invitation," *The New York Times,* March 20, 1990, p. A12.

6. *Ibid.* See also Zimmerling and Zimmerling, eds., *Neue Chronik DDR,* Vol. 6, p. 6.

7. *Frankfurter Allgemeine Zeitung,* March 21, 1990.

8. As early as January 10, 1990, Interior Minister Schäuble warned in a cabinet session in Bonn that the escalating migration might lead to serious social conflicts in the West as well as to "bleeding and bankruptcy of the GDR." It even might sweep away the reformers in all of Eastern Europe, including Mikhail Gorbachev, Schäuble said. The figures, according to Schäuble, were dramatic indeed: On Monday, January 8, alone 2,298 people had come from the GDR, in addition to 8,910 resettlers of German origin from Eastern Europe and the Soviet Union. See Teltschik, *329 Tage,* p. 103; "DDR: 'Sie fühlen sich betupft.' Bonn rechnet mit 500,000 neuen Übersiedlern," *Der Spiegel,* January 15, 1991, p. 16.

9. Serge Schmemann, "Kohl Is Called Intent on Slowing Reunification With East Germans," *The New York Times,* March 20, 1990, p. A12.

10. *Bild,* January 24, 1990, p. 1.

11. Teltschik, *329 Tage,* p. 114.

12. Other GDR politicians, such as the chairman of the DSU, Hans-Wilhelm Ebeling, also were afraid that the East German economy now might collapse quickly. See "Ich fürchte den Kollaps," *Der Spiegel,* January 29, 1990.

13. Modrow, *Aufbruch und Ende,* p. 119.

14. Statement of the GDR prime minister at a press conference on February 1, 1990, to explain his concept "Für Deutschland, einig Vaterland," in: Modrow, *Aufbruch und Ende*, Annex 5, pp. 184-85. Verbatim text of the concept in: Ingo von Münch, ed., *Dokumente der Wiedervereinigung Deutschlands. Quellentexte zum Prozess der Wiedervereinigung von der Ausreisewelle aus der DDR über Ungarn, die CSSR und Polen im Spätsommer 1989 bis zum Beitritt der DDR zum Geltungsbereich des Grundgesetzes der Bundesrepublik Deutschland im Oktober 1990* (Stuttgart, 1991), pp. 79-81.

15. Modrow, *Aufbruch und Ende*, pp. 119-20.

16. *Ibid.*, pp. 122-23. See also Arnold, *Die ersten hundert Tage*, pp. 97-98; and Francis X. Clines, "Wary Gorbachev Sees Momentum Toward Germans' Reunification," *The New York Times*, January 31, 1990, p. A1.

17 *Frankfurter Allgemeine Zeitung*, January 31, 1990, p. 1. See "Einheit in diesem Jahr," *Der Spiegel*, February 5, 1990, p. 17.

18. Teltschik, *329 Tage*, p. 120.

19. *Ibid.*, p. 121. Similarly, Foreign Minister Genscher noted in a speech at the Evangelical Academy in Tutzing, where Egon Bahr had coined the slogan "change through rapprochement" in 1963, that Gorbachev's statements "opened the way for a constructive policy in Europe and Germany" to provide "dynamism in stability." Quoted from: *Süddeutsche Zeitung*, January 31, 1990, p. 1.

20. "Coalition Disagrees on Role of NATO in a United Germany," *The Week in Germany*, February 2, 1990, pp. 1-2.

21. *Ibid.*

22. Modrow, *Aufbruch und Ende*, p. 124.

23. *Der Tagesspiegel*, February 2, 1990.

24. "Coalition Disagrees on Role of NATO in a United Germany," p. 2.

25. See Teltschik, *329 Tage*, p. 124.

26. *Ibid.*, p. 126. See also "Wir brechen bald zusammen," *Der Spiegel*, February 12, 1990, pp. 16-20.

27. Teltschik, *329 Tage*, p. 127.

28.   "'Ein Kollaps ist nicht auszuschliessen.' Der Vorsitzende der Ost-CDU, Lothar de Maizière, über den Zustand der DDR," *Der Spiegel*, February 5, 1990, p. 20.

29.   Teltschik, *329 Tage*, p. 128.

30.   *Frankfurter Allgemeine Zeitung*, February 8, 1990.

31.   *Süddeutsche Zeitung*, February 10, 1990.

32.   Serge Schmemann, "2 German Chiefs Prepare to Meet: A Steamroller vs. a Lame Duck?" *The New York Times*, February 13, 1990, p. A10.

33.   Teltschik, *329 Tage*, pp. 137-38.

34.   *Ibid.*, p. 139.

35.   *Ibid.*, pp. 139-40.

36.   TASS, February 11, 1990.

37.   *Süddeutsche Zeitung*, February 12, 1990. On the same day, the *Münchner Merkur* commented: "Kohl's trip to Moscow represented the end of the post-war order. . . . Gorbachev returned the key to the solution of the German question to the Germans—without any preconditions." On February 21, Kohl's advisor Horst Teltschik, speaking before the Bund für Lebensmittelrecht und Lebensmittelkunde in Bonn, also argued that the key to the unification of Germany was no longer in Moscow. "The Chancellor has collected the key," Teltschik said. "It is now in Bonn." Reacting to a statement by the Soviet foreign minister that German unity was still "years away," Teltschik replied that Shevardnadze would be surprised; now it was up to the Germans to decide how fast the unification of their country would proceed. See "Bonner Schlüssel," *Der Spiegel*, February 26, 1990, p. 20.

38.   "Botschaft an alle Deutschen." Statement by Chancellor Kohl in Moscow, February 10, 1990, in: *Bulletin*, No. 24 (1990), p. 189.

39.   Schmemann, "2 German Chiefs Prepare to Meet," p. A1.

40.   Modrow, *Aufbruch und Ende*, p. 131.

41.   This complaint was confirmed by Karl-Heinz Arnold, senior advisor to Prime Minister Modrow, in a conversation with the author, December 19, 1991.

42.   Schmemann, "2 German Chiefs Prepare to Meet," p. A10.

43. See "Das war wie eine Ohrfeige," *Der Spiegel,* February 19, 1990, pp. 19-20.

44. Statement by Chancellor Kohl at a joint press conference with Prime Minister Modrow in Bonn, February 13, 1990, in: *Bulletin,* No. 25 (1990), p. 194. The supplementary budget submitted by Finance Minister Theo Waigel on February 6, 1990, increased expenditures of the 1990 federal budget by almost DM7 billion, of which about DM6 billion were to go toward aid for the GDR and costs for resettling Germans and ethnic Germans from the East bloc. However, apart from DM2.1 billion for the travel money fund, the GDR would receive only DM1 billion directly, in the form of low-interest credits for such areas as environmental protection and health care. A further D2 billion in additional expenditures were blocked temporarily by the finance minister and reserved for unforeseeable "immediate measures based on the current developments in the GDR as well as the influx of resettlers from the East." See "Stand der Soforthilfe der Bundesregierung für die DDR." Speech by Finance Minister Waigel before the Bundestag, February 7, 1990, in: *Bulletin,* No. 22 (1990), p. 175.

45. See Teltschik, *329 Tage,* p. 145.

46. Christa Luft, economics minister in the Modrow government, later stated that the "meager result" of the Bonn meeting, namely the establishment of an expert commission for the implementation of a currency union between the two German states, could also have been agreed upon "by telephone." See Christa Luft, *Zwischen Wende und Ende. Eindrücke, Erlebnisse, Erfahrungen eines Mitglieds der Modrow-Regierung* (Berlin, 1991), p. 171.

47. Schmemann, "2 German Chiefs Prepare to Meet," p. A10.

48. "Milliarden auf Jahre hinaus. Gefahr für die Mark: Wiedervereinigung wird zum Wirtschaftsabenteuer," *Der Spiegel,* February 12, 1990, p. 25.

49. *Ibid.*

50. Craig R. Whitney, "Bonn's Top Banker Urges Caution," *The New York Times,* March 3, 1990, p. D1.

51. "'Wir werden sehr aufpassen.' SPIEGEL-Gespräch mit Bundesbank-Präsident Karl Otto Pöhl über die Währungseinheit mit der DDR und die Folgen," *Der Spiegel,* February 26, 1990, p. 106. It seems likely that at that time the decision had not yet been taken.

52. "Central Banks, Institute Skeptical on Monetary Union," *The Week in Germany,* February 9, 1990, p. 4. On February 7, the German Institute for Economic

Research in Berlin (West) also expressed strong reservations about a quick monetary union between the two German states. In a report summing up the findings of a working group of economists from both sides of Berlin, the institute lent its support to a currency association similar to the European Monetary System. A quick unification of the currencies, the report stated, would not bring economic advantages. See *Berichte des Deutschen Instituts für Wirtschaftsforschung,* February 7, 1990.

53. *Frankfurter Allgemeine Zeitung,* February 8, 1990.

54. "Milliarden auf Jahre hinaus," p. 26.

55. Speech by Economics Minister Haussmann before the Bundestag, February 7, 1990, in: *Bulletin,* No. 22 (1990), p. 176.

56. Ferdinand Protzman, "Bonn Panel to Plan for Common Currency With East," *The New York Times,* February 8, 1990, p. A15.

57. Deutsche Bank Group, *Fixed Income Research Market Trends: A Weekly Review,* Vol. 4, No. 6, February 12, 1990, p. 5.

58. Peter Passell, "Monetary Union: Would It Help?" *The New York Times,* February 9, 1990, p. D1.

59. "Milliarden auf Jahre hinaus," p. 26.

60. *Ibid.,* pp. 26-27.

61. Luft, *Zwischen Wende und Ende,* p. 167.

62. "Sie lernt ja täglich dazu. Zu lange gezögert, zu kurz gedacht—DDR-Wirtschaftsministerin Christa Luft ist gescheitert," *Der Spiegel,* February 12, 1990, p. 112. Chancellery Minister Seiters stated in this regard before the Bundesrat on February 16 that it would have been useless to invest DM15 billion in emergency aid requested by the Modrow government in a "decrepit socialist economy."

63. Statement by Chancellor Kohl at a joint press conference with Prime Minister Modrow in Bonn, February 13, 1990.

64. "Monetary Union Moves Closer," *The Week in Germany,* February 16, 1990, p. 4.

65. *Ibid.*

66. "Wirtschaftskonferenz 'Solidarität mit der DDR.'" Statement by Chancellor Kohl after talks with business and trade union representatives in Bonn, February 20, 1990, in: *Bulletin*, No. 28 (1990), p. 224.

67. "Monetary Union Moves Closer," p. 4.

68. Franz Steinkühler, "Wir mischen uns jetzt ein," *Metall*, No. 3, February 9, 1990, p. 3. Steinkühler stated that "We are going to interfere now . . . The German question is no longer open. The answer of the people is clear. . . . It is our task to bring into play the interests of the workers, those of the GDR and those of the Federal Republic."

69. "Business, Unions Support Kohl's Economic Steps in GDR," *The Week in Germany*, February 23, 1990, p. 4. Interestingly enough, Breit himself eventually signed a "Joint Declaration for a United Economic and Social Order in the two German States" with the president of the German Employers' Associations (BDA), Klaus Murmann, on March 9 in Düsseldorf to prepare for German unity. See Manfred Wilke and Hans-Peter Müller, *Zwischen Solidarität und Eigennutz. Die Gewerkschaften des DGB im deutschen Vereinigungsprozess* (Melle, 1992).

70. *Frankfurter Allgemeine Zeitung*, February 21, 1990.

71. "Der Plan für den Tag X," *Der Spiegel*, March 5, 1990, pp. 16-17.

72. "Monetary Commission Meets," *The Week in Germany*, March 9, 1990, p. 4.

73. Zimmerling and Zimmerling, eds., *Neue Chronik DDR. Berichte. Fotos, Dokumente*, Vol. 4-5, pp. 234-38.

74. "Es gibt keine DDR mehr," *Der Spiegel*, March 19, 1990, pp. 20-33. See also "'Wir brauchen sinnvolle Übergänge.' Der Vorsitzende der DDR-CDU, Lothar de Maizière, über die Folgen des Wahlsiegs," *Ibid.*, pp. 122-25. See also de Maizière's inaugural address of April 19, 1990, in: Münch, ed., *Dokumente der Wiedervereinigung Deutschlands*, pp. 190-213.

75. "Cabinet Sets Date for Currency Union, Ends Resettler Benefits," *The Week in Germany*, March 23, 1990, pp. 1-2.

76. *Ibid.*

77. *Frankfurter Rundschau*, March 20, 1990.

78. "Die drücken uns an die Wand," *Der Spiegel*, March 26, 1990, p. 132.

79. "Going for Broke: The Daring Plan to Rebuild the East," *Business Week,* April 2, 1990, p. 51.

80. *Augsburger Allgemeine,* April 2, 1990.

81. *Handelsblatt,* April 2, 1990; "Bundesbank Recommends 2:1 Exchange Rate," *The Week in Germany,* April 6, 1990, p. 4.

82. *Ibid.*

83. *Ibid.* See also "Ohne 1:1 werden wir nicht eins," *Der Spiegel,* April 9, 1990, p. 17.

84. Teltschik, *329 Tage,* pp. 191-92.

85. *Bunte Illustrierte,* April 8, 1990.

86. "Wachstumsschub dank Wirtschaftsunion: Frühjahrsgutachten der deutschen Forschungsinstitute," *Neue Zürcher Zeitung,* April 14, 1990, p. 13. In addition, Bonn was also counting on help from the European Community. Kohl's monetary advisor, Bundesbank director Hans Tietmeyer, said on April 6 that in the Federal as well as in the EC budget priorities had to be redefined and funds could be shifted. Solidarity, he stressed, was "not a one-way street." On the other hand, German unity would strengthen economic growth EC-wide, he stated, noting that since the beginning of 1990 financial markets had been reacting positively in the wake of developments in Eastern Europe and especially in the GDR.

87. *Neue Zürcher Zeitung,* April 10, 1990.

88. Teltschik, *329 Tage,* pp. 203-4.

89. *Ibid.,* p. 202.

90. "Angebot der Bundesregierung für den Staatsvertrag mit der DDR zur Gründung einer Währungsunion mit Wirtschafts- und Sozialgemeinschaft," April 23, 1990, in: *Bulletin,* No. 47 (1990), p. 374. See also "Gleichberechtigte Partnerschaft?" *Der Spiegel,* April 23, 1990, p. 14.

91. Ferdinand Protzman, "Bonn Offers East a Generous Rate in Unifying Money," *The New York Times,* April 24, 1990, p. A1.

92. "Meinungsaustausch des Bundeskanzlers mit Ministerpräsident de Maizière in Bonn," April 24, 1990, in: *Bulletin,* No. 48 (1990), p. 381. See also Rudolf Seiters, "Erklärung der Bundesregierung zum Stand der Verhandlungen mit der DDR," April 27, 1990, in: *Ibid.,* pp. 378-79.

93. See, for instance, Peter Passell, "Experts Fear a German Inflation Rise," *The New York Times*, April 25, 1990, p. A14, and "An der Grenze des Vertretbaren," *Der Spiegel*, April 30, 1990, p. 18.

94. Ferdinand Protzman, "German Leaders Agree on a July 2 Unification Date," *The New York Times*, April 25, 1990, p. A14.

95. "Einigung über die Einführung der Währungs-, Wirtschafts- und Sozialunion." Statement by Minister Seiters in Bonn, May 2, 1990, in: *Bulletin*, No. 50 (1990), pp. 393-94. See also "Grundsatzeinigung zwischen Bonn und Ostberlin. Differenzierte Lösung für die Währungsumstellung," *Neue Zürcher Zeitung*, May 3, 1990, p. 1, and "Die Eckwerte der deutschen Währungsunion. Bonn und Ostberlin über die Umtauschrelation einig," *Neue Zürcher Zeitung*, May 3, 1990, p. 33. Horst Teltschik noted in his diary on May 2 that with the announcement of the currency union, the chancellor had reached a "decisive political goal" in regard to the upcoming local elections in the GDR on May 6. "I am impressed time and again," Teltschik added, "how carefully he [the Chancellor] combines government decisions with election considerations." See Teltschik, *329 Tage*, p. 214.

96. During the talks in Moscow, the Soviets pointed out that 35 percent of the GDR's foreign trade was with the Soviet Union. See "Zustimmung in Ostberlin." Positive Bewertung der Moskauer Gespräche de Maizières," *Neue Zürcher Zeitung*, May 3, 1990, p. 1.

97. *Frankfurter Allgemeine Zeitung*, May 4, 1990.

98. Hans Klein, "Zeitplan für den Staatsvertrag über die Währungs-, Wirtschafts- und Sozialunion," May 3, 1990, in: *Bulletin*, No. 52 (1990), p. 412.

99. Serge Schmemann, "Germanys Finish Pact on Merging Economies," *International Herald Tribune*, May 14, 1990, p. 2.

100. *Frankfurter Allgemeine Zeitung*, May 17, 1990.

101. *Ibid.*

102. "Vertrag über die Schaffung einer Währungs-, Wirtschafts- und Sozialunion zwischen der Bundesrepublik Deutschland und der Deutschen Demokratischen Republik," May 18, 1990, in: *Bulletin*, No. 63 (1990), pp. 517-44.

103. Text of the statements by Chancellor Kohl and Prime Minister de Maizière in: *Europa-Archiv*, Vol. 45, No. 13-14 (1990), pp. D323-27. See also Ferdinand Protzman, "Germanys Sign Pact Binding Economies," *The New York Times*, May 19, 1990, p. A5.

104. "Vertrag über die Schaffung," pp. 517-19.

105. Protzman, "Germanys Sign Pact," p. 5.

106. *Frankfurter Rundschau,* May 22, 1990.

107. " 'Ich rechne mit dem Schlimmsten': Interview mit der Ost-Berliner Arbeits-
     ministerin Regine Hildebrandt über die Folgen der bevorstehenden Währungs-
     union für die DDR," *Der Stern,* No. 21, May 17, 1990, pp. 216-19. See also "East
     Germans Voice Concern on Merger," *International Herald Tribune,* May 11,
     1990, p. 1.

108. Deutscher Bundestag, 11. Wahlperiode, 212. Sitzung, May 23, 1990, in:
     Verhandlungen des Deutschen Bundestages. Stenographische Berichte, Vol. 153, pp.
     16667 and 16678; *Der Spiegel,* May 28, 1990.

109. "Progress Reported Toward Agreement on Currency Union Treaty," *The
     Week in Germany,* June 1, 1990, p. 1.

110. Youssef M. Ibrahim, "Hastily Arranged European Community Summit to
     Discuss the Extraordinary Changes in East Bloc," *The New York Times,*
     November 15, 1989, p. A14.

111. "Ein Staatenbund? Ein Bundesstaat?" *Der Spiegel,* December 11, 1989, p. 25.

112. "Die Siegermächte warnen Bonn," *Der Spiegel,* December 11, 1989, p. 17.

113. *Ibid.* Similarly, Luc Rosenzweig, correspondent of the French daily *Le Monde* in
     Bonn, prophesied in a heated conversation with Horst Teltschik on December
     1 that France now had to return to "earlier constellations" and that the
     Franco-German cooperation would come to an end. See Teltschik, *329 Tage,*
     p. 61.

114. *Le Figaro* (Paris), November 13, 1989, p. 1.

115. "Die Siegermächte warnen Bonn," pp. 17-18; "Ein Staatenbund? Ein Bundesstaat?"
     p. 25.

116. "Ein Staatenbund? Ein Bundesstaat?" p. 25. Regarding the background of the
     US position, see Elizabeth Pond, *After the Wall: American Policy toward Germany*
     (New York, 1990), passim.

117. James A. Baker, Interview with CNN, December 4, 1989, in: *Europa-Archiv,*
     Vol. 45 (1990), pp. D52-54.

118. Teltschik, *329 Tage,* pp. 76-78. Dumas's speech before the French National Assembly published in: *Journal Officiel,* Assemblée Nationale, 2e séance du 12 décembre 1989, p. 6379. Text of Baker's speech of December 12, 1989, in: *U.S. Policy Information and Texts* (USIS Bonn), No. 154, December 13, 1989.

119. See communiqué of the North Atlantic Council ministers' conference in Brussels, December 14-15, 1989, in: *Europa-Archiv,* Vol. 45 (1989), p. D152. The formulation originated in a letter of August 12, 1970, from the Federal Republic's foreign minister, Walter Scheel, to Soviet counterpart Andrei Gromyko.

120. *Neues Deutschland,* December 21, 1989, p. 1.

121. See Karl Kaiser, *Deutschlands Vereinigung: Die internationalen Aspekte* (Bergisch Gladbach, 1991), p. 61. Regarding Gorbachev's position earlier in the year, see Hannes Adomeit, "Gorbachev and German Unification: Revision of Thinking, Realignment of Power," *Problems of Communism* (July-August 1990), pp. 1-24.

122. See Teltschik, *329 Tage,* p. 96.

123. Confidential telegram, published in: *Frankfurter Allgemeine Zeitung,* January 4, 1990.

124. See Teltschik, *329 Tage,* pp. 98-99.

125. *Ibid.,* p. 100.

126. *Ibid.,* pp. 100-1.

127. *Ibid.,* p. 105.

128. See Kaiser, *Deutschlands Vereinigung,* pp. 53-54.

129. Teltschik, *329 Tage,* p. 109. Gorbachev had made this statement during a telephone conversation with Mitterrand in December 1989. See "Psychische Narben," *Der Spiegel,* April 9, 1990, p. 158.

130. Teltschik, *329 Tage,* p. 110.

131. *Izvestiia,* January 22, 1990. Shevardnadze's article was entitled "Europe—From Division to Unity."

132. *The Wall Street Journal,* January 28, 1990.

133. Teltschik, *329 Tage*, p. 116.

134. Elizabeth Pond, "Die Entstehung von Zwei-plus-Vier," *Europa-Archiv,* Vol. 47 (1992), p. 622.

135. Thomas L. Friedman and Michael R. Gordon, "Steps to German Unity: Bonn as a Power," *The New York Times,* February 16, 1990, p. A9.

136. *Ibid.* The extent to which the British continued to be torn by developments in Germany was made plain on February 8, when Prime Minister Thatcher stated in a speech before the House of Commons that the unification of Germany was now "likely," while her foreign policy advisor at No. 10 Downing Street, Charles Powell, let the Germans know on the same day that Mrs. Thatcher still felt "uneasy" about the prospect of a large and strong Germany. See Teltschik, *329 Tage,* p. 134.

137. See Pond, "Die Entstehung von Zwei-plus-Vier," p. 627.

138. Friedman and Gordon, "Steps to German Unity," p. A9.

139. Helmut Kohl, "Europe—Every German's Future," Statement at the World Economic Forum, Davos, February 3, 1990, in: *Statements & Speeches,* Vol. 13, No. 4, February 6, 1990, p. 2.

140. *Ibid.,* p. 4.

141. See Friedman and Gordon, "Steps to German Unity," p. A9.

142. *Ibid.*

143. Teltschik, *329 Tage,* pp. 137-38. See also Wolfgang Pfeiler, "Die Viermächte-Option als Instrument sowjetischer Deutschlandpolitik," *Interne Studien* Nr. 25/1991 (Forschungsinstitut der Konrad-Adenauer-Stiftung), April 1991, passim.

144. Teltschik, *329 Tage,* p. 141.

145. "Botschaft an alle Deutschen." Statement by Chancellor Kohl in Moscow, February 10, 1990, cited in *Ibid.,* p. 189.

146. Schmemann, "2 German Chiefs Prepare to Meet," p. A10.

147. Friedman and Gordon, "Steps to German Unity," p. A9.

148. *Ibid.*

149. *Ibid.*

150. Kommuniqué der Aussenminister der Bundesrepublik Deutschland, der Deutschen Demokratischen Republik, Frankreichs, des Vereinigten Königreichs, der Sowjetunion und der Vereinigten Staaten von Amerika, abgegeben am Rande der "Open Skies"-Konferenz in Ottawa, February 13, 1990, in: *Bulletin*, No. 27 (1990), p. 215.

151. For West Germany, the political director of the Foreign Office, Dieter Kastrup, was commissioned to prepare the negotiations. See Gerhard Spörl, "Die Last mit Lust und Laune tragen. Der Bonner Diplomat Dieter Kastrup bereitet sich auf schwierige Monate vor," *Die Zeit,* April 13, 1990, p. 2.

152. *Frankfurter Allgemeine Zeitung,* February 14, 1990. Earlier in the day, Genscher had assured conference delegates in a speech that the two German states would not negotiate on unification "behind the backs of the four powers" but would "respect the rights and responsibilities of the four powers which bear the responsibility for Germany as a whole."

153. *Ibid.*

154. James Baker, Speech before the Berlin Press Club, December 12, 1989, in: *U.S. Policy Information and Texts* (USIS Bonn), No. 154, December 13, 1989.

155. "Für Deutschland, einig Vaterland," in: Modrow, *Aufbruch und Ende,* Annex 5, pp. 184-85.

156. Hans-Dietrich Genscher, "Zur deutschen Einheit im europäischen Rahmen," Speech at the Evangelic Academy Tutzing, January 31, 1990, in: *Der Bundesminister des Auswärtigen informiert, Mitteilung für die Presse,* No. 1026/90, January 31, 1990.

157. Al Kamen, "Baker Said to Back Bonn Unification Plan," *The Washington Post,* February 7, 1990, p. A19.

158. *Ibid.*

159. Teltschik, *329 Tage,* p. 132. See also "Bizzares Szenario. Das Bonner Aussenministerium entwirft Pläne für den Status eines vereinten Deutschlands," *Der Spiegel,* February 12, 1990, p. 23.

160. For the background of the Soviet foreign minister's reasoning, see Eduard Schewardnadse (Shevardnadze), *Die Zukunft gehört der Freiheit* (Reinbek, 1991), pp. 235-36.

161. Eduard Shevardnadze, Address before the External Affairs and Defense Committees of the Canadian Parliament, February 15, 1990, quoted from: Paul Lewis, "Shevardnadze Calls for Meeting This Year on German Unification," *The New York Times*, February 16, 1990, p. A9.

162. *Ibid.*

163. Under the Italian proposal, all 35 CSCE nations would agree to respect each other's sovereignty and observe human rights. More important, however, the plan envisaged that the East European countries would gradually move away from Moscow and closer to the 12 European Community nations, strengthening their economic and political ties with Western Europe, thus providing the basis for a pan-European, collective security order.

164. See, for instance, "'Für militärische Neutralität': Gorbatschows Deutschland-Experte Walentin Falin über die deutsche Einheit," *Der Spiegel*, February 19, 1990, pp. 168-72. Gorbachev himself also voiced new reservations on German unity in a *Pravda* interview on February 21, 1990, saying that "the reunification of Germany should take account of . . . the inadmissability of disrupting the military-strategic balance."

165. Craig R. Whitney, "Moscow's Last Hope: Diplomats Believe Gorbachev Wants to Salvage Access to West's Economy," *The New York Times*, February 16, 1990, p. A8.

166. *Ibid.*

167. Schmemann, "2 German Chiefs Prepare to Meet," p. A1.

168. Deutscher Bundestag, 11. Wahlperiode, 197. Sitzung, February 15, 1990, in: *Verhandlungen des Deutschen Bundestages. Stenographische Berichte*, Vol. 152, pp. 15103-4.

169. See Hans-Dietrich Genscher, Speech before the General Assembly of the United Nations, September 27, 1989, in: *Europa-Archiv*, Vol. 44 (1989), p. D654.

170. Resolution of the German Bundestag regarding German-Polish relations, November 8, 1989, in: *Europa-Archiv*, Vol. 44 (1989), p. D672.

171. See Teltschik, *329 Tage*, p. 14.

172. *Ibid.*, p. 160, and Thomas L. Friedman, "West Berlin Mayor Critical of Kohl on Boundary Issue," *The New York Times*, February 27, 1990, p. A8.

173. *Ibid.* Some 11.7 million Germans had been evicted after the war from Pomerania, Silesia, East Prussia, the Baltic states, and the Sudetenland, with about 10 million of them eventually settling in West Germany.

174. *Europa-Archiv,* Vol. 45 (1990), p. Z 56.

175. John Kifner, "Warsaw Fights for Role in German Unity Talks," *The New York Times,* February 28, 1990, p. A12.

176. Teltschik, *329 Tage,* p. 153.

177. See "Unehrlich und zweideutig," *Der Spiegel,* March 5, 1990, pp. 23-24; and Thomas L. Friedman, "Senators Complain to Bush Over Kohl's Border Policy," *The New York Times,* February 28, 1990, p. A12. See also Jürgen Krönig, "Lieber bremsen als lenken. Margaret Thatcher macht aus ihrer Ablehnung der deutschen Einheit kein Hehl," in: *Die Zeit,* March 9, 1990, p. 2.

178. Teltschik, *329 Tage,* pp. 163-64.

179. *Ibid.,* p. 164.

180. Serge Schmeman, "Kohl Takes Tentative Step On Polish Border Proposal," *The New York Times,* March 1, 1990, p. A16.

181. Deutscher Bundestag, 11. Wahlperiode, 200. Sitzung, March 8, 1990, in: *Verhandlungen des Deutschen Bundestages. Stenographische Berichte,* Vol. 152, p. 15429.

182. *Europa-Archiv,* Vol. 45 (1990), p. Z65; and "Überall Unruhe," *Der Spiegel,* March 12, 1990, pp. 171-73. Regarding the French position, see also "'Seit Attila 60 Invasionen,': Der französische Verteidigungsminister Jean-Pierre Chevènement über die deutsche Einigung und Europa," *Der Spiegel,* March 12, 1990, pp. 190-95; and Roland Dumas, "One Germany—If Europe Agrees," *The New York Times,* March 13, 1990, p. A29.

183. Teltschik, *329 Tage,* p. 172.

184. *Ibid.,* pp. 172-75.

185. Bush actually urged Mazowiecki to come to an agreement with the chancellor, whom the former said he would not oppose. Information based on a telephone call between Bush and Kohl on March 27, 1990. *Ibid.,* pp. 179-83.

186. *Ibid.,* p. 184.

187. Alan Riding, "France Urges West Germany to Speed Unification," *The New York Times*, March 21, 1990, p. A17. See also "Don't Panic: The EC and a United Germany," *The Economist*, March 24, 1990, pp. 51-52.

188. Teltschik, *329 Tage*, p. 179.

189. *Der Tagesspiegel*, March 9, 1990.

190. Robert Pear, "Neutral-Germany Stand By Soviets Is Softening," *The New York Times*, March 21, 1990, p. A16.

191. *Die Welt*, March 20, 1990.

192. "Kritische Gemütslage," *Der Spiegel*, March 26, 1990, p. 25.

193. Hans-Dietrich Genscher, Speech at the meeting of the Western European Union, Luxembourg, March 23, 1990, in: *Statements & Speeches*, Vol. 13, No. 8, March 30, 1990, p. 3.

194. Helmut Kohl, Letter to Hans-Dietrich Genscher, March 26, 1990. See Teltschik, *329 Tage*, pp. 182-83.

195. Genscher urged US President Bush and Secretary of State Baker, for instance, during talks in Washington on April 4 to give a "new quality" to European-American relations.

196. In this respect, Shevardnadze even went so far during talks with Secretary of State Baker in Washington on April 6 as to repeat an earlier suggestion that Germany could also be a member in both alliances—an idea that was in fact probably more an expression of Soviet helplessness than a serious political proposal. Dual membership of a united Germany in both NATO and the Warsaw Pact had also been supported by some intellectuals, however—for instance, by John Lewis Gaddis, professor of history at Ohio State University. See John Lewis Gaddis, "One Germany—in Both Alliances," *The New York Times*, March 21, 1990, p. A27.

197. Teltschik, *329 Tage*, pp. 185-86.

198. *Ibid.*, p. 190.

199. *Ibid.*, pp. 205-6. See also "Wir brauchen einen Vertrag," *Der Spiegel*, April 23, 1990, pp. 17-20.

200. Teltschik, *329 Tage*, p. 206.

201. On the eve of the first round of the two-plus-four negotiations in Bonn, a *Pravda* article also stated that "a German membership in NATO, which now seems likely, would not be a worldwide catastrophe." See *Pravda*, May 3, 1990, p. 1.

202. Thomas L. Friedman, "Baker Is Off to Europe, Ready to Sell Soviets on United Germany in NATO," *The New York Times*, May 2, 1990, p. A10. By this time, the West German SPD had also formally adopted the concept of NATO membership for a united Germany. See "Von der Konfrontation der Blöcke zu einem Europäischen Sicherheitssystem," SPD position paper, April 25, 1990.

203. Friedman, "Baker Is Off to Europe." See also Baker's statement at the opening of the two-plus-four negotiations in Bonn on May 5, 1990, in: *U.S. Policy Information and Texts*, No. 60, May 7, 1990.

204. *Der Tagesspiegel*, May 4, 1990.

205. Regarding the background of President Bush's decision, see Andrew Rosenthal, "Bush, Europe and NATO: Bowing to the Inevitable as a New Germany Rises," *The New York Times*, May 4, 1990, p. A8.

206. See *Europa-Archiv*, Vol. 45 (1990), p. Z87.

207. Thomas L. Friedman, "NATO Adopts Plans to Revamp Itself for German Unity," *The New York Times*, May 4, 1990, p. A8.

208. Rosenthal, "Bush, Europe and Nato," p. A8.

209. *Ibid.*

210. Manfred Wörner, Statement at press conference in Brussels, May 3, 1990, in: Friedman, "NATO Adopts Plan," p. A8.

211. *Ibid.*

212. Serge Schmemann, "New Europe: The Armies. As Germany Reunites, East and West Seek A System for Future Security on Continent," *The New York Times*, April 10, 1990, p. A1. In a communiqué issued at the conclusion of an EC summit meeting in Dublin, Ireland, on April 28, the heads of state and government of the European Community also expressed the desire to secure a "smooth and harmonious" integration of a united Germany into the EC. See "Europäischer Rat in Dublin." Sondertagung der Staats- und Regierungschefs der EG," April 28, 1990, in: *Bulletin*, No. 51 (1990), p. 401.

213. *Time*, March 26, 1990, p. 33. On May 6, 1990, Secretary of State Baker brought the Polish government a formal letter from Foreign Minister Genscher on behalf of all six participants of the two-plus-four negotiations, inviting Poland to join the two-plus-four session in Paris in July on the border issue.

214. Teltschik, *329 Tage*, p. 217.

215. *Ibid.*, pp. 220-21. In his memoirs, Foreign Minister Shevardnadze himself strictly avoided mentioning the backstage financial negotiations in Bonn on May 4-5, 1990. See Shevardnadze, *Die Zukunft gehört der Freiheit*, esp. pp. 244-47.

216. Teltschik, *329 Tage*, p. 221.

217. *Ibid.*, p. 227. The "special responsibility" of Germany with regard to the Soviet economy also stemmed from the fact that East Germany supplied 40 percent of all agricultural machinery to the Soviet Union, 40 percent of its cosmetics and medicines, 30 percent of imported clothing, and an untold amount of military equipment, among other things.

218. See Eberhard Schneider, "Die Einführung des Präsidialsystems," in: Bundesinstitut für ostwissenschaftliche und internationale Studien, ed., *Sowjetunion 1990-91: Krise-Zerfall-Neuorientierung* (Munich, 1991), pp. 56-64.

219. Thomas L. Friedman, "Is U.S.S.R. Nearing Collapse?" *International Herald Tribune*, May 7, 1990, p. 1.

220. Teltschik, *329 Tage*, pp. 227-28.

221. *Ibid.*, pp. 230-34.

222. Quoted from: Serge Schmemann, "Soviets Unyielding on a New Germany in Western Orbit," *The New York Times*, May 6, 1990, p. A20.

223. *Ibid.*; Shevardnadze, *Die Zukunft gehört der Freiheit*, pp. 244-47.

224. Marc Fisher, "Soviets Reach Dead End on German Plan," *International Herald Tribune*, May 9, 1990, p. 1. See also Serge Schmemann, "German Coalition Leaders Split on Soviet Proposal for Unification," *The New York Times*, May 9, 1990, p. A12.

225. Fisher, "Soviets Reach Dead End," p. 1.

226. Regarding the generally weak position of the GDR after the elections of March 18, see Martin Mantzke, "Eine Republik auf Abruf. Die DDR nach den Wahlen vom 18. März 1990," *Europa-Archiv*, Vol. 45 (1990), pp. 287-92.

227. *Ibid.*, p. 217.

228. The political inexperience and insecurity of the new East German government had also been demonstrated by a visit by Prime Minister Lothar de Maizière to the Soviet embassy on April 16 at Soviet request, when Ambassador Kochemasov had made "clear" to de Maizière who still had "the say" in the GDR. Two mistakes at once, the West Germans felt: first, the ambassador should have gone to the prime minister, not vice versa; and second, de Maizière should not have accepted Kochemasov's icy language, which now belonged to a distant past. See Teltschik, *329 Tage*, p. 198.

229. "Kohl Asserts Last Hurdle to Unity Is Lifted," *International Herald Tribune*, May 7, 1990, p. 1. See also Helmut Kohl, Policy Statement to the Bundestag, May 10, 1990, in: *Statements & Speeches*, Vol. 13, No. 14, May 14, 1990, passim.

230. Hans-Dietrich Genscher, Policy Statement to the Bundestag on the May 3 Conference of NATO Foreign Ministers Conference and the May 5, 1990 "Two plus Four" Talks, in: *Statements & Speeches*, Vol. 13, No. 13, May 14, 1990, p. 1.

231. "Kohl, Bush Confer on German Unification Process," *The Week in Germany*, May 18, 1990, p. 1. East German Prime Minister Lothar de Maizière, in contrast, merely stated in a speech before the European Parliament in Strasbourg on May 16 that a united Germany had "the right" to be a member of the Western alliance. *Frankfurter Allgemeine Zeitung*, May 17, 1990.

232. Teltschik, *329 Tage*, p. 237.

233. *Ibid.*, p. 243.

234. *Ibid.*, p. 244.

235. "Genscher Meets with 'Two Plus Four' Participants," *The Week in Germany*, May 25, 1990, p. 1; Teltschik, *329 Tage*, p. 249.

236. *Die Welt*, May 30, 1990.

237. Kommuniqué der Ministertagung des Verteidigungsplanungs- Ausschusses in Brüssel, May 22-23, 1990, in: *Europa-Archiv*, Vol. 45 (1990), pp. D445-47.

238. "Ein geeintes Deutschland als Gewinn für Stabilität und Sicherheit in Europa." Speech by Chancellor Kohl before the Inter-Parliamentary Disarmament Conference in Bonn, May 25, 1990, in: *Bulletin*, No. 68 (1990), pp. 586-87.

239. "Genscher Addresses Concerns About United Germany," *The Week in Germany*, June 1, 1990, p. 1.

240. Teltschik, *329 Tage*, p. 247.

241. *Izvestiia*, May 29, 1990.

242. News Conference of President Bush and President Mikhail Gorbachev of the Soviet Union, June 3, 1990, in: *Public Papers of the Presidents of the United States: George Bush: 1990: Book I: January 1 to June 30, 1990* (Washington, DC, 1991), p. 756. The public impression of Gorbachev's attitude was still different, though, as a comment of the West German daily *Die Welt* demonstrated: "They say about the Bourbons that they had learned nothing, nor had they forgotten anything. As far as Gorbachev is concerned, one is tempted to say that he has learned and forgotten selectively. The way in which he belabored an allegedly continuing German danger in Washington must seem curious to all those who remember the 'Gorby, Gorby' cries during his visit in Germany." *Die Welt,* June 6, 1990.

243. Thomas L. Friedman, "U.S. Will Press the Soviets to Accept Plan on Germany," *The New York Times,* June 5, 1990, p. A17.

244. *Ibid.*

245. George Bush, Telegram to Helmut Kohl, June 4, 1990. See Teltschik, *329 Tage*, pp. 257-58. During the talks, Gorbachev's delegation also had suggested that if a united Germany were to join NATO, the Soviet Union should be invited to join NATO as well. According to a senior administration official, when that notion had been broached, Bush had reminded the Soviets that if they seriously thought of applying for membership, they might want to keep in mind that the commander of NATO was always an American. See Thomas L. Friedman, "Soviets Promise to Pull Back Some Tactical Nuclear Arms," *The New York Times,* June 6, 1990, p. A10.

246. *Europa-Archiv,* Vol. 45 (1990), pp. Z146-47.

247. See Francis X. Clines, "Warsaw Pact Pronounces the End Of Ideological Conflict With West," *The New York Times,* June 8, 1990, pp. A1 and 6.

248. James A. Baker, Remarks at the North Atlantic Council Minister's Conference in Turnberry, Scotland, June 7, 1990, in: *US Information Service,* File Date/ID: 06/07/90 TX-406, Text Link 142071, p. 6.

249. Quoted from: Thomas L. Friedman, "Now, NATO Is in Search of a New Self," *The New York Times,* June 8, 1990, p. A6.

250. *Ibid.* See also Kommuniqué der Ministertagung des Nordatlantikrats am 7. und 8. Juni 1990 in Turnberry (Grossbritannien), in: *Europa-Archiv,* Vol. 45 (1990), pp. D447-53.

251. Helmut Kohl, Letter to Mikhail Gorbachev, June 12, 1990, in: Teltschik, *329 Tage,* p. 265.

252. "Bonn and Moscow Ministers Consult on Germany," *The New York Times,* June 12, 1990, p. A11.

253. Teltschik, *329 Tage,* p. 267.

254. Bill Keller, "Gorbachev Yields On Alliance Roles In a New Germany," *The New York Times,* June 13, 1990, p. A1.

255. The fact that Gorbachev called for "dual membership" for Germany in the competing alliances again, but this time was not insisting on equal membership, was clear proof of the shift. Under the new concept, according to Gorbachev, "the Bundeswehr would, as before, be subordinate to NATO, and the East German troops would be subordinate to the Government of the new Germany." In other words, the proposal would have left a united Germany free to use East Germany's army any way it saw fit—including abolishing it. See *Ibid.,* p. A18.

256. George Bush, Letter to Helmut Kohl, June 21, 1990, in: Teltschik, *329 Tage,* p. 282.

257. See Gemeinsame Entschliessung des Deutschen Bundestages und der Volkskammer der Deutschen Demokratischen Republik zur deutsch-polnischen Grenze, June 21, 1990, in: Münch, *Dokumente der Wiedertvereinigung Deutschlands,* pp. 280-81.

258. See *Der Tagesspiegel,* June 23, 1990, p. 1; Clifford Krauss, "Goodbye Charlie, Beige Symbol of the Cold War," *The New York Times,* June 23, 1990, p. A4.

259. Shevardnadze, *Die Zukunft gehört die Freihert,* pp. 248-49. Text of Shevardnadze's East Berlin declaration published by TASS, June 22, 1990. See also Erklärung des sowjetischen Aussenministers, Eduard Shevardnadze, abgegeben beim zweiten Zwei-plus-Vier-Aussenministertreffen am 22. Juni 1990 in Ost-Berlin, in: Kaiser, *Deutschlands Vereinigung,* Document 41, pp. 233-38.

260. Teltschik, *329 Tage,* p. 285.

261. Serge Schmemann, "Shevardnadze Seeks Curbs on Forces in New Germany," *The New York Times,* June 23, 1990, p. A4.

262. *Ibid.*

263. On June 26, Robert Blackwill of the National Security Council even called the Chancellery in Bonn to ask the Germans to coordinate the draft exclusively

with the French, as Thatcher would give in only if she was confronted with a united front of the Americans and continental Europeans. A visit by Teltschik, Kastrup, and Major General Klaus Naumann from the Ministry of Defense to Washington was canceled, however, since the British might have been offended if the "special relationship" between Washington and Bonn became known.

264. Teltschik, *329 Tage,* pp. 294-96.

265. NATO Press Service, Press Communiqué S-1(90)36. See also "Londoner Erklärung" der Gipfelkonferenz der Staats- und Regierungchefs der NATO-Mitgliedstaaten am 5. und 6. Juli 1990, in: *Europa-Archiv,* Vol. 45 (1990), pp. D456-57.

266. *Ibid.,* pp. D458-60.

267. Shevardnadze, *Die Zukunft gehört der Freiheit,* p. 251.

268. "Auf eiserne Art: Moskaus Ex-Aussenminister Schewardnadse hat enthüllt, dass die deutsche Vereinigung gewaltsam verhindert werden sollte," *Der Spiegel,* April 15, 1991, p. 41.

269. "Europäischer Rat in Dublin. Tagung der Staats- und Regierungchefs der EG," June 25-26, 1990, in: *Bulletin,* No. 84 (1990), pp. 720-21. See also Craig R. Whitney, "European Leaders Back Kohl's Plea to Aid Soviets," *The New York Times,* June 27, 1990, p. A1. On July 3, Poland, too, turned to the Federal Republic for financial support. At the same time that Foreign Minister Skubiszewski was demanding negotiations on a border treaty prior to German unification, Prime Minister Mazowiecki sent a personal letter to Kohl asking the chancellor to support Poland's efforts to reduce its foreign debt.

270. Gorbachev had also appealed to President Bush earlier in the month to support his reform program at the G7 meeting. See Mikhail Gorbachev, Letter to George Bush, July 4, 1990, in: *Europa-Archiv,* Vol. 45 (1990), pp. D437-38.

271. Political Declaration, July 10, 1990, in: *Bulletin,* No. 91 (1990). See also Erklärungen der Staats- und Regierungchefs der Bundesrepublik Deutschland, Frankreichs, Grossbritaniens, Italiens, Japans, Kanadas und der Vereinigten Staaten sowie Vertretern der Europäischen Gemeinschaften zum Weltwirtschaftsgipfel in Houston (Texas) vom 9. bis zum 11. Juli 1990, in: *Europa-Archiv,* Vol. 45 (1990), esp. pp. D430-31.

272. Teltschik, *329 Tage,* pp. 317-18.

273. *Ibid.,* pp. 319-24.

274. *Ibid.,* p. 334.

275. Kohl and Gorbachev had already discussed the issue during the flight from Moscow to Stavropol, where Kohl had mentioned the figure 370,000 and explained the reasons why the ceiling should not be lower. The Soviet president eventually accepted the figure, although he had expected a larger reduction.

276. Teltschik, *329 Tage,* p. 338.

277. See Erklärung des Bundeskanzlers der Bundesrepublik Deutschland, Helmut Kohl, über die Ergebnisse seines Besuchs in der Sowjetunion, abgegeben vor der Presse in Schelesnowodsk am 16. Juli 1990, in: *Europa-Archiv,* Vol. 45 (1990), p. D480. Press conference of Soviet President Mikhail Gorbachev regarding the visit of Chancellor Kohl, in: *Pravda,* July 18, 1990 (German translation in: *Sowjetunion heute,* No. 8, August 1990). See also Pfeiler, "Die Viermächte-Option," pp. 55-56.

278. Shevardnadze, *Die Zukunft gehört der Freiheit,* p. 252.

279. *Ibid.,* p. 253.

280. Erklärung zum Abschluss der dritten Runde der Zwei-plus-Vier-Verhandlungen, abgegeben vom Bundesminister des Auswärtigen der Bundesrepublik Deutschland, Hans-Dietrich Genscher, in Paris am 17. Juli 1990, in: *Europa-Archiv,* Vol. 45 (1990), pp. D504-5.

281. Eduard Shevardnadze, Letter to Hans-Dietrich Genscher, August 27, 1990.

282. Teltschik, *329 Tage,* pp. 352-53.

283. See *Europa-Archiv,* Vol. 45 (1990), p. Z190. During a press conference on the same day in the White House, President Bush proposed an "international cost coordination in the Gulf region" to collectively support those countries that sustained the heaviest losses as a result of the embargo against Iraq, especially Turkey, Egypt, and Jordan.

284. Teltschik, *329 Tage,* p. 358.

285. *Ibid.,* pp. 359-62. In the end, Bonn agreed to pay DM3 billion for the stationing costs until 1994, DM1 billion for the transportation of Soviet troops from East Germany to the Soviet Union, DM200 million for advanced education of soldiers, and DM7.8 billion for the housing program. The additional interest-free loan of DM3 billion could be used by the Soviet Union to cover its share of the stationing costs.

286. See Kaiser, *Deutschlands Vereinigung*, pp. 75-76.

287. Shevardnadze, *Die Zukunft gehört der Freiheit*, p. 259.

288. Vertrag über die abschliessende Regelung in bezug auf Deutschland, September 12, 1990, in: *Bulletin*, No. 109 (1990), pp. 1153-56.

289. "Allies Suspend Their Rights in Germany: Treaty Leaves East and West Free to Reunify in October," *International Herald Tribune*, September 13, 1990, p. 1. See also Christoph Bertram, "Ein Weltrekord der Diplomaten," *Die Zeit*, No. 37, September 7, 1990, p. 4.

290. For details, see the documentation in: Kaiser, *Deutschlands Vereinigung*, pp. 260-383. Regarding the "new situation" after two-plus-four see Pfeiler, "Die Viermächte-Option," pp. 71-79.

291. A detailed account of the subject is provided in Schäuble, *Der Vertrag: verhandelte*, passim. Interior Minister Schäuble was the Federal Republic's principle negotiator on the "Einheitsvertrag" (Treaty on Unity) with the GDR.

292. Grundgesetz für die Bundesrepublik Deutschland vom 23. Mai 1949, in: Bundesgesetzblatt 1949. Article 23 declared after naming the states (Länder) in which the Basic Law would become effective immediately: "In other parts of Germany, it is to be implemented following their acccession." Article 146 said: "The Basic Law becomes void on the day on which a constitution chosen by free decision of all the German people becomes effective."

293. Teltschik, *329 Tage*, p. 152.

294. Serge Schmemann, "How to Hammer Germany Back Together: The Nuts and Bolts," *The New York Times*, February 27, 1990, p. A8.

295. On February 19, the Central Round Table in East Berlin also rejected the "annexation of the GDR or individual states of the GDR" according to Article 23. See *9. November: Das Jahr danach. Vom Fall der Mauer bis zur ersten gesamtdeutschen Wahl. Eine Chronik in Dokumenten und Bildern* (Munich, 1990), p. 69.

296. "Angst vor dem Ende," *Der Spiegel*, No. 9, February 26, 1990, p. 100.

297. Schmemann, "How to Hammer Germany Back Together," p. A8.

298. Zimmerling and Zimmerling, eds., *Neue Chronik DDR. Berichte-Fotos-Dokumente*, Vol. 3, p. 58.

299. Schäuble, *Der Vertrag*, p. 29.

300. *Ibid.*, pp. 54-55. See also "'Anschluss ist ein falscher Begriff,'" Innenminister Wolfgang Schäuble und Markus Meckel, Vize der DDR-SPD, über die künftige Verfassung," *Der Spiegel*, No. 12, March 19, 1990, pp. 48-51.

301. Schmemann, "How to Hammer Germany Back Together," p. A8.

302. Robert Leicht, "Einheit durch Beitritt. Warum am Grundgesetz rühren?— Eine neue Verfassung kann nur schlechter werden," *Die Zeit*, No. 9, March 2, 1990, p. 3.

303. *Ibid.* When Chancellor Kohl discussed the pros and cons of Article 23 and Article 146 with Klaus Stern, Dieter Blumenwitz, Josef Isensee, Rupert Scholz, and Hans-Hugo Klein on the evening of March 5 at the Chancellery bungalow, these experts on public and constitutional law took the same position as Leicht and unanimously spoke in favor of Article 23. See Teltschik, *329 Tage*, p. 167.

304. "Legal Scholars for German Unity According to Article 23," *The Week in Germany*, March 30, 1990, pp. 6-7.

305. *Ibid.*, p. 7.

306. Schäuble, *Der Vertrag*, p. 297.

307. *Frankfurter Allgemeine Zeitung*, April 19, 1990.

308. Schäuble, *Der Vertrag*, p. 300.

309. The East German federal states Saxony, Saxony-Anhalt, Mecklenburg-Near Pomerania, Brandenburg, and Thuringia were formally installed by a decision of the People's Chamber on July 22, 1990. The first state elections were held in the five new Länder on October 14, 1990.

310. Teltschik, *329 Tage*, p. 220.

311. *Ibid.*, p. 224.

312. *Frankfurter Allgemeine Zeitung*, May 16, 1990.

313. See "Dann wird der Kampf heiss," *Der Spiegel*, No. 21, May 21, 1990, p. 20.

314. Schäuble, *Der Vertrag*, p. 137.

315. *Ibid.*, pp. 136-37.

316. Gemeinsame Erklärung der Regierungen der Bundesrepublik Deutschland und der Deutschen Demokratischen Republik zur Regelung offener Vermögensfragen vom 15. Juni 1990, in: *Dokumente der Wiedervereinigung Deutschlands*, p. 277.

317. "Bonn Expects Compensation for Nationalized Assets in GDR," *The Week in Germany,* April 6, 1990, p. 4.

318. *Ibid.*, pp. 4-5.

319. This meant that the delegations from East and West comprised of some 50 persons each. See Schäuble, *Der Vertrag,* pp. 115, 185.

320. See Abkommen zwischen der Regierung der Bundesrepublik Deutschland und der Regierung der Deutschen Demokratischen Republik über die Aufhebung der Personenkontrollen an den innerdeutschen Grenzen vom 1. Juli 1990, in: *Dokumente der Wiedervereinigung Deutschlands*, pp. 282-91.

321. Schäuble, *Der Vertrag,* pp. 124-25.

322. *Ibid.*, pp. 126-31.

323. *Ibid.*, pp. 130-35. Prime Minister de Maizière later also said that the treaty on German unity should be "supported," not just "endured," by the people of both German states. See Zimmerling and Zimmerling, eds., *Neue Chronik DDR,* Vols. 7-8, p. 130.

324. The date was eventually confirmed during a joint session of the "German Unity" committees of the Bundestag and Volkskammer on July 26.

325. See Vertrag zur Vorbereitung und Durchführung der ersten gesamtdeutschen Wahl des Deutschen Bundestages zwischen der Bundesrepublik Deutschland und der Deutschen Demokratischen Republik vom 3. August 1990, in: *Dokumente der Wiedervereinigung Deutschlands*, pp. 324-26. On September 29, 1990, the Constitutional Court of the Federal Republic decided, however, that the treaty was unconstitutional and that the 5 percent clause could be applied in the two parts of Germany separately only.

326. Zimmerling and Zimmerling, eds., *Neue Chronik DDR,* Vols. 7-8, p. 179.

327. Beschluss der Volkskammer der Deutschen Demokratischen Republik über den Beitritt der Deutschen Demokratischen Republik zum Geltungsbereich des Grundgesetzes der Bundesrepublik Deutschland, August 23, 1990, in: *Dokumente der Wiedervereinigung Deutschlands*, p. 326.

CHAPTER 5

1. Hans-Dietrich Genscher, Speech at the Second Meeting on the Human Dimension of the CSCE, Copenhagen, June 5, 1990, in: *Bulletin*, No. 72 (1990), p. 624.

2. Helmut Kohl, Day of German Unity Message to all Governments of the World, October 3, 1990, in: *Bulletin*, No. 118 (1990), p. 1.

3. Richard von Weizsäcker, Speech at the Day of German Unity State Ceremony in Berlin, October 3, 1990, in: *Europa-Archiv*, Vol. 45 (1990), p. D543.

4. See Peter M.E. Volten, "Security Dimensions of Imperial Collapse," *Problems of Communism* (February 1992), pp. 136-47.

5. See Angela Stent, "The One Germany," *Foreign Policy*, No. 81 (Winter 1990-91), pp. 53-70.

6. Gordon A. Craig, a professor of history at Stanford University and a longtime expert on Germany, warned as early as 1989 that in the case of German unification there would be "a new thinking, a new pride, and a new perception of what the Germans are and what their role in Europe should be." Professor Craig therefore recommended keeping Germany divided and creating a neutralized confederation of two independent democratic German states. See "Zu gross für Europa? Der amerikanische Historiker Gordon A. Craig über ein wiedervereinigtes Deutschland," *Der Spiegel*, No. 46, November 13, 1989, p. 185.

7. See Helmut Herles, *Nationalrausch—Szenen aus dem deutschen Machtkampf* (Munich, 1990); Hajo Funke, *"Jetzt sind wir dran . . ." Nationalismus im geeinten Deutschland. Aspekte der Einigungspolitik und nationalistische Potentiale in Deutschland* (Berlin, 1991); and Peter Glotz, *Der Irrweg des Nationalstaats— Europäische Reden an ein deutsches Publikum* (Stuttgart, 1990).

8. Jeff Thinnes, "Germany's Foreign Policy After Unification," *Aspen Institute Berlin Conference Report*, March 19-21, 1991, p. 4.

9. *Ibid.,* p. 5.

10. The expression was used as early as in April 1990 by Jacques Calvet, chairman of French auto giant Peugeot, with regard to plans to have a single market functioning within the EC by 1992. See "One Germany," *Business Week*, April 2, 1990, p. 48.

11. Robert Gerald Livingston, "United Germany: Bigger and Better," *Foreign Policy*, No. 87 (Summer 1982), p. 157.

12. Thinnes, "Germany's Foreign Policy After Unification," p. 7. See also Gilbert Ziebura et al., *Deutschland in der neuen Weltordnung. Unbewältigte Herausforderung* (Opladen, 1992), chap. 1.

13. See Gregor Schöllgen, *Die Macht in der Mitte Europas. Stationen deutscher Aussenpolitik von Friedrich dem Grossen bis zur Gegenwart* (Munich, 1992), chap. 1; and "German Assertiveness Is Supported by U.S.," *International Herald Tribune,* January 22, 1992.

14. Daniel Hamilton, "A More European Germany, A More German Europe," *Journal of International Affairs* (Summer 1991), p. 129.

15. Prior to the unification of Germany, Arnulf Baring, professor of contemporary history at the Free University of Berlin, had already launched an early warning against Germany's leaving the trustworthy Western community. See Arnulf Baring (with Volker Zastrow), *Unser neuer Grössenwahn: Deutschland zwischen Ost und West* (Stuttgart, 1988), esp. pp. 248-53.

16. See Zbigniew Brzezinski, "Postkommunistischer Nationalismus," *Europa-Archiv,* Vol. 44 (1989), p. 733.

17. Theo Sommer, "Nackenschlag zur Wiederbelebung. Treibt das Gespenst des Rechtsextremismus die alten Parteien endlich zum Handeln?" *Die Zeit,* No. 16, April 10, 1992, p. 1.

18. Stent, "The One Germany," p. 62.

19. *Ibid.,* p. 63.

20. See Gill and Schröter, *Das Ministerium für Staatssicherheit;* Schell and Kalinka, *Stasi und kein Ende;* Worst, *Das Ende eines Geheimdienstes.*

21. Hans-Dietrich Genscher, "Opening Remarks," May 5, 1990, *Statements & Speeches,* Vol. 13, No. 11, May 8, 1990.

22. See, for instance, Brandt, *Friedenspolitik in Europa,* p. 146: "The question concerning the future of Germany and the position of the Germans in Europe is the question of a durable European peace order. Only in a peacefully structured Europe that has accomplished the bridge building between East and West and in which the nations, as equals among equals, compete for peace, justice and well-being for all, can the past be overcome positively."

23. Richard von Weizsäcker, *A Voice From Germany* (London, 1985), p. 78.

24. Brandt, *Friedenspolitik,* p. 134.

25. See again Willy Brandt, "Die Verantwortung der Deutschen gegenüber Europa," Lecture at the Annual Conference of the Board of Trustees of the Friedrich Ebert Foundation, Dusseldorf, November 30, 1967, in: Willy Brandt, *Aussenpolitik- Deutschlandpolitik- Europapolitik: Grundsätzliche Erklärungen während des ersten Jahres im Auswärtigen Amt,* 2nd ed. (Berlin, 1968), pp. 149-64.

26. Similarly, Horst Teltschik wrote on the eve of German unity that a united Germany should strive for a new Europe: "The result could be a Europe from the Atlantic to the Bug [River], a Europe of free democratic countries with the same economic system and currency, a Europe of fatherlands that culminates in a united Europe with federal structures." *Die Welt,* September 22, 1990.

27. See Der Vertrag von Maastricht. Vertrag über die Schaffung der Europäischen Union, unterzeichnet von den Aussen- und Finanzministern der Europäischen Gemeinschaft am 7. Februar 1992 in Maastricht (Niederlande), in: *Europa-Archiv,* Vol. 47 (1992), pp. D 177-254.

28. See Hanns W. Maull, "Zivilmacht Bundesrepublik Deutschland. Vierzehn Thesen für eine neue deutsche Aussenpolitik," *Europa-Archiv,* Vol. 47 (1992), pp. 276-77, and Hans-Peter Schwarz, *Die gezähmten Deutschen. Von der Machtbesessenheit zur Machtvergessenheit* (Stuttgart, 1985), pp. 105-51.

29. Thinnes, "Germany's Foreign Policy," p. 8.

30. Livingston, "United Germany," p. 166.

31. C. Michael Aho and Gregory F. Treverton, "German Integration Will Delay 1992," *The New York Times,* November 19, 1989.

32. "Rush to unity may put brakes on 1992 process," *Financial Times* (London), March 19, 1990, p. 3.

33. *La Repubblica,* March 18, 1990.

34. Helmut Kohl, Policy Statement to the Bundestag, May 10, 1990, in: *Statements & Speeches,* Vol. 13, No. 14, May 14, 1990, p. 1.

35. *Ibid.*

36. Alan Riding, "Europe United? 12 Community Members Do Not Agree On How Much Sovereignty to Give Up," *The New York Times,* April 28, 1990, p. 5. Experts also agreed that a unified Europe would not mean a "homogenized" Europe, but would be based on the "principle of subsidiarity," by which the common authority of the union would be empowered as necessary in a number of crucial areas, while a large margin of initiative would be left to the

national governments and to private citizens. See, for instance, "The Case for Euro-Optimism. A Conversation with Mark Eyskens," *European Journal of International Affairs*, Vol. 7 (Winter 1990), p. 34.

37. See Alan Riding, "Europe Seeking Greater Unity by '93," *The New York Times*, May 3, 1990, p. A16.

38. See *Der Vertrag von Maastricht*, p. D254.

39. Livingston, "United Germany," p. 158.

40. See Markus Jachtenfuchs, "Die EG nach Maastricht. Das Subsidiaritätsprinzip und die Zukunft der Integration," *Europa-Archiv*, Vol. 47 (1992), pp. 279-87.

41. The expression "European Civil War" was coined by Ernst Nolte in his book *Der europäische Bürgerkrieg 1917-1945. Nationalsozialismus und Bolschewismus* (Frankfurt am Main, 1987). After the end of Nazism and Bolshevism, the term would have to be redefined. But, as recent events in former Yugoslavia have shown, the potential for civil war in Europe still exists.

42. See Livingston, "United Germany," p. 168.

43. Obviously, this provision does not apply to the highly advanced industrial states of the former European Free Trade Association (EFTA), such as Austria, Switzerland, Finland, and Sweden, which are expected to become full members of the EC rather soon.

44. Clemens Geissler, "Neue Völkerwanderungen in Europa," *Europa-Archiv*, Vol. 47 (1992), p. 569. See also Hans-Joachim Hoffmann-Novotny, *Die neue Völkerwanderung: Ein makroskopischer, soziologischer Rahmen für siedlungskulturelle Überlegungen* (Zurich, 1991).

45. Data according to a study by KPMG Peat Marwick and *Bloc* magazine, cited in: *International Herald Tribune*, December 24-25, 1990. See also Hamilton, "A More European Germany," p. 135.

46. Livingston, "United Germany," pp. 167-68.

47. Giles Merritt, "The E.C. Can't Afford to Let Eastern Europe Flounder," *International Herald Tribune*, December 7, 1990.

48. Hamilton, "A More European Germany," p. 137.

49. "Perspectives for Trade with the East," *Deutsche Bank Bulletin* (December 1990).

50. For details, see Stephen F. Szabo, *The Changing Politics of German Security* (New York, 1990), pp. 137-63.

51. See, for instance, Maull, "Zivilmacht Bundesrepublik Deutschland," p. 269.

52. See Curt Gasteyger, "Ein gesamteuropäisches Sicherheitssystem?" *Europa-Archiv*, Vol. 47 (1992), p. 475; Daniel Hamilton and James Clad, "Germany, Japan, and the False Glare of War," *Washington Quarterly* (Autumn 1991), pp. 39-49.

53. Helmut Kohl, Speech before the American Council on Germany, New York, June 5, 1990, in: *Bulletin*, No. 74 (1990), pp. 638-41.

54. Helmut Kohl, Speech at commencement ceremonies at Harvard University, June 7, 1990, in: *Bulletin*, No. 74 (1990), p. 642. A detailed analysis of U.S.-German relations after unification provides Ronald D. Asmus, "Germany and America: Partners in Leadership?" *Survival* (November-December 1991).

55. Volten, "Security Dimensions of Imperial Collapse," p. 137.

56. See *Ibid.*, p. 144.

57. This does not mean, of course, that the only remaining superpower, the United States, will not try to perpetuate its position and deter any nation or group of nations from challenging US primacy. The case for a world dominated by one superpower has in fact already been made in a 46-page document that was circulated at the highest levels of the Pentagon in February and March 1992. See "Pentagon's New World Order: U.S. to Reign Supreme," *International Herald Tribune*, March 9, 1992, p. 1. Yet the argument here is that, on the contrary, a single power is not likely to succeed in establishing a new order in a world of unprecedented complexity.

58. Livingston, "United Germany," pp. 169-70.

59. "Germany, Europe, and the Future Security System for the 1990's," Report prepared by Hope Harrison, Aspen Institute Berlin, November 1990, p. 18. For the future role of CSCE, see also Ian M. Cuthbertson, ed., *Redefining the CSCE: Challenges and Opportunities in the New Europe* (New York, 1992).

60. See Manfred Wörner, "European Security Will Need Both NATO and CSCE," Address before The Netherlands Atlantic Commission on the occasion of its 40th anniversary, February 12, 1992, in: *US Policy Information and Texts* (USIS Bonn), No. 20, February 14, 1992, p. 23.

61. For details, see David P. Calleo, "NATO: Reconstruction or Dissolution?" *FPI New World-New Direction Series* (Washington, DC, 1992). US President Bush also stated that "even as NATO gives more emphasis to its political mission, its guarantee of European security must remain firm." Cited from: *International Herald Tribune*, May 5-6, 1990, p. 1.

62. Arnulf Baring, *Deutschland, was nun? Ein Gespräch mit Dirk Rumberg und Wolf Jobst Siedler* (Berlin, 1991), p. 118.

63. Wörner, "European Security," p. 24.

64. Ambassador John Kornblum, head of the US delegation to the CSCE, agreed in a February 27, 1992, television interview that "NATO has transformed itself tremendously and has become increasingly a part of the overall structures of security in Europe. Cooperative security is clearly the future goal of everyone, and NATO is becoming increasingly important in this role." Quoted from: "Kornblum Sees the Future of Europe as a Bright One," *US Policy Information and Texts* (USIS Bonn), No. 26, February 28, 1992, p. 35.

65. Wörner, "European Security," pp. 24-25. See also Livingston, "United Germany," p. 170.

66. See Wörner, "European Security," p. 25.

67. See Gipfelkonferenz der Staats- und Regierungschefs der NATO-Mitgliedstaaten am 7. und 8. November 1991 in Rom (mit dem neuen Strategischen Konzept und anderen Erklärungen), in: *Europa-Archiv*, Vol. 47 (1992), pp. D52-75.

68. "Gipfelerklärung von Helsinki," *Europa-Archiv*, Vol. 47 (1992), p. D534.

69. See "Beschlüsse von Helsinki," *Europa-Archiv*, Vol. 47 (1992), pp. D539-76.

70. See "CSCE Helsinki Document 1992: The Challenge of Change," July 10, 1992, *US Policy Information and Texts*, No. 87, July 13, 1992, p. 11. For a detailed analysis, see also Michael R. Lucas, "The Challenges of Helsinki II," in: Cuthbertson, *Redefining the CSCE*, pp. 259-301.

71. Robert Leicht, "Flotter Abschied vom Genscherismus," *Die Zeit*, No. 32, July 31, 1992, p. 1.

72. See "Nahe dran am echten Krieg," *Der Spiegel*, Vol. 46 (1992), pp. 22-29.

73. See Jacques Delors, "European Integration and Security," *Survival* (March-April 1991), pp. 99-109.

74. Presseerklärung über die Aufstellung eines Europäischen Korps, veröffentlicht zum Abschluss der 59. deutsch-französischen Konsultationen in La Rochelle, May 22, 1992, in: *Europa-Archiv*, Vol. 47 (1992), pp. D454-55. See also David S. Yost, "France and West European Defence Identity," *Survival* (July-August 1991), pp. 327-51.

75. Volten, "Security Dimensions of Imperial Collapse," p. 146.

76. Gerhard Wettig of the Bundesinstitut für ostwissenschaftliche und internationale Studien in Cologne explicitly warns against a transformation of NATO, which he thinks would lead to a renationalization of European politics and a loss of protection against aggression. See Gerhard Wettig, "Deutsche Vereinigung und europäische Sicherheit," *Aussenpolitik*, Vol. 42 (1992), p. 17.

77. Wörner, "European Security," p. 26. See also Reinhard Wolf, "Kollektive Sicherheit und das neue Europa," *Europa-Archiv*, Vol. 47 (1992), pp. 365-74.

78. Wörner, "European Security," p. 27.

79. Eckart Arnold, "German Foreign Policy and Unification," *International Affairs* (London), No. 3 (1991), p. 470.

80. See also "The New Superpower," *Newsweek*, February 26, 1990, pp. 18-20.

81. *Ibid.*, p. 19. See also Louis Uchitelle, "East Europe Tries a Mild Capitalism," *The New York Times*, December 11, 1989, p. D10.

82. Bernhard Felderer, "Kein Sprung ins kalte Wasser," *Frankfurter Allgemeine Zeitung*, January 27, 1990, p. 13.

83. "The New Superpower," p. 23.

84. Uchitelle, "East Europe Tries a Mild Capitalism," and "1991 Economic Trends in the Federal Republic of Germany: Implications for the United States," Position Paper, United States Embassy Bonn, August 1991, p. 5. See also Hans-Heribert Derix, "Bürokratisch regulierte Marktwirtschaft zwischen Beharrung und Liquidation," *Aussenpolitik*, Vol. 41, 1990, No. 4, p. 351.

85. Treuhandanstalt, *The Chance of the 90's: Investing in Eastern Germany* (Berlin, 1991), p. 7.

86. "Unternehmensgründungen in Deutschland," *Die Zeit*, No. 15, April 3, 1992, p. 36 (source: Institut für Mittelstandsforschung). See also "1991 Economic Trends in the Federal Republic of Germany," pp. 5-6.

87. *Ibid.,* p. 6.

88. A critical account of the history and activities of the Treuhandanstalt is provided in Heinz Suhr, *Der Treuhandskandal. Wie Ostdeutschland geschlachtet wurde* (Frankfurt am Main, 1991), passim. Regarding Modrow's "Genossen-Treuhand," see *Ibid.,* pp. 44-61.

89. Treuhandanstalt, *The Chance of the 90's,* p. 9.

90. *Ibid.*

91. Karl C. Thalheim, *Die wirtschaftliche Entwicklung der beiden Staaten in Deutschland,* 3rd ed. (Berlin, 1988), p. 79.

92. Kuno Kruse and Birgit Schwarz, "Wem gehört die DDR?" *Die Zeit,* No. 12, March 23, 1990, p. 7.

93. Treuhandanstalt, *The Chance of the 90's,* pp. 7 and 9.

94. Data as of July 1, 1993, provided by the Treuhandanstalt, August 23, 1993. Of the privatized companies, some 2,364 were taken over by their respective management and employees (management buyouts); about 700 were acquired by foreign investors. In comparison, privatization in other formerly state-planned economies in Eastern Europe had not exceeded 20 to 25 percent by this time.

95. Gerlinde Sinn and Hans-Werner Sinn, *Kaltstart: Volkswirtschaftliche Aspekte der deutschen Vereinigung* (Tübingen, 1991), passim.

96. Heinz D. Kurz, "Sozialpakt am Abgrund," *Die Zeit,* No. 12, March 13, 1992, p. 47.

97. Suhr, *Der Treuhandskandal,* p. 199; "Sabotage an der Einheit," *Der Spiegel,* No. 13, March 23, 1992, pp. 24 and 26. Another comparison also illustrates the dilemma: West German capital stock grew by some DM200 billion in the year before German unification. About five times the amount would be necessary to balance the capital deficit of East Germany arithmetically. It seems obvious that this cannot be done quickly.

98. *Der Tagesspiegel,* June 20, 1992, p. 21.

99. "Leistungen der westdeutschen öffentlichen Haushalte für Ostdeutschland," *Die Zeit,* No. 14, March 27, 1992, p. 32 (Source: Deutsche Bundesbank).

100. Treuhandanstalt, *The Chance of the 90's,* p. 7.

101. "1991 Economic Trends in the Federal Republic of Germany," p. 6.

102. Quoted from: Dieter Feddersen, "Die ostdeutschen Bundesländer heute," Lecture at the Atlantik-Brücke, June 11, 1991, in: *Rundschreiben* Nr. 5/1991 (Atlantik-Brücke), p. 2.

103. "Sabotage an der Einheit," p. 25.

104. *Ibid.*

105. *Ibid.*, p. 26.

106. Plans call for dismantling scores of obsolete, polluting factories and reviewing the 15,000 mostly illegal dumps of dangerous toxic waste. If West German laws were applied, 70 percent of East German industry would have to shut immediately. Providing East Germany with relatively clean energy alone is expected to cost $20 billion. See Marlise Simons, "West Germans Get Ready to Scrub The East's Tarnished Environment," *The New York Times*, June 27, 1990, p. A6.

107. Treuhandanstalt, *The Chance of the 90's*, p. 8.

108. Feddersen, "Die ostdeutschen Bundesländer Heute," p. 2. Official unemployment in the new Länder was 1.2 million, or 15 percent, on July 1, 1992. The true extent of the joblessness was disguised, however, as 494,000 people were working part time, while another 505,000 were in state-paid retraining schemes and 782,000 in early retirement, adding up to 33 percent of East Germany's work force. See Livingston, "United Germany," p. 162. One year later, on July 1, 1993, official unemployment in the East German Länder was still 14.4 percent—affecting 1,099,700 people—although some economic indicators showed signs of improvement. See *Die Zeit*, July 23, 1993, p. 22.

109. "1991 Economic Trends in the Federal Republic of Germany," p. 1.

110. Sources: Institut der Deutschen Wirtschaft, Cologne, and EC Commission, Brussels. See *Berliner Morgenpost*, March 10, 1992, p. 4. In comparison, the highly praised European Bank for Reconstruction and Development, a $12 billion institution established in May 1990 by representatives of 40 nations in London to help revive Eastern Europe's economy, provided a mere DM1.26 billion during its first year in business, according to its president, Jacques Attali, a former advisor to French president Mitterrand. See "Manager und Märkte," *Die Zeit*, No. 15, April 3, 1992, p. 36.

111. OECD Report of December 1991. Quoted from: "Sabotage an der Einheit," p. 27. See also Roland Sturm, *Staatsverschuldung* (Opladen, 1992).

112. "1991 Economic Trends in the Federal Republic of Germany," p. 7.

113. *Ibid.*, p. 4.

114. A report by the US Central Intelligence Agency, entitled "Eastern Europe: Long Road Ahead to Economic Well-Being," predicted in 1990 that the emerging democracies of Eastern Europe faced daunting economic problems that would require their citizens to tolerate high unemployment and financial hardship for years as the countries tried to move from centralized planned economies to market-oriented systems. "Although many East Europeans clearly have shown impressive boldness and courage in pushing ahead with reforms, significant growth and improvement in living standards in the region, at best, will take years," the report stated. See "East's Economies: A Bleak Forecast," *International Herald Tribune*, May 17, 1990, p. 1.

115. See August Pradetto, "Europa nach der Revolution. Ost und West vor säkularen Herausforderungen," *Aus Politik und Zeitgeschichte. Beilage zur Wochenzeitung Das Parlament*, B 6/92, January 31, 1992, p. 3.

116. Francis Fukuyama, "The End of History," *National Interest*, No. 16 (Summer 1989).

117. "Germany After the Two States: A Conversation with Joachim Fest," *European Journal of International Affairs* (Winter 1990), p. 75.

118. *Ibid.*, p. 88.

119. Daniel Hamilton, "In Europe, the Walls Go up Again," *The Baltimore Sun*, May 22, 1991.

120. David Anderson, ed., "Crisis Management in Eastern Europe," Yugoslavia—A Case Study, *Aspen Institute Berlin Conference Report* (March 1992), p. 14.

121. See James Baker, "The Euro-Atlantic Architecture: From West to East," Address at the Aspen Institute Berlin, June 18, 1991, in: *US Policy Information and Texts* (USIS Bonn), No. 85, June 19, 1991, p. 20.

122. *Ibid.*, p. 21. See also Peter Glotz, "Die Einheit und die Spaltung Europas: Die Auswirkungen der mitteleuropäischen Revolution von 1989 auf Gesamteuropa," *Aus Politik und Zeitgeschichte. Beilage zur Wochenzeitung Das Parlament*, B 6/92, January 31, 1992, pp. 58-59. Glotz is less optimistic about the future and foresees a new division of Europe, with regressing prosperity in the West and a zone of economically underdeveloped authoritarian dictatorships in the East; he also sees the continuing predomination of nation-states as the most significant political units.

123. Jean Monnet, *Erinnerungen eines Europäers: Vorwort von Bundeskanzler Helmut Schmidt* (Munich, 1980), p. 661. An early example of reflections about a new Europe was Count Coudenhove-Kalergi's book on a European federation, first published in 1923. See Richard Coudenhove-Kalergi, *Weltmacht Europa* (Stuttgart, 1971).

124. Baker, "The Euro-Atlantic Architecture," p. 21-22. See also Andrej Cima, "New Democracies in East Central Europe: Expectations for the EC and the CSCE," in: Cuthbertson, ed., *Redefining the CSCE*, pp. 179-206.

125. Glotz, "Die Einheit und die Spaltung Europas," p. 60.

126. See Heinz Kramer and Friedemann Müller, "Die wirtschaftlichen Voraussetzungen für eine erfolgreiche Assoziation," in: *Die EG und die jungen Demokratien: Ein gemeinsamer Bericht westeuropäischer Aussenpolitik-Institute* (Baden-Baden, 1991), pp. 29 and 38.

127. Konrad Seitz, *Die japanisch-amerikanische Herausforderung: Deutschlands Hochtechnologie-Industrien kämpfen ums Überleben* (Stuttgart, 2nd ed., 1991), p. 353.

128. See Michael Brie and Dieter Klein, eds., *Umbruch zur Moderne: Kritische Beiträge* (Hamburg, 1991), pp. 153-54.

129. See, for instance, Jerzy Holzer, "Polen nach dem Kommunismus— quo vadis?"; Pavel Smutny, "Die Tschechoslowakei—eine Rückkehr zu sich selbst"; and Máté Szabó, "Probleme der Demokratisierung in Ungarn," in: *Aus Politik und Zeitgeschichte: Beilage zur Wochenzeitung Das Parlament, B 6/92,* January 31, 1992, pp. 11-49.

■ SELECTED BIBLIOGRAPHY ■

DOCUMENTS

DDR: Dokumente zur Geschichte der Deutschen Demokratischen Republik 1945-1985. Ed. by Hermann Weber. Munich: Deutscher Taschenbuch Verlag, 1986.

Dokumente des geteilten Deutschland: Quellentexte zur Rechtslage des Deutschen Reiches, der Bundesrepublik Deutschland und der Deutschen Demokratischen Republic. Ed. by Ingo von Münch. Stuttgart: Kroener Verlag, 1974.

Dokumente der Wiedervereinigung Deutschlands: Quellentexte zum Prozess der Wiedervereinigung von der Ausreisewelle aus der DDR uber Ungarn, die CSSR und Polen im Spätsommer 1989 bis zum Beitritt der DDR zum Geltungsbereich des Grundgesetzes der Bundesrepublik Deutschland im Oktober 1990. Ed. by Ingo von Münch. Stuttgart: Kroener Verlag, 1991.

Iche liebe euch doch alle! Befehle und Lageberichte des MfS January-November 1989. Ed. by Armin Mitter and Stefan Wolle. Berlin: BasisDruck Verlagsgesellschaft, 1990.

Kaiser, Karl. *Deutschlands Vereinigung: Die internationalen Aspekte—Mit den wichtigen Kokumenten.* Bergisch Gladbach: Gustav Lübbe Verlag, 1991.

Neue Chronik DDR. Ed. by Zeno and Sabine Zimmerling. 8 vols. Berlin: Treptower Verlagshaus, 1990-91.

Und diese verdammte ohnmacht: Report der unabhängigen Untersuchungskommission zu den Ereignissen vom 7./8. Oktober 1989 in Berlin. Berlin: BasisDruck Verlagsgesellschaft, 1991.

Wir sind das Volk: Die DDR zwischen 7. Oktober und 17. Dezember 1989—Eine Chronik. Ed. by Hannes Bahrmann and Christoph Links. Berlin: Aufbau Verlag, 1990.

Memoirs

Andert, Reinhold, and Wolfgang Herzberg. *Der Sturz: Erich Honecker im Kreuzverhör.* Berlin: Aufbau Verlag, 1990.

Arnold, Karl-Heinz, *Die ersten hundert Tage des Hans Modrow.* Berlin: Deitz Verlag, 1990.

Brandt, Willy. *Erinnerungen.* Berlin: Ullstein Verlag, 1989.

Honecker, Erich. *Aus meinem Leben,* 14th ed. Berlin: Deitz Verlag, 1989.

Janka, Walter. *Schwierigkeiten mit der Wahrheit.* Reinbek: Rowohlt Taschenbuch Verlag, 1989.

————. *Spuren eines Lebens.* Berlin: Rowohlt Verlag, 1991.

Krenz, Egon (with Hartmut König and Gunter Rettner). *Wenn Mauern fallen: Die Friedliche Revolution—Vorgeschichte, Ablauf, Auswirkungen.* Vienna: Paul Neff Verlag, 1990.

Luft, Christa. *Zwischen Wende und Ende: Eindrücke, Erlebnisse, Erfahrungen eines Mitglieds der Modrow-Regierung.* Berlin: Aufbau Taschenbuch Verlag, 1991.

Mittag, Günter. *Um jeden Preis: Im Spannungsfeld zweier Systeme.* Berlin: Aufbau Verlag, 1991.

Modrow, Hans. *Aufbruch und Ende.* Hamburg: Konkret Literatur Verlag, 1991.

————. "Bilanz nach 150 Tagen." *Die Zeit,* April 13, 1990.

Schabowski, Günter. *Der Absturz.* Berlin: Rowohlt Verlag, 1991.

————. *Das Politbüro: Ende eines Mythos. Eine Befragung.* Ed. by Frank Sieren and Ludwig Koehne. Reinbek: Rowohlt Taschenbuch Verlag, 1990.

Schäuble, Wolfgang. *Der Vertrag: Wie ich über die deutsche Einheit verhandelte.* Stuttgart: Deutsche Verlags-Anstalt, 1991.

Schwardnadse, Eduard. *Die Zukunft gehört der Freiheit*. Reinbek: Rowohlt Verlag, 1991.

Schmidt, Helmut. *Menschen und Mächte*. Berlin: Siedler Verlag, 1987.

————. *Die Deutschen und ihre Nachbarn: Menschen und Mächte II*. Berlin: Siedler Verlag, 1990.

Strauss, Franz Josef. *Die Erinnerungen*. Berlin: Siedler Verlag, 1989.

Teltschik, Horst. *329 Tage: Innenansichten der Einigung*. Berlin: Siedler Verlag, 1991.

Wolf, Markus. *In eigenem Auftrag: Bekenntnisse und Einsichten*. Munich: Schneekluth Verlag, 1991.

————. *Die Troika*. Berlin: Aufbau Verlag, 1989.

BOOKS AND ARTICLES

Historical Dimensions of the German Question
Albertini, Luigi. *The Origins of the War of 1914*. London: Oxford University Press, 1952.

Barkin, Kenneth D. *The Controversy over German Industrialization, 1890-1902*. Chicago: University of Chicago Press, 1970.

Barraclough, Geoffrey. *The Origins of Modern Germany*. New York: Capricorn Books, 1963 (reprint).

Bracher, Karl-Dietrich. *The German Dictatorship: The Origins, Structure, and Effects of National Socialism*. New York: Praeger, 1970.

Bullock, Alan. *Hitler: A Study in Tyranny*. New York: Harper & Row, 1962.

Calleo, David. *The German Problem Reconsidered: Germany and the World Order, 1870 to the Present*. Cambridge: University Press, 1978.

Craig, Gordon. *Deutschland, 1866-1945*. Munich: Beck Verlag, 1980.

————. *Über die Deutschen.* Munich: Beck Verlag, 1982.

Dehio, Ludwig. *Germany and World Politics in the Twentieth Century.* New York: Norton & Company, 1959.

Eyck, Erich. *Bismarck and the German Empire,* 3rd ed. London: Unwin University Books, 1968.

Fest, Joachim C. *Hitler.* New York: Harcourt Brace Jovanovich, 1974.

Fischer, Fritz. *Germany's Aims in the First World War.* New York: Norton, 1967.

————. *The War of Illusions.* New York: Norton, 1975.

Gall, Lothar. *Bismarck. Der weisse Revolutionär.* Frankfurt and Berlin: Ullstein Verlag, 1980.

Gay, Peter. *Weimar Culture: The Outsider as Insider.* New York: Harper & Row, 1968.

Geiss, Imanuel. *German Foreign Policy, 1871-1914.* London: Routledge and Kegan Paul, 1976.

Görtemaker, Manfred. *Deutschland im 19. Jahrhundert. Entwicklungslinien.* Opladen: Leske Verlag und Budrich, 1983.

Haffner, Sebastian. *Anmerkungen zu Hitler.* Munich: Kindler Verlag, 1978.

————. *Von Bismarck zu Hitler: Ein Rückblick.* Munich: Kindler Verlag, 1987.

Hildebrand, Klaus. *The Foreign Policy of the Third Reich.* Berkeley: University of California Press, 1973.

Holborn, Hajo. *A History of Modern Germany, 1840-1945.* New York: Alfred Knopf, 1970.

Hubatsch, Walter. *Die Ära Tirpitz. Studien zur deutschen Marinepolitik 1880-1918.* Gottingen: Vandenhoeck und Ruprecht, 1955.

Jarausch, Konrad H. *The Enigmatic Chancellor: Bethmann-Hollweg and the Hubris of Imperial Germany.* New Haven: Yale University Press, 1973.

Kehr, Eckart. *Battleship Building and Party Politics in Germany 1894-1901.* Chicago: University of Chicago Press, 1973.

Krüger, Peter. *Die Aussenpolitik der Republik von Weimar.* Darmstadt: Wissenschaftliche Buchgesellschaft, 1985.

Laqueur, Walter. *Weimar: A Cultural History.* New York: G.P. Putnam's, 1974.

Michalka, Wolfgang, and Marshall M. Lee (ed.). *Gustav Stresemann.* Darmstadt: Wissenschaftliche Buchgesellschaft, 1982.

Nichols, J. Alden. *Germany after Bismarck: The Caprivi Era 1890-1894.* New York: Norton, 1968.

Nolte, Ernst. *Der europäische Bürgerkrieg 1917-1945: Bolschewismus und Nationalsozialismus.* Frankfurt: Ullstein Verlag, 1987.

——. *Der Faschismus in seiner Epoche: Die Action francaise. Der italienische Faschismus. Der Nationalsozialismus.* Munich: Piper Verlag, 1963.

——. *Die Krise des liberalen Systems und die faschistischen Bewegungen.* Munich: Piper Verlag, 1968.

Palmer, Alan. *Bismarck.* London: Weidenfeld and Nicolson, 1976.

Schoenbaum, David. *Hitler's Social Revolution.* New York: Doubleday, 1966.

Schulze, Hagen. *Weimar: Deutschland 1917-1933.* Berlin: Siedler Verlag, 1982.

Sheehan, James J. (ed.). *Imperial Germany.* New York: Watts, 1976.

Stern, Fritz: *Gold and Iron: Bismarck, Bleichröder and the Building of the German Empire.* New York: Knopf, 1977.

Stolper, Gustav. *The German Economy: 1870 to the Present.* New York: Harcourt Brace Jovanovich, 1967.

Stürmer, Michael. *Das ruhelose Reich. Deutschland 1866-1918.* Berlin: Siedler Verlag, 1983.

Taylor, A. J. P. *Bismarck, the Man and the Statesman.* London: Hamilton, 1955.

Thamer, Hans-Ulrich. *Verführung und Gewalt: Deutschland 1933-1945.* Berlin: Siedler Verlag, 1986.

Treviranus, Gottfried Reinhold. *Das Ende von Weimar. Heinrich Bruning und seine Zeit.* Düsseldorf: Econ Verlag, 1968.

Wehler, Hans-Ulrich. *Das deutsche Kaiserreich.* Göttingen: Vandenhoeck & Ruprecht, 1975.

The Two Germanys After World War II

Bandulet, Bruno. *Adenauer zwischen West und Ost: Alternativen der deutschen Aussenpolitik.* Munich: Weltforum Verlag, 1970.

Baring, Arnulf. *Aussenpolitik in Adenauers Kanzlerdemokratie: Bonns Beitrag zur Europäischen Verteidigungsgemeinschaft.* Munich: Oldenbourg Verlag, 1969.

————. *Der 17. Juni 1953.* Mit einem Vorwort von Richard Löwenthal. 2nd ed. Stuttgart: Deutsche Verlags-Anstalt, 1983.

Besson, Waldemar. *Die Aussenpolitik der Bundesrepublik. Erfahrungen und Masstäbe.* Munich: Piper Verlag, 1970.

Catudal, Honoré M. *Kennedy and the Berlin Wall Crisis: A Case Study in US Decision Making.* Berlin: Berlin Verlag, 1980.

Dennis, Mike. *The German Democratic Republic: Politics, Economics and Society.* London: Pinter, 1988.

Doering-Manteuffel, Anselm. *Die Bundesrepublik Deutschland in der Ära Adenauer: Aussenpolitik und innere Entwicklung, 1949-1963.* Darmstadt: Wissenschaftliche Buchgesellschaft, 1983.

Feis, Herbert. *Between War and Peace. The Potsdam Conference.* Princeton: University Press, 1960.

Gotto, Klaus, et al. *Konrad Adenauer. Seine Deutschland- und Aussenpolitik 1945-1963.* Munich: Deutscher Taschenbuch Verlag, 1975.

Graml, Herman. *Die Alliierten und die Teilung Deutschlands. Konflikte und Entscheidungen 1941-1948.* Frankfurt: Fischer Taschenbuch Verlag, 1985.

Griffith, William E. *The Ostpolitik of the Federal Republic of Germany.* Cambridge: MIT Press, 1978.

Grosser, Alfred. *Germany in Our Time: A Political History of the Postwar Years.* New York: Praeger, 1973.

Haftendorn, Helga. *Sicherheit und Entspannung. Zur Aussenpolitik der Bundesrepublik Deutschland, 1955-1982.* Baden-Baden: Nomos Verlagsgesellschaft, 1983.

Hanrieder, Wolfram F. *The Stable Crisis: Two Decades of German Foreign Policy.* New York: Harper & Row, 1970.

Hillgruber, Andreas. *Deutsche Geschichte 1945-1982. Die "deutsche Frage" in der Weltpolitik,* 4th ed. Stuttgart: Kohlhammer Verlag, 1983.

Jacobsen, Hans-Adolf et al. (ed.). *Drei Jahrzehnte Aussenpolitik der DDR: Bestimmungsfaktoren, Instrumente, Aktionsfelder,* 2nd ed. Munich: Oldenbourg Verlag, 1980.

Klessmann, Christoph. *Die doppelte Staatsgründung: Deutsche Geschichte, 1945-1955.* 3rd ed. Bonn: Bundeszentrale für politische Bildung, 1984.

————. *Zwei Statten, eine Nation: Deutsche Geschichte, 1955-1970.* Bonn: Bundeszentrale für politische Bildung, 1988.

Koch, Peter. *Willy Brandt: Eine politische Biographie.* Berlin: Ullstein Verlag, 1988.

Krisch, Henry. *The German Democratic Republic: The Search for Identity.* Boulder: Westview Press, 1985.

Müller-Enbergs, Helmut. *Der Fall Rudolf Herrnstadt: Tauwetterpolitik vor dem 17. Juni.* Berlin: LinskDruck Verlag, 1991.

Noack, Paul. *Deutsche Aussenpolitik seit 1945.* Stuttgart: Kohlhammer Verlag, 1972.

Reed, John A., Jr. *Germany and NATO.* Washington, DC: National Defense University Press, 1987.

Richardson, James L. *Germany and the Atlantic Alliance: The Interaction of Strategy and Politics.* Cambridge, MA: Harvard University Press, 1966.

Schwarz, Hans-Peter. *Vom Reich zur Bundesrepublik: Deutschland im Widerstreit der aussenpolitischen Konzeptionen in den Jahren der Besatzungsherrschaft, 1945-1949,* 2nd ed. Stuttgart: Klett-Cotta Verlag, 1980.

―――. *Die Ära Adenauer: Gründerjahre der Republik, 1949-1957.* Stuttgart: Deutsche Verlags-Anstalt, 1981.

―――. *Die Ära Adenauer: Epochenwechsel, 1957-1963.* Stuttgart: Deutsche Verlags-Anstalt, 1983.

Shlaim, Avi. *The United States and the Berlin Blockade, 1948-1949: A Study in Crisis Decision-Making.* Berkeley: University of California press, 1989.

Staritz, Dietrich. *Die Gründung der DDR: Von der sowjetischen Besatzungsherrschaft zum sozialistischen Staat.* Munich: Deutscher Taschenbuch Verlag, 1984.

―――. *Geschichte der DDR, 1949-1985.* Frankfurt: Suhrkamp Verlag, 1985.

Steininger, Rold. *Eine vertane Chance: Die Stalin-Note vom 10. März 1952 und die Wiedervereinigung.* Berlin: Verlag J.H.W. Dietz Nachf., 1985.

Stutterlin, James S., and David Klein. *Berlin: From Symbol of Confrontation to Keystone of Stability.* New York: Praeger, 1989.

Weber, Hermann. *Geschichte der DDR.* Munich: Deutscher Taschenbuch Verlag, 1985.

Wettig, Gerhard. *Entmilitarisierung und Wiederbewaffnung in Deutschland, 1943-1955: Internationale Auseinandersetzungen um die Rolle der Deutschen in Europa.* Munich: Oldenbourg Verland, 1967.

Willis, F. Roy. *Germany and the New Europe.* Stanford: Univresity Press, 1968.

New Ostpolitik and Inner-German Relations

Baring, Arnulf. *Machtwechsel: Die Ära Brandt-Scheel.* Stuttgart: Deutsche Verlags-Anstalt, 1982.

Baring, Arnulf (with Volker Zastrow). *Unser neuer Grössenwahn: Deutschland zwischen Ost and West.* Stuttgart: Deutsche Verlags-Anstalt, 1988.

Bender, Peter. *Offensive Entspannung: Möglichkeit für Deutschland.* Cologne: Kiepenheuer und Witsch, 1964.

————. *Die Ostpolitik: Vom Mauerbau bis zum Moskauer Vertrag.* Munich: Deutscher Taschenbuch Verlag, 1986.

————. *Neue Ostpolitik: Vom Mauerbau bis zum Moskauer Vertrag.* Munich: Deutscher Taschenbuch Verlag, 1986.

Brandt, Willy. *A Peace Policy for Europe.* New York: Holt, Rinehart and Winston, 1969.

Brinkschulte, Wolfgang, et al. *Freikaufgewinnler: Die Mitverdiener im Westen.* Frankfurt: Ullstein Verlag, 1993.

Carr, Jonathan. *Helmut Schmidt.* Düsseldorf: Econ Verlag, 1985.

Gaus, Günther. *Wo Deutschland liegt: Eine Ortsbestimmung.* Hamburg: Hoffmann und Campe Verlag, 1983.

Haftendorn, Helga. *Sicherheit und Stabilität. Aussenbeziehungen der Bundesrepublik zwischen Ölkrise und NATO-Doppelbeschluss.* Munich: Deutischer Taschenbuch Verlag, 1986.

Kaiser, Karl. *German Foreign Policy in Transition: Bonn Between East and West.* London: Oxford University Press, 1968.

Martin, Ernst. *Zwischenbilanz: Deutschlandpolitik der 80er Jahre*. Stuttgart: Verlag Bonn aktuell, 1986.

McAdams, A. James. *East Germany and Detente: Building Authority After the Wall*. Cambridge: University Press, 1985.

Nawrocki, Joachim. *Relations Between the Two States in Germany: Trends, Prospects and Limitations*. Stuttgart: Verlag Bonn aktuell, 1985.

Rehlinger, Ludwig A. *Freikauf: Die Geschäfte der DDR mit politisch Verfolgten, 1963-1989*. Berlin: Ullstein Verlag, 1991.

Schröder, Karsten. *Egon Bahr. Mit einem Bertrag von Günter Grass*. Rastatt: 1988.

Schütz, Wolfgang W. *Rethinking German Policy*. New York: Praeger, 1967.

Vali, Ferenc. *The Quest for a United Germany*. Baltimore: Johns Hopkins University Press, 1967.

Whetten, Lawrence L. *Germany's Ostpolitik: Relations Between the Federal Republic and the Warsaw Pact Countries*. New York: Oxford University Press, 1971.

Whitney, Craig R. *Advocatus Diaboli: Wolfgang Vogel—Anwalt zwischen Ost und West*. Berlin: Siedler Verlag, 1993.

Windsor, Philip. *German Reunification*. London: Elek Books, 1969.

————. *Germany and the Management of Détente*. London: Chatto and Windus, 1971.

Zündorf, Benno. *Die Ostverträge: Die Verträge von Moskau, Warschau, Prag, das Berlin-Abkommen und die Verträge mit der DDR*. Munich: Beck Verlag, 1979.

The Collapse of the GDR and German Unification

Adomeit, Hannes. "Gorbachev and German Unification: Revision of Thinking, Realignment of Power." *Problems of Communism*, July-August 1990.

Bahr, Eckhard. *Sieben Tage im Oktober: Aufbruch in Dresden.* Leipzig: Forum Verlag, 1990.

Bahro, Rudolf. *Die Alternative: Zur Kritik des real existierenden Sozialismus.* Cologne: Europäische Verlagsanstalt, 1977.

Bortfeldt, Heinrich. *Washington-Bonn-Berlin: Die USA und die deutsche Einheit.* Bonn: Bouvier Verlag, 1993.

Ehring, Klaus, and Martin Dallwitz. *Schwerter zu Pflugscharen: Friedensbewegung in der DDR.* Reinbek: Rowohlt Verlag, 1982.

Fricke, Karl Wilhelm. *Die DDR-Staatssicherheit: Entwicklung, Strukturen, Aktionsfelder,* 3rd ed. Cologne; Verlag Wissenschaft und Politik, 1989.

Friedman, Thomas L., and Michael R. Gordon. "Steps to German Unity: Bonn as a Power." *The New York Times,* February 16, 1990.

Gauck, Joachim. *Die Stasi-Akten: Das unheimliche Erbe der DDR.* Reinbek: Rowohlt Verlag, 1991.

Gill, David, and Ulrich Schröter. *Das Ministerium für Staatssicherheit: Anatomie des Mielke-Imperiums.* Berlin: Rowohlt Verlag, 1991.

Glaessner, Gert-Joachim (ed.). *Die DDR in der Ära Honecker: Politik-Kultur-Gesellschaft.* Opladen: Leske Verlag und Budrich, 1988.

Grosser, Dieter (ed.). *German Unification. The Unexpected Challenge.* Oxford: University Press, 1992.

Hamilton, Daniel. "After the Revolution: The New Political Landscape in East Germany," *Germany Issues* (American Institute for Contemporary German Studies), Vol. 7, 1990.

Henkys, Reinhard (ed.). *Die evangelischen Kirchen in der DDR: Beiträge zu einer Bestandsaufnahme.* Munich: Kaiser Verlag, 1982.

Israel, Jürgen (ed.). *Zur Freiheit berufen: Die Kirche in der DDR als Schutzraum der Opposition, 1981-1989.* Berlin: Aufbau Taschenbuch Verlag, 1991.

Kaiser, Karl. *Deutschlands Vereinigung. Die internationalen Aspekte.* Bergisch Gladbach: Lübbe Verlag, 1991.

Koch, Egmont R. *Das geheime Kartell: BND, Schalck, Stasi & Co.* Hamburg: Hoffmann und Campe Verlag, 1992.

Lang, Jochen von. *Erich Mielke: Eine deutsche Karrierre.* Berlin: Rowohlt Verlag, 1991.

Maaz, Hans-Joachim. *Der Gefühlsstau: Ein Psychogramm der DDR.* Berlin: Argon Verlag, 1990.

Maleck, Bernhard. *Wolfgang Ullmann: "Iche werde nicht schweigen"— Gespräche mit Wolfgang Ullmann.* Berlin: Dietz Verlag, 1991.

Mantzke, Martin. "Eine Republik auf Abruf. Die DDR nach den Wahlen vom 18. Marz 1990," *Europa-Archiv,* Vol. 45, 1990.

Meyer, Gerd. *Die DDR-Machtelite in der Ära Honecker.* Tübingen: Francke Verlag, 1991.

Müller-Enbergs, Helmut, et al. (eds.) *Von der Illegalität ins Parlament: Werdegang und Konzept der neuen Bürgerbewegungen.* Berlin: LinksDruck Verlag, 1991.

Musiolek, Berndt, and Carola Wuttke, eds. *Parteien und politische Bewegungen im letzten Jahr der DDR (Oktober 1989 bis April 1990).* Berlin: BasisDruck Verlagsgesellschaft, 1991.

Pfeiler, Wolfgang. "Die Viermächte-Option als Instrument sowjetischer Deutschlandpolitik," *Interne Studie* (Forschungsinstitut der Konrad-Adenauer-Stiftung), No. 25/1991, April 1991.

Pond, Elizabeth. *Beyond the Wall: Germany's Road to Unification.* Washington, DC: The Brookings Institution, 1993.

————. "Die Entstehung von Zwei-plus-Vier," *Europa-Archiv,* Vol. 47, 1992.

Przybylski, Peter. *Tatort Politbüro: Die Akte Honecker.* Berlin: Rowohlt Verlag, 1991.

————. *Tatort Politbüro, Vol. 2: Honecker, Mittag und Schalck-Golodkowski.* Berlin; Rowohlt Verlag, 1992.

Ramet, Pedro. "Church and Peace in the GDR." *Problems of Communism,* Vol. 33, July-August 1984.

Schell, Manfred, and Werner Kalinka. *Stasi und kein Ende: Die Personen und Fakten.* Frankfurt: Ullstein Verlag, 1991.

Süss, Walter. "Bilanz einer Gratwanderung: Die kurze Amtszeit des HAns Modrow," *Deutschland Archiv,* Vol. 24, 1991.

————. "Mit Unwillen zur Mächt: Der Runde Tisch in der DDR der Übergangszeit." *Deutschland Archiv,* Vol. 24, 1991.

Thaysen, Uwe. *Der Runde Tisch—Oder: Wo blieb das Volk?* Opladen: Leske Verlag und Budrich, 1990.

Wettig, Gerhard. *Changes in Soviet Policy Towards the West.* London: Pinter, 1991.

————. "Die Rolle der UdSSR bei der Vereinigung Deutschlands." In: Konrad Löw (ed.). *Ursachen und Verlauf der deutschen Revolution 1989.* Berlin: Duncker & Humbolt, 1991.

Wilke, Manfred, and Hans-Peter Müller. *Zwischen Solidarität und Eigennutz. Die Gewerkschaften des DGB im deutschen Vereinigungsprozess.* Melle: Knoth Verlag, 1991.

Worst, Anne. *Das Ende eines Geheimdienstes—Oder: Wie lebendig ist die Stasi?* Berlin: LinksDruck Verlag, 1991.

The Unified Germany and the New Europe
Arnold, Eckart. "German Foreign Policy and Unification." *International Affairs* (London), No. 3, 1991.

Asmus, Ronald D. "Germany and America: Partners in Leadership?" *Survival,* November-December 1991.

Baring, Arnulf. *Deutschland, was nun? Ein Gespräch mit Dirk Rumberg und Wolf Jobst Siedler.* Berlin: Siedler Verlag, 1991.

Brzezinski, Zbigniew. "Postkommunistischer Nationalismus." *Europa-Archiv,* Vol. 44 (1989).

Calleo, David P. *NATO: Reconstruction or Dissolution?* Washington, DC: *EPI New World-New Direction Series,* 1992.

Cuthbertson, Ian M. (ed.). *Redefining the CSCE: Challenges and Opportunities in the New Europe.* New York: Institute for EastWest Studies, 1992.

Derix, Hans-Heribert. "Bürokratisch regulierte Marktwirtschaft zwischen Beharrung und Liquidation." *Aussenpolitik,* Vol. 41, 1990, No. 4.

Fritsch-Bournazel, Renata. *Europa und die deutsche Einheit,* 2nd ed. Stutgart: Verlag Bonn aktuell, 1991.

Funke, Hajo. *"Jetzt sind wir dran . . ."—Nationalismus im geeinten Deutschland: Aspekte der Einigungspolitik und nationalistische Potentiale in Deutschland.* Berlin: Aktion Suhnezeichen, 1991.

Gasteyger, Curt. "Ein gesamteuropäisches Sicherheitssystem?" *Europa-Archiv,* Vol. 47, 1992.

Geissler, Clemens. "Neue Völkerwanderungen in Europa." *Europa-Archiv,* Vol. 47, 1992.

Glotz, Peter. "Die Einheit und die Spaltung Europas: Die Auswirkungen der mitteleuropäischen Revolution von 1989 auf Gesamteuropa." *Aus Politik und Zeitgeschichte.* Beilage zur Wochenzeitung Das Parlament, B 6/92, January 31, 1992.

Hamilton, Daniel. "A More European Germany, A More German Europe." *Journal of International Affairs,* Summer 1991.

Hamilton, Daniel, and James Clad. "Germany, Japan, and the False Glare of War." *The Washington Quarterly,* Autumn 1991.

Harrison, Hope (ed.). "Germany, Europe, and the Future Security System for the 1990's." *Aspen Institute Berlin Conference Report,* November 1990.

Jachtenfuchs, Markus. "Die EG nach Maastricht: Das Subsidiaritätsprinzip und die Zukunft der Integration." *Europoa-Archiv,* Vol. 47, 1992.

Jesse, Eckard, and Armin Mitter (eds.). *Die Gestaltung der deutschen Einheit: Geschichte, Politik, Gesellschaft.* Bonn: Bundeszentrale fur politische Bildung, 1992.

Livingston, Robert Gerald. "United Germany: Bigger and Better." *Foreign Policy,* No. 87, Summer 1982.

Mathiopoulos, Margarita (ed.). *Das neue Europa: Ein europäisch-amerikanischer Dialog an der Humboldt-Universität.* Bonn: Bouvier Verlag, 1992.

Maull, Hanns W. "Zivilmacht Bundesrepublik Deutschland: Vierzehn Thesen für eine neue deutsche Aussenpolitik." *Europa-Archiv,* Vol. 47, 1992.

Murswiek, Dietrich et al. (eds.). *Die Vereinigung Deutschlands: Aspekte innen-, aussen- und wirtschaftspolitischer Beziehungen und Bindungen.* Berlin: Mann Verlag, 1992.

Pradetto, August. "Europa nach der Revolution: Ost und West vor säkularen Herausforderungen." *Aus Politik und Zeitgeschichte.* Beilage zur Wochenzeitung Das Parlament, B 6/92, January 31, 1992.

Schöllgen, Gregor. *Die Macht in der Mitte Europas. Stationen deutscher Aussenpolitik von Friedrich dem Grossen bis zur Gegenwart.* Munich: Beck Verlag, 1992.

Schwarz, Hans-Peter. *Die gezähmten Deutschen: Von der Machtbesessenheit zur Machtvergessenheit.* Stuttgart: Deutsche Verlags-Anstalt, 1985.

Sinn, Gerlinde, and Hans-Werner Sinn. *Kaltstart: Volkswirtschaftliche Aspekte der deutschen Vereinigung.* Tübingen: Mohr Verlag, 1991.

Stent, Angela. "The One Germany." *Foreign Policy,* No. 81, Winter 1990-91.

Stollreither, Konrad. *Das vereinigte Deutschland. Grundlagen und Veränderungen.* Berlin: Landeszentrale für politische Bildungsarbeit, 1991.

Sturm, Roland. *Staatsverschuldung.* Opladen: Leske Verlag und Budrich, 1992.

Suhr, Heinz. *Der Treuhandskandal: Wie Ostdeutschland geschlachtet wurde.* Frankfurt am Main: Eichborn Verlag, 1991.

Szabo, Stephen F. *The Changing Politics of German Security.* New York: St. Martin's Press, 1990.

Thalheim, Karl C. *Die wirtschaftliche Entwicklung der beiden Staaten in Deutschland,* 3rd ed. Berlin: Landeszentrale für politische Bildungsarbeit, 1988.

Thinnes, Jeff. "Germany's Foreign Policy After Unification." *Aspen Isntitute Berlin Conference Report,* March 19-21, 1991.

Volten, Peter M.E. "Security Dimensions of Imperial Collapse." In: *Problems of Communism,* February 1992.

Wettig, Gerhard. "Deutsche Vereinigung und europäische Sicherheit." *Aussenpolitik,* Vol. 42, 1992.

Wolf, Reinhard. "Kollektive Sicherheit und das neue Europa." *Europa-Archiv,* Vol. 47, 1992.

Yost, David S. "France and West European Defence Identity." *Survival,* July-August 1991.

Ziebura, Gilbert et al. *Deutschland in der neuen Weltordnung: Unbewältigte Herausforderung.* Opladen: Leske Verlag und Budrich, 1992.

■ INDEX ■